Empowering Students and Maximising Inclusiveness and Equality
through ICT

Studies in Inclusive Education

Series Editor

Roger Slee (*University of Leeds, UK*)

Editorial Board

Mel Ainscow (*University of Manchester, UK*)
Felicity Armstrong (*Institute of Education, University of London, UK*)
Len Barton (*Institute of Education, University of London, UK*)
Suzanne Carrington (*Queensland University of Technology, Australia*)
Joanne Deppeler (*Monash University, Australia*)
Linda Graham (*Queensland University of Technology, Australia*)
Levan Lim (*National Institute of Education, Singapore*)
Missy Morton (*University of Auckland, New Zealand*)

VOLUME 49

The titles published in this series are listed at *brill.com/stie*

Empowering Students and Maximising Inclusiveness and Equality through ICT

Edited by

Mbulaheni Maguvhe, Ramashego Shila Mphahlele and
Sharon Moonsamy

BRILL
SENSE

LEIDEN | BOSTON

All chapters in this book have undergone peer review.

Library of Congress Cataloging-in-Publication Data

Names: Maguvhe, Mbulaheni, editor. | Mphahlele, Ramashego Shila Shorty, editor. | Moonsamy, Sharon, editor.
Title: Empowering students and maximising inclusiveness and equality through ICT / Mbulaheni Maguvhe, Ramashego Shila Mphahlele and Sharon Moonsamy.
Description: Leiden ; Boston : Brill | Sense, 2021. | Series: Studies in inclusive education, 2542-9825 ; volume 49 | Includes bibliographical references and index.
Identifiers: LCCN 2021006715 (print) | LCCN 2021006716 (ebook) | ISBN 9789004432505 (paperback) | ISBN 9789004432536 (hardback) | ISBN 9789004447226 (ebook)
Subjects: LCSH: Inclusive education--South Afirca. | Inclusive education--Technological innovations. | Students with disabilities--South Africa--Computer-assisted instruction. | Educational equalization--South Africa. | Assistive computer technology.
Classification: LCC LC1203.S6 E67 2021 (print) | LCC LC1203.S6 (ebook) | DDC 371.9/0460968--dc23
LC record available at https://lccn.loc.gov/2021006715
LC ebook record available at https://lccn.loc.gov/2021006716

Typeface for the Latin, Greek, and Cyrillic scripts: "Brill". See and download: brill.com/brill-typeface.

ISSN 2542-9825
ISBN 978-90-04-43250-5 (paperback)
ISBN 978-90-04-43253-6 (hardback)
ISBN 978-90-04-44722-6 (e-book)

Copyright 2021 by Koninklijke Brill NV, Leiden, The Netherlands.
Koninklijke Brill NV incorporates the imprints Brill, Brill Hes & De Graaf, Brill Nijhoff, Brill Rodopi, Brill Sense, Hotei Publishing, mentis Verlag, Verlag Ferdinand Schöningh and Wilhelm Fink Verlag.
All rights reserved. No part of this publication may be reproduced, translated, stored in a retrieval system, or transmitted in any form or by any means, electronic, mechanical, photocopying, recording or otherwise, without prior written permission from the publisher. Requests for re-use and/or translations must be addressed to Koninklijke Brill NV via brill.com or copyright.com.

This book is printed on acid-free paper and produced in a sustainable manner.

Contents

List of Figures and Tables IX

Notes on Contributors XI

Introduction: Empowering Students and Maximising Inclusiveness and Equality through ICT 1
  Ramashego Shila Mphahlele and Mbulaheni Maguvhe

PART 1
Identification and Support of Barriers to Learning in School and Open Distance and e-Learning

1 Inclusivity, Equality and Equity: Student (Em)Power(ment) through ICT Mediated Learning 11
  Roshini Pillay and Najma Agherdien

2 Barriers to Teaching and Learning through Open Distance and e-Learning 27
  Shonisani Agnes Mulovhedzi

3 Early Identification of Barriers to Learning as the First Step in the Inclusion Process 40
  Shonisani Agnes Mulovhedzi and Ndileleni Paulinah Mudzielwana

4 The Role of Information and Communication Technologies in the Identification of Barriers to Teaching and Learning 57
  Ramashego Shila Mphahlele

5 The Role of ICT in Supporting Students at Risk for Academic Literacies in Higher Education 73
  Sharon Moonsamy and Anniah Mupawose

6 Using Information Communication Technologies and Assistive Technologies to Address Specific Barriers to Teaching and Learning in Schools 88
  Andries du Plessis

7 The Role of ICT in Supporting Students Experiencing Barriers to Learning in the ODeL 114
Anniah Mupawose, Sharon Moonsamy and Skye Nandi Adams

8 Using ICT in Higher Education for Student Empowerment: An Academic Perspective Using Critical Pedagogies 134
Nazira Hoosen and Andrew Crouch

PART 2
The Use of ICT to Empower Students in Different Areas

9 The Role Played by ICT in Mathematics and Science Teaching and Learning Mediation 161
Mapula Gertrude Ngoepe

10 Conceptualising the Use of ICTs in ODL through Mathematical Participation Model for Community of Practice to Overcome Students' Barriers to Learning 184
Moshe Moses Phoshoko

11 The Uses of Augmentative and Alternative Communication Technology in Empowering Learners Overcome Communication Barriers to Learning 203
Munyane Mophosho and Khetsiwe Masuku

12 Teleaudiology as Part of Efforts to Enhance Inclusivity and Equality through ICT in South African Schools: Some Considerations 223
Katijah Khoza-Shangase, Ben Sebothoma and Nomfundo Floweret Moroe

13 Educational Audiology within the Classroom: The Use and Importance of Information and Communication Technologies 244
Dhanashree Pillay and Ben Sebothoma

14 Information and Communication Technologies to Facilitate Cognitive Skills Development of Learners Experiencing Barriers to and Learning 260
Nkhensani Susan Thuketana

CONTENTS

VII

15 Empowering Students Experiencing Barriers to Learning through ICT to Ensure Inclusiveness and Equality 277
Mbulaheni Maguvhe

16 Summary 291
Mbulaheni Maguvhe and Ramashego Shila Mphahlele

Index 295

Figures and Tables

Figures

1.1 Summary of Ravjee's competing perspectives on the relation of ICTs and higher education. 16

1.2 Student views on the use of ICTs for teaching and learning at Wits University. 21

3.1 The process of early identification of learning barriers as part of SIAS (images by K. Ratshilumela, 2015–2017). 45

4.1 Types of barriers to teaching and learning with factors that may cause them. 59

6.1 IMS Global Consortium Accessibility Parts (adapted from http://www.imsglobal.org/activity/accessibility). 92

6.2 Bronfenbrenner's bio-ecological model (Source: https://commons.wikimedia.org/wiki/File:Bronfenbrenner%27s_Ecological_Theory_of_Development_(English).jpg). 96

10.1 The Mathematical Participation Model (MP-model) (from Phoshoko, 2013, p. 86). 190

10.2 The MP-model and mathematical proficiency (from Phoshoko, 2013, p. 90). 192

10.3 Three-dimensional MP-model. 194

10.4 The relationship between the MP-model and mathematical proficiency. 195

10.5 The relationship between the MP-model and TPACK. 196

11.1 BigMac. 208

11.2 Eye-gaze alphabet board. 208

11.3 Go-Talk 4. 209

11.4 Go-Talk 32. 209

11.5 AAC process. 211

Tables

3.1 Early intervention strategies for learners with barriers to learning. 48

4.1 Factors, manifestations and barriers to teaching and learning. 62

4.2 Instruments used to identify reading difficulties in the FSS. 65

4.3 Possible contributing factors towards reading difficulties. 66

4.4 Use of ICTs to identify learners experiencing reading difficulties. 67

5.1 Challenges and solutions of ICT that support academic literacy. 83

6.1 Summary of AT available to Deaf and hard-of-hearing learners. 102

6.2	Summary of solutions related to learners with visual impairment.	104
6.3	Some learning impairments and examples of assistive technologies.	106
8.1	The interplay between structure, culture and agency.	152

Notes on Contributors

Skye Nandi Adams
is an Associate Lecturer of Speech-Language Pathology at the University of the Witwatersrand in Johannesburg, South Africa. She has been working in the department since 2016. She is currently a PhD candidate and is supported by the Consortium for Advanced Research Training in Africa (CARTA) doctoral fellowship programme. Prior to that, she obtained her BSc in Speech-Language Pathology from the University of Cape Town, South Africa, and her MSc in Language Sciences from the University College London, United Kingdom. Recently, she initiated a range of projects focusing on transformative practices in higher education, targeting both teaching and learning and research. She has also been working on research related to decolonisation in the speech and language department with regard to the clinical and academic curriculum.

Najma Agherdien
is the Curriculum and Teaching Team Leader at the Centre for Learning, Teaching, and Development at the University of Witwatersrand in Johannesburg, South Africa. She holds a PhD in Education Studies and a Masters in Computer-based education (cum laude). She has experience as a Programme Specialist in the area of Learning design and has led several projects involving curriculum and materials development, monitoring and evaluation, and research. She is passionate about social justice issues and takes a keen interest in critical pedagogies, the use of technologies for learning and teaching, and generally learning from and connecting with others in the field. Part of her professional development and personal learning network (PLN) includes tweeting regularly (see @agherdien).

Andrew Crouch
is the Vice-Chancellor and Principal of Sol Plaatje University in Kimberley, South Africa. He is a professional chemist, but for the past fifteen years has been operating within the senior management of universities, the last 11 years being at the University of the Witwatersrand (Wits) in Johannesburg as Dean of Science and as Deputy Vice-Chancellor Academic respectively. At Wits, he championed the digitalization of teaching and learning, including the use of ICTs in teaching and learning. He earned a BSc in Chemistry and Biochemistry and a BSc Honours from the University of the Western Cape in Bellville, South Africa before proceeding to complete a PhD in Chemistry from Concordia University in Montreal, Canada. He has extensive teaching experience in Chemistry at all levels at various universities, including the University of the Western

Cape, Stellenbosch University, and various Universities abroad. He has more than 25 years of research experience in environmental electrochemistry and its applications, being the author/co-author of more than 140 research papers, conference proceedings, and presentations and one patent in the area of Electrochemistry and Analytical Chemistry. He received many awards during his academic career, the most notable being the Ernst Oppenheimer Memorial Trust Fellowship and Gold Medal (1998) from the Anglo American Chairman's Fund, as well as the "Excellence in Teaching and Research Award" from the International Society of Electrochemistry (ISE) for his contribution to the field of Environmental Electrochemistry in South Africa.

Andries du Plessis

has completed his BA (Ed) with majors in History and Afrikaans at the University Potchefstroom (currently the North-West University). He went on to complete his Honors in History followed by an MA Dissertation (History) at the then Rand Afrikaans University (currently the University of Johannesburg). By 2006 he was awarded a DPhil(Information Science) from the University of Pretoria. In this study, he explored online social networks using Social Network Analysis (SNA). Dr. du Plessis currently holds a position as Senior Lecturer in the Faculty of Education at the University of Mpumalanga's Siyabuswa campus. He is responsible for several undergraduate modules in the School of Early Childhood Education's BEd Foundation Phase programme. His research interests are mainly technology-focussed. He has published several chapters, contributed to textbooks, and presented at conferences. His research interests remain grounded in social networks, digital knowledge, and organisational learning, as well as the enabling effects of technology in educational environments. He also continues to explore developments related to efforts to bridge the digital divide, especially in developing economies.

Nazira Hoosen

is a Lecturer and educational developer at the Centre for Learning, Teaching, and Development at Wits. She was previously a researcher at the Wits School of Governance. She holds a Master's Degree from Wits University and is busy completing her PhD in Digital Transformation Studies (Interdisciplinary Digital Knowledge Economy) at the University of Witwatersrand. She has consulted in government and taught widely in Finance and Business Management in South Africa and the Middle East. She was part of the team that implemented and facilitated the blended learning platforms in the Middle East, being specifically located in The Kingdom of Saudi Arabia. Her research interests include critical digital pedagogies, policy in higher education, and continuous professional development.

NOTES ON CONTRIBUTORS

Katijah Khoza-Shangase

is the 2017 Business Women Association of South Africa's Finalist – Academic Category. She is an Associate Professor and former Head of the Speech Pathology and Audiology Department at the University of the Witwatersrand. She has played an important leadership role in the Health Professions Council of South Africa. Khoza-Shangase has won numerous awards, principally in the area of research and research supervision, and for contributions to the field of audiology. She has several publications to her name, including peer-reviewed journal articles, technical and research reports, book chapters, and co-edited books. *Black Academic Voices: The South African Experience* (HSRC Press, 2019) is her most current contribution to the transformation and decolonisation project, which is the winner of the 2020 Humanities and Social Sciences Award (Non-fiction category). Her edited books *Early Detection and Intervention in Audiology: An African Perspective* by Wits University Press will be published in February 2021, and *Preventive Audiology: An African Perspective* (AOSIS) later in 2021. She also co-edited a Special Issue for the *South African Journal of Communication Disorders* (2020) titled *Occupational Hearing Loss in Africa: An Interdisciplinary View of the Current Status*. Her forthcoming outputs include *Occupational Noise-Induced Hearing Loss: An African Perspective* and *Complexities and Challenges in Preventive Audiology: An African Perspective,* both by AOSIS Book Publishers.

Mbulaheni Maguvhe

is a special educationist who professes in inclusive education. What makes him a researcher is not only his advanced education with training in rigorous research, but also his involvement in some book chapters, community engagement projects (most interestingly on the education of children in schools for the visually impaired), and many articles published in peer-reviewed journals of standing, such as the century-old *Journal of Visual Impairment and Blindness*. Professor Maguvhe writes on various topics, the common focus of which is the empowerment of learners with disabilities, particularly those with visual impairment (including the Deaf-blind). He has published numerous articles on community-based rehabilitation (CBR) and the empowerment of learners with visual impairment, augmentative and alternative communication (AAC) systems, the teaching of science to learners with visual impairment, inclusive education (IE), orientation and mobility for blind and partially sighted persons, curriculum adaptation for learners with visual impairment, adult education and training (AET), and the adaptation of examination materials for learners with sensory impairments. The spectrum of his research interests is broad, yet focused on the empowerment of learners with visual impairment through unhindered access to education and training. In his latest book, Professor Maguvhe devotes a chapter to university access for students with disabilities in addition to the areas mentioned above. These academic and practical initiatives make him a researcher of note, particularly in sub-Saharan Africa where most educated persons with visual impairment do not engage in research because of the considerable demands it makes.

Khetsiwe Masuku

is a Lecturer in the Department of Speech Pathology at the University of the Witwatersrand. She teaches and supervises Speech Pathology students at both undergraduate and postgraduate levels. She has a Master's degree in Public Health and a PhD in Augmentative and Alternative Communication (Severe Disability). Her research focuses on disability, specifical access for persons with disabilities, caregivers of persons with disabilities, and the implementation of disability policies within the African context. Her other research interests include research in Aphasia and Deafblindness. She has published several articles in peer-reviewed journals and written book chapters.

Sharon Moonsamy

is a Speech-Language Pathologist, Audiologist, and Remedial Education Consultant. She is an Associate Professor in Speech Pathology at Wits University, and currently holds the position of the Head of the School of Human & Community Development. Her professional experience relates to education, health, and higher education. Her teaching and research, in the areas of child language, literacy, and cognition are centered on social justice. She believes that all individuals given the opportunity can achieve according to their potential. Thus, creating access to services for those from marginalized populations furthers this perspective. Teacher-therapist workshops, conference presentations, and journal and book publications contribute to her scholarly profile.

Munyane Mophosho

is a Senior Lecturer in the Department of Speech-Language Pathology at Wits University. She worked as a lecturer at the Centre for Augmentative and Alternative Communication (CAAC) at the University of Pretoria and joined Wits in 2004. Her professional experience is in inclusive education, disabilities, transformation in the Speech and hearing professions, and health. She is involved in teaching a course on academic service-learning, augmentative, and alternative communication (AAC), educational principles, and practices. Her PhD was on Health communication in the profession of speech-language therapy. She is a member of the local and international association, including the South African Speech-Language and hearing Association (SASLHA), and the International Augmentative and Augmentative Association (ISAAC). She has made presentations at local and international conferences and published articles and book chapters.

Nomfundo Floweret Moroe

is a Senior Lecturer and current Head of Discipline (Audiology) at the University of the Witwatersrand. She is part of the Department of Higher Education and Training's NGap Programme – a programme that involves the recruitment of highly capable scholars as new academics, against carefully designed and balanced equity considerations and in light of the disciplinary areas of greatest need. She is a passionate researcher, with an interest in Occupational Audiology, Complex Interventions, Deaf culture, and Deafblindness. She is a CARTA Fellow (Consortium for Advanced Research Training in Africa), a highly competitive programme that trains young and emerging researchers in Africa. She is currently conducting post-doctoral research which is funded by this consortium. She has published several peer-reviewed articles and book chapters; and has presented at both national and international conferences. She has co-edited a special issue for the *Journal for the South African Journal of Communication Disorders* (2020) titled *Occupational Hearing Loss in Africa: An Interdisciplinary View of the Current Status.* Her upcoming outputs include a co-edited book *Occupational Noise-Induced Hearing Loss: An African Perspective* by AOSIS Press.

Ramashego Shila Mphahlele

is a Lecturer at the University of South Africa in Early Childhood Education. She obtained the following qualifications DEd: Psychology of Education (UNISA), MEd: Inclusive Education (UNISA), BEd Honours: Inclusive Education (UNISA), Inclusive Education Certificate (UJ), ACE: Educational Management (TUT), Adult Basic Education & Training Certificate (UNISA), Senior Primary Teachers Diploma (Kwena Moloto College of Education). She taught for twelve years in different schools at Limpopo and Gauteng Provinces of South Africa respectively offering services at Primary Schools, Secondary Schools, and one Special School. She worked as a Senior Education Specialist for six years in the Gauteng Department of Education before being promoted as the Deputy Chief Education Specialist (Researcher) in 2016. She joined the University of South Africa in June 2018. Dr. Mphahlele presented papers, posters, and Pecha-Kucha at different conferences both nationally and internationally. She published and co-published several research outputs in accredited publishing institutions nationally and internationally. She won a research award in 2018 named: Data Champion for First term 2018 awarded by New Leaders Foundation. She is currently nominated for the Women in Research emerging researcher prize.

Ndileleni Paulinah Mudzielwana

is an Associate Professor in Early Childhood Education. She holds a PhD degree in Early Childhood Education from the University of Pretoria. She is a member of South African Research in Early Childhood Education (SARAECE) and the Literacy Association of South Africa (LITASA). Recent publications include a chapter on "Teachers' practice of shared reading as a strategy" in the book *From Words to Ideas: The Role of Literacy in Enhancing Young Children's Development* (British Council, 2018). She is a coordinator of the Early Childhood Development project. At present, Professor Mudzielwana is the Head of the Department in Early Childhood Education at the University of Venda.

Shonisani Agnes Mulovhedzi
holds a PhD degree in Early Childhood Education from the University of Pretoria. She is a committee member of South African Research in Early Childhood Education (SARAECE) and a coordinator of the Univen-Model Preschool. Her research and teaching focus primarily on special issues relating to Early Childhood Education with an emphasis on leadership, Life Skills, and Administration and Management in the Foundation Phase. She won Vice-Chancellors excellence awards in teaching and learning. Shonisani has written and published book chapters and articles in accredited journals. She has authored and co-authored numerous articles. At present, Dr. Mulovhedzi is working as a senior lecturer at the University of Venda.

Anniah Mupawose
is a Senior Lecturer in the Speech Pathology and Audiology Department of the Witwatersrand University. Anniah has worked as a Speech language pathologist in a variety of settings that have included preschools, primary schools, rehabilitation centers and hospitals in the United States from 1993 to 2000. In 2001, she ran her own speech therapy practice in Zimbabwe providing services to both adults and children. In 2002, Anniah started working at the Witwatersrand University as a lecturer. She obtained her MA in Speech Language Pathology from California State University, Fresno. In 2012 Anniah graduated with her PhD entitled 'The Cognitive – Linguistic Abilities of Adults Living with HIV/AIDS before and after HAART'. Additionally, in 2017 she earned a PG Diploma in Health Science Education. She has managed various administrative portfolios and positions in the department including Head of department. Her primary research thrust is transformative teaching and learning methods at tertiary level. Her other research interests include cognition, language and literacy development in preschool and school age children, learning disabilities especially dyslexia and stuttering.

Mapula Gertrude Ngoepe
is an Associate Professor and former Chair of the Department of Mathematics Education at the University of South Africa, South Africa. She holds a Doctor of Mathematics Education from the Curtin University of Technology, Australia

which focuses on investigating classroom practices in disadvantaged schools in multilingual classrooms. Her MEd in Mathematics Education is from the University of Birmingham, UK. Her undergraduate and postgraduate studies are from the University of the North in Limpopo. Her career started as a high school teacher, a lecturer at a college of education, a statistician at the department of education, and a post-graduate assistant. She leads a community engagement project 'Mathematics Teaching and Learning Intervention Programme' (MTLIP) and a member of the United Nations number sense project. Her research interest includes Teaching practice research in Open Distance Learning (ODeL) and ICT, Classroom practice in a multilingual context, Professional development of mathematics teachers, Curriculum studies, Mathematics education pedagogy, and Mathematics Teacher education.

Moshe Moses Phoshoko

is an Associate Professor of mathematics education in a department in the College of Education at the University of South Africa (UNISA). He holds the following professional and/or academic qualifications: Secondary Teachers' Diploma (Transvaal College of Education); BSc degree at UNISA; Hons BEd & MEd at University of Witwatersrand and PhD in Mathematics, Science & Technology Education at UNISA. A mathematics teacher who has taught at high school, serving in different capacities as the subject head (mathematics), head of department (mathematics & science), deputy principal (academic), acting principal, he also was the project leader of the research team conducting customer satisfaction survey for the Gauteng Shared Services (GSSC) in the period 2005 to 2006. As a lecturer at the tertiary level from the beginning of 2007, he served as the chairperson of the following departmental committees: teaching & learning, quality assurance & evaluation, and ethics applications reviews. He has developed modules for undergraduate & postgraduate programmes and also taught these whilst supervising Masters and Doctoral students. His research interest is in the areas of the teaching and learning of mathematics in contexts and his recent work is *Teachers Views on Revisiting the Operation of Signed Numbers Using Contexts: A Case of Three African Teachers* (Adonis & Abbey Publishers, 2018). He is currently one of the executive committee members of the Department of Mathematics Education in the institution.

Dhanashree Pillay

is an Audiologist and Senior Lecturer at the University of the Witwatersrand. She has worked in rural KZN and has been involved in the Red Cross Air Mercy Service outreach programs within Northern KZN. She is a board member of the PADI (People for the Awareness of Disability Issues) organisation in South Africa and she is a member of the Standards Division at the SABS (South African

Bureau of Standards) where she is involved in the writing up of policies and procedures. Dr. Pillay has published in scholarly journals and has presented at both national and international conferences. She is a reviewer for Speech Pathology and Audiology journals. Dr. Pillay's research interests focus on the areas of Amplification, Spirituality, Religion, Traditional beliefs and practices, Sports Medicine, and Noise.

Roshini Pillay

is a Senior Lecturer in Social Work at the University of the Witwatersrand since June 2009. She holds a PhD from the University of the Western Cape. She has worked in the field of social work for 20 years before joining the academy. Her research interests are meso practice/social work with group work, social work education, and Occupational Social Work. She is a teacher and practitioner first. Roshini is curious and knows that learning occurs through pedagogies of discomfort, activity, cognition, and affect. She enjoys exploring ways to decolonise the curriculum using blended learning in course design.

Ben Sebothoma

has an MA (Audiology), is a qualified and registered clinical audiologist and an Associate Lecturer in the Department of Speech Pathology and Audiology at the University of the Witwatersrand. He has lectured and supervised students at both undergraduate and postgraduate levels. He completed his undergraduate training at the University of Cape Town and his Master of Arts Degree in Audiology at the University of the Witwatersrand. He is a current PhD fellow (Audiology), with a focus in middle ear pathologies in HIV/AIDS at the University of the Witwatersrand. He has published several scientific papers in accredited journals and chapters; and has presented in local and international conferences. His areas of research interest include prevention, identification, and management of middle ear pathologies across the lifespan in low- and middle-income countries.

Nkhensani Susan Thuketana

is a Lecturer and the Learning Support modules coordinator at the Faculty of Education, University of Pretoria (UP). The modules focus specifically on learners' school readiness and facilitate students' knowledge and understanding of Inclusive Education and the insights into the causes of learning barriers. Before her current employment, Dr. Thuketana worked in special education, coordinated the School-Based Support Team, and served in the District Based Support Team. She holds a Master's degree in Augmentative and Alternative Communication (AAC) from the University of Pretoria inSouth Africa, a PhD in Early Childhood Education (ECE), specializing in Inclusive Education. Her research interests pertain to children's development, learning difficulties, and learner support.

INTRODUCTION

Empowering Students and Maximising Inclusiveness and Equality through ICT

Ramashego Shila Mphahlele and Mbulaheni Maguvhe

1 Introduction and Brief Background

Access to and participation in education are critical issues in contemporary South Africa. Awareness of the importance of inclusion and equality is not recent, having possibly first been described at the dawn of the millennium by the United Nations Educational, Scientific, and Cultural Organization (UNESCO). Educational problems encountered by individuals experiencing barriers to learning in the 21st century can be attributed to, among other things, lack of empowerment, exclusion, inequality, inaccessible ICT, and a lack of recognition of the support provided by teachers when using technology. This book on inclusive open distance and e-learning (ODeL) education evaluates a topic central to education in South Africa and the world over, emphasizing the role played by information communication technology (ICT) in ensuring the identification of barriers to teaching and learning in order to give relevant support and to maximise access and participation.

Drawing from current framings in the Southern African development community (SADC) education system, we argue that ICT has a key role to play in the transformation, Africanisation, and decolonisation of education. Through ICT, students can be empowered to access and freely participate in teaching and learning activities. It should be borne in mind that ICT can serve as a powerful tool to normalise the conditions of students in general, and especially those experiencing barriers to learning. The design and development of new technologies has, however, sometimes reinforced experiences of social exclusion in the academic context. This book is an attempt to show how technological advances can play an instrumental role in the integration of people experiencing barriers in all fields of education and employment.

Even as ICTs are becoming the norm rather than exception in many classrooms, students experiencing barriers to learning believe they are deprived of general assistive technologies which would provide accommodations to learning environments, and ICTs which help in the facilitation of many learning encounters. The book hopes to dispel the misconceptions and attitudes of

© KONINKLIJKE BRILL NV, LEIDEN, 2021 | DOI: 10.1163/9789004447226_001

many people who still believe that ICTs do not have a role to play in the education and life of people experiencing barriers.

ICTs can be used to promote and ensure inclusiveness and the equality of students experiencing barriers to learning in open distance electronic learning environments. This book discusses diverse topics on ICTs and ICT best practices. We felt compelled to write this book because, as academics, we wish to suggest the direction institutions of learning should move towards, especially those offering distance learning when it comes to the use of ICT in education and other spheres of life.

In order for education to truly be a tool for empowerment, inclusiveness, and equality, all students (including those experiencing barriers to learning) have to be exposed to new technologies and enabled to fully participate to the digital world. Having thus outlined some of the main orientations of this book, let us now describe the book's organisation and content in detail.

2 Book Organisation

The goal of the editors of this book was to bring a different focus to discussions of support of students, approaching this through an empowerment lens. We identified two themes which formed the basis of this book's contributions: barriers to teaching and learning and empowering students and ensuring inclusiveness and equality. These themes also frame the overall division of the book.

2.1 Part 1: Identification and Support of Barriers to Learning in School and Open Distance and e-Learning

There is a growing body of literature that recognises the importance of empowering pre-service teachers with the skills to identify and support individuals experiencing barriers to learning. Agyei and Voogt (2011) advocate for teacher preparation programmes to avoid several obstacles that teachers experience in classrooms. This book focuses the readers' attention towards student empowerment, suggesting that pre-service teachers who are in the ODeL environment have the knowledge and skills to use ICT to identify and support students experiencing barriers to teaching and learning. This is the focus of the first eight chapters of this book as outlined below.

Chapter 1: The authors focus on higher education (HE) in South Africa, paying particular attention to:

- Recent developments (e.g. fees must fall movement) which highlight the need for a more inclusive, student-centred approach to teaching and learning, by making use of ICT;

EMPOWERING STUDENTS AND MAXIMISING INCLUSIVENESS

– The responsibility of HE to contribute to social justice, development, and democratic citizenship.

Challenges encountered (such as massification and stratification) highlight the need for HE institutions to critically examine the values, practices, and policies standing in the way of social justice and inclusion. This chapter conceptualises inclusivity, equality, and equity as follows:

> Inclusion refers to being included within a group or structure. In SA, it goes beyond only physical inclusion and refers to opening up and providing access to previously disadvantaged students so that they can have equal opportunities for academic success and empowerment. In the process, the role of lecturers must change as they have to relinquish their positions of power and authority and be open to understanding the pain of structural exclusion which so many people have experienced.

This requires inclusive curricula, practices, and learning environments (guided by ethical open practices), and identification of inequitable structural arrangements that have led to exclusion on the one hand, and privileging of some students on the other. It considers these issues in relation to issues of equity and equality. *Equality* is a state of being equal in status, rights, or opportunities; the capacity to function as a human being. Things described as fundamentally unjust, immoral, and damaging to human dignity refer to vital inequality (unequal life changes, such as where they grew up, live and access technology), resource inequality (unequal distribution and access to resources), existential inequality (social capital, circles of influence). Equality demands that boys and girls access the same opportunities. *Equity* refers to fairness and justice, providing special encouragement and support for those who were disadvantaged in the past. Equity is concerned with matters of justice and/or injustice. Individual and group needs differ and that implies that to be fair, students' needs have to be considered.

Chapter 2: This chapter begins with an introduction to, and background on, open distance and e-learning (ODeL) systems and the challenges that institutions using them experience. This chapter promotes ODeL as a teaching and learning mode that is accessible "from anywhere, at any time, by anyone, with high impact due to its flexibility". The versatility of ODeL is the reason for its rapid expansion, but with its application, a number of barriers and challenges have to be considered. The chapter discusses the barriers, advantages, and disadvantages of ODeL, which sets the scene for both the chapter and the publication.

Chapter 3: The aim of this chapter is to explore the ways in which student teachers can be empowered with the skills necessary for the early identification of barriers to learning to ensure inclusiveness and equality in education through information and communication technology (ICT). The authors examine recent scholarship to discuss the importance of early identification, the factors of influence, and the challenges faced when providing effective inclusive education. The chapter recommends an extensive training programme on ICT be created to empower pre-service teachers to teach in inclusive classes.

Chapter 4: Barriers to teaching and learning which are intrinsic (within the learner) or extrinsic (within the system) can manifest at any level or phase of education and should therefore be identified as early as possible. Identifying the barriers that learners may experience is fundamental to the success of teaching and the learning process. This chapter argues that there is little capacity provided to teachers to do proper identification, hence the reliance on psychometric assessments. The focus of this chapter is on the role played by ICTs in identifying barriers to teaching and learning in the classroom. The author connects this to the role played by ODeL in capacitating the pre-service teachers to be empowered with skills and knowledge to identify barriers to teaching and learning.

Chapter 5: The focus of this chapter is on higher education in South Africa and concerns the performance of students, their diverse backgrounds, English as medium of instruction, the level of academic literary skills, their limited ability to read and write subject matter, and also the potential of ICT to address these concerns. The authors acknowledge the assumption that students who enter higher education can read effectively. However, they argue that most students might not be exposed to the intricacies of writing from a reader's perspective at the high school level. This is especially challenging for first year students who have to adapt to greater demands of cognitive skills when processing information. This chapter suggests that ICT is an avenue for enhancing academic literacies. The authors view ICT as an ideal resource for ODeL universities to use to overcome the limitations experienced when working with students. The authors show that conventional institutions are beginning to apply ICT strategies and online learning.

Chapter 6: The author refers to the main purpose of the education system, namely to provide quality education, and then refers to the international move from exclusivity to inclusivity, also within the South African context. This chapter argues that despite the correct policy positions and documents, the failure of inclusive education to ensure equality and equity is largely due to a lack of resources and funding, negative attitudes, and a lack of clarity around the means to implement the policy. The author perceives a lack of knowledge of ICT amongst administrators and teachers as being a barrier to technological integration at the classroom-level, especially in the more rural parts of

South Africa. He recommends possible ICT devices that can be used and outlines the benefits they could have for the different categories of learners with disabilities.

Chapter 7: South African universities have a mandate to transform and decolonise the curriculum in order to accommodate the students who come from the previously marginalised and disadvantaged Black African population. The authors make reference to one of the ODeL institutions in South Africa where they highlighted the fact that barriers that can hinder the use of ICT are within students' contexts, the structure of the learning environment, content, and didactics. However, this chapter considers the benefits of ICT, such as giving students the opportunity to engage in critical discourse with others over the learning content while learning at their own pace.

Chapter 8: Higher education in South Africa has gone through significant change since 1994, with a new model of university emerging which uses ICTS to engage in teaching, research, and service delivery. When incorporating ICTS into the teaching and learning process, academics are challenged and forced to rethink their pedagogy. The authors showed that universities in South Africa, and globally, have to cope with large student numbers, poverty, inequality, diverse student needs, high costs, the attainment of measurable outcomes, student unrest or dissatisfaction, and the ability of academics to engage in alternative approaches in teaching and learning. This chapter theorises ICT in teaching and learning as a cost-effective means to facilitate education to a wide range of remote audiences and as a means to generate additional revenue through increased enrolment, improved affordability, saving on classroom space, and providing flexibility in student access.

2.2   *Part 2: The Use of ICT to Empower Students in Different Areas*

This part swings the discussion towards the main goal of this book, which is to illuminate the use of ICT as an empowerment tool in specific fields of learning, including mathematics, speech language pathology and audiology. The last seven chapters demonstrate the different roles of ICT in empowering students who experience barriers to teaching and learning. The use of ICT has received considerable critical attention, recently due to the COVID-19 pandemic. Many scholars (such as Kozma, 2003; Ghavifekr, Kunjappan, Ramasamy, & Anthony, 2016; Kler, 2015) hold the view that ICTS can do a lot of things in the classroom, but one of their most important impacts is the ability to put the power of learning in the hands of students.

Chapter 9: This chapter highlights the importance of ICT in the teaching and learning of mathematics and science to empower students to learn better and with deeper comprehension. The author problematises the different needs that are displayed by teachers and students in their use of ICT. Students yearn for constructivist ICT use while teachers are more comfortable with traditional teacher-centred approaches. The author conceptualised some the functions ICT serves in the teaching and learning of mathematics and science, which includes the display of abstract scientific ideas through images, graphs, animations and simulations; to display natural events; summarise experimental results or ideas; and identify patterns or draw conclusions. The author recommends that ICTs be used to improve the quality of science education, keeping in mind the way that socio-economic challenges can impact the successful use of ICT.

Chapter 10: Community of practice (CoP) is fundamental to the enhancement of mathematical participation in ODeL institutions to promote mathematical proficiency. At the core of teaching is the facilitation of learning. ICTs are used to promote the five strands of mathematical proficiency: conceptual understanding, procedural fluency, strategic competency, adaptive reasoning, and productive disposition. The author raises a concern regarding the lack of policies to guide the development, and implementation, of open and distance learning (ODL) programmes in SADC countries. The chapter uncovers the use of ICT in ODL through a mathematical participation model for communities of practice to overcome students' barriers to learning.

Chapter 11: The focus of this chapter is on the barriers which students with little or no functional speech often experience. There is a need for high level support to enable them to function and participate fully. The authors demonstrate the role of ICTs in bridging the gap created by underutilisation of available technologies due to policy, practice, limited educator skills, lack of awareness and inequalities in education, health and social development. The chapter outlines the value and use of ICTs and augmentative and alternative communication (AAC) technology in school settings to assist with language development, communication, and the social participation of children who struggle to develop speech, language, and literacy. ACC can be used to facilitate communication between teachers and children with special education needs and help children develop the ability to conceptualise ideas and comprehend all sorts of communicating information.

Chapter 12: Teleaudiology is the use of telecommunication technologies to reach out to patients, to reduce barriers, to access specialists and services, and to save on travel. This chapter considers the relevance of teleaudiology in the education sector by applying computer-based technology and connectivity to reach children who experience barriers to learning in various communities. The authors argue that through teleaudiology early identification of hearing problems in children can be done to identify hearing loss, outer ear cell functioning, auditory nerve functioning, allowing support to be provided to reduce or prevent impact in the long term. Universities are urged to empower students by introducing telehealth programmes into their training programmes of health professionals.

Chapter 13: Learners with atypical auditory systems often have difficulty accessing auditory information in the classroom, especially when the infrastructure is poor and acoustics unfavourable due to limited resources for amplification (such as hearing aids and cochlear implants). This chapter focuses on the use and importance of ICTs in the South African education setting to improve learner access to auditory information. The authors argue that deaf education requires a visual channel of input and, as a result, they recommend the design of ICT methods that can attract and keep the learners' attention.

Chapter 14: This chapter focuses on student teachers and in-service teachers (to assist with the development of understanding regarding cognitive skill development, and the effect it has on learning) and scholars (to initiate debate on cognitive skill development).

In this chapter, reference is made to the following conditions which are commonly found in children with special education needs: dyslexia, dysgraphia, and dyscalculia. The author maintains that with appropriate assessment and relevant intervention strategies such children can access their prescribed curriculum. The author recommends differentiated teaching and assessment methods to accommodate children's different learning styles and to support their abilities.

Chapter 15: The author provides an analysis of the impact that ICTs as empowering tools have on the reasonable accommodation of students with disabilities, in inclusive education settings, and the use of ICTs to eliminate or minimise barriers to learning. The author problematises the design of most computer hardware and software which accommodates mainly the mainstream population and which could result in the exclusion of students with special education needs. The chapter focuses on (1) those students who experience barriers to learning where assistive technology (AT) and ICT are not integrated into the teaching and learning, and the effect that has, and (2) the use of AT and ICT in addressing learning barriers and the benefits they can have, based on connectivism theory.

Chapter 16: This is a concluding chapter aimed to bring the diverse topics of the fifteen chapters together. The chapter highlights the intentions and presents the common thread identified from the fifteen chapters. It includes a summary of all chapters and a call for action to the readers.

References

Agyei, D. D., & Voogt, J. (2011). ICT use in the teaching of mathematics: Implications for professional development of pre-service teachers in Ghana. *Education and Information Technologies, 16*(1), 423–439. https://doi.org/10.1007/s10639-010-9141-9

Cha, H., Park, T., & Seo, J. (2020). What should be considered when developing ICT-integrated classroom models for a developing country? *Sustainability, 1*(2967), 1–19.

Ghavifekr, S., Kunjappan, T., Ramasamy, L., & Anthony, A. (2016). Teaching and learning with ICT tools: Issues and challenges from teachers' perceptions. *Malaysian Online Journal of Educational Technology, 4*(2), 38–57.

Kozma, R. B. (2003). Technology and classroom practices: An international study. *Journal of Research on Technology in Education, 36*, 1–14.

PART 1

Identification and Support of Barriers to Learning in School and Open Distance and e-Learning

∵

CHAPTER 1

Inclusivity, Equality and Equity: Student (Em)Power(ment) through ICT Mediated Learning

Roshini Pillay and Najma Agherdien

Abstract

The #FeesMustFall movement and the recent COVID-19 containment in South African higher education institutions (HEIs) has highlighted the need for a more inclusive, student-centred approach to teaching and learning using information and communication technologies (ICTs). Moreover, higher education (HE) is held as the mirror of society and this comes with the responsibility of furthering the ideals of social justice, equity, development, and socially responsible citizenship. Often this contribution is neither foregrounded nor enacted. As educators working in HE, we find that the development of personhood and existential equality is essential for social justice and inclusion within HE. Thus, critical realism and social justice are useful lenses to understand the learning and teaching environment. We employ these complementary lenses to make recommendations towards the (em)power(ment) of students in the online learning and teaching space. In addition, student voice (agency) serves to illuminate some of the barriers of using ICT for the development of responsible citizenship and academic student success.

Keywords

critical realism – empowerment – equality – equity – inclusivity – Information and Communication Technologies

•••

Digital technologies are transforming the world. Their potential for reducing poverty and accelerated growth is enormous, but access

© KONINKLIJKE BRILL NV, LEIDEN, 2021 | DOI: 10.1163/9789004447226_002

to technology on its own is insufficient to reduce poverty, if it is not backed-up by reforms ...

QIMIAO FAN (World Bank Press Release)

∴

1 Introduction

The international and local higher education (HE) landscape has faced consistent critique for its commodification of approaches and practices (Rajeev, 2007). Current challenges relate to massification (rapid student enrolment increase) and stratification (inequitable grouping or categorisation) as white students perform better than black students (Czerniewicz, 2018; Walker, 2018b). These challenges highlight a dire need for a "public good" approach, requiring critical examination of the values, practices, and policies of social justice and inclusion within HE (Leibowitz, 2012). Moreover, public good and decoloniality align with social justice, redistribution, recognition, and inclusion. Therbon (2013) correctly identifies family wealth and/or poverty and race as factors that influence the development of an often-neglected aspect of existential development and personhood, self-formation (Walker, 2018b).

1.1 ICT Increases the Digital Divide

Students in higher education range in socio-economic status which results in unequal distribution regarding access to technology and connectivity (Broekman, Enslin, & Pendlebury, 2002). In addition, the COVID-19 pandemic highlighted the deep gaps in access and equality in the student body. Another factor that contributes to the divide is unequal access to internet connectivity and electricity as well as spaces to work when students are at home during the COVID-19 lockdown period.

In an attempt to address related challenges, higher education institutions (HEIS) continue to turn to information communication technologies (ICTS) to create learning experiences that mirror changing times. We agree with Veletsiano and Moe (2017) that seeing technology as a solution to the threats facing education is a technicist approach. From our experience, the use of ICTS in education has not revolutionied HE as envisioned by many, nor has it improved equitable outcomes in regards to student success. We propose socially just and pedagogically sound use of ICTS, informed by student agency, to enable inclusivity, equality, and equity to address persistent educational barriers.

1.2 *The Affordances of ICT*

ICT is ubiquitous and when used ethically can result in helping people all over the world (Johnson & Wetmore, 2009). Important to the use of ICT for learning and teaching is the provision of rich multimedia environments. Another affordance of this technology is the flexibility created whereby use may occur beyond the walls of a face-to-face classroom at times and in asynchronous spaces suitable to the consumer of the information. Technology provides a collaborative space whereby all are allowed a voice on features such as chats, discussion forums, and other collaborative tools. These collaborative tools may result in a community of practice where learning is passed between more knowledgeable others and novices (Lave & Wenger, 2001). When there is good design of learning, with ICT used as a cognitive tool, it can result in several affordances.

More information on how ICT can be used to support learning can be found in the authentic learning framework which includes elements to encourage multiple perspectives and roles, good scaffolding and coaching, collaborative construction of knowledge, reflection, and access to expert performances all within the use of a complex real-world task (Herrington, Oliver, & Reeves, 2010).

While this book focuses on the role of ICT in ensuring the identification of barriers to teaching and learning, this chapter aims to highlight the need for critical scrutiny of HEI values, practices, and policies against the notions of social justice and inclusion. The argument is that if not addressed, the barriers remain and opportunities to provide the relevant support and to maximise access and participation will not be realised. The target audiences of this chapter are educators, students, parents, the Department of Higher Education, Council for Higher Education, policy makers, funders and university administration, including support staff.

2 Towards Conceptualizing Inclusivity, Equality, and Equity

Two and a half decades into post-apartheid HE in South Africa, much emphasis remains on inclusion and equality, oftentimes at the expense of equity. The aim of this chapter is not to provide answers but to prompt thinking and discourse. The authors, as educators at the University of the Witwatersrand (Wits), start this chapter with a brief overview of concepts to work towards conceptual clarity. We include questions for the reader to reflect upon and to encourage deeper engagement in what can be considered a cursory overview of concepts.

2.1 Inclusion beyond Widening Physical Access

While the Oxford University Press Online Dictionary (2019) defines inclusion as "The action or state of including or of being included within a group or structure", in a South African HE context, it involves opening physical access to previously disadvantaged students. This entails access beyond the physical space, to that of equal opportunities for academic success and (em)power-ment. (Em)powering students means relinquishing our power as academics and opening ourselves up to understanding the pain of structural exclusion felt by students. Walker (2018a) adds that public good and development of per-sonhood is about mutual recognition and social inclusion, we become who we are with and through others and build something better by working together. These concepts resonate with the value of Ubuntu (Msila, 2015).

Opening access requires inclusive curricula, practices, and learning envi-ronments. Inclusion also demands the examination of inequitable structural arrangements that result in exclusion and the privileging of some students (Walton, Bekker, & Thompson, 2015). For practical examples of how inclusion could be enacted, see Danowitz and Tuitt's (2011) careful deliberation, promot-ing inclusivity through engaged pedagogy.

Some questions that need deeper reflection include:

- What inclusionary and/or exclusionary cultures and structures exist in HEIS?
- Why is inclusion of student voice (not) enough?
- How might ICTs mediate inclusive practices or increase or decrease the digital divide?

2.2 Equality and Human Dignity

Equality is defined as "The state of being equal, especially in status, rights, or opportunities" (Oxford University Press Online Dictionary, 2019). Therborn (2013) advances a more useful explanation of equality as "the capability to function as a human being" (p. 41) and inequality is thus fundamentally unjust, immoral, and damaging to human dignity. Distinguishing between different types of inequality is useful (Therborn, 2013). Vital inequality refers to unequal life chances and includes considering where students live and how they access technology. Resource inequality refers to unequal distribution and access to resources; included as resources are people one might turn to for help when troubled and the psychological and political resources at one's disposal. Exis-tential inequality includes aspects of social capital, circles of influence, how one requests help, and one's social circles. It further considers respect, dignity, recognition, and personhood (Walker, 2018b). As far as the development of personhood goes, existential equality links directly with decoloniality as it is concerned with rehumanizing or "liberating humanity" (Walker, 2018a, p. 560).

Notions of equality vs equity in higher education are often conflated. Samoff (1996, pp. 266–267) offers a useful distinction between the concepts: Achieving equality requires insuring that children [students] are not excluded or discouraged from the tracks that lead to better jobs because they are girls. Equity, however, has to do with fairness and justice, where there has been a history of discrimination, justice may require providing special encouragement and support for those who were disadvantaged in the past.

For further reflection, think about the following questions:
– How do HEI structures (policies and physical spaces) reproduce inequalities?
– What possible interventions may assist "equality of attainment"?
– How could ICTs enable equality of access and success?

2.3   Equity as a Matter of (In)justice

Equity is concerned with matters of justice and/or injustice. The Oxford University Press Online Dictionary (2019) defines equity as "The quality of being fair and impartial". However, individual and group needs differ, and this implies that to be fair, consideration of student needs is imperative. The reality is that inequities pertaining to race, gender, religion, and/or ethnicity means that not all are equal and, by implication, that starting points would be different. Thus, inclusion without equity is not effective, but more importantly, not socially just.

Equity refers to both fairness of distribution and procedure (Espinoza, 2007) and comprises different levels, such as equity for equal needs, equal potential, and equal achievement (output). These levels can be examined in relation to the educational process, which Espinoza (2007) sees as including resources, access, survival, output, and outcomes.

A few reflective questions include:
– How do we ensure that current inequities are highlighted in academic practice and scholarship?
– How can equity and social justice in HEI be actioned?
– How can ICTs address the digital divide?

To conclude this section, we suggest that becoming intentional about inclusivity, equality, and equity in HEIs (curricula, spaces, and practices) is imperative. The next section explores two useful lenses that guides one's thinking around ICT mediated learning.

3 Useful Lenses in Examining ICT Mediated Learning

Theoretical and conceptual frameworks help one make sense of the world. Thompson (2018) explains, "A theory is just a way of explaining, of saying how things relate to each other, why they are the way that they are, and how they relate to other things" (p. 6). That said, two useful lenses that guide our thinking and understanding (as educational practitioners and scholars) are social justice and critical realism. See Figure 1.1 for a representation of other lenses or perspectives.

FIGURE 1.1   Summary of Ravjee's competing perspectives on the relation of ICTs and higher education

We see social justice and critical realism as lenses extending the cultural politics of an e-learning perspective. These lenses are not competing, but rather complementary.

3.1   *Social Justice*

According to Fraser (2003), social justice refers to matters of equitable distribution of resources and includes participation. Through participatory parity, all have equal opportunity to participate and overcome economic as well as sociocultural injustices (Fraser, 2003). In this perspective, discomfort, ambiguity, and vulnerability are embraced (Zembylas & Bozalek, 2017). Additionally, Agherdien and Pillay (2018) suggest that a social justice perspective includes,

> being critical of the unspoken rule that students leave everything they have been taught, believed and valued behind, to uncritically accept a foreign, western, culture which exists at many South African universities. (p. 351)

Social justice is hampered when oppressive structures abound. Bozalek, Watters, and Gachago (2015) found that if equitable power relations between a student and an academic exists, student agency is maintained. However, if student agency is not valued by the academic, epistemic injustice results. Bali (2019) describes the concept this way:

> Epistemic injustice is all about hearing/listening and about how some people don't get heard because the hearer has prejudice against their credibility or because social systems have made it more difficult for them to be understood. (p. 5)

Unfortunately, students experiencing injustice often do not have the power, nor the access to resources, opportunities, and practices, that will allow them to overcome it. Thus, if students feel that their contribution "suffers from a deficit of credibility" they are prevented from becoming who they are as they are not recognised as the knowers (Walker, 2018a, p. 561).

3.2 Critical Realism

Social realist Archer (1988) and critical realist Bhaskar (1998) theorise causal mechanisms to make sense of and/or analyse society. In general, realists recognise the empirical/experiences, the actual/events, and the real (the mechanisms that explain the actual and empirical as layers of reality). Realists acknowledge that not everything can be known (Sayer, 2000, p. 2).

The aim of critical realism is the integration of the natural sciences, social sciences and the humanities, considering the link to a "sustainable future" (Huckle, 2004, p. 2). Thus, critical realism is a theory that considers three main domains: the empirical, the real, and the actual as well as the generative mechanism that may be unobserved (Bhaskar, 1998). Blom and Moren (2019) expanded the theory to include context, actor, intervention, mechanisms, and results influenced by politics, stakeholders, institutional considerations, and management.

The framework of critical realism offers an innovative and challenging way to foreground structures, power, ideology, emancipation, and a dialectic materialism that considers the role of social, global and economic factors (Van Rensberg et al., cited in Huckle, 2004, p. 5). Unlike the silo mentality of the past, a narrow view where cognitive bias resulted in the development of multiple academic departments as disciplines, based on professions (Friedman & Friedman, 2018), greater focus is placed on the interconnections between structure, processes, and causal powers. Moreover, critical realism supports the understanding of student voice and the interplay with ICTs for teaching and learning. Leibowitz, Bozalek, Schalwyk, and Winberg (2014) remind us that within the South African context, socio-economic factors do require focus and there is no "predictive" relationship between university type and outcome.

Critical realism considers the various relationships and interrelationships that occur with a culture, a history, and a social structure (Leibowitz et al., 2014). However, relationships are entangled, multidirectional, and thus difficult to map out. Wheelahan (2007) proposes using a critical realism lens, which calls for examining the "underlying causal mechanisms" that shape the world, especially since individual understanding of the world is limited. We now turn our attention to how blended learning is informed by these lenses.

4 Student (Em)power(ment) in the Blended Teaching and Learning Space

In simple terms, blended learning refers to a combination of face-to-face and online (ICT mediated) learning, facilitated through student-centred activities to develop and (co)create knowledge and digital fluency (Salmon, 2013). A critical realist view of blended learning would foreground the institutional structures and culture and student vs. academic agency aspects whilst a social justice view would foreground inclusion, participation, equality, and equity.

Blended learning, and more recently remote learning, is actively promoted at the University of the Witwatersrand (Wits), an IT savvy and "an internationally leading research-intensive university located in Africa" (Crouch, 2018, p. 2). Wits encourages the digital competencies of students and staff using innovative curricula and the creation of 21st century learning and teaching environments (University of the Witwatersrand, 2014). Challenges identified in the use of blended learning include "ICT technical support, capacity development of staff and students and access to reliable ICT infrastructure that supports anytime, anywhere using of any device learning and teaching" (University of the Witwatersrand, 2014, p. 8).

A central question in this chapter is: How can students be (em)powered to embrace democratic learning experiences and blended learning spaces and flourish in the world beyond HEI? We argue that some clues might be found in examining institutional structures and culture and student vs. academic agency. In this chapter, we use the University of the Witwatersrand not as a case study, but rather to provide a contextual example to advance our argument.

4.1 Wits Institutional Structures: Policy on ICT Use
The Wits 2018–2022 Humanities Undergraduate Studies and Teaching and Learning Profiles have seven priority areas that complement the Teaching and

Learning Plan: 2015–2019. Four of these priorities include (1) the recruitment of a diverse student body, (2) increasing good quality throughout, (3) curricula that "incorporates the diverse learning histories and strengths" (2–4) and the use of best available technologies to support teaching and learning. Priority four translates into staff practices where the University Learning Management System (LMS) is used for "distribution of material, communication with students and design appropriate learning tasks" (University of the Witwatersrand, 2014, p. 6). Moreover, there is some consideration of the diversity of the student body as objective f) notes:

> upon entry, computer literacy instruction should be provided for any student who does not have such skills, through the FYE (First Year Experience) computer literacy programme and perhaps through the use of online teaching programmes licensed to the faculty. (University of the Witwatersrand Strategy, 2018–2022, p. 6)

However, we question whether this objective considers the existential inequality of students who hail from schools and homes that have had limited or no access to ICT infrastructure. The zeal for using ICTs should be tempered by the desire to hear and support student voice regarding their competence in using ICTs and by an understanding of the various inequalities that exist. Students need to be active agents in the use of ICTs for their learning and the university should assimilate these views into its policy.

We argue that ensuring equity instead of equality is necessary so that all students from different social classes are able to competently use and access ICTs on and off campus. These considerations become acute as South Africa has the unenviable title of being the most unequal society based on the Gini Coefficient of .68, as more than half the country's population live below the national average of R922 per month (Statistics South Africa, 2017). Moreover, aspects of cultural domination, non-recognition, unequal allocation of personhood (autonomy, dignity, degree of freedom, right to respect, and self-hood) must be foregrounded (Therbon, 2013). Hence, Wits as a 97-year-old historically advantaged HEI is morally obligated to uphold equity and existential equality in students accessing ICTs for learning. To this end, Wits has negotiated 30 Gigs of free data, selected zero-rated sites, and has allocated and delivered 5000 laptops to underprivileged students during the COVID 19 containment period (University of the Witwatersrand, 2020).

While Wits Teaching and Learning Plan (2014–2019) does embrace decoloniality and the development of critical skills of students, more can be done to ensure existential equality, resource equality, and the development of personhood. Through valuing agency and equity, the institution can forge a path that embraces multiple perspectives. Understanding the need to develop person-hood is vital so that all students can take their rightful seat at the round table to become public good citizens.

4.2 *The Wits Culture*

The vision of Wits is "to be a leading world-class research-intensive university firmly embedded among international top league universities by 2022" (University of the Witwatersrand, 2018, p. 5). Despite its research focus, much effort is directed at learning and teaching, including transformed learning. The Centre for Learning, Teaching and Development (CLTD) supports staff in embracing blended learning approaches, engages in curriculum renewal efforts, and generally encourages transformed practices. The Deputy Vice Chancellor (DVC) academic vociferously supports the efforts of this centre to be relevant and responsive to the needs of academic staff and students. Nevertheless, change management is a challenge and discontent remains.

Symptomatic of the wider HEI community, much student protest action has plagued the institution as it continues to battle with racial integration, equitable student outcomes, and student poverty. Recently a hardship fund to the value of R13 million (Wits news, 2019) was established to help those students in serious need of registration assistance. The planned high tech e-learning spaces and smart classroom projects are being established to ensure that Wits and all associated with it adopt a culture of innovation and success.

4.3 *Student Agency*

In terms of student agency, Bozalek et al. (2015) posit that student involvement and agency disrupt hierarchical power relations and offer students choice and access in the use of ICTs. Agherdien and Pillay (2018) and Leibowitz, Garraway, and Farmer (2014) concur that student agency shapes students' responses to their learning. By implication, students take responsibility for their learning, beyond the HEI to extend to their personal and social existence in this world. Student agency occurs through self-reflective and intentional action and interaction within the context (Klemenčič, 2015).

Paying particular attention to power differentials and student (em)power (ment) (both social justice and critical realist concerns) are necessary. Figure 1.2 presents Wits student views on the use of ICTs. While this is not a case study, we feel the inclusion of this data is necessary to advance our argument.

The views of Wits students regarding the use of ICTs for learning compels educators to be student-centred and to be mindful of how they use and access ICTs. In response to the question of technologies/ICTs in their respective faculty and/or classroom, the ideas of unequal resourcing, skill sets (that of

At a Wits Teaching and Learning conference held in 2018, student views on the use of ICTs were explored in a panel discussion and their responses are offered here. While their views, in some ways, contradict the policies that are developed, the institution needs to continue to address issues of diversity, inclusion, equality and equity.	**Question 1: What are your views on the use of academic technologies in your faculty and/or classroom?** ICT is both a boon and a bane Some student need help to use ICT, especially when used for high stakes assessment and should be scaffolded into the process gradually particularly at first-year level Some faculties are better resourced than others Some educators need greater training to use ICT effectively
	Question 2: How accessible are the technologies used? ICT access and Wi-Fi on campus is good although not all lecture venues have internet access International students indicated that compared to the rest of Africa , South Africa has good technologies but data is expensive There is limited use of augmented reality such as second life
	Question 3: What student support initiatives are needed? Students are diverse therefore computer literacy tests are recommended to help support student who had little or no access to ICT Resources and training should be extensive disciple- specific and made compulsory for students Students should be inducted in the eZone spaces Students should be encouraged to form a community of practice
	Question 4: What are some suggestions for enhancing student learning through academic technologies? Educators should [be] more hands-on for students to use ICT in computer laboratories Educators should make explicit the value of the technology for learning Clickers are used often in first year due to large class size but should extend beyond Educators need to be aware of how students access ICT both on and off campus as some students do not have wifi outside the university

FIGURE 1.2   Student views on the use of ICTs for teaching and learning at Wits University

students and educators), and support came to the fore. It also became apparent that ICT use is not only seen as an enabler but also a constraint. Students commented on how ICTs are used mainly for assessment. We were encouraged by students' willingness and courage to contest the notion of purely positive ICT adoption.

In terms of accessibility of ICTs, responses suggested that limited access to resources (a.k.a resource inequality) such as data and Wi-Fi constrained participation. It is suggested that limitations extended to the way ICTs were used and the availability (or rather lack) of more advanced tools.

Regarding support, computer literacy tests were cited as a support need, and so was the need for customised or personalised support. The student support unit CCDU, together with the CLTD, has taken up this task. Coupled with this was a need for induction into the use of high-tech spaces and lastly, a need for collaborative communities of practice. Again, CLTD has undertaken the capacity building responsibility. Interestingly, regarding the recommendations, students referred to the role of educators in making the value of ICTs explicit, in having more hands-on approaches, and in taking student resource needs into account.

Not making assumptions regarding student knowledge of ICTs is vital so that every effort is made to ensure equity and inclusion. Despite the constraints, some factors that can be seen as enabling are the appointment of a DVC for Teaching and Learning that is championing the use of ICTs at the institution and the use of writing intensive programmes that support teaching and learning initiatives.

Going beyond the institutional LMS is another way to (em)power student learning. Much of the current and emerging ICTs offers various opportunities for underrepresented students to collaborate (locally and globally) and learn in new ways. (See Agherdien and Pillay (2018) for an example of how ICTs were directed at promoting social justice.) If sound institutional ICT polices are in place, but do not translate into practice, social injustices may result.

To conclude this section, we offer three practical guidelines to infusing equality in ICT mediated learning (based on Therborn's (2013) types of inequality).

- *Existential Inequality*: Manage the shift in culture from fully contact to blended learning and/or remote learning. Buy-in from the senior executive team, staff, and students is crucial, but offering compassion, empathy, and care are equally important. Active encouragement of this shift needs to include self-regulation on the part of students to prioritise the successful completion of their studies by engaging with set tasks and communicating challenges and inculcating a sense of responsible citizenship to make a positive difference in society.
- *Vital Inequality*: Provide ICT training through a partnership between institutional ICT units, student support units, and learning and teaching centres. Regular check-ins (e.g. surveys) or reviews will ensure that just-in-time changes result, and no one is left behind, especially those in remote areas. Additionally, establish partnerships in the private and public sector.
- *Resource Inequality*: Arrange zero-rated sites, free data, and provide laptops (on loan) if needed. As a safety precaution, add a condition that if the device is stolen, missing, or damaged, a certain amount will be added to the student fees account.

5 Recommendations: Towards Socially Just Use of ICT Mediated Learning for Student (Em)power(ment)

Respecting student voice and/or agency honours the role of students in how ICTs translate, both inside and outside, learning and teaching spaces. Veletsiano and Moe (2017) caution that there is a need for greater collaborative efforts and deeper understandings of learning and teaching, otherwise the promise of ICTs for learning may not be realised. Decolonisation of the internet is another aspect to consider as ICTs are value-laden, both politically and ideologically (Veletsiano & Moe, 2017). Further, to empower students to use ICTs optimally, it is essential that we remain critical of the goals of ICT usage and its learning and teaching implications. Moreover, we should ensure that technology-rich learning environments are not restricted to resource rich students.

Universities should not make any assumptions about the computer, digital, or information literacies and skills of students. Rather, learning analytics could be used to identify students who require different types of support through tracking performance from the first test they write through to considering absenteeism.

At a fundamental level, access to WiFi and ICT use and support should be established based on the individual needs of students and if students have access to computers outside university. The recent #FeesMustFall movement and COVID-19 lockdown saw many students expressing critical condemnation of blended and remote learning on equity grounds. Czerniewicz and Rother (2018) add that blended learning is associated with exclusion.

Students must be prepared to enter the world of work upon graduation, but within that context little consideration is given to resource inequality compared to social capital such as connections, community presence, and privacy. The fourth industrial revolution is upon us, thus understanding the metacognitive skills required for ICT use and becoming part of an on-going community of practice needs deliberation.

Careful design of ICT mediated, authentic, assessments is key to scaffold first-year students into assessments. We encourage educators to use ICTs to foster active, collaborative tasks and discussions, enabling students to become co-creators of knowledge.

6   Final Word

Examining ICT access (inclusivity) vs. equality and equity should ideally be a matter of paramount concern. This ideal should not be lost in the face of multiple demands faced by HEIs. As authors, we hope that this chapter and the reflective questions posed in it result in deeper engagement regarding the use of ICTs and its related barriers. A checklist that can be used by HEIs for reflection can be found in Table 1.1.

TABLE 1.1   Checklist

Reflections on	Yes	No	Comment
Inclusion beyond widening physical access			
Explore mindfully the inclusionary and/or exclusionary cultures, practices and structures that exist in HEIs.			
(PS! A Critical Realism lens could be useful).			
Develop methods that encourage student voice.			
Deliberate on how ICT might mediate inclusive practise or increase the digital divide.			
Equality and human dignity			
Examine if/how HEI structures (policies and physical spaces) reproduce inequalities.			
Explore the possible interventions that may contribute to "equality of attainment".			
Collaboratively consider how ICTs enable equality of access and success.			
Equity as a matter of (in)justice			
Ensure current inequities are highlighted in academic practice/scholarship			
Explore how equity and social justice in HEI can be actioned to promote responsible citizenship.			
Conduct regular evaluation of how ICTs impact on the digital divide.			

References

Agherdien, N., & Pillay, R. (2018). Enabling transformation through socially just critical pedagogies in a health and wellbeing course: A South African case study. *Journal of Human Behavior in the Social Environment, 28*(3). https://doi.org/10.1080/10911359.2017.1423252

Archer, M. (1988). *Culture and agency: The place of culture in social theory.* Cambridge University Press.

Bali, M. (2019). *Listening and epistemic injustice.* https://blog.mahabali.me/writing/listening-and-epistemic-injustice/

Bhaskar, R. (1998). Philosophy and scientific realism. In M. S. Archer, R. Bhaskar, A. Collier, & T. Lawson (Eds.), *Critical realism: Essential readings* (pp. 16–47). Routledge.

Blom, B., & Moren, S. (2019). *Theory for social work practice.* Studenlitteratur.

Bozalek, V., Watters, K., & Gachago, D. (2015). Power, democracy and technology: The potential dangers of care for teachers in higher education. *Alternation, 16*(*Special Edition*), 22(1), 259–282.

Broekman, I., Enslin, P., & Pendlebury, S. (2002). Distributive justice and information communication technologies in higher education in South Africa. *South African Journal of Higher Education, 16*(2), 29–25.

Crouch, A. (2018). *Wits digital learning and teaching strategy* [PowerPoint slides council presentation]. http://intranet.wits.ac.za/_layouts/15/WopiFrame.aspx?sourcedoc=/ Documents/Digital%20Learning_Teaching%20Strategy%20% 20Implementation.pptx&action=default&DefaultItemOpen=1

Czerniewicz, L. (2018, October). *Digital inequalities* [PowerPoint slides]. Paper presented at University of the Witwatersrand CLTD Conference, Johannesburg, South Africa.

Czerniewicz, L., & Rother, K. (2018). Institutional educational technology policy and strategy documents: An inequality gaze. *Research in Comparative and International Education, 13*(1), 27–45. https://doi.org/10.1177/1745499918761708

Danowitz, M. A., & Tuitt, F. (2011). Enacting inclusivity through engaged pedagogy: A higher education perspective. *Equity & Excellence in Education, 44*(1), 40–56.

Espinoza, O. (2007). Solving the equity–equality conceptual dilemma: A new model for analysis of the educational process. *Educational Research, 49*(4), 343–363.

Fraser, N. (2003). Social justice in the age of identity politics: Redistribution, recognition and participation. In N. Fraser & A. Honneth (Eds.), *Redistribution or recognition? A political philosophical exchange* (pp. 7–106). Verso.

Friedman, H. H., & Friedman, L. W. (2018). Does growing the number of academic departments improve the quality of higher education? *Psychosociological Issues in Human Resource Management, 6*(1), 96–114.

Herrington, J., Reeves, T., & Oliver, R. (2010). *A guide to authentic e-learning.* Routledge.

Huckle, J. (2004). Critical realism: A philosophical framework for higher education In P. Corcoran & A. Wals (Eds.), *Higher education and the challenge of sustainability: Problems promise and practice* (pp. 33–46). Kluwer Academic Publishers.

Johnson, D. G., & Wetmore, J. M. (2009). *Technology and society: Building our sociotechnical future.* MIT Press.

Klemenčič, M. (2015). What is student agency? An ontological exploration in the context of research on student engagement. Student engagement in Europe. *Society, Higher Education and Student Governance,* 11–29.

Lave, J., & Wenger, E. (2001). Legitimate peripheral participation in communities of practice. In J. Clarke, A. Hanson, R. Harrison, & F. Reeve (Eds.), *Supporting lifelong learning* (pp. 121–136). Routledge.

Leibowitz, B. (2012). *Higher education for the public good: Views from the south.* Sun Press.

Leibowitz, B., Bozalek, V., van Schalkwyk, S., & Winberg, C. (2015). Institutional context matters: The professional development of academics as teachers in South African higher education. *Higher Education, 69,* 315–330.

Leibowitz, B., Garraway, J., & Farmer, J. (2014). Influence of the past on professional lives: A collective commentary. *Mind, Culture, and Activity, 22*(1), 23–36.

Msila, V. (2015). *Ubuntu: Shaping the current workplace with (African) wisdom.* Knowres Publishing.

Oxford University Press Online Dictionary. (2019). Homepage. https://en.oxforddictionaries.com/

Ravjee, N. (2007). The politics of e-learning in South African higher education. *International Journal of Education and development using ICT, 3*(4), 27–41.

Salmon, G. (2013). *E-tivities: The key to active online learning*. Routledge.

Sayer, A. (2000). *Realism and social science*. Sage.

Statistics South Africa. (2017). *Poverty trends in South Africa: An examination of absolute poverty between 2006 and 2015*. Statistics South Africa.

Therborn, G. (2013). *The killing fields of inequality*. Polity.

Thompson, P. (2018). *Theory fright part one*. https://patthomson.net/2018/11/12/theory-fright-part-one/

University of the Witwatersrand. (2014). *Learning and teaching plan 2015–2019*. https://www.wits.ac.za/media/wits-university/teaching-and-learning/documents/ReviewTeachingLearning2015-2019.pdf

University of the Witwatersrand. (2018). *Vision 2022 strategic framework*. https://www.wits.ac.za/media/wits-university/footer/about-wits/governance/documents/Wits%20Vision%202022%20Strategic%20Framework.pdf

University of the Witwatersrand. (2018). *Strategy 2018–2022 Humanities: Undergraduate studies and teaching & learning portfolios*.

University of the Witwatersrand. (2020, April 14). *Wits switches to remote online teaching and learning from 20 April 2020*. https://www.wits.ac.za/covid19/covid19-news/latest/wits-switches-to-remote-online-teaching-and-learning-from-20-april-2020.html

Veletsianos, G., & Moe, R. (2017). The rise of educational technology as a sociocultural and ideological phenomenon [Blog post]. *Educause Review*. http://er.educause.edu/articles/2017/4/the-rise-of-educational-technology-as-a-sociocultural-and-ideological-phenomenon

Walker, M. (2018a). Dimensions of higher education and the public good in South Africa. *High Educ, 76*, 555–569.

Walker, M. (2018b). Aspirations and equity in higher education: Gender in a South African university *Cambridge Journal of Education, 48*(1), 123–139.

Walton, E., Bekker, T., & Thompson, B. (2015). South Africa: The educational context. In S. Moonsamy & H. Kathard (Eds.), *Speech-language therapy in a school context: Principles and practices* (pp. 15–31). Van Schaik.

Wheelahan, L. (2007). *What are the implications of an uncertain future for pedagogy, curriculum and qualifications?* In M. Osborne, M. Houston, & N. Toman (Eds.), *The pedagogy of lifelong learning: Understanding effective teaching and learning in diverse contexts* (pp. 143–153). Taylor and Francis.

Zembylas, M., & Bozalek, V. (2017). Re-imagining socially just pedagogies in higher education: The contribution of contemporary theoretical perspectives. *Education for Change, 21*(2), 1–3.

CHAPTER 2

Barriers to Teaching and Learning through Open Distance and e-Learning

Shonisani Agnes Mulovhedzi

Abstract

The open, distance and e-learning (ODeL) approach is a new and innovative way of providing flexible access to education. It has been adopted by different institutions and may bring down barriers to teaching and learning in education. Institutions are faced with the e-learning challenges of students who are studying through distance or e-learning platforms. This makes the internet, email, and other information communication technologies (ICTs) crucial teaching and learning tools. This chapter presents the advantages, disadvantages, and barriers to the use of ICT in ODeL. Recent research shows that the graduates of ODeL institutions from developing countries are treated as second class graduates. This chapter discusses the barriers to the use of ICT in open distance e-learning and works to foster an inclusive agenda in education. Barriers include the lack of infrastructure, inadequate time and staff available to assist students, lack of funds and technical knowledge, psychological barriers, and attitudes and beliefs towards ODeL. Educational stakeholders such as students, teachers, governments, and institutions must jointly work to mitigate the impact of barriers to ODeL delivery in empowering students and ensuring inclusiveness and equality through ICT. The chapter ends with a discussion of solutions and recommendations.

Keywords

barriers – developed countries – distance education – education – e-learning – e-teaching – online learning

1 Introduction

Open, distance and e-learning (ODeL) is promoted as learning that is accessible from anywhere, at any time, by anyone and which is expected to have high impact due to its flexibility. This is the learning system that separated lecturer and student from a mode of physical contact. Guri Rosenbit (2009) states that the rapid expansion of ODeL is attributed to many factors, among them: challenges faced by institutions of higher learning and universities, the speed of development of modern and faster communication technologies, and an unquenched demand for education (p. 105). However, Minnaar (2013) indicates that the promise of ODeL has not been realised in many universities as its successful launch is beset by numerous challenges.

Muuro, Wagacha, Oboko, and Kihoro (2014) opine that even when students had positive attitudes towards online learning, they are faced with some challenges including difficulty in communication and the absence of real-time feedback. This chapter aims to examine the barriers to the use of open distance e-learning through the application of information and communication technologies (ICTs). Students, teachers, curriculum developers, researchers, and officials in the Department of Education would benefit immensely by reading this chapter as it fits within the overall scope of the book, working to address the barriers that hinder teaching and learning through ODeL in order to empower students and ensure inclusiveness and equality through ICT.

2 Background on Barriers to Teaching and Learning through Open Distance and e-Learning

The world is constantly changing, as change is inevitable. The process of teaching and learning has changed significantly over the past decades as open distance and e-learning (ODeL) has become one of the most significant avenues for teaching and learning (Simonson, 2012; Simonson, Smaldino, & Zvacek, 2014; Landsberg, Krüger, & Swart, 2019). Ehlers and Schneckenberg (2010) assert that a large number of tertiary institutions and colleges are adopting ODeL globally. Teachers and students, including learners with disabilities, are among those experiencing barriers to teaching and learning through ODeL as increasingly teachers are using ICT to teach learners/students through ODeL.

The teaching and learning system has evolved from the traditional teaching approach to a more nontraditional teaching process. The traditional learning process involves the usage of a paper-based learning approach where the teacher and the student have to be in the same classroom or learning environment, experiencing a series of physical contacts. However, the nontraditional approach includes the use of a "physical contactless" approach where teachers and students do not have to be in a physically confined environment or engaged in a paper-based teaching approach. The nontraditional teaching approach knows no boundaries in its efficiency in teaching and learning deliveries and helps meet the needs of diverse groups of students. Simonson (2012) argues that in the nontraditional approach students do not consider schools to be central to their lives as the majority of them have very different needs as they are older, and prefer attending classes part time while they hold relevant jobs to gain practical experience or raise funds to take care of themselves and their families. This is unlike the traditional student who is on campus full time and prefers the instructor to be onsite and physical.

According to Bates (2015) the structure of teaching and learning has been transformed as a result of the advent of information and communications technology with its "round the clock" society. With regard to education systems and institutions keeping abreast of societal change and needs, institutions need to provide flexible learning opportunities to suit the diverse needs of students and this can only be accomplished through the ODeL process. These institutions must focus on the needs of students and provide opportunities for the development of skills and knowledge that extend beyond the time of formal studies.

In a rapidly changing world, universities need to adopt learning and teaching strategies that accommodate learning in ways that the students are accustomed to in their daily lives. However, there are no innovations without shortcomings and the ODeL process is faced with several limiting factors that present themselves as barriers and bottlenecks that reduce the effectiveness of the teaching and learning process.

3 Review of Related Literature on Barriers to Teaching and Learning through Open Distance and e-Learning

The special concern of this chapter is the advantages and benefits and disadvantages of ODeL for teachers and students in developing countries such as South Africa. These are discussed in relation to relevant literature on the topic.

3.1 Definition and Context of Open Distance and e-Learning

A brief discussion of the underlying principles behind ODeL is necessary to understand the associated barriers. The foundation of open distance e-learning can be traced back as far as the 1990's. Moore and Tait (2002) discuss the concept of independent study as a significant foundation of ODeL. They suggest that successful teaching can take place even though the teacher and the student are physically separated during the learning process and this separation can occur in several ways depending on the nature of the course content and delivery medium.

In a rapidly changing world, the needs of students can only be met through innovative teaching delivery strategies. Open distance e-learning continues to grow as it is seen to be an effective and creative teaching strategy to meet the diverse needs of students. Darinskaia and Molodtsova (2019) define ODeL as the type of teaching and learning that gives students who have to fulfil multiple roles and are affected by the barriers of distance, cost, and time, an opportunity to pursue their studies online. Simonson and Schlosser (2009) state that open distance e-learning is institution-based, formal education where the learning group is separated, and where interactive telecommunications systems are used to connect students, resources, and instructors. Simonson and Schlosser (2009) further explain that open distance e-learning is carried out by an institution and, therefore, is not synonymous with self-study or a non-academic learning context. This means that institutions are accredited to offer this kind of nontraditional learning. Also, geographical differences, distance, and time are major factors considered in open distance e-learning.

A well designed open distance e-learning programme is expected to mitigate the problem of intellectual, cultural, social, and religious differences between students.

Furthermore, communication media are of paramount importance in open distance e-learning as communication between teachers and students becomes less dependent upon physical proximity as communication in ODeL is largely dependent on internet, cell phones, and emails which contribute immensely to the growth of distance education. Finally, open distance education also established a learning group called a virtual learning community, where students from different locations could engage in dialogue, post questions, opinions, comments, and critiques to their instructors and teachers. Open distance e-learning grew more rapidly as a result of technology.

On the one hand, e-learning can be understood as any type of learning delivered electronically. From a broader perspective, this form of teaching and learning process can encompass learning products delivered by computer, intranet, internet, satellite or other remote technologies such as Skype and Zoom, YouTube, and Microsoft Teams (Pangeni, 2016). On the other hand, Bejjar and Boujelbene (2016) define e-learning as the use of ICT, online media, and web technologies for learning. One of the best definitions of e-learning would be one which covers a wide set of applications and processes, such as web-based learning, computer-based learning, virtual classrooms, and digital collaboration. It includes the delivery of content via internet, intranet/extranet, audio and videotape, satellite broadcast, interactive TV, CD-ROM, and more. They further explain e-learning as constituting instructions popularly delivered electronically by a web browser, through the internet or an intranet.

Bejjar and Boujelbene (2016) classify e-learning into synchronous or asynchronous. Both terms refer to the extent to which a course is bound by place and/or time. Synchronous simply means that two or more events occur at the same time, while asynchronous means that two or more events occur at separate or independent times. For example, when you attend live training, such as a class or workshop, then the event is synchronous, because the event and the learning occur at the same time. Asynchronous learning occurs when a person takes an online course in which events are completed at different times. This is when communication occurs via time delayed email or in discussion list postings.

3.2 *Disadvantages of Teaching and Learning in Open Distance e-Learning in the Institutions*

However, there are some disadvantages to using ODeL in teaching and learning. Clover (2017) identifies some of these disadvantages, which include:

- The face-to-face learning experience is missing.
- Most of the online assessments are limited to questions that are only objective in nature.
- There is also the issue of the security of online learning modules.
- The assessments that are computer marked generally have a tendency of being only knowledge-based and not necessarily practicality-based.
- Poor network connectivity, especially in disadvantage areas.
- The high cost of purchasing data for accessing internet. (p. 4)

ODeL also has the possibility of imposing undue stress on students as it does not offer conventional human interaction, especially if students are accustomed to traditional human interpersonal experiences for learning. This can greatly impede their learning ability.

3.3 *Cost Effectiveness*

Balula and Moreira (2014) report that the ODeL system has proven to be cost effective for both the student and for institutions. Graninger (2013) argues that the challenge of having to travel daily to the site of the physical campus is reduced and saves costs. This means that students can easily enroll at an institution from different countries or continents. Also, students can easily attend their classes online and submit their assignments and tasks online via email or other online platform. Additionally, teachers are able to upload student tasks and course materials on online platforms such as Blackboard, where they will be accessible to all registered students and the teacher can monitor the students' activities without having to be physically present. This saves students and teachers the cost of having to travel almost daily and other associated costs. Bates (2015) adds that institutions save costs in an ODeL situation because they do not need physical resources such as offices, libraries, and classrooms where students and teachers interact.

4 Barriers to Teaching and Learning in Open Distance and e-Learning

Although teaching and learning provided from a distance and via internet or email serves as a strategic substitute to a physical learning space, a number of impediments need to be addressed in order for a viable teaching and learning process to be achieved through ODeL. Landsberg, Krüger, and Swart (2019) define a barrier "as an obstacle that keeps people or things apart and it prevents communication and advancement". According to Hodgkinson-Williams (2010), barriers to teaching and learning are problems, impediments, and/ or situations that prevent an effective teaching and learning process. These barriers limit the effectiveness of the students, teachers, and the institution involved in ODeL. Barriers to teaching and learning through ODeL are complex and diverse among various stakeholders.

Chen (2009) suggests that the barriers from the students' perspective could be emotional, mental, physical health issues, attitudinal, financial, legal, mobility, family crisis, and social imbalances. Most of these student barriers may be categorised under student motivation and attitudes towards distance learning or e-learning in particular, or attitudes towards learning in general. From the teachers' perspective, the major barrier to teaching and learning was the adoption of the usual traditional course delivery system which practically failed. Most of these teachers and instructors do not have the technical skills to deliver courses through ODeL (Harlow, 2007). A significant barrier to ODeL from an institutional perspective is an institution's understanding of what ODeL is. Many institutions that adopted ODeL early believe that it will drastically improve students' performance and they rushed into investing and adopting an ODeL system without proper readiness and orientation. This has left a lot of those institutions disappointed as ODeL is seemingly not performing the "magic" they all anticipated (Chen, 2009).

Earlier studies into the barriers of teaching and learning through ODeL conducted by Rezabek (2000) classified the barriers into the following groups: situational, institutional, dispositional, and epistemological. Other studies categorise theme as legal, cultural, and ethical. Berge, Muilenburg, and Haneghan (2002) came up with an updated list of ten learning barriers of ODeL which

BARRIERS TO TEACHING AND LEARNING THROUGH OPEN DISTANCE 33

are, administrative structure, organisational change, technical know-how, social interaction, time, technology risks, legal factors, evaluation, access, and student back end support. Shortly after that, Muilenburg and Berge (2005) conducted further research and concluded that there are only four major barriers to learning through ODeL which the identified as social interaction, administrative issues, student motivation, and time and support for studies.

A number of leading recent researchers (Hatakka, 2009; Hodgkinson-Williams, 2010; Hoosen, 2012; Percy & Belle, 2012; Ngimwaa & Wilsona, 2012; Samzugi & Mwinyimbegu, 2013) summarised learning barriers of ODeL, especially in developing countries into five categories. This includes limited technology, legal, relevance, social, and institutional and national policies. Ngugi (2011) is of a similar opinion that the major barriers to teaching and learning through ODeL in developing countries, such as South Africa, is inadequate financial infrastructure and limited skills and competence. An elaborate discussion of the barriers to teaching and learning through ODeL is provided next.

4.1 Lack of Infrastructure

Infrastructure involves the basic facilities needed for an effective operation of a programme or project. Teaching and learning through ODeL is negatively affected because of a lack of much needed infrastructure. The majority of students who enroll through ODeL do so because of its flexibility and do not have adequate access to basic infrastructure. Gulbahar (2007) reports that the vast majority of the students on open distance e-learning lack access to computers, a stable power supply, printers, scanners, and internet facilities. He further reports that information and communication technology (ICT) is the backbone for e-learning and inadequate access to basic technology would impede teaching and learning. Furthermore, ODeL requires up-to-date electronic hardware and application software. Similarly, Assareh and Bidokht (2011) argue that one of the major barriers to teaching and learning through ODeL is the lack of access to ICTs such as the internet and computers.

4.2 Insufficient Funds

Most students who enroll through ODeL are struggling financially and see that open distance e-learning will eradicate the cost of travelling from one location to another for lectures. However, their financial constraints impede effective teaching and learning as the majority of the students are unable to afford the necessary course materials for distance learning or the technological gadgets that will enhance their studies (Ngugi, 2011). Afshari, Bakar, and Su-Luan et al. (2009) state that effective teaching and learning through ODeL is dependent upon the availability of software and hardware and the accessibility of these resources to students, teachers, and administrative staff of institutions. The costs attached to these gadgets, accessories, and services are quite unaffordable to many, especially in developing countries as the necessary funds are not readily available.

4.3 Teachers and Students' Limited Knowledge and Skills in the Use of ODeL

The success of teaching and learning through ODeL requires necessary skills and technical know-how on the part of the student and the teacher with regard to the subject matter. Tinguely (2010) reports that teachers' lack of knowledge and skills is one of the main barriers to teaching and learning in both developed and developing countries. Ihmeideh (2009) argues that the majority of the teachers that are hired to deliver online classes are not experts in the use of hardware and software or other technological tools used to deliver course content to students. He further explains that most students also lack the skills needed in operating needed technological accessories such as computers, scanners, and interactive application software. Therefore, the lack of knowledge regarding the use of technology in teaching and learning in ODeL is a major barrier.

4.4 Lack of Time Due to a Shortage of Teachers and/or Overcommitted Teachers

Another major barrier to teaching and learning through ODeL is insufficient time on the part of teachers. Ngimwa and Wilson (2012) report that many institutions have a shortage of teachers who are already burdened with the workload of traditional classroom routine programmes. Some of the institutions, especially in developing countries, have adopted e-learning systems alongside traditional teaching systems which has increased teacher workload while the number of teachers has not increased to meet new demands. Moreover, some teachers are also tasked with administrative duties. This has left the teachers with little or no time to adequately prepare and design viable course materials suitable for open distance or e-learning. Also, the teachers have no time to equip themselves with the necessary skills needed to effectively use the technological tools involved in e-learning (Ihmeideh, 2009).

4.5 Psychological Barriers

In addition to the funding, technical, and infrastructural barriers, there are also psychological barriers on the part of both students and teachers. Assareh and Hosseini Bidokht (2011) argue that students are easily confused, anxious, frustrated, and lose focus when learning through ODeL as they require prompt feedback from their teachers regarding course content, assignments, research papers, and a lot more. They further explain that the majority of teachers do not notice the frustration and impatience of their students regarding feedback and, thus, are not able to adequately deal with the frustrations of their students. The expected level of interaction between students and between students and teachers is decreasing due to the open distance teaching and learning compared to the traditional classroom setting. Tinguely (2010) suggests that students' feelings of isolation through ODeL have affected teaching and learning negatively.

4.6 Stakeholders' Negative and Nonchalant Attitudes and Beliefs towards ODeL

Teachers' and students' attitudes towards ODeL have been found to be a major predictor of success in teaching and learning (Afshari et al., 2009). Students with positive attitudes towards online classes, technology, and flexible learning systems exercise better concentration, participation, and collaboration in teaching and learning through ODeL. Teachers with a positive disposition towards learning technological tools and upgrading their teaching skills with an awareness of their benefits also contribute greatly to the success of teaching and learning. Therefore, a negative and nonchalant attitude towards ODeL is a major barrier to teaching and learning.

4.7 Strategies That Focus on Training and Guidance to Address the Barriers

People living with disabilities belong to a vulnerable group that is in need of vocational training and skill development through the following support system:
- Family members are significant support to assist in meeting some needs.
- Initiate community rehabilitation programmes to enhance inter-sectoral collaboration.
- Implementing public awareness campaign to promote social integration.
- Engage them in projects and activities that facilitate de-institutionalisation and re-integration into family.

4.8 Strategies Necessary to Re-train or Upskill Persons with Disabilities Graduates

- Offer expanded number and range of learnership to improve daily living skills.
- Encourage and capacitate youth empowerment by broaden the identified gaps.
- Impart technical capabilities.
- Establish a network and strategic partnership.

5 Solutions and Recommendations

It is apparent that the overarching solution to the aforementioned barriers include making available adequate infrastructure. This will enhance ODeL teaching and learning systems. Assareh and Hosseini Bidokht (2011) report that students and teachers can only make the best use of ODeL if there is adequate infrastructure in place. Students and teachers should be well trained in the usage and efficacy of ODeL tools if their use is to be effective. It is desirable that ODeL institutions adopt an integrated approach to learning and skill development which provides ample opportunities for merging theory with practice.

The training modes should also be driven by a strong partnership between training institutions and industry to avoid the churning out of "half-baked" graduates. These constitute the group of unemployed certificate holders who roam the streets in many developing nations. An effective internship ODeL may also need to be developed to ensure those people who graduate from distance learning institutions which rely on ICT are afforded more practice. It may further be made mandatory for graduates of such institutions to be retrained after spending some time, say 5 years, unemployed.

More interactive sections should be made available for distance learning. This will create a conducive learning community for the distance students and reduce the psychological barriers and feelings of isolation that are prominent when learning through an ODeL learning system (Tinguely, 2010). Therefore, it is recommended that the students, teachers, and other stakeholders be reoriented towards the importance and efficacy of ODeL in this ever-changing era. Teachers should identify all students with disabilities and their individual or special needs, then identify computer programmes, games, or activities that can be used to meet the needs of such learners. It is essential that teachers liaise with caregivers or service providers at home to assist in the implementation and monitoring of assigned tasks. This would help to alleviate the barriers students encounter in ODeL through using information and communication technologies. Institutions should provide all the necessary support systems, including financial and moral support through the teaching and learning processes of ODeL, as this will enhance the acceptance and effectiveness of ODeL. The financial challenge could be overcome by seeking funding from government agencies, non-governmental organisations, the private sector, and other interested parties. Therefore, below is a summary of possible solutions and recommendations:

- Provision of adequate infrastructure.
- Offer effective training to students and teachers in the use of ODeL tools.

- Re-organise students, teachers, and other stakeholders regarding the importance and efficacy of ODeL.
- Provide training in the use of ODeL to all stakeholders, and support to institutions.
- The latter includes financial and moral support.

6   Conclusion

Open distance and e-learning is not a new concept, it has been adopted by a vast majority of institutions globally because of its effectiveness and significance. It has allowed teaching and learning to become more flexible and accessible for students and has given rise to a larger number of people enrolling for distance learning.

However, ODeL systems or platforms have their special kinds of barriers, which include lack of infrastructure, inadequate time and staff, lack of funds, cultural barriers, lack of technical know-how, psychological barriers, and attitudes and beliefs about ODeL learning systems. Partnerships between industry and ODeL institutions can help all work towards the provision of an integrated curriculum which fosters the merging of theory and practice. Learners with disabilities can benefit from the use of ICT while undergoing ODeL through exposing them to computer games that are co-supervised by teachers and caregivers at home.

References

Afshari, M., Bakar, K. A., Luan, W. S., Samah, B. A., & Fooi, F. S. (2009). Factors affecting teachers' use of information and communication technology. *Online Submission, 2*(1), 77–104.

Assareh, A., & Bidokht, M. H. (2011). Barriers to e-teaching and e-learning. *Procedia Computer Science, 3,* 791–795.

Balula, A., & Moreira, A. (2014). *Evaluation of online higher education: Learning, interaction and technology.* Springer.

Bates, A. W. (2015). *Teaching in a digital age: Guidelines for designing teaching and learning.* Tony Bates Associates Ltd.

Bejjar, M. A., & Boujelbene, Y. (2016). E-learning and web 2.0: A couple of the 21st century advancements in higher education. *In Mobile Computing and Wireless Networks: Concepts, Methodologies, Tools, and Applications* (pp. 2150–2170). IGI Global.

Berge, Z. L. (2013). Barriers to communication in distance education. *Turkish Online Journal of Distance Education, 14*(1).

Berge, Z. L., Muilenburg, L. Y., & Haneghan, J. V. (2002). Barriers to distance education and training: Survey results. *The Quarterly Review of Distance Education, 3*(4), 409–418.

Casey, J., & Wilson, P. (2005). A practical guide to providing flexible learning in further and higher education. *Quality Assurance Agency for Higher Education Scotland, Glasgow.* http//www.enhancementthemes.ac.uk/documents/flexibleDelivery/FD_Flexible_Learning_JCaseyFINALWEB.pdf

Chen, B. (2009). Barriers to adoption of technology mediated distance education in higher-education institutions. *Quarterly Review of Distance Education, 10*(4).

Clover, I. (2017). *Advantages and disadvantages pf eLearning.* https://elearningindustry.com/advantages-and-disadvantages-of-elearning

Darinskaia, L. A., & Molodtsova, G. I. (Eds.). (2019). *Modern technologies for teaching and learning in socio-humanitarian disciplines.* IGI global.

Ehlers, U. D., & Schneckenberg, D. (Eds.). (2010). *Changing cultures in higher education: Moving ahead to future learning.* Springer Science & Business Media.

Grainger, B. (2013). *Massive Open Online Course (MOOC) report 2013.* University of London.

Gülbahar, Y. (2007). Technology planning: A roadmap to successful technology integration in schools. *Computers & Education, 49*(4), 943–956.

Guri-Rosenblit, S. (2009). Distance education in the digital age: Common misconceptions and challenging tasks. *Journal of Distance Education, 23*(2), 105–122.

Harlow, J. (2007). Successfully teaching biblical languages online at the seminary level: Guiding principles of course design and delivery. *Teaching Theology & Religion, 10*(1), 13–24.

Hatakka, M. (2009). Build it and they will come? Inhibiting factors for reuse of open content in developing countries. *The Electronic Journal of Information Systems in Developing Countries, 37*(1), 1–16.

Higher Education Academy. (2016). *Flexible learning in higher education.* AdvanceHE. https://www.heacademy.ac.uk/workstreams-research/themes/flexible-learning

Hodgkinson-Williams, C. (2010). *Benefits and challenges of OER for higher education institutions (Open Educational Resources (OER) Workshop for Heads of Commonwealth Universities).* Commonwealth of Learning (COL), Capetown, South Africa.

Hoosen, S. (2012). *Survey on governments' Open Educational Resources (OER) policies.* Commonwealth of Learning. http://hdl.handle.net/11599/291

Ihmeideh, F. M. (2009). Barriers to the use of technology in Jordanian pre-school settings. *Technology, Pedagogy and Education, 18*(3), 325–341.

Landsberg, E., Krüger, D., & Swart, E. (Eds.). (2019). *Addressing barriers to learning: A South African perspective: Identification and assessment of barriers to learning* (4th ed.). Van Schaik Publisher.

Minnaar, A. (2013). Challenges for successful planning of Open and Distance Learning (ODL): A template analysis. *The International Review of Research in Open and Distributed Learning, 14*(3), 81–108.

Moore, M., & Tait, A. (2002). *Open and distance learning: Trends, policy and strategy considerations* [Electronic version]. UNESCO, Division of Higher education. Retrieved August 31, 2007, from https://unesdoc.unesco.org/ark:/48223/pf0000128463

Muilenburg, L. Y., & Berge, Z. L. (2005). Student barriers to online learning: A factor analytic study. *Distance Education, 26*(1), 29–48.

Muuro, M. E., Wagacha, W. P., Oboko R., & Kihoro, J. (2014). Student's perceived challenges I an online collaborative learning environment: A case of higher learning institution in Nairobi, Kenya. *International Review of Research in Open and Distance Learning, 15*(6), 132–161.

Ngimwa, P., & Wilson, T. (2012). An empirical investigation of the emergent issues around OER adoption in Sub-Saharan Africa. *Learning, Media and Technology, 37*(4), 398–413.

Ngugi, C. N. (2011). OER in Africa's higher education institutions. *Distance Education, 32*(2), 277–287.

Pangeni, S. K. (2016). Open and distance learning: Cultural practices in Nepal. *European Journal of Open, Distance and E-Learning, 19*(2), 32–45.

Percy, T., & Van Belle, J. P. (2012, September). Exploring the barriers and enablers to the use of open educational resources by university academics in Africa. In *IFIP International Conference on open source systems* (pp. 112–128). Springer.

Rezabek, R. J. (2000, January). Online focus groups: Electronic discussions for research. *Forum Qualitative Sozialforschung/Forum: Qualitative Social Research, 1*(1).

Samzugi, A. S., & Mwinyimbegu, C. M. (2013). Accessibility of open educational resources for distance education students: The case of The Open University of Tanzania. *HURIA: Journal of The Open University of Tanzania, 14*, 76–88.

Simonson, M., & Schlosser, L. A. (2009). *Distance education 3rd edition: Definition and glossary of terms.* Iap.

Simonson, M., Smaldino, S., & Zvacek, S. M. (Eds.). (2014). *Teaching and learning at a distance: Foundations of distance education.* Iap.

Tinguely, S. (2010). *Issues in distance education: Communication.* http://learning-with-sara.blogspot.com/2010_07_27_archive.html

CHAPTER 3

Early Identification of Barriers to Learning as the First Step in the Inclusion Process

Shonisani Agnes Mulovhedzi and Ndileleni Paulinah Mudzielwana

Abstract

The process of identifying students experiencing barriers to learning is a critical step towards the provision of effective inclusive education. Teachers with a clear understanding of the need for identifying such barriers are predisposed to institute appropriate intervention programmes to identified individuals. As such, universities, as one of the teacher training institutions, are expected to produce teachers who can deliver on that mandate. It is the aim of this chapter to explore ways in which student teachers can be empowered with the skills to identify early barriers to learning to ensure inclusiveness and equality in education through information and communication technology (ICT). This chapter uses a theoretical review of literature to discuss the importance of early identification, factors of influence, and challenges faced, among other issues. It is recommended that urgent and extensive training programmes on ICT be conducted to make sure that student teachers are empowered to teach inclusive classes. Terms considered key in this chapter are defined as the discussion unfolds.

Keywords

barriers to learning – early identification – inclusion – information and communication technology – intervention strategies

1 Introduction

The inability to identify barriers to learning accurately is one of the many problems facing educational institutions today. In the majority of cases, it has been difficult to locate with certainty the challenges experienced by learners in schools. It is common for both qualified and student teachers to label students who encounter barriers to learning as mentally retarded, emotionally

© KONINKLIJKE BRILL NV, LEIDEN, 2021 | DOI: 10.1163/9789004447226_004

disturbed, behaviourally disordered, and slow learners. This failure by these practitioners to accurately identify experienced barriers to learning in their classes justifies their need to acquire relevant theoretical knowledge and skills.

There are many ways to explain the inability of student teachers to accurately detect barriers to learning. According to Gal, Schreur, and Engel-Yeger (2010), this has created problems in the delivery of educational mandates regarding learners with diverse educational needs such as visual, sensory, physical, and psychological needs. Owing to this, some learners have been misplaced in special classes, made to repeat grades, or dropped out of school. This scenario is disempowering to learners and works against the commitment by the South African government to offer an education curriculum which advances inclusiveness and equality (Education White Paper 6, 2001).

It is therefore imperative for student teachers to be prepared in their training to identify barriers to learning early in the lives of learners so that assistance and support services can be provided. There is also a need to use available identification tools that are contextually relevant before any decision for intervention is made (Adelman & Taylor, 2002; Purdue, 2009). This chapter is designed for student teachers; however, a wide range of other practitioners such as pre-service teachers, administrators, researchers, curriculum designers, and policy makers may benefit as well.

2   Definition and Causes of Barriers to Learning

According to Gutuza and Mapolisa (2015), barriers to learning are defined as obstacles that hinder effective acquisition of academic knowledge by learners. The Department of Education (2005) concurs by explaining that "barriers to learning are difficulties which arise within the education system as a whole, the learning site and/or within the learner him/herself which prevent both the system and the learner needs from being met" (p. 6). Visser (2002) also emphasises that these barriers have adverse effects on academic content acquisition. The causes of experienced barriers to learning can be internal or external in nature.

2.1   *Internal Barriers to Learning*
According to Donald, Lazarus, and Lolwana (2006), internal barriers to learning refer to intrinsic factors which mainly operate within the individual while external barriers operate outside of the individual. Intrinsic barriers to learning are inherent to learners. This means they are born with obstacles to learning

which may be visible physically in the form of deformities and paralysis (Adelman & Taylor, 2012). There are also neurological barriers which relate to delays in the intellectual and developmental progression of children. Similarly, learners may be limited in their ability to learn because they experience difficulty with regard to the functioning of the senses. This kind of obstacle is referred to as a "sensory barrier".

Internal barriers can also be diseases which impair the disposition of learners to learn such as pneumonia, tuberculosis, infections, malnutrition, measles, and diabetes. Physical obstacles to learning may include improper functioning of skeletal and motor systems, lack of stamina, poor coordination, and malfunctions in the senses (Kruger, 2019). Learners experiencing challenges in using psycho-motor skills struggle to participate in group activities such as sports and games. This may also result in poor handwriting. The cumulative effect of internal barriers to learning may coalesce to create feelings of anger, stress, lack of confidence, depression, and eventual disinterest in learning (Gal, Schreur, & Engel-Yeger, 2010).

2.2 *External Barriers to Learning*

External barriers to learning are obstacles which exist in the environment of the learner, such as family, school, and the community. These impact the physical and emotional conditions of learners (Adelman & Taylor, 2012). The socio-economic environment in the family shapes the readiness of learners to learn. Children from families that are safe, supportive, and secure exhibit high propensity to engage in academic activities. On the other hand, poverty and lack of basic services exert negative influences on learners which hinder their inclusion in education. Inclusion denotes a process of restructuring school programmes and activities in such a way that all pupils have equal access to all educational and social opportunities at school (Mittler, 2012).

Martinez, Mcmahon, Coker, and Keys (2016) identify a lack of well trained teachers and a lack of a positive attitude to teaching and learning as constituting major barriers to learning. This means that student teachers should not only be equipped with skills to identify barriers to learning but attitudinal issues must also be considered. There are also various aspects of the curriculum which play a significant part in ensuring that all learners are included in educational provision. These focus on the nature of the content, teaching resources, language and methods used, available time, and forms of evaluation (Hoskins, 2015). It is important that student teachers are prepared for the early identification of barriers to learning so that they meet the requisite standards upon entering the profession.

3 The Basis of Early Identification

Students with barriers to learning may be informally identified then referred to specialists for detailed analysis. The process of identifying barriers to learning is designed to specify the nature, degree, and context of the barrier so that correct early intervention strategies can be applied. Intervention strategies denote well-structured, specific, and well-coordinated learning activities and processes meant to address identified barriers to learning (Singleton, 2009; Falth, 2013). Alliston (2007) asserts that early identification assumes that when relevant services and support are provided earlier in an individual's life, then the better the chances of him or her overcoming associated future challenges.

The Department of Education Education White Paper 6 (2001) states that a child who requires educational support should be identified early. The Comprehensive Child Development Service (CCDS) (2008) asserts that it is precisely the plasticity of child's brain development that makes early identification and intervention important. The early identification of the child's developmental barriers to learning prompt referral and help us understand and support the child's conditions and learning needs. This implies that the barriers that learners experience in learning at school can be resolved through engaging them in an inclusion process (National Joint Committee on Learning Disabilities, 2019). Furthermore, ICANCharity (2016) adds that, early identification is everyone's responsibility. This means that parents, teachers, and other relevant stakeholders must work collaboratively to identify learners with barriers to learning and the unique challenges they face.

According to the Department of Basic Education (2014), the main policy that is used in the South African education system to identify barriers to learning is called the Screening Identification Assessment Support (SIAS). Its mandate is to provide a framework for the process of identifying students who need support and providing early interventions. These refer to suitable programmes for all learners who require additional assistance to fully participate and be included in all school activities. The early identification of barriers to learning helps to improve access to quality education for vulnerable learners and those who experience difficulties due to family problems, language issues, poverty, and any other disabilities. SIAS also ensures proper management of teaching and learning processes for learners who face challenges in learning within the framework of the National Curriculum Statement Grades R–12.

Furthermore, DBE (2014) notes that the SIAS policy is closely aligned with the Integrated School Health Policy (ISHP) (2012) in the establishment of a system which ensures early identification and effective intervention to minimise learning breakdown and potential dropout. The SIAS policy further includes a protocol as well as a set of official forms to be used by teachers, school-based support teams and district-based support teams in the process of the screening, identifying, and analysing of barriers to learning. This leads to planning of intervention programmes and monitoring systems.

4 A Brief Overview of the Process of Early Identification of Barriers to Learning

In South Africa the Department of Education, White Paper No 6 (2001) states that from Grade R to Grade 12, admission requirements should be holistic and cover all learners in terms of their learning problems, physical challenges, and other factors. The screening of learners for early identification of barriers to learning include aspects of the physical, social, mental, and emotional wellbeing of a child. Purdue (2006) suggests that teachers who promote inclusive and equality focused education practices are taking steps towards actively identifying barriers to learning and then using this information as a basis to improve their classroom practice. Figure 3.1 shows the stages that denote the process of early identification of barriers to learning for inclusion.

Figure 3.1 shows that student teachers enrolled at universities should be empowered with theoretical knowledge and skills on the early identification of barriers to learning. The knowledge acquired must then be tested in practice during the Work Integrated Learning (WIL), where student teachers are exposed to direct teaching experience. It is through teaching and learning discourses that they are able to first screen, then identify, those with barriers to learning. Student teachers should then be able to infuse ICT skills into their teaching to enhance inclusiveness and educational equality.

Early identification involves the use of screening tools. In South Africa, the SIAS policy framework provides a set of forms which offer a checklist of issues to be considered in the identification and intervention process (DoE, 2014). The identification exercise should be done only after the qualified or student teacher has made observations, read the profile of the learner, and met with parents. The identification of at risk learners is soon followed by instituting early interventions as informed by the needs of individual learners. The SIAS protocol, however, relies on the scores from class observations which do not reflect the nature of a particular barrier to learning.

In America, the most used tool is the Systematic Screening of Behaviour Disorders (SSBD) (Sprague & Walker, 2000). It focuses on the use of multiple gates or screens, that are sequential in nature and linked to each other, to

LEARNING AS THE FIRST STEP IN THE INCLUSION PROCESS 45

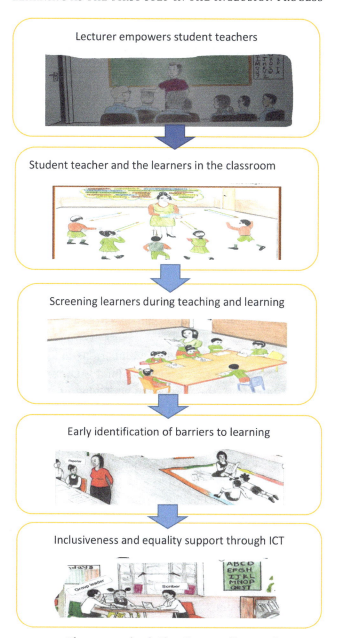

FIGURE 3.1   The process of early identification of learning barriers as part of SIAS (images by K. Ratshilumela, 2015–2017)

accomplish a set goal or task. The three gates of the SSBD are: teacher nominations, teacher ratings of the desired behavioural responses of the learner, and the direct behaviours observed in class and outdoor plays. The School Archival

Records Search (SARS) procedure is another option which requires teachers to analyse the archival school records of learners to capture information on specific things, such as attendance, disciplinary referrals, and negative verbal statements.

In Japan, the department of education developed a tool for screening for use by class teachers. This is a ten-minute exercise which is done at the end of the year for each learner. The check list was precisely developed for the purpose of identifying learners who experience barriers to learning. The information gathered reflects the daily observations of the teacher about the learner without testing being done. The strategy was to develop a time saving tool which is also more objective (Leung, Lindsay, & Lo, 2007).

After training in such tools, student teachers will be expected to implement early intervention strategies in response to information collected from the identification process to facilitate inclusion.

5 The Importance of Early Identification of Barriers to Learning

This may be done to identify or distinguish learners with barriers to learning from the larger school or class population. The National Joint Committee on Learning Disabilities (2019) states that "the purpose of early identification is to determine which learners have developmental learning problems that may be an obstacle to learning" (p. 1). This means that, in picking up learners with learning barriers, service providers should be biased towards identifying those barriers that hinder successful learning in inclusive settings. Moats (2014) adds that early identification does not only help teachers and other interested parties to discover learners with learning needs but also assists them in verifying individual requirements and evaluating the extent of the impact of the identified conditions ion inclusion and quality learning. Early identification of learning barriers aids teachers by helping them:

Understand the uniqueness of learners: The administration of early identification services for learners experiencing barriers to learning can help schools and teachers understand their uniqueness. This means that, after selecting a group of individuals with barriers to learning, it is noble for teachers to then identify and differentiate the types of needs that the learners have. These needs may be shaped by hearing, visual, emotional, or physical disabilities or students who are slow learners or experience psychological obstacles. It is also prudent for teachers to verify the severity of the particular condition. This might suggest the type of intervention needed and the level of urgency required in offering the support service. Spiker, Hebbeler, and Mallik (2005) also note that the individual learning styles of different learners can also be identified through an early identification procedure. Shriver (2018) suggests some of the following as behaviours that diverse learners with barriers to learning may exhibit:

> Acting without really thinking about possible outcomes (impulsiveness); acting out in school or social situations; difficulty staying focused; being easily distracted; difficulty saying out a word correctly, loud or expressing thoughts; problems with school performance from week to week or day to day; speaking like a younger child; using short, simple phrases; or leaving out words in sentences; having a hard time listening; problems dealing with changes in schedule or situations; develop low self-esteem and problems understanding words or concepts. (Shriver, 2018, p. 1)

Facilitate referrals: Early identification helps teachers make referrals of learners with barriers to learning for more detailed scrutiny. Some learners need to be thoroughly screened using multi-disciplinary procedures and teams before decisions are made on the type of assistance to be rendered.

Design and implement relevant interventions: The Department of Education and Skills (2001) emphasises the need for early identification of barriers to learning and stresses that the earlier this is done, the earlier an intervention can be provided. This means that early identification of barriers to learning is crucial as it facilitates an immediate action towards inclusion and the provision of quality education. The Education Review Office (2016) indicates that students whose barriers to learning are identified early are likely to be provided with an education which is relevant to their needs. Johnston and Dixon (2008) concur that identification is the first step towards the provision of quality education in inclusive settings.

Furthermore, the Center for Leadership in Disability (2014) states that the ability of teachers to institute early identification of barriers to learning, enhances their understanding of and the value of implementing correct interventions. Early identification further facilitates placement of an individual with barriers to learning in a particular programme for further assistance (Mittler, 2012). This could be a remedial programme or service. Moats (2014) indicates that teachers can use evidence-based instruction until the child becomes successful. Similarly, Reif (2019) suggests the following early intervention strategies that can be implemented by student teachers in teaching inclusive classes. These are shown in Table 3.1.

Prevent barriers to learning: This inhibits the worsening of the barrier to learning in an individual. It is believed that most children encounter various barriers to learning when they first start school, therefore, it might not be necessary to consider these as problems that need early identification unless they influence the learners' ultimate academic achievement. Once conclusions are

TABLE 3.1   Early intervention strategies for learners with barriers to learning

Strategy	Intervention activities
Monitoring	Providing learner support inside and outside the school, using various teaching strategies, moving around in the classroom to maintain visibility.
Teaching thematically	Break lesson content into themes, allowing for integration of ideas/concepts and connections to be made.
Preparation of well-structured lesson presentation	Present at a lively, brisk pace, be prepared, avoid lag time, use pictures, diagrams, gestures, manipulatives, and high interest materials.
Direct instruction	Use direct instruction techniques and other methods of questioning that allow for high response opportunities.
Encourage strong participation	Alter the way learners are called on to make responses. Instead, have learners respond by telling their partners, writing down or drawing their responses, or other alternatives.

made about the barrier to learning, intervention can immediately be given so as to retard its progress. Ntsanwisi (2010) further clarifies that early identification helps to reduce the learning gaps before the barrier to learning becomes more profound and entrenched. Above all, early identification can prevent the development of further learning barriers in later years. This suggests that when early identification is done, the likelihood is high that interventions will be given, and these will further address barriers before they develop into a more complicated learning disability.

Ensure quality access to the regular school curriculum: Early identification of learners who experience barriers to learning helps teachers implement strategies that ensure that affected individuals gain adequate access to the regular school curriculum. According to Ntsanwisi (2010), quality education for learners with identified barriers to learning helps them improve their participation in inclusive classroom activities. This enhances the learners' ability to experience a successful future both inside and outside of the school. To ensure that children experiencing barriers to learning gain access to the mainstream curriculum, The Understood Team (2014) suggests that schools should offer:
– Differentiated instruction where teachers meet the individual needs of learners.

LEARNING AS THE FIRST STEP IN THE INCLUSION PROCESS   49

- Supportive teaching strategies that improve the academic progress of learners.
- Counselling services that help reduce stigma and encourage learners to talk about how everyone learns in their way.
- Teaching and learning resources that can motivate learners and aid them to learn easily.

6   Use of Information Communication Technology in Early Identification of Barriers to Learning

Bingimlas (2009) observes that "the use of ICT in the classroom is very important for providing opportunities for learners to learn to operate in an information age. Studying the obstacles to the use of ICT in education may assist both qualified/student teachers to overcome barriers to learning and become successful technology adopters in the future" (p. 1). Lake (2019) outlines the following important reasons for bringing ICT into the inclusion classroom:
- Help qualified/student teachers identify barriers among learners.
- Help track progress to help left-behind learners.
- Support qualified/student teachers' efforts to increase learners' access to learning opportunities.
- Identify the obstacles learners face in accessing education and the challenges schools face in retaining learners.

Therefore, the effectiveness of any intervention programme largely depends on good diagnostic information and this justifies the use of diagnostic activities in inclusive education. Mkhuma (2012) observes that while the role of the diagnosis of barriers to learning cannot be overemphasised, it is complicated, time consuming, depends on the experiences of teachers, and typically involves mastery of several complex tools which most regular class teachers do not have. Nonetheless, Singleton (2004) notes that, in recent years, the introduction of information and computer technology to identify barriers to learning has ameliorated the setbacks posed by conventional methods of diagnosis.

7   Factors Influencing Early Identification of Barriers to Learning

There are various factors that should be considered in early identification of barriers to learning. They include the knowledge of teachers about different learning obstacles, parental involvement, use of a variety of early identification tools and multiple diagnosis procedures before decision making. These are discussed below.

7.1 Knowledge of Qualified/Student Teachers about Different Barriers to Learning

The ability of student/qualified teachers to identify early barriers to learning is crucial in the inclusion process. Generally, teachers are seen as having inadequate knowledge or training to successfully screen learners experiencing barriers to learning to ensure inclusiveness and equality of education is achieved by schools. This implies that student teachers should be aware of indicators that suggest the existence of barriers to learning (Ladbrook, 2009). They should also be able to differentiate the diverse learning difficulties and needs of different learners. Such knowledge and skills form the basis for proper decision making and intervention. Mkhuma (2012) observes that one of the challenges encountered by teachers in the early identification of barriers to learning is their lack of awareness and knowledge of indicators that suggest the presence of barriers to learning. Ideally, student teachers should keep abreast of new and innovative ways of identifying and implementing strategies to limit the effect of barriers to learning. This calls on student teachers to adopt integrated methods of teaching, when in schools, which involve infusion of ICT to enhance inclusion in classrooms.

7.2 Parental Involvement in Early Identification of Barriers to Learning

The Department of Education and Skills (2001) requires all members of a multidisciplinary team, which includes parents, to play a significant role in the entire process of early identification of barriers to learning. Parents can provide basic information regarding the life history of their children. This assists student teachers to connect their findings in the identification of learners with barriers to learning with information obtained from parents. Anastasiou and Polychronopoulou (2009) describe the family as having a notable function in the early identification of learners experiencing barriers to learning. Kilgore (2013) indicates that inclusive practices are supported and better promoted when there is meaningful family engagement in the education of their children.

The Understood Team (2014) indicates that "in an inclusive classroom, teachers and parents work together to meet the needs of learners" (p. 1). El Shourbagi (2017) suggests that the involvement of parents leads to improvements in attitudes, behaviour, and school attendance as well as the mental health of learners. It is also reported to improve parent-teacher relations, teacher morale, and the school climate. The participation of parents in their children's education has been associated with increased confidence, satisfaction with parenting, as well as increased interest in their education (The Early Intervention Foundation, 2019).

Similarly, Jacob, Olisaemeka, and Edozie (2015) note that the involvement of the family in early identification of barriers can, among other things, improve parenting skills, reduce costs of special education and rehabilitation, reduce stress, and improve the development of the child. Parents also form part of Individual Education Plan (EIP) team of their children as a required step in the process of receiving special education services. The purpose of IEP is to help parents and qualified/student teachers meet the learner's needs based on the learner's development. It is vital that student teachers be aware of the role of parents in the identification process and consult whenever needed.

8   Challenges Faced by Schools in the Early identification of Barriers to Learning

There are several challenges which are encountered in the process of the early identification of barriers to learning among students. The most troubling one is inadequate knowledge on the part of both student-teachers and qualified teachers regarding inclusive education, and early identification of barriers to learning in particular. They have to be conversant with the specialised terminology used in the field prior to identifying individuals in the class. The proper use of terminology renders it possible for teachers to design appropriate interventions for specific barriers (Kavale, 2010).

Usually student teachers experience challenges that emanate from their training, which mainly focuses on teaching in mainstream classes. This explains why, in some cases, they may successfully manage to identify exhibited barriers but fail to provide suitable interventions. Mkhuma (2012) suggests that most teachers may not struggle with identifying indicators of barriers to learning, although what is required beyond this detection appears to be where the problem begins.

Most schools are faced with large enrolments and high teacher-learner ratio. This scenario is not conducive for effective identification of barriers to learning because it may be difficult for the student teachers to diagnose the needs of every learner (Ntsanwisi, 2010). Such experiences do not exempt student teachers. The pressure of having to deal with many learners causes them to develop negative attitudes towards inclusion. According to Gwala (2008), such negative attitudes may arise as a consequence of insufficient knowledge and skills in ensuring inclusivity and equality of education. This is further worsened by the need for classroom practitioners to infuse ICT into their teaching practices.

Mkhuma (2012) further contends that the shortage of resources in inclusive classes frustrates the performance of student teachers in their conduct of expected duties. They should be afforded enough time to plan, teach, and collaborate with colleagues in order to deliver quality teaching. It is prudent to hold discussions pertaining to strategies of identifying learners with barriers, the nature of available barriers, and possible options for interventions (Mensah & Shayar, 2016). There is also the lack of effective quality support from district-based support teams and ICT tools for use in schools.

9 Solutions to the Challenges

In order to solve the challenges that are faced in the early identification of barriers to learning, teacher training institutions and universities may consider intensifying the rollout of inclusive programmes in their curriculum. This would create a deeper and broader understanding of the purpose of delivering inclusive education, such as providing quality and equitable education for all learners. Furthermore, the Department of Basic Education, through districts and schools, should periodically conduct workshops aimed at improving the knowledge of both qualified and student teachers and other relevant stakeholders in early identification of barriers to learning, inclusion and equality of education, as well as providing relevant services to the affected learners.

Universities should collaborate with schools to ensure that student teachers are assisted in developing the skills to identify barriers to learning. A consideration of the reduction of teacher-learner ratio in mainstream schools must be made so that learners experiencing barriers to learning may easily be recognised. Parental involvement in identifying and providing support to needy learners must be intensified in schools. Furthermore, School Management Teams (SMTs) should ensure the provision of flexible timetables so that adequate time for the early identification of barriers to learning is provided. Above all, the government must consider allocating funds to schools for the provision of adequate ICT equipment.

10 Recommendations

This chapter recommends that barriers to learning should be identified as early as possible. This implies that teachers should receive adequate training to implement the provisions of early identification of obstacles to learning. They will use this knowledge throughout their teaching career. Teacher assistants are also needed to give support, especially in the teaching of overcrowded classrooms. The Department of Basic Education should supply adequate early identification and intervention materials for successful inclusion in schools. It is also recommended that schools should closely collaborate with the Department of Education to convert all primary schools into what are called full-service schools. There should be a marked reduction in the trend of transferring learners from normal schools to special institutions to foster the new philosophy of inclusion.

Parents with learners that experience barriers to learning need to be exposed to programmes aimed at encouraging their active involvement in the learning of their children. Early identification of learners who experience barriers to learning, and the offering of related support services, should ultimately constitute inclusive education. There should be an urgent and extensive programme to empower teachers with ICT skills for use in inclusive classes.

11   Conclusion

This chapter discusses the process of early identification for an effective inclusion process. It is essential that both student and qualified teachers have adequate knowledge to identify learners who experience barriers to learning at an early stage. This will help prevent the worsening of a problem while also necessitating the provision of suitable early intervention strategies. Schools should also develop good relations with parents so that there is continual learning from school to home. It is critical that ICT should permeate the entire process of inclusion, beginning with early identification of barriers to learning, through to ensuring inclusiveness and equality of education.

References

Adelman, H. S., & Taylor, L. (2002) Building comprehensive, multifaceted, and integrated approaches to address barriers to student learning. *Childhood Education, 78*(5), 261–268.

Adelman, H. S., & Taylor, L. (2012). Mental health in schools: Moving in new directions. *Contemporary School Psychology, 16*(1), 9–18.

Alliston, L. (2007). *Principles and practices in early intervention: A literature review for the Ministry of Education.* https://www.educationcounts.govt.nz/pdf

Bingimlas, K. A. (2009). Barriers to the successful integration of ICT in teaching and learning environments: A review of the literature. *Eurasia Journal of Mathematics, Science & Technology Education, 5*(3), 235–245.

Center for Leadership in Disability. (2014). *Early identification and screening.* Georgia State University.

Comprehensive Child Development Service. (2008). *Pre-primary learners development and behaviour management.* https://www.edb.gov.hk/en/edu-system/preprimary-kindergarten/comprehensive-child-development-service/index.html

Department for Education and Skills. (2001). *Special educational needs code of practice.* DfES Publications.

Department of Basic Education. (2010). *Guidelines for Inclusive Teaching and Learning: Education Building an Inclusive Education and Training System.* Government Printers.

Department of Basic Education. (2014). *Policy on screening, identification, assessment and support.* Government Printer.

Department of Education. (2001). *Education White paper 6, special needs education: Building on inclusive education and training.* Department of Education.

Donald, D., Lazarus, S., & Lolwana, P. (2006). *Educational psychology in social context.* Oxford University Press.

Education Review Office. (2016). *Inclusion of learners with special needs in early childhood services: Introduction.* https://www.ero.govt.nz/publications/inclusion-of-children-with-special-needs-in-early-childhood-services/

El Shourbagi, S. (2017). Parental involvement in inclusive classrooms for students with learning disabilities at Omani schools as perceives by teachers. *Journal of Psychology Cognition, 2*(2), 133–137.

Falth, L. (2013). *The use of interventions for promoting reading development among struggling readers.* Linnaeus University Press.

Gal, E., Schreur, N., & Engel-Yeger, B. (2010). Inclusion of children with disabilities: Teachers' attitudes and requirements for environmental accommodations. *International Journal of Special Education, 25*(2), 89–99.

Gutuza, R. F., & Mapolisa, T. (2015). Challenges of assessment of learners with special learning needs. *Journal of Humanities and Social Sciences, 4*(2), 1–3.

Gwala, Q. V. (2006). *Challenges facing the implementation of inclusive education in primary schools* (Unpublished theses). University of Zululand.

Hatch, J. A. (2002). *Qualitative research in educational settings.* State University of New York Press.

Health Basic Education. (2012). *Integrated school health policy.* Government Printer.

Hoskins, G. A. (2015). *Exploring the learning experiences of grade 6–9 dyslexic school learners in a long-term remedial school.* University of South Africa.

ICANcharity. (2016). *Early identification and intervention.* http://blog.ican.org.uk/2016/09/early-identification-and-intervention/

Jacob, U. S., Olisaemeka, A. N., & Edozie, I. S. (2015). Developmental and communication disorders in learners with intellectual disability: The place of early intervention for effective inclusion. *Journal of Education and Practice, 6*(36), 42–56.

Johnston, M., & Dixon, D. (2008). Current issues and new directions in psychology and health: What happened to behaviour in the decade of behaviour? *Psychology and Health, 23*(5), 509–513.

Kavale, A. K. (2010). Identifying specific learning disability: Is responsive to intervention the answer? *Journal of Learning Disabilities, 38*(6), 553–562.

Kilgore, K. (2018). *10 steps to implementing effective inclusive practices: A guide for schoolsSite leaders*. The SUNS Center.

Ladbrook, M. W. (2009). *Challenges experienced by educators in the implementation of inclusive education in primary schools in South Africa* (Unpublished thesis). University of South Africa.

Lake, A. (2019). *How ICTs can help overcome the barriers that stand between millions of children and an education.* https://news.itu.int/icts-can-overcome-barriers-that-stand-between-millions-children-education/

Landsberg, E., Krüger, D., & Swart, E. (Eds.). (2019). *Addressing barriers to learning: A South African perspective: Identification and assessment of barriers to learning* (4th ed.). Van Schaik Publisher.

Leung, C., Lindsay, G., & Lo, S. K. (2007). Early identification of primary school students with learning difficulties in Hong Kong: The development of a checklist. *European Journal of Special Needs Education, 22*(3), 327–339.

Martinez, A., Mcmahon, S. D., Coker, C., & Keys, C. B. (2016). Teacher behaviour practices: Relations to student risk behaviours, learning barriers and school climate. *Psychology in the Schools, 53*(8), 817–830.

Mensah, A. A., & Shayar, J. B. (2016). Identification of special educational needs for early childhood inclusive education in Ghana. *Journal of Education and Practice, 7*(11), 1–8.

Mittler, P. (2012). *Working towards inclusive education: Social contexts*. Routledge.

Mkhuma, I. L. (2012). *The challenges experienced by teachers in identifying learners who experience barriers to learning in a rural full-service school in KwaZulu-Natal.* University of South Africa.

Moats, L. (2014). What teachers don't know and why they aren't learning it: Addressing the need for content and pedagogy in teacher education. *Australian Journal of Learning Difficulties, 19*(2), 75–91.

National Joint Committee on Learning Disabilities. (2019). *Learning disabilities and young learners: Identification and intervention.* http://www.ldonline.org/article/11511/

Ntsanwisi, L. N. (2010). *The identification of barriers to learning by grade 3 teachers in the Ritavi district of the Limpopo province.* University of Limpopo.

Purdue, K. (2006). Learners and disability in early childhood education: "Special" or inclusive education? *Early Childhood, 10*(2), 12–15.

Reif, S. F. (2019). *The educators 'guide to learning disabilities and ADHD.* https://nevadaadrc.com/resources/learn-about/item/607-individualized-education-program-the-process

Shriver, E. K. (2018). *What are some signs of learning disabilities.* https:/nichd.nih.gove/health/topic/learning/conditions/signs

Singleton, C. (2004). Using computer-based assessment to identify learning problems. In L. Florian & J. Hegarty (Eds.), *ICT and special educational needs: A tool for inclusion* (pp. 46–63). Open University Press.

Singleton, C. (2009). *Intervention for dyslexia. A review of published evidence on the impact of specialist dyslexia teaching.* DfES Publications.

Spiker, D., Hebbeler, K., & Mallik, S. (2005). Developing and implementing early intervention programs for children with established disabilities. In M. J. Guralnick (Ed.), *The developmental systems approach to early intervention* (pp. 305–349). Paul H. Brookes Publishing Co.

Sprague, J., & Walker, H. (2000). Early identification and intervention for youth with antisocial and violent behavior. *Exceptional Children, 66*(3), 367–379.

The Early Intervention Foundations. (2019). *What is early intervention?* https://www.eif.org.uk/why-it-matters

The Understood Team. (2014). *Benefits of inclusion classrooms. Understood for learning & attention issues.* Understood For All Inc.

Visser, T. (2002). *Personality traits of learners with special education needs: Implementations in an inclusive education setting* (Unpublished M.Ed. dissertation). University of South Africa.

CHAPTER 4

The Role of Information and Communication Technologies in the Identification of Barriers to Teaching and Learning

Ramashego Shila Mphahlele

Abstract

One of the dominant assumptions made about the identification of barriers to teaching and learning is that only psychological and medical tests can be used. Research indicate that the identification of barriers to teaching and learning begins with continuous assessment during the presentation of lessons in the classroom by the teacher. However, there is little capacity provided to teachers to do proper identification, hence the reliance on psychometric assessments. The focus of this chapter will be on the role played by information and communication technologies (ICTs) in identifying barriers to teaching and learning in the classroom. The use of health and medical practitioners in identifying teaching and learning barriers in the classroom has created a gap which took away the role of teachers in identifying and addressing teaching and learning barriers. This gap will be explored with the question in mind of whether the identification of barriers should be understood from an inclusion perspective or a psychological/ medical perspective. This chapter will argue that ICTs have a comprehensible role in identifying barriers to teaching and learning and to align that with the role of open distance and e-learning education in capacitating pre-service teachers.

Keywords

barriers to teaching and learning – continuous assessment – information communication technologies

1 Introduction

The identification of barriers to teaching and learning is an important component of the South African education system and plays a key role in the implementation of an inclusive education system. It is believed that one

© KONINKLIJKE BRILL NV, LEIDEN, 2021 | DOI: 10.1163/9789004447226_005

cannot mention inclusive education without alluding to Education White Paper 6 (EWP6), "Building an inclusive education and training system".[1] The EWP6 served as a vehicle for inclusive education for many years. Ten years after South African democracy, the Department of Education renewed interest in the implementation of inclusive education by introducing the Screening Identification Assessment and Support (SIAS) policy.[2] The SIAS policy was introduced to improve access to quality education for vulnerable learners and for those who experience barriers to teaching and learning. Previous studies mostly refer to barriers to learning. Despite its common usage, in this chapter I refer to barriers to teaching *and* learning because teaching and learning have a circular relationship with mutual benefit which derives from this circularity (Harpaz, 1973).

Although identification of barriers to teaching and learning is seen as the second step of the SIAS process, it should be noted that it is rather the first step. During the teaching and learning process the teacher can identify barriers to teaching and learning even though he or she might not be able to specify the type or form of the barrier, hence screening should be done. Drawing from the principles of support from the Department of Basic of Education (2014), it would seem that the role of screening is to eliminate diagnosis of learners by medical and psychological staff which leads to remediation rather than support. In this chapter I view identification of barriers to teaching and learning in higher education institutions as equally important as in basic education institutions.

It should be noted that barriers to teaching and learning may arise at any level or phase of education. This chapter focuses on identification of barriers to teaching and learning in primary schools so that learners can be supported as early as possible in order to be empowered throughout their education career. First, this chapter outlines the types of barriers and the factors that may cause barriers to teaching and learning. Second, it provides context through a discussion of five primary school teachers' experiences to demonstrate how they used different instruments including ICTs to identify different types of barriers to teaching and learning. Finally, the use of ICTs in the identification of barriers to teaching and learning is discussed in relation to the reading difficulties experienced in five primary schools in Gauteng Province.

2   Types and Factors That May Cause Barriers to Teaching and Learning

Chapter 2 of this book delineated barriers to teaching and learning in open, distance and e-learning (ODeL). This chapter discussions in more depth the types of barriers, some of which are outlined in detail in Chapter 2, for the purpose of clarifying which barriers can be or cannot be identified through instruments such as tests or information and communication technologies (ICTs). There is a consensus among different researchers that barriers to teaching and learning are either intrinsic or extrinsic. Linking up with the title of this book, *Empowering Students and Ensuring Inclusiveness and Equality through ICT*, this chapter argues that pre-service teachers in ODeL institutions should be empowered with knowledge and skills to identify barriers to teaching and learning. I base this argument on Reid and Came's (2009) view that it is important to obtain an understanding of the type of difficulties experienced by learners and to identify how these difficulties can be minimised. With that in mind, it is safe to conclude that pre-service teachers in ODeL need not only learn about what they will teach to the learner, but also what the learner can or cannot do. Figure 4.1 illustrates the two types of barriers to teaching and learning together with factors that may cause these barriers.

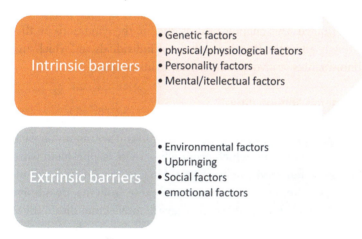

FIGURE 4.1   Types of barriers to teaching and learning with factors that may cause them

It can be seen in Figure 4.1 that there are two types of barriers to teaching and learning: intrinsic and extrinsic. Intrinsic barriers are defined by various scholars as barriers that are within the learner, meaning some of them are barriers learners are born with. Extrinsic barriers are those found outside the learner such as fear and hunger. In this chapter I focus on the intrinsic barriers to teaching and learning because they are within the learner and they require some instruments to be identified. This need for identification is discussed in the section on identifying barriers to teaching and learning below. It is essential that pre-service teachers in ODeL are aware of the existence of barriers to teaching and learning and know how to identify them. As recommended by (Sánchez, de Haro Rodríguez, & Martínez, 2019) pre-service teachers should be capable of proposing changes and improvements that eliminate barriers to teaching and learning in order to offer inclusive responses to learners. Empowering pre-service teachers with skills to identify barriers to teaching and learning will ensure that they do not perpetuate or develop them when they are in practice. In the following section I discuss the examples of barriers to teaching and learning presented in Figure 4.1.

2.1 Genetic Conditions That May Cause Barriers to Teaching and Learning

Many medical scholars hold the view that some genetic conditions are inherited from the parents, while other genetic conditions are caused by acquired changes or modifications in a pre-existing gene or group of genes. According to Stöppler (2018), a genetic condition is any disease that is caused by an abnormality in an individual's genome, which is the person's entire genetic makeup. There are different types of genetic conditions as outlined by Stöppler (2018), namely, single gene inheritance, multifactorial inheritance, chromosome abnormalities, and mitochondrial inheritance. This chapter focuses only on the conditions on the above list that strongly affect the learning abilities of individuals and which are chromosome abnormalities or involve mitochondrial inheritance.

2.1.1 Chromosome Abnormalities

Examples of chromosome abnormalities include Down syndrome, Turner syndrome, Klinefelter syndrome and cri-du-chat syndrome and are mainly caused by abnormalities in chromosomes which occur when there is a problem with cell division. Most of the full-service schools (FSS)[3] in Gauteng Province admit students with Down syndrome[4] and a majority of these students are admitted into the special schools for students with severe intellectual disabilities. When children with Down syndrome are admitted to ordinary schools or FSS it might not be easy for the teachers to identify their barriers to teaching and learning, especially in the foundation phase. It should be noted that the identification of teaching and learning barriers should not be based on assumptions or perceptions; rather, the identification of barriers to teaching and learning requires knowledge, skill, and relevant tools. Sometimes it may also require certain medical assessments.

2.1.2 Mitochondrial Inheritance

Mitochondrial inheritance can influence the development of genetic conditions that are caused by changes in the non-nuclear DNA of mitochondria. Mitochondria are small round or rod-like organelles that are involved in cellular respiration and are found in the cytoplasm of plant and animal cells. Each mitochondrion may contain 5 to 10 circular pieces of DNA. Egg cells, but not sperm cells, keep their mitochondria during fertilisation. One of the examples of a condition involving mitochondrial inheritance which is common in the teaching and learning situation is epilepsy. Conditions such as epilepsy can only be diagnosed medically; however, the teacher can identify the symptoms if he or she is educated about them. It has medically been proven that epileptic seizures can stop memory from working properly. Since memory aids in the encoding, storing, retaining, and recalling of information during the learning process, it is worth considering how epilepsy might create barriers to teaching and learning.

2.2 Physical/Physiological Conditions That Can Cause Barriers to Teaching and Learning

Physical/physiological barriers to teaching and learning may result from individuals' discomfort, caused by ill health, poor eye sight, hearing difficulties, or language difficulties. Omollo (2015) noted that physical/physiological barriers to teaching and learning are related to the limitations of the human body and the human mind (memory, attention, and perception).

2.3 Personality Traits That Can Cause Barriers to Teaching and Learning

Soto (2018) has proposed a taxonomy of personality traits based on common language descriptors called Big Five personality traits. He based his idea on the association between words and not on neuropsychological experiments. In this Big Five personality traits approach, Soto (2018) suggests five broad dimensions commonly used to describe the human personality, namely: openness to experience, conscientiousness, extraversion, agreeableness, and neuroticism. Drawing from Soto's argument that possession of the afore-mentioned personality traits could make someone more likely to participate in certain activities, it is possible that the lack of these traits can cause barriers to teaching and learning. For instance, lack of openness to experience might be due to fear of embarrassment, doubt, and inadequacy, all of which can lead to a student or a learner not participating in teaching and learning activities.

2.4 Mental/Intellectual Conditions That Can Cause Barriers to Teaching and Learning

There is some evidence from medical researchers to suggest that mental and intellectual conditions are often caused by various genetic disorders and infections. Australian Disability Clearing House on Education and Training (ADCET) (2019) describes mental and intellectual conditions as those which significantly reduce an individual's ability to understand new or complex information, learn new skills, and to cope independently, including in regard to social functioning. ADCET also argues that there are many types of mental and intellectual conditions, with varying degrees of severity. When it comes to their effect on teaching and learning activities, ADCET (2019) highlights a number of common characteristics that may have a significant impact on an individual's learning, including:

– Difficulty understanding new information.
– Difficulties with communication and social skills.
– Slow cognitive processing time.
– Difficulty in the sequential processing of information.
– Difficulties comprehending abstract concepts.

These are just some of the intrinsic barriers to teaching and learning that can be identified. The factors mentioned in Figure 4.1 may manifest in different ways to different students and may also cause different barriers which are summarised in Table 4.1.

TABLE 4.1   Factors, manifestations and barriers to teaching and learning

Examples of factors that may cause the barrier	Manifestation	Barriers to learning
Lack of sleep (due to overindulgence in entertainment/too much noise at home)	Sleeping in the classroom Tiredness Lack of concentration	Incomplete learning activities Reading difficulties
Visual impairment	Clumsiness Holding reading material very close or far away from eyes	Writing difficulties Reading difficulties
Auditory impairment	Inattentiveness Lip reading Turns head to listen	Misinterpretation of teaching and learning instructions Spelling problems
Trauma/emotional factors	Changed behaviour (withdrawn/ hyperactive) Lack of concentration Forgetfulness Less interest in academic activities Difficulty following simple instructions	Mathematical difficulties Incomplete learning activities Reading difficulties Study difficulties (in senior and FET phases)

THE ROLE OF INFORMATION AND COMMUNICATION TECHNOLOGIES   63

3   Identifying Barriers to Teaching and Learning

In many instances, barriers to teaching and learning are noticed by the teacher in the classroom when the student is struggling or unable to do academic activities as expected, especially to his or her level. Table 4.1 indicates the manifestations of some examples of barriers shown in Figure 4.1 and the type of barriers to teaching and learning that they may cause.

A teacher who noticed any of the manifestations shown in Table 4.1 in a particular student might want to find out more about what is causing the barrier. That is when the teacher might want to screen the student to identify the possible cause and the effect the barrier has on the student's learning. It should be noted that the manifestations listed in Table 4.1 are not only limited to the factors they are associated within the table as the manifestations might be a result of one or more factors including those that were indicated in Figure 4.1. For example, the learner might be sleeping in the classroom because of trauma or other social or emotional factors. Before proceeding to the identification of barriers to teaching and learning, one should be informed about the different ways to identify different barriers.

This chapter focuses on the identification of barriers to teaching and learning which can be identified by the teacher in the classroom. The previous section put forward and briefly described the different intrinsic factors that may cause barriers to teaching and learning. It should be noted that genetic, physical/physiological and mental and intellectual conditions are medical conditions, therefore only medical practitioners can diagnose them. However, in relation to physical/physiological barriers, the teacher can screen the student for the extent and nature of the barriers to teaching and learning. This brings us to the processes and instruments that can be used to identify barriers to teaching and learning.

3.1   *Processes and Instruments Used to Identify Barriers to Teaching Learning*

It has commonly been assumed that identifying barriers to teaching and learning is largely based on evaluations, assessments, and screening tests that are mostly psychologically oriented and were mostly referred to as diagnostic assessments. A great deal of previous research into the use of diagnostic assessments to identify barriers to teaching and learning including the work of Nel, Nel, and Lebeloane (2013) has theorised that it requires a multidisciplinary or collaborative approach that involves different professionals and parents. In this process mostly, standardised tests[5] are used. There are also some informal scholastic tests that are used to identify barriers to teaching and learning such as those identifying spelling, reading, and writing difficulties. An example of such a test are Informal Reading Inventories (IRIS). Mphahlele (2018) explained IRIS as instruments mostly used to identify reading difficulties, such as word recognition, fluency, comprehension, and overall reading levels.

Drawing from the study conducted by Mphahlele (2018), this section discusses the instruments used in schools to identify barriers to teaching and learning, with special attention to reading difficulties. Reading difficulties are one of the barriers to teaching and learning presented in column three of Table 4.1. It can be seen from Table 4.1 that reading difficulties can be caused by almost all the factors listed in column one. This study was conducted in five FSS in Gauteng Province where 47 teachers were given a structured questionnaire with several variables. This chapter only focuses on three of the ten variables: the instruments used to identify reading difficulties, the possible contributing factors to reading difficulties, and the use of ICTs to identify learners experiencing reading difficulties. Table 4.2 presents the instruments used by teachers in the five selected FSS to identify reading difficulties and the frequency of their use.

It is apparent from Table 4.2 that some individual tools were used more extensively (e.g. guided reading with a 59.57% often/always response), while other tools were used less often/seldom (e.g. ICTs with a 70.21% never/seldom response) and there was great variability in use. The limited used of ICTs in this instance was attributed to the availability of ICTs, where another variable indicated that by far the majority of teacher-participants (73.4% overall never/seldom response) stated that all ICT-related tools and appliances are not freely available. Without getting into the details of the study, I want to point to the possible contributing factors to reading difficulties (in Table 4.3) which were identified in the five FSS in an effort to provide insight into some of the possible causes of reading difficulties and to communicate the importance of identifying exactly what is the cause in order to provide proper support.

It appears from Table 4.3 that some of the factors discussed in the previous section and the examples of factors presented in Table 4.1 form part of the possible contributing factors towards reading difficulties. This serves as confirmation that one barrier to teaching and learning might be caused by different factors. The only way to know the factors is to assess or screen for identification. The individual response patterns (individual row frequencies and percentages in Table 4.3) were further investigated through the Chi-square test. The fact that the Chi-square test30 statistic for this distribution is statistically significant at the 0.1% level of significance, implies that some of the individual response patterns (individual rows of the table), over the proportions, differ in a statistically significant way from other response patterns. In this case, language, socio-economic factors, and social problems stand out as factors that

THE ROLE OF INFORMATION AND COMMUNICATION TECHNOLOGIES 65

TABLE 4.2   Instruments used to identify reading difficulties in the FSS

Items	Frequency of use			Total
Frequency row percentage	Never/seldom	Sometimes	Often/always	
Informal reading inventories	17 36.17	12 25.53	18 38.30	47
Norm reference tests	22 46.81	12 25.53	13 27.66	47
Standard-based tests	22 46.81	10 21.28	15 31.91	47
Portfolios	21 44.68	14 29.79	12 25.53	47
Rubrics	13 27.66	13 27.66	21 44.68	47
Response to intervention	12 25.53	17 36.17	18 38.30	47
Language experience approach	17 36.17	8 17.02	22 46.81	47
Guided reading	8 17.02	11 23.40	28 59.57	47
Integrated approach	14 29.79	8 17.02	25 53.19	47
ICTS	33 70.21	8 17.02	6 12.77	47
Total	179 38.09%	113 24.04%	178 37.87%	470

Note: The probability of the Chi-square statistic assuming the value of $53.54 < 0.001$***
Significance legend: *: statistical significance is on the 5% level; **: statistical significance is on the 1% level; ***: statistical significance is on the 0.1% significance level
SOURCE: MPHAHLELE (2018)

affect learners experiencing reading difficulties most acutely since proportions of over 40% "substantial/great proportion of learners" were indicated in these instances. Turning now to the use of ICTs to identify learners experiencing reading difficulties, it should be noted that the relevance of this information to this chapter is to highlight one of the roles of ICTs in identification of barriers to teaching and learning.

TABLE 4.3   Possible contributing factors towards reading difficulties

Items	Proportion of learners possibly affected by listed factors			Total
Frequency row percentage	Almost none/ small proportion	Approx. 50%	Substantial great proportion	
Intellectual factors	30 63.83	11 23.40	6 12.77	47
Language problems	16 34.04	12 25.53	19 40.43	47
Learning factors	19 40.43	14 29.79	14 29.79	47
Physical/medical factors	36 76.60	9 19.15	2 4.26	47
Hearing problems	43 91.49	3 6.38	1 2.13	47
Visual problems	41 87.23	6 12.77	21 44.68	47
Socio-economic problems	19 40.43	7 14.89	21 44.68	47
Social problems	16 34.04	10 21.28	21 44.68	47
Cultural problems	26 55.32	11 23.40	10 21.28	47
Hereditary influences	34 72.34	7 14.89	6 12.77	47
Total	280 59.57%	90 19.15%	100 21.28%	470

Note: The probability of the Chi-square statistic assuming the value of 106.27 < 0.0001***
Significance legend: *: statistical significance on the 5% level; **: statistical significance on the 1% level; ***: statistical significance on the 0.1% significance level
SOURCE: MPHAHLELE (2018)

4   The Use of ICTs in the Identification of Barriers to Teaching and Learning

It has been shown by several studies, such as in the work of Masango (2014) and Mishra, Sharma, and Selinger (2001), that ICTs have a potential to add value to and positively impact teaching and learning activities. However, little is documented about the use of ICTs in the identification of barriers to teaching and learning. Mphahlele (2018) describes ICTs as any communication device or application, including radio, television, cellular phone, computer, and network hardware and software, satellite systems as well as services and other applications associated with them such as video-conferencing. In teaching and learning situations the devices indicated above are mainly used

THE ROLE OF INFORMATION AND COMMUNICATION TECHNOLOGIES 67

to support the teaching and learning processes for learners experiencing barriers to learning and there are several studies to confirm that (Adam & Tatnall, 2010; Bagon & Vodopivec, 2016; Benmarrakchi, Kafi, & Elhore, 2017).

From the study mentioned in the previous section by Mphahlele (2018), there was evidence of the use of ICTs in identifying reading difficulties. Table 4.1 emphasised reading difficulties as one of the barriers to teaching and learning that is caused by different factors. Table 4.4 illustrates the experiences of teachers in the five selected FSS when using ICTs to identify learners experiencing reading difficulties.

TABLE 4.4   Use of ICTs to identify learners experiencing reading difficulties

Items	Frequency of use			Total
Frequency row percentage	Never/seldom	Sometimes	Often/always	
Download screening tools to	32	9	6	47
ID reading difficulties	68.09	19.15	12.77	
Design reading screening tools	29	10	8	47
to ID reading difficulties	61.70	21.28	17.02	
Upload and save designed	26	17	4	47
screening tools	55.32	36.17	8.51	
For identifying the reading	19	20	8	47
levels of students	40.43	42.55	17.02	
Classify students according to	15	22	10	47
reading levels	31.91	46.81	21.28	
Identifying the type of reading	14	21	12	47
support students require	29.79	44.68	25.53	
Identifying the level of	13	23	11	47
support students require	27.66	48.94	23.40	
Total	171	138	67	376

Note: The probability of the Chi-square statistic assuming the value of 34.40 = 0.002***
Significance legend: *: statistical significance is on the 5% level; **: statistical significance is on the 1% level; ***: statistical significance is on the 0.1% significance level
SOURCE: MPHAHLELE (2018)

As shown in Table 4.4, generally the majority of teacher-participants do not use ICTs extensively to identify learners experiencing reading difficulties (an overall 45.48% never/very seldom and a 36.70% sometimes response was reported). In particular, more than approximately 50% (68.09% to 48.94%) of participants offered a never/very seldom response to:

- Downloading of pre-loaded reading screening tools.
- Selecting of relevant screening tools for different reading difficulties.
- Design of reading screening tools to identify reading difficulties.
- Uploading & saving designed reading screening tools.

A somewhat more frequent response was reported for the items of:

- Learner classification by reading ability.
- Identification of reading support required.
- The level of support required to assist reading difficulties.

From Table 4.4, it can be seen that ICTs are very seldom used and that may be attributed to a number of factors, including limited ICTs in the participating schools. This might also indicate that the value of ICTs in identifying barriers to teaching and learning might be not known or acknowledged. It is also safe to conclude that teachers might not be familiar with the different types of ICTs and their special application fields, this should be explained to and shared with teachers. An ICTs guide is the ideal place to introduce and explain the various ICTs available to assist in identifying barriers to teaching and learning. Against this backdrop, this chapter argues that maximised ICT access for teachers would increase the interest in and the level of computer skills which are needed to use ICTs to identify barriers to teaching and learning. Thus far, Table 4.4 painted a picture that ICTs to a certain extent are used to identify barriers to teaching and learning. The section that follows moves on to summarise the gaps and issues identified regarding the role of ICTs in the identification of barriers to teaching and learning and further presents recommendations for moving forward.

5 Recommendations

This study set out to explore the role of ICTs in the identification of barriers to teaching and learning, with the question in mind of whether identification of barriers to teaching and learning should be understood from an inclusion perspective or a psychological/medical perspective. It is worth noting that most children are sent to primary school without any information regarding barriers to teaching and learning that they might experience. Whether the barriers to teaching and learning are of a medical or psychological nature, the first person

THE ROLE OF INFORMATION AND COMMUNICATION TECHNOLOGIES 69

who should identify such barriers is the teacher. As a result, the pre-service teacher in ODeL should be empowered to be able to identify learners experiencing teaching and learning barriers, without diagnosing students, so that the learner can then be referred to medical practitioners for diagnosis.

Table 4.2 illustrated a variety of instruments that can be used to identify barriers to teaching and learning, this chapter recommends that all the instruments listed in Table 4.2 be used in conjunction with ICTs. Taking Table 4.4 into consideration, some of the instruments mentioned in Table 4.2 can be downloaded from the internet, some can be designed, such as IRS using ICTs, and uploaded to the computer screening programmes for future use. The pre-service teachers in ODeL should be taught the skills of downloading, designing, and uploading the screening tools using ICTs. When the identification instruments involve the use of ICTs the following advantages can be realised:

– Safety and ease of access: Seeing that most of the instruments are in the form of paper, they can be destroyed, misplaced, or when the storage is locked some teachers might be unable to access them.
– Quick and reliable feedback: After inputting data into the ICT tool that is loaded with the instrument you are likely to get instant feedback which is accurate unlike when you have to sit and analyses the data in order to write a report.
– Identification of majority of the learners in a short period: Due to the availability of ICTs in some schools more than one learner can be screened at the time.
– Determination of the level of the barrier to teaching and learning: It is imperative for the teacher to know the level of the barrier before planning the support or intervention. With the relevant settings the ICTs can be able to determine the level of the barrier the learner is experiencing.
– Cost effectiveness: Not lot of printing or photocopying of instruments is needed when using ICTs and the instruments can be re-used over and over without extra costs.

This chapter recommends that identification of barriers to teaching and learning should be informed by the observation of manifestations such as those listed in Table 4.1. Pre-service teachers in ODeL should take note that a learner could exhibit many signs that can make the teacher want to identify the causes of the barriers to teaching and learning the learner is experiencing. There is some evidence to suggest that learners, especially in the primary schools, enjoy using ICTs. That being the case, the teacher may not struggle to get learners to cooperate during the identification process.

6 Conclusion

This chapter attempted to argue that ICTs have a role to play in identifying barriers to teaching and learning. This chapter began with a discussion of how the types of barriers to teaching and learning can be delineated followed by how they should be identified, and lastly how ICTs could be used to identify barriers to teaching and learning. Drawing from Table 4. specifically, one can see that the role of ICTs aligns well with that of the teacher in the sense that the teacher has to use the ICTs to download, select, design, and upload the identification instruments. To answer the question raised in the introduction section: Whether identification of barriers should be understood through an inclusion perspective or psychological/medical perspective? Tables 4.1, 4.2, and 4.4 provide a clear picture that identification of barriers to teaching and learning should start in the classroom, which guarantees an inclusion perspective. Proper identification by the teacher leads to learner support while identification from a psychological/medical perspective leads to remediation. According to Department of Education (2001) there is a need for support strategies and interventions that will assist teachers in coping with a diversity of learning and teaching needs to ensure that transitory learning difficulties are ameliorated. The use of ICTs to identify barriers to teaching and learning is one of the strategies that responds to the implementation of inclusive education as outlined in the EWP6 and SIAS policy. This book focuses on the appropriateness of ICTs in promoting and ensuring inclusiveness and equality for students experiencing barriers to learning in ODeL. This chapter, however, brought an angle that aims to empower pre-service teachers in ODeL, so that when barriers to teaching and learning are identified as early as primary school, relevant support can be provided, leading to the empowerment of that learner throughout his or her education.

Notes

1 The Education White Paper 6: "Building an inclusive education and training system" is an inclusion policy that was introduced in response to the post-apartheid state of special needs and support services in education and training in South Africa (Department of Education, 2001).

2 Screening, Identification, Assessment and Support is a policy that provides standardised procedures for supporting students to ensure that *all* children may access quality education and achieve to the best of their ability (DoBE, 2014).

3 Full Service School is described as a support strategy which is based on the implementation of Education White Paper 6 for students who require mild to moderate levels of support (Mphahlele, 2018).

4 Down syndrome is a common disorder that occurs when a person has three copies of chromosome 21 (Stöppler, 2018).

5 Standardised test is defined as a form of test that that is administered and scored in a consistent, or "standard", manner to measures a student's progress and abilities throughout their education journey (Rozon, 2014).

References

Adam, T., & Tatnall, A. (2010). Use of ICT to assist students with learning difficulties: An actor-network analysis. In N. Reynolds & M. Turcsányi-Szabó (Eds.), *Key Competencies in the Knowledge Society (KCKS 2010)* (pp. 1–10). Springer. https://doi.org/10.1007/978-3-642-15378-5_1

ADCET. (2019). *Intellectual disability.* https://www.adcet.edu.au/inclusive-teaching/specific-disabilities/intellectual-disability/

Bagon, S., & Vodopivec, J. L. (2016). Motivation for using ICT and pupils with learning difficulties. *International Journal of Emerging Technologies in Learning, 11*(10), 70–75. https://doi.org/10.3991/ijet.v11i10.5786

Benmarrakchi, F., Kafi, J. E., & Elhore, A. (2017). Communication technology for users with specific learning disabilities. *Procedia Computer Science, 110*, 258–265. https://doi.org/10.1016/j.procs.2017.06.093

Department of Education. (2001). *Education White paper 6: Special needs education, building an inclusive education and training system.* Department of Education. https://doi.org/10.5663/aps.v1i1.10138

DoBE. (2014). *Draft policy on screening, identification, assessment and support.* Pretoria. http://www.education.gov.za

Harpaz, Y. (1973). *Teaching and learning: Analysis of the relationships.* http://yoramharpaz.com/pubs/en_learning/teaching-and-learning-analysis.pdf

Masango, M. M. (2014). *instruction and learning and the availability of ICT.* University of Pretoria.

Mishra, M., & Sharma, V. (2016). *ICT as a tool for teaching and learning in respect of learner with disability.* Wikieducator.Org. http://wikieducator.org/images/7/7b/SJ_M.P.Mishra.pdf

Mphahlele, R. S. S. (2018). *Information communication techonologies as a support mechanism for learners experiencing reading difficulties in full service schools.* University of South Africa. http://uir.unisa.ac.za/bitstream/handle/10500/24465/thesis_mphahlele_rs.pdf?sequence=1&isAllowed=y

Nel, N., Nel, M., & Lebeloane, O. (2013). Assessment and learner support. In N. Nel, M. Nel, & A. Hugo (Eds.), *Add to bag learner support in a diverse classroom: A guide for foundation, intermediate and senior phase teach.* Van Schaik.

Omollo, D. O. (2015). *Barriers of communication.* https://agrieconomics.uonbi.ac.ke/sites/default/files/cavs/agriculture/agriecon/barriers%20of%20communication%202.pdf

Prinsloo, E. (2007). Socio-economic barriers to learning in contemporary society. In E. Landsberg, D. Kruger, & N. Nel (Eds.), *Addressing barriers to learning: A South African perspective.* Van Schaik.

Reid, G., & Came, F. (2009). Identifying and overcoming the barriers to learning in an inclusive context. In G. Reid, E. Gad, J. Everatt, J. Wearmouth, & D. Knight (Eds.), *The Routledge companion to dyslexia* (pp. 193–202). Routledge. doi:10.4324/9780203549230-23

Rozon, O. B. (2014). Standardized tests: What factors affects how a student does on these exams? In *Modern classroom assessment* (pp. 329–352). https://doi.org/10.4135/9781506374536.n13

Sánchez, P. A., de Haro Rodríguez, R., & Martínez, R. M. M. (2019). Barriers to student learning and participation in an inclusive school as perceived by future education professionals. *Journal of New Approaches in Educational Research, 8*(1), 18–24. doi:10.7821/naer.2019.1.321

Selinger, M. (2001). Learning information and communications technology skills and the subject context of the learning. *Journal of Information Techology for Teacher Education, 10*(1–2), 143–156. doi:10.1080/14759390100200108

Soto, C. J. (2018). Big five personality traits. In M. H. Bornstein (Ed.), *The Sage encyclopedia of lifespan human development.* https://doi.org/10.4135/9781506307633.n93

Stöppler, M. C. (2018). *Genetic disease (inherited) symptoms, causes, treatments, and prognosis.* MedicineNet.

CHAPTER 5

The Role of ICT in Supporting Students at Risk for Academic Literacies in Higher Education

Sharon Moonsamy and Anniah Mupawose

Abstract

Education globally is on the cusp of change. This chapter aims to explore the role of ICT as a tool to support and enhance student academic literacies, whilst revolutionizing teaching pedagogy, within higher education. The authors argue for both teaching and learning, as change will not be realised if academic support is only focused on the student's competencies, or lack thereof. Hence, institutional practice needs to be examined, so that a developmental trajectory rather than a deficit track is promoted. This methodology aligns with the transformed curriculum the South African education system is pursuing, to make the content and the pedagogy contextually relevant, as well as globally recognised. The chapter explores academic literacies in South African higher education, especially as the majority of students are learning through the medium of English, which may frequently not be their home language. ICT as a tool ties in with the overall purpose of the book, as institutions of higher education are stepping into the 4IR, and no student should be left behind. The content of this chapter should be of interest to stakeholders in higher education, including students, lecturers and policymakers.

Keywords

academic literacies – higher education – ICT – pedagogy – teaching – learning

1   Introduction

Students attending universities in South Africa are often first in their families to do so. They come from diverse backgrounds and given the history of our education system, many students are differently prepared, experiencing various challenges at the university. Thus, a growing concern has erupted around South African students' performance in academic literacies (Bharuthram,

2012); consequently, throughput in higher education is not as expected, with a high failure rate amongst first year students. The challenge of throughput is compounded by socio-economic factors, struggles to adapt to new ways of knowing, and the language of learning and teaching (LOLT). Students, since the "fees must fall" campaign, have championed for a transformed curriculum, as the learning needs of most students are not being met. The current curriculum is not reflective of a relevant and transformed pedagogy for South Africa. Furthermore, Prensky (2001) states that students' approaches to learning have changed, thus teaching pedagogies must change too.

To develop students' literacy skills, which are foundational for all learning, a change in teaching and learning strategies is needed. Hence, educators need to transform their teaching practices, whilst students need to actively engage in text comprehension and text production for effective learning. The authors argue that the role of ICT as a tool should improve student success, when it is applied correctly, as well as increase motivation and interest, as we enter the Fourth Industrial Revolution (4IR). Furthermore, ICT will build on student-centeredness rather than teacher-centeredness, enhancing a flexible learning medium. Given this background, changes in education should aim at improving content and process, so that relevant practices are promoted. For this chapter, the socioeconomic factors are not explored further, as literature supports the implications socioeconomic factors have on education. Nevertheless, a focus on epistemological access and language as a medium of instruction for teaching and learning are discussed.

2 Epistemological Access

Students in higher education, whether they are English first language speakers or English as additional language speakers, experience difficulties with academic literacies (Bharuthram, 2012). According to Weiderman (2018) academic literacy is a complex network of constructs and includes among others, comprehension of vocabulary specific to discipline knowledge, understanding inter-relationships between text structures, making meaning beyond the level of the sentence, as well as applying cognitive processing to engage with information. Hence, students entering institutions of higher learning need to engage with this specific level of academic literacy. Students who experience difficulty making sense of their discipline specific knowledge may have a negative impact on the expected throughput. This may be reflective of students from the current basic education system in South Africa.

Since 1994, the South African government has increased formal access to higher education institutions, in line with the Constitution of South Africa (1996). Increased formal access was one avenue to redress the past inequalities experienced by many Black students. However, according to Walton, Bekker, and Thompson (2015), formal access does not promise access to learning. Morrow (2007) refers to the concept "access to learning" as "epistemological access" (p. 2). This he defines as access to knowledge that is provided by the institution, and is the responsibility of educators (teachers, lecturers and tutors). The institutions and their educators are accountable for the pedagogy selected and the manner in which the content is delivered and knowledge constructed. Walton et al. (2015) state that "the task of enabling epistemological access is the heart of teaching and is a more complex task than is realised" (p. 18).

Access to higher education demands more than learning content. According to Beekman (2015), students need to approach their studies with a different mind-set, where insights and judgments are generated. Application of new knowledge to novel situations and adopting a perspective on issues raised are also expected. Beekman (2015) refers to these learning requirements as "deep learning", where higher order processing is required. Copious amounts of content can hinder some students' access to knowledge construction, making it difficult for them to making sense of the information. Students display difficulty organising information and interpreting and making sense of content, indicating a difficulty for some students in knowing how to adapt from learning at school to learning at higher education institutions. According to Paxton and Frith (2014), this mismatch with the expectations of higher education is reflected in the students' less than adequate ability to read and write subject matter, and to access and construct knowledge. A student's construction of knowledge is influenced by the pedagogy selected. Thus, the educator should be sensitive to students' learning styles as well as to their context; this should enable the student to adapt to new ways of knowing. Students also have difficulty engaging with academic literacies, as several sources of information need to be processed simultaneously while the student also needs to access numerous resources, especially in this digitalised environment. Students therefore describe a sense of feeling overwhelmed by heaps of information.

Furthermore, the majority of students experience difficulty with academic literacies as a result of pursuing their studies in a language that is neither their first language nor their mother tongue. Their competency in the LOLT will influence their tertiary experience. According to Nizonkiza and van Dyk (2015) first year students at North West University are given the Test of Academic Literacy Levels (TALL) so students can be provided with different levels of support. In addition, students at risk of not completing their studies in the required time can be identified. The support provided by North West University to first year students is aimed at assisting students in developing their vocabulary and academic literacy, as a correlation exists between vocabulary and academic literacy (Nizonkiza & van Dyk, 2015). Many university programmes have been put in place or are in the process of providing some form of academic support. Haggis (2006) proposes that the conceptualisation of student support should go beyond seeing the problem as only residing within the student and should interrogate the goals of the institution as well. This trajectory is key to transforming teaching and learning practices and tackling under preparedness and differently prepared students entering university. Such a focus will be transformative in practice, altering systemic issues, while supporting the student through their studies.

3 Language Policy

English is the medium of instruction in most institutions of higher education. A mismatch in the performance of students to the expectations of universities may relate to the students' competency in the LOLT. Currently, there is a debate on the language policy in the country, with several institutions encouraging students to include learning an African language as part of their degree. Wits University has taken the first steps towards implementing the African language policy proposed by the current minister of higher education and training, Dr. Blade Nzimande. Wits' language policy outlines provisions for isiZulu and Sesotho to be included in the requisite curricula of all degrees should the government declare this mandatory in tertiary institutions.

The head of the African languages department, Dr Brenda Mhlambi, says, "In order to build positive sustainable development of African languages we need to focus students on the historic, political and economic elements of the language, such as its translation and usage in the workplace and for their own economic needs" (Wits Language Policy, 2018). This is part of being inclusive and striving to address issues of transformation, as well as to redress negative attitudes to African languages experienced during the apartheid period. Language competency is foundational for learning and is known as the "vehicle which drives the curriculum"; thus, educators need to be cognisant of this and support students in developing their academic literacies, whilst acquiring their discipline specific knowledge.

Consequently, to understand the role that ICT plays in bolstering academic literacies in higher education, the theories that undergird teaching and learning, as well as the concepts linked to academic literacies and ICT, are deconstructed next.

4 Theories in Teaching and Learning

Vygotsky's (1978), Feuerstein's (cited in Tzuriel, 2013), and Mezirow's (1997) theories are foundational in understanding transformation in teaching and learning. The student and the educator need to actively engage in the teaching and learning process to make sense of information. Therefore, the authors argue that the constructivist theory would ground the pedagogy of ICT use in academic literacy (Kosnik et al., 2017). Moll and Drew (2008) indicate that such active engagement leads to new knowledge construction. Vygotsky (1978) referred to active engagement as social constructivist theory and Feuerstein (cited in Tzuriel, 2013) spoke of mediated strategies. Thus, the student, with the guidance of the mediator, reflects on their learning, thereby internalising it. The learning spiral described by Moll and Drew (2008) involves cognition, metacognition, language and learning, and these are foundational and provide access to epistemological knowledge. Such learning processes can be achieved effectively through ICT, as the more knowledgeable other (educator) would be constructing the materials and activities that provoke critical thinking. Furthermore, through discussion forums, peer exchange, synchronous and asynchronous learning platforms (such as chat rooms, Microsoft Teams, Skype, zoom, WhatsApp), knowledge construction can be established.

Learning occurs when the student interprets information based on their perceptions, beliefs, and experiences. Mezirow (1997) asserts that learning occurs when frames of reference (beliefs and experiences) are disrupted and the student is forced to interrogate their thinking. This interrogation, or disruption, of the thought process is an active and constructive process, also referred to as cognitive dissonance. Knowledge can also be constructed socially via how a student interacts with the environment and with the people in it, as suggested by Vygotsky (1978), Mezirow (1997) and Feuerstein (cited in Tzuriel, 2013). Ahsan and Smith (2016) who advocate a social constructivist approach have identified practices that support academic literacy, including:

– Social interaction and dialogue.
– Environments deeply rooted in culture.
– More Knowledgeable Others (MKOs) helping students.
– Scaffolding of learning.
– Progressing through the zone of proximal development (ZPD).
– Constructive and timely feedback.
– Collaboration among students.

When a constructivist approach is utilised to undergird academic literacy, it fosters an environment of "safe learning" (Kosnik et al., 2017). Students who experience a mismatch between their spoken language and LoLT need a safe learning environment so that their vulnerabilities in their academic literacy can be nurtured. Construction of knowledge generally will not occur if students do not experience a safe community to simply be. This is true for many of South African students because learning in a second or third language may adversely affect their success and, in turn, self-worth and well-being (Eybers, 2018). Ultimately, literacy practices are "embedded in socially constructed epistemological principles" (Street, 2006, cited in Eybers, 2018, p. 255), because it is reliant on student-to-student, student-to-educator, and student-to-institution interactions. Thus, constructivism and social constructivism as theoretical underpinnings must be considered in relation to ICT as a tool to develop academic literacies and to support students with barriers to learning.

5   Academic Literacies in Higher Education

Academic skills, including academic literacies, are important as a life-long skills, for both tertiary education and work placement (Beekman, 2011). Academic literacies refer to the ability to use language and cognition to meet the demands of higher education (Cummins, 2000; van Dyk & Weideman, 2004; Jacobs, 2006). In addition, academic literacies, include media and technology literacies, numerical, and information literacies. Academic literacies thus provide the student with a set of knowledges and skills to navigate the higher education context. This chapter focuses on students' language and cognition, and their application to accessing and constructing knowledge, as well as digital competencies

Academic literacies in higher education are experiencing new challenges due to the diverse learning needs and competencies of students (Goodfellow & Lea, 2013). Higher education institutions assume that students entering their gates can read effectively, but Bharuthram (2012) indicated that even though decoding skills may be present, comprehension of texts should not be assumed. Most students in high schools are not exposed to the intricacies of writing from a reader's perspective. Therefore, it can be more difficult for first year students to be successful in higher education as they must contend with new terminology in their specific subject or discipline and then make sense of these concepts before applying them. Students require the basic skills of reading for meaning to be able to engage critically with textual information. Moreover, the expository text genre, of which all higher education content is constructed, requires greater demand of cognitive skills when processing. Critical skills of analysis, evaluation, comparison, deduction, and creation, along with other cognitive skills, are necessary to navigate learning in higher education. Comprehension of information must be translated or communicated for others to understand.

Hence, writing skills are required for students to express their understanding of the content. Written language is based on oral language competency, thus, a student who is not sufficiently competent in the (LOLT) will experience difficulties writing in that language. Academic literacies create a conscious application of required skills in tasks. Thus, the need for metacognition, where reflection, monitoring, and evaluation are key to presenting the best outcome, are necessary (Moonsamy, 2015).

Based on the above discussion, the majority of students who experience challenges in epistemological access in higher education, often due to limited academic literacy, should be supported in developing their academic literacies for success. Weideman (2003) suggests that institutions must do more to develop the skills of students who are at risk because of issues around academic literacy. This chapter argues that ICT are useful tools for enhancing academic literacies. However, for ICT to be effectively utilised, students must exhibit digital literacy in order to develop their academic literacy.

6   ICT as a Tool to Support Students in Higher Education

In the current social and educational context, a new communicative framework for learning has been adopted, that of ICT. Rao (n.d.) suggests ICT as an ideal resource for open and distant universities and as it can help in overcoming the limitations experienced when working with students on a large scale. Moreover, Daniels (2002) states that ICT in a short period have become key building blocks of the modern world. This has become a visible, global reality in the unprecedented circumstances of the COVID-19 pandemic (personal communication, 2020).

Conventional or face-to-face institutions are beginning to apply ICT strategies, engaging learners in webinars, discussion forums, and online learning. This has allowed classroom discussion to engaging students in idea beyond the content of their discipline. Previously, content has been the focus, but with the introduction of ICT, teaching and learning has taken on a new trajectory, as information no longer relies on memory and recall but rather on the application of information (Ragusa & Crampton, 2018). Similarly, ICT has the potential to support students' academic literacy skills, which for a long period have been focused on rehearsing content. ICT's flexibility and innovative technological platforms allow students to be stimulated, keeping them motivated to learn.

Amin (2013) cites Davis and Tearle (1996) in supporting the claim that ICTs have a revolutionary impact on education, and he states that ICTs have the potential to innovate, accelerate, enrich, and deepen skills, to motivate and engage students, to help relate school experience to work practices, create economic viability for tomorrow's workers, and strengthen teaching and help schools change.

In addition, Klimova (2011) indicates the potential use of ICT in enhancing academic literacies in higher education, particularly as it relates to their online course aimed at improving written language. It begins with planning and drafting to presenting a completed text for publication. Klimova (2011) states that as students are digital natives, this experience is exploited to develop the student's writing skills. However, Prensky (2001) in earlier research has suggested that exploiting students' interest in digital technology in developing writing has little empirical evidence to support it. Nevertheless, it can be argued that the current generation of students would be highly motivated as they are the generation of the information age. Students' interest in technology will keep them focused for longer periods, thus making digital platforms ideal. Clark and Mayer (2008) further assert that they want students to transition from an "Information Age to an Interaction Age", using ICT. The positive influence of ICT on academic literacies would be supported if all students had access to devices and connectivity. This problem has been identified in developing countries, which continue to experience digital inequity. The role of ICT in education should, therefore, not be underestimated, and the challenges of effective application of an ICT communication framework needs to be explored.

7 Influence of ICT on Academic Literacies

As ICT as a tool to support academic literacies in higher education is the focus of this chapter, we also need to look at the challenges that may influence acquisition of academic literacy, including digital competencies. Guzman-Simon, García-Jimienez, and Lopez-Cobo (2017) describe digital competence as more than just digital skills, but as a holistic experience in which higher education institutions involve the students in the academic discourse. Governments globally support the introduction of ICT in higher education to improve student performance (Karamti, 2016). As ICT could be beneficial for all students, ICT can be used to identify barriers in developing effective academic literacies.

Students in higher education are transitioning into ICT domains as their daily learning contexts. ICT environments require the student to shift roles in literacy practices away from decoding and engaging printed text to a role of a navigator, interpreter, designer, and interrogator of multimodal information (Serafini, 2012, cited in Tungka, 2018). This shift in paradigm assumes that students will engage with academic literacies more effectively. However, some students may not transition effectively into ICT contexts, as online presentations are tied to sociocultural identities. The undergraduate students in a study by Guzman-Simon et al. (2017) seemed to benefit from reading text online when there were visual images and videos which complemented their understanding. This could also indicate that the audio and visual information may have kept their attention, which resulted in better comprehension. This was also reported by South African students at one institution, who requested that online slides have voice overs to aid their understanding (personal communication, Moonsamy, 2020). These findings confirm that multimodal online presentations are preferred (Guzman-Simon et al., 2017). Furthermore, students in the Guzman-Simon et al. (2017) study did not use a variety of reading strategies and continued to apply the same strategies used in printed text to online text, hence not using hybrid strategies in their reading and writing practices.

Tungka (2018) confirmed that participants in her study in Indonesia were also varied in their use of multimodal resources, despite the guided reading strategies that were provided. It seems evident from these studies (Guzman-Simon et al., 2017; Tungka, 2018) that students do not access a variety of hybrid strategies to deepen their learning for academic purposes, as they would for social purposes, such as looking for information when making a purchase. Nevertheless, students' given guided literacy instruction should be able to navigate their disciplines' content, ensuring learning. Empirical evidence, however, has not been consistent regarding the impact that ICT has on learning. This is especially so in developing countries, as published research of positive impacts has emerged from developed countries (Karamti, 2016). The reason for the paucity of published research has been reported as methodological limitations. Therefore, the ICTs selected must be grounded in theory and empirical studies should be conducted, globally, for better practice. The quality of the programme when using ICT requires sound pedagogical foundations, so that all students can access the content and engage in learning.

Amin (2013) presents the concept of ICT for education, which implies that ICT is developed especially for teaching and learning purposes. Asynchronous and synchronous engagement builds collaboration and sharing of knowledge linking the pedagogy to the constructivist argument. Technology can make this possible. A variety of ICTs are available to support the different dimensions of learning and for a range of learners with different needs, such as accessing and understanding content, content creation and interaction, and organisation and memory (Kanwar & Cheng, 2017). Evidence shows that active learning in ICT focuses more on understanding and other higher order functions, rather than mere knowledge retention (Ritchhart, Church, & Morrison, 2011), which is what sound pedagogy refers to and would support academic literacies. We thus support the paradigm-shift from a teacher-centred to a student-centred approach in online learning. Tungka (2018) posits that guided literacy instruction should be formulated taking the students' experiences into account, as students have more established knowledge about the terrain around ICT. However, more research on the outcomes of ICT use in education, especially in developing academic literacy, needs to be explored.

8   Challenges, Solutions, and Recommendations

The challenges and solutions of ICT to support academic literacy are presented in Table 5.1 and are recommended for stakeholders including lecturers, students, Department of Education, and others, to action.

The above challenges prevent the promotion of ICT as a tool to support academic literacies, which is required for successful and life-long learning. Prinsloo and Van Rooyen (2007) indicated, "the question of access to these support services and technologies often overshadows other concerns such as the essential integration of these technologies in creating sensorially and conceptually rich environments for active learning" (p. 52). Thus, it is not only about adding another technology or sending out more material, but rather making the learning experience more applicable and ensuring that students make sense of the information.

Mphahlele and Nel (2018) also noted the limited access to ICT in their study, where teachers indicated that they were enthusiastic about aiding the learners to read, but that ICT resources were insufficient. The latter speaks to the systemic challenges South Africa faces; thus, it is recommended that the Department of Education and the Government of South Africa prioritise ICT resources so that students learning in the 21st century are prepared for the workplace and for life. Online learning provides opportunities for higher education to deliver services to people continuing their education, to leverage technology to reduce the burden on teachers, and to use improved pedagogies better suited to maintaining student engagement (Feedback Fruits, 2020). This is the social responsibility of government and business, to redress past inequalities and work towards a social justice agenda.

THE ROLE OF ICT IN SUPPORTING STUDENTS AT RISK 83

TABLE 5.1   Challenges and solutions of ICT that support academic literacy

Challenges	Solutions	Action
Slow progress in incorporating ICT into HE	Staff member/s who have a fixed mind-set and do not want to explore ICT as a tool for student learning add further inhibitors to the process Workshops and seminars to develop a growth mindset is essential, as change to include the digital age is inevitable	Staff in higher education, especially younger staff who are digitally savvy need to be brought to the fore and centres of teaching and learning at higher education need to support staff development
Focus on copious amounts of content in courses	To develop appropriate material for ICT, as the course work needs to be grounded in a constructivist paradigm It is also important that relevant material are the focus, reducing content redundancy	Consult digital designers so that the quality of the course is appropriate for online learning
Students experience overload of information	Materials to be developed require application approaches	Lecturers and course designers
Limited digital competencies	Students may have the digital skills, but the culture of learning online may not be effectively developed	Lecturers, course designers and central teaching and learning staff
Limited application of online reading strategies	Students need to be introduced to online literacy strategies so that they are not limited to only printed material strategies	Lecturers, support mentors and students
Systemic issues of connectivity and wider access	Increase access to connectivity. Provide a wider access across communities	Lecturers, support mentors and students
Student access to hardware	Provide students in their first year with loan digital devices.	Service providers and communities.
Limited research in ICT and academic literacies	Engage in more research on ICT and academic literacies in HE	Staff and students in institutes of higher education

9 Conclusion

Rapid changes in technology are creating a revolution in HE learning. This chapter aimed to describe ICT's role in identifying barriers to learning and to develop academic literacies in students. From the above discussion, it can be deduced that ICT has a role in supporting students in HE in developing academic literacies to navigate their learning experience. Studies have shown how ICT is supportive of students' academic literacy (Rao, n.d; Kanwar, 2017). The conception of academic literacy as reading and writing of printed materials should expand to include multimedia and computer-based text (Hugo, 2003). Pedagogically, multimodal text can be a meaningful learning resource that students can use to gain a range of knowledges and language resources beyond the classroom. Higher education needs to prepare students for the workplace, where different types of information such as facts, viewpoints, analyses, critiques, and demonstrations are processed. ICT can therefore serve as a curricular tool that helps develop these different genres of information processing, increasing flexibility and critical thought.

ICT has the potential to increase access for marginalised populations, despite the technological and digital divide in SA. This has been evident where educational lockdown due to COVID-19 has propelled us into ICT teaching and learning (personal communication, 2020). Big business and government have also been moved into action to provide devices to students in higher education. With education reshaping itself and being inclusive of digitalisation, ICT is promoted as it is student-centred and in keeping with the transformed curriculum. ICTs are an integral part of educational contexts and many workplaces in the 21st century. Education is evolving; many more students are accessing ICT as a means of learning, thus appropriate training of human resources is necessary to design content to maximise learning. Even though the move towards ICT is a fundamental shift in education, some issues and challenges in technical infrastructure, and to a lesser extent human capacity, are evident and will need to be considered in planning a new curriculum.

Harris (2002) states that the benefits of ICT will only be realised when teachers demonstrate confidence and are willing to explore new opportunities for changing their classroom practices by using ICT. In the words of former president Mr. Nelson Mandela: "Those who can't imagine change reveal the deficits of their imaginations, not the difficulty of change". Hence, we as educators need to embrace change in pedagogy in education and include ICT as a tool to support a constructivist paradigm in our teaching practices so that students' academic literacies will be enhanced, and barriers to learning can be identified early for appropriate intervention.

References

Amin, S. (2013). An effective use of ICT for education and learning by drawing on worldwide knowledge, research and experience: ICT as a change agent for education (a literature review). *Scholarly Journal of Education, 2*(4), 38–45.

Ahsan, S., & Smith, W. (2016). Facilitating student learning: A comparison of classroom accountability and assessment. In W. Smith (Ed.), *The global testing culture: Shaping education policy perceptions, and practice* (pp. 131–152). Symposium Books.

Beekman, L. (2015). Understanding and engaging in academic study. In L. Beekman, C. Dube, & J. Underhill (Eds.), *Academic Literacy*. Juta Press.

Bharuthram, S. (2012). Making a case for the teaching of reading across the curriculum in higher education. *South African Journal of Education, 32*, 205–214.

Clark, R., & Mayer, R. (2008). *E-learning and the science of instruction: Proven guidelines for consumers and designers of multimedia learning.* Pheiffer.

Cummins, J. (2001). Bilingual children's mother tongue: Why is it important for education. *Sprogforum, 7*(19), 15–20.

Daniels, J. S. (2002). Foreword. In *Information and communication technology in education – A curriculum for schools and programme for teacher development.* UNESCO.

Eybers, O. O. (2018). Friends or foes? A theoretical approach towards constructivism, realism and students' well-being via academic literacy practices. *South African Journal of Higher Education, 32*, 251–269. http://dx.doi.org/10.20853/32-6-2998

Feedback Fruit. (2020). *The rise of online classes after COVID-19: Best practices based on literature.* https://feedbackfruits.com/blog/the-rise-of-online-classes-after-covid-19-best-practices-based-on-literature

Goodfellow, R., & Lea, M. R. (2013). *Literacy in the digital university. Critical perspective on learning, scholarship, and technology.* Routledge.

Haggis, T. (2006). Pedagogies for diversity: Retaining critical challenge amidst fears of dumbing down. *Studies in Higher Education, 31*(5), 521–535.

Hallett, F. (2013). Study support and the development of academic literacy in higher education: A phenomenographic analyses. *Teaching in Higher Education, 18*(5), 518–530. http://doi.org/10.1080/13562517.2012.752725

Harris, S. (2002). Innovative pedagogical practices using ICT in schools in England. *Journal of Computer Assisted Learning, 18*, 449–458.

Hugo, A. (2003). From literacy to literacies: Preparing higher education in South Africa for the future. *South African Journal of Higher Education, 17*(2), 46–53.

Jacobs, C. (2006). *Negotiated understandings of the academic literacy practices of tertiary educators University of Kwa-Zulu Natal* (Unpublished doctoral degree). Faculty of Education, College of Humanities, at the University of KwaZulu-Natal, South Africa.

Kanwar, A., & Cheng, R. Z. (2017). *Making open and distant learning inclusive: The role of technology*. Keynote address presented at the 6th International Conference on Information and Communication Technology and Accessibility. http://oasis.col.org/bitstream/handle/11599/2827/2017_Kanwar-Cheng_Making-ODL-Inclusive_

Karamti, C. (2016). Measuring the impact of ICTs on academic performance: Evidence from higher education in Tunisia. *Journal of Research and Technology in Education, 48*(4), 332–337. http://doi.org/10.1080/15391523.2016.1215176

Klimova, B. F. (2011). Making academic writing real with ICT. *Procedia Computer Science, 3*, 133–137. doi:10.1016/j.procs.2010.12.023

Kosnik, C., Menna, L., Dharamshi, P., & Beck, C. (2018). Constructivism as a framework for literacy teacher education courses: The cases of six literacy teacher educators. *European Journal of Teacher Education, 41*(1), 105–119. doi:10.1080/02619768.2017.1372742

Mezirow, J. (1997). Transformative learning: Theory to practice. *New Directions for Adult and Continuing Education, 74*, 5–12.

Mohamedbhai, G. (2020). COVID-19: What consequences for higher education? *University World News: Africa Edition*. https://www.universityworldnews.com/post.php?story=20200407064850279

Moll, I., & Drew, S. (2008). *How people learn: A learning spiral*. South African Institute for Distant Education.

Moonsamy, S. (2015). Metacognition: A tool for strategic-thinking teachers when mediating in the classroom. In E. Walton & S. Moonsamy (Eds.), *Making education inclusive* (pp. 113–129). Cambridge Scholars Publishing.

Morrow, W. (2007). *Learning to teach in South Africa*. HSRC Press.

Mphahlele, S., & Nel, N. (2018). Information communications technologies: As a support strategy for learners experiencing reading difficulties. *Per Linguam, 34*(2), 1–13. http://dx.doi.org/10.5785/34-2-807

Nizonkiza, D., & van Dyk, T. (2015). Academic literacy of South African higher education level students: Does vocabulary size matter? *Stellenbosch Papers in Linguistics, 44*(1), 147–174. doi:10.5774/44-0-159

Paxton, M., & Frith, V. (2014). Implications of academic literacies research for knowledge making and curriculum design. *Higher Education, 67*, 171–182.

Prensky, M. (2001). Digital natives, digital immigrants. *On the Horizon, 9*(5), 1–6.

Prinsloo, P., & van Rooyen, A. A. (2007). Exploring a blended learning approach to improving student success in the teaching of second year accounting. *Accountancy Research, 15*(1), 51–69. https://doi.org/10.1108/10222529200700004

Ragusa, A. T., & Crampton, A. (2018). Sense of connection, identity and academic success in distance education: Sociologically exploring online learning environments. *Rural Society, 27*(2), 125–142.

Rao, M. A. M. (n.d.). *ICT in open distance learning: Issues and challenges.* Indira Gandhi National Open University. https://wikieducator.org/images/4/49/A._Murali_M_Rao.pdf

Ritchhart, R., Church, M., & Morrison, K. (2011). *Making thinking visible: How to promote engagement, understanding, and independence for all learners.* Jossey-Bass.

Roehl, A., Reddy, S. L., & Shannon, G. J. (2013). The flipped classroom: An opportunity to engage millennial students through active learning strategies. *Journal of Family & Consumer Sciences, 105*(2), 44–49.

Tungka, N. F. (2018). Guided literacy instruction: Helping students read multimodal English-medium texts. *Indonesian Journal of Applied Linguistics, 8*(2), 345–357. doi:10.17509/ijal.v8i2.13281

Tzuriel, D. (2013). Mediated learning experience and cognitive modifiability. *Journal of Cognitive Education and Psychology (JCEP), 12*(1), 59–80.

Van Dyk, T., & Weidman, A. (2004). Switching constructs on the selection of an appropriate blueprint for academic literacy assessment. *Journal for Language Teaching, 38*(1), 1–13. doi:10.4314/jlt.v38i1.6024

Vygotsky, L. (1978). *Mind in society: The development of higher psychological processes.* Harvard University Press.

Walton, E., Bekker, T., & Thompson, B. (2015). South Africa: The educational context. In S. Moonsamy & H. Kathard (Ed.), *Speech-language therapy in a school sontext* (pp. 15–38). Van Schaik Publishers.

Weideman, A. (2003). Assessing and developing academic literacy. *Per Linguam, 19*(1–2), 55–65.

Weideman, A. (2018). *Academic literacy: Five new tests.* Geronimo Distribution.

CHAPTER 6

Using Information Communication Technologies and Assistive Technologies to Address Specific Barriers to Teaching and Learning in Schools

Andries du Plessis

Abstract

The aim of this chapter is to explore barriers to teaching and learning in the South African context by placing them against the background of international trends related to achieving inclusion using information communication technologies (ICTs). Inclusion has to be ensured from the outset for all digital content. However, specialised assistive technologies (ATs) are necessary for learners with special educational needs. In this chapter, attention is given to the most prevalent barriers, namely auditory impairments, visual impairments, and a limited number of other types of barriers to teaching and learning. By adhering to the central theme of this book, this chapter aims to guide student teachers along universal design principles that offer ways to ensure broad-based inclusion, but also to by-pass and reduce the effects of certain impairments. Reference is made to institutions like universities, companies, and non-profit organisations that provide specialist assistance and training with regard to AT solutions.

Keywords

assistive technologies – barriers to teaching and learning – inclusive education – inclusion – Information Communication Technologies – technology

1   Introduction

The main purpose of any education system is to provide quality education for all learners to enable them to reach their full potential and contribute meaningfully to, and participate fully in, society throughout their lives (Education White Paper 6, 2001). The difficulty of attaining such a goal lies in the fact that

© KONINKLIJKE BRILL NV, LEIDEN, 2021 | DOI: 10.1163/9789004447226_007

learners, in common with any other group of people, have different talents and abilities, which affect the way they perceive and process information about themselves, others, and their environment. These differences give rise to a diverse mix of learners, each with their own educational needs (Lewis & Doorlag, 2006). By using ICTs, high levels of personalisation in teaching and learning are possible, a development that does not only apply to learners with special educational needs, but to all learners (Lai, 2010; Svetsky et al., 2010).

Education, however, has a very long history of exclusion, which means that institutions such as schools, colleges, and universities have for a considerable period catered only to those who fit into the mainstream, i.e. learners considered to be "normal" (Lloyd et al., 2007). Using Loopoo and Singh's (2010) two distinct categories, "normal" learners have "ordinary needs". Consequently, those falling outside the definition of "normal" are those learners with "barriers to teaching and learning", i.e. learners who require special measures to help overcome barriers to teaching and learning. Other factors have also contributed to exclusion in the past and thereby perpetuated the notion of "otherness" for some members of society. Conway (2017) argues that "[inclusion] is a transformation, intrinsically and extrinsically, as it involves adopting a philosophy, a set of values and beliefs and a passion" (p. 1). Transformation cuts across many layers. In South Africa, transformation includes, among other things, the Africanisation and decolonisation of education (Badat & Sayed, 2014). Transformation can also involve efforts to modernise teaching and learning in light of constant advancements in ICTs.

Advancements in ICTs cause societal shifts that place new demands on education. However, ICTs also create new possibilities and offer solutions. It is notable that the changes brought about by ICTs have been so profound that they have changed approaches to teaching and learning itself; something that is evident in new learning theories and teaching strategies that rely on technology (Ezziane, 2007; Fee, 2009; Reisier, 2002; Webb et al., 2011). To stay abreast of advancements requires teachers to be researchers and life-long learners. This is in fact one of the seven roles assigned to South African teachers (DBE & DHET, 2011) and rests upon the premise that there is a reciprocal relationship between research and practice (Albion et al., 2015).

This chapter seeks to make student teachers aware of the legal and ethical obligations to meet all learners' educational needs. Teachers' use of ICT-based solutions needs to adhere to internationally accepted specifications aimed at inclusion. However, to achieve inclusion using ICT solutions requires more than first-hand knowledge of the technology, a deep understanding of relevant theoretical frameworks, and appropriate instructional design principles.

2 Background

The move from exclusivity to inclusion in education is rooted in major historical developments that have also affected advances in human rights, especially after the Second World War (1939–1945). As a key institution, the United Nations (UN) has since its inception after the war played a significant role in advancing the ideals of freedom for all, equity and social justice, all of which are core building blocks of the human rights movement. Education and the rights of the vulnerable, especially women and children, started to receive considerable attention. Over time, international declarations followed, which formed the basis for inclusive education in most countries, especially those who subscribe to the ideals of a free world. Examples of declarations include The Charter of the United Nations (1945), the Universal Declaration of Human Rights (1948), the International Covenant of Economic, Social and Cultural Rights (1966), and the International Covenant on Civil and Political Rights (1966).

The United Nations Convention on the Rights of a Child (1989) helped to advance inclusive education further by revising the 1959 version of the charter. However, significant international events, such as the demise of the Soviet Union (USSR) and the end of the Cold War in 1991 helped reframe the human rights movement. Phasha (2018) notes that by 1993 the equal rights to education of all children, youth, and adults with disabilities were reaffirmed by Rule 6 of the United Nations Standard Rules on the Equalization of Opportunities for Persons with Disabilities. Rule 6 also emphasises that education should be provided in "integrated school settings" and in "general school settings". In fact, the Salamanca Statement following the World Conference of Special Needs Education in 1994 re-emphasised the role of schools. An important acknowledgement was that strengthening the capacity of education systems would also benefit diversity (Motitswe, 2012). The Right to Education for Persons with Disabilities (2001) further cemented efforts to help ensure a move towards inclusion for all. This had been preceded a year earlier by the adoption of Education for All (EFA), a global movement led by UNESCO. Adopted by the Dakar Framework in 2000 the primary goal was that all children should have started to receive primary education by 2015. Despite the fact that clarity about the "all" in Education for All remains elusive, the EFA movement merely reaffirmed the vision and commitment of the Universal Declaration of Human Rights, which dates back to 1948. Article 26 states the following: first, everyone has the right to education; second, education shall be directed to the full development of the human personality and to the strengthening of respect for human rights and fundamental freedoms (United Nations, 2008).

Advances with human rights issues and inclusive education should not be seen in isolation from other factors that affect society. Since the second-half of the 20th century, for example, advancements in the field of ICT gave rise to the Third Industrial Revolution (3IR). This ushered in the Information Age and with it the notion that the world has become a global village (Castells, 2011). Because of the 3IR and the stellar rise of mass social media (MSM), society also changed in other ways. Anytime, anywhere communication helped to connect people who would otherwise have been isolated, thereby displaying people's diversity. Together with advancements in hardware and internet connectivity across the globe, social media channels such as Facebook, LinkedIn, Twitter, Instagram, and YouTube brought "otherness" into the mainstream. Many examples exist of people with impairments who share their extraordinary feats at beating the odds, such as the South African-born Martin Pistorius, also known as the ghost boy (Pistorius, 2015). However, perhaps the best-known example of someone who succeeded in continuing with his life and work despite a debilitating illness is Stephen Hawkins (Wood, 2018), someone whose life story and scientific contributions to society continue to inspire millions across the globe.

The rise of ICTs in the late 20th century affected education in profound ways, especially since media formats became digital (Fu, 2013; Jang & Chen, 2010; Solomon & Schrum, 2007). Digital media, together with applications on affordable smart devices afforded accessibility to the mass market. With the capacity to support learners generally, specialist ATs drawing from broad-based technological advancements opened ways for learners with special education needs to get assistance for or bypass their impairments. It is important to note that from the outset of the 3IR the Word Wide Web Consortium (W3C) was quick to set standards to help ensure that the World Wide Web (WWW) became accessible to all people. This effort was also a move to accommodate those with special needs (W3C, 2019). Likewise, the Institute Management Systems – Accessibility (IMS-ACC) include the W3Cs standards in their specifications (IMS, n.d.). In fact, the IMS has developed a Learner Information Package (LIP) that goes beyond their IMS AccesForAll specifications (IMS, n.d.). In terms of ICT generally and ATs specifically, teachers and content providers have to ensure that digital content adheres to the W3C's standards while also taking heed of the IMS AccessForAll specifications (de Macedo & Ulbricht, 2013). The multi-faceted nature of the IMS's various accessibility parts is displayed in Figure 6.1.

Student teachers should remain mindful of each part and its place in the bigger whole – something that Newhouse's conceptual framework of ICT in education illustrates quite clearly (2002). In the case of the IMS' Accessibility Parts, each part entails a host of detail, which relies upon broad-based knowledge

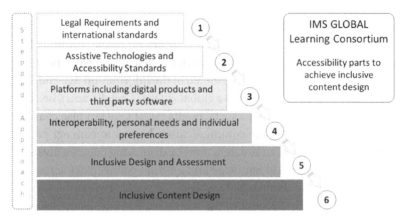

FIGURE 6.1   IMS Global Consortium Accessibility Parts (adapted from http://www.imsglobal.org/activity/accessibility)

about ICT on the one hand, and specialist technological pedagogical content knowledge on the other hand. For example, to unpack Part 3 on digital products, knowledge about the so-called pedagogical wheel of applications (Carrington, 2020) and Bloom's revised taxonomy would be required, together with first-hand knowledge about application suites such as Microsoft365 (McGhie-Richmond & de Bruin, 2015; Sideeg, 2016). All these work together along with chosen approaches to teaching and learning, which in turn depend on learning theories such as constructivism (Anderson, 2016).

However, staying abreast of developments in ICT remains a daunting task for most teachers. Recognition must also be given to the staggered implementation of ICTs that results in some schools still coming to terms with technologies associated with the 3IR (Davis, 2016). The net result is a widening digital divide with dire consequences if left unchecked (Choung & Manamela, 2018; Ho & Tseng, 2006). Currently, advances in artificial intelligence (AI), machine learning, and automation have given rise to the notion of an unfolding Fourth Industrial Revolution (4IR). We are thus likely to experience a far greater degree of synergy between humans and machines, which will result in even greater benefits for people with special needs (Lynch, 2018). One development, for example, that holds great promise is neuralink, a human-machine interface conceptualised by the tech entrepreneur Elon Musk. It is envisaged that once initial trials have proven to be successful that the first beneficiaries will be humans with special needs, such as those who are paralysed, or people who have lost the ability to communicate (Neuralink: Complete Presentation by Elon Musk, 2019). As may be expected, these and other developments will require adjustments to existing specifications and legislation that governs human-machine interactions.

One positive outcome of AI's use in education (AIEd) is the way it has lowered some costs associated with individualizing learning. Artificial intelligence will put individualised learning within almost everybody's reach (Akbaba-Altun, 2006; Holmes et al., 2019). This development has a direct impact on, for example, the IMS's accessibility parts numbers 4–6 as illustrated in Figure 6.1. AIEd would also help with mainstreaming learners with special needs—a term that is used as an "informal way of describing the practice of including special needs [learners] in regular classrooms and giving them the exact same opportunities as any other [learner] to enjoy every aspect of the school experience—from academics, to socialization" (What Is Meant by Mainstreaming?, 2020).

3　Inclusivity in South Africa Since 1994

Following decades of segregationist policies based on race in South Africa, first under colonial rule and later under the apartheid system (1948–1994), the introduction of a new democratically elected government in 1994 resulted in large-scale transformation across all sectors of society. Education became a focal point for efforts to ensure that the country's human capital would be developed fully (Beckmann, 2011). The right to education became enshrined in the country's new constitution. Section 29(1) states: "Everyone has the right: (a) to a basic education, including adult basic education; and (b) to further education, which the state, through reasonable measures, must make progressively available and accessible" (South Africa, 1996).

Following the new constitution, a revised legal framework-initiated change at all levels of the education system of which the then Department of Education (DoE), later known as the Department of Basic Education (DBE), became the custodian (DBE, 2005). Inclusive education has been embraced fully and a number of policies have been developed to guide the transition towards it (Conway, 2017). Education White Paper 6 remains a key policy document to help ensure that all educational practices follow the same set of principles. It affirms that all learners can learn if given the necessary and relevant support.

These principles, which hold schools responsible for providing workable solutions and adequate support, safeguard learners' rights to education in inclusive classrooms. It represents a major departure from how children with special needs and their learning once was viewed in South Africa. Following international trends, the special needs (medical) model made way for an inclusive education model (Lloyd et al., 2007). This introduced the notion that support for learners should be based on the levels of support needed for overcoming individual learners' barriers to teaching and learning, rather than on the categorisation of learners according to their (dis)abilities (DBE, 2005).

However, inclusion has come to mean different things to different people with variations of the concept found in different educational contexts across the globe. To signal that inclusion is in place, Swart et al. (2019) cite Florian (2014) who has done an analysis of the different definitions of inclusion. Three approaches have to be present at every level to justify using the term inclusion, namely a person centred approach to teaching and learning, school improvement, and special education practices. Inclusion along the three above mentioned approaches also bring mainstreaming to the fore, which is an approach that stems from Scandinavian countries (Swart & Pettipher, 2019).

White Paper 6 makes provision for the introduction of a range of services. Schools have also been categorised into either mainstream schools, full-service schools, or special schools (Conway, 2017). At its core is the need for teachers and schools to resolve barriers to teaching and learning as a way to ensure inclusion in education. Full service schools, which are particularly relevant to this chapter, are defined as schools that are "first and foremost mainstream education institutions that provide quality education to all learners by supplying the full range of learning needs in an equitable manner" (DBE, 2010, p. 7).

Questions that are relevant to full-service schools, include: (1) How should we transform educational institutions? (2) What is required to empower teaching staff who must serve the learning needs of all learners? (3) Which solutions exist to best resolve specific sets of barriers that arise from the curriculum? Although these and other questions are explored in Guidelines for Full-service/Inclusive Schools (DBE, 2010), one must remain mindful of these questions' universal applicability. For example, all educational institutions who endeavour to achieve inclusion in accordance with the W3Cs' specifications or the IMS' Accessibility Parts (see Figure 6.1) ought to relate to these questions. These questions are also relevant when applying frameworks such as Universal Design for Learning (UDL). At a classroom-based level, a practical example that relates to question three above would be a decision-chart for a teacher who must select appropriate sets of applications to help ensure that all learners achieve a certain set of outcomes (Lee & Cherner, 2015).

4 Conceptual Framework for Understanding Barriers to Teaching and Learning

Any number of multifaceted factors may cause learners to have special educational needs (see Figure 6.2). However, based upon the social model of disability, for learners their impairments remain barriers to teaching and learning until the barriers are resolved through active interventions, a responsibility that rests primarily on teachers. However, in South Africa a wide range of unaddressed issues continue to hamper learners' access to meaningful and fully accessible education, something that is not limited to learners with special educational needs. This state of affairs reflects a deficient system and not deficient learners (Loopoo & Singh, 2010).

When viewed holistically, poor service delivery affects all learners in some way during any given point in their education. However, learners with special educational needs are affected to a far greater extent. Conway (2017) notes that the Assessment Guidelines for Inclusion (DoE, 2002) describes three main groups of barriers to learning: (1) Those barriers which are caused by differing abilities (physical, neurological, sensory or cognitive); (2) Barriers to learning caused by inflexible teaching methods, unsuitable forms of assessment and underfunded support for the educators; and (3) Barriers caused by socioeconomic factors (e.g. severe poverty, absenteeism, schools with insufficient support materials, inadequate facilities or overcrowded classrooms). Left unresolved, these barriers thus result in the exclusion of some learners. Furthermore, it results in low levels of learner engagement and overall poor performance and/or high dropout rates at both school and later tertiary levels (CHE, 2010; Naidoo, 2005; Spaull, 2015).

As mentioned earlier in this chapter, teachers are required to have a deep understanding of the shaping agents that affect their learners' lives. This will assist with making adjustments at both institutional and classroom levels, the latter would involve decisions about teaching strategies and best practices in as far as it relates to the use of ICT applications (Kay, 2018). Bronfenbrenner's bio-ecological model provides a solid theoretical base for such an understanding (see Figure 6.2). According to this model, various contexts play an influential role in an individual's development (Bronfenbrenner, 1979).

Swart and Pettipher (2019) remark that the significance of this model for inclusion lies in its potential to explain the nature and dynamics of implementing a large-scale change process that might aim to achieve inclusion across a whole education system. Such a change process would most likely draw upon the principles of UDL as well as the IMS Accessibility Parts model (see Figure 6.1). The bio-ecological model has had a significant influence on the development of adaptations to attain inclusion, such as the one postulated by Engelbrecht (1999, as cited in Swart & Pettipher, 2019).

It is also notable that a growing interest in an Afrocentric philosophy holds particular promise for the development of an African perspective along Bronfenbrenner's model. While moving away from Euro-Western perspectives about

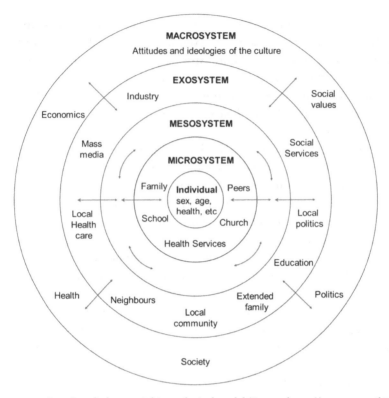

FIGURE 6.2 Bronfenbrenner's bio-ecological model (Source: https://commons.wikimedia.org/wiki/File:Bronfenbrenner%27s_Ecological_Theory_of_Development_(English).jpg)

educational problems, finding answers for questions that would inevitably arise from thinking about an Afrocentric philosophy is imperative. Oyeshile (2008), for example, discusses issues pertaining to an Afrocentric philosophy per se, and includes reference to the various problems that arise from attempts to define it. However, Phasha and Moichela (2011) state that an Afrocentric view is important for inclusive education, since "philosophies, which validate and address the experiences of the local people, could be relevant and appropriate for responding to their educational problems, and in particular, the implementation of inclusive education" (p. 373). As a result, when considering inclusion from an Afrocentric perspective three common values form the bedrock of attitudes and approaches to help ensure that learners who experience barriers are in fact accommodated. These are interdependence, communalism, and humanism.

Earlier in this chapter, it was mentioned that ICTs have had, and continue to have, a profound impact on society and its various sectors, including education. Notably, the prevalence of ICTs in education has given rise to new learning theories and instructional design models. Across all levels of the educational spectrum, such as teaching, instruction, and training three important theoretical perspectives provide a framework with which we can make sense of the role of ICTs generally and ATs specifically when attempting to address barriers to teaching and learning.

Rowlands (2015) explains how the Cultural Historical Activity Theory (CHAT) addresses the central tenet of assistive technology (AT). According to CHAT, when given the correct tools to enable interaction, learners (in context) who experience any number of barriers to their learning can be enabled to interact with resources/artefacts through technology and thus build their learning experiences and knowledge. A second theory, Wellness Theory, explores the role of ATs along different dimensions, i.e. physical, intellectual, emotional, social, spiritual, and occupational wellness. A third theory worthy of our attention when exploring ways to ensure that all learning content is accessible to everyone is Universal Design (UD). UD has been making considerable inroads across all spheres of design (e.g. buildings, products). When applied to teaching and learning, Universal Design for Learning (UDL) seeks to ensure that anything related to learning must be accessible by any user, no matter what the user's abilities are (Curry, 2003; Dalton et al., 2012; Nepo, 2017; Spencer, 2011).

5 Addressing Barriers to Teaching and Learning

Developments in ICTs have thus far directly impacted advancements in ATs, although it is necessary to make a clear distinction between the two concepts. Rowlands (2015) defines AT as "[a]ny device, piece of equipment or product which can be made by an individual and customised to suit a particular need, or obtained via commercial purchase, which is designed to enhance, increase, maintain, or improve the functional capabilities of students or individuals with exceptionality or a disability" (p. 13).

Over the past 40 years the use of ATs has made considerable inroads in mostly developed countries (Starcic & Bagon, 2014). However, ensuring that education remains both accessible and meaningful to all learners as envisioned in South African educational policy documents, most notably White Paper 6, would require extraordinary efforts, especially on the part of teachers of whom it is expected to develop transformative pedagogic skills and competencies (Tchombe, 2017). As pointed out already, problems with providing enabling environments have their origins higher up in the system. Conway (2017) notes that "[t]he failure of inclusive education to achieve the impact envisioned in policies is largely due to a lack of resources and funding, negative attitudes and a lack of clarity around the means to implement the policy" (p. 17).

In South Africa, a lack of accessibility to and knowledge of high-tech solutions among some sections of society prohibit technological integration at classroom-based level (Afshari et al., 2009; Chisholm, 2011). Those affected by the so-called digital divide are mostly historically disadvantaged schools, most notably those situated in rural areas (Ndlovu & Lawrence, 2012; Nkula & Krauss, 2014). A lack of access to devices, caused by so-called first-order barriers to technology persists well into the 21st century (Hodgkinson-Williams, Sieborger, & Terzoli, 2007; du Plessis & Webb, 2012; Singh, 2010), despite repeated promises to equip learners, teachers and schools with ICTs (Goosen, 2016; Mnisi, 2015). The result has been that many South African public schools are lagging in terms of the advances made elsewhere in the field of ICTs (Chetty et al., 2017; Van Wyk, 2012). The effects hereof have recently been crystallised when South Africa, like many other countries, opted for a complete lockdown in the wake of a COVID-19 pandemic. With all educational institutions closed, e-learning became the solution of choice, a decision which highlighted the numerous voids, but above all the realities of digital exclusion. It also highlighted the extent to which ICTs have not been integrated into teaching and learning in everyday schooling, despite policy directives such as the national whitepaper on e-learning (DoE, 2004; Nkula & Krauss, 2014).

The backlog in terms of broad-based ICT integration in school-based education also has a bearing on the use of ICTs and ATs to achieve inclusion. With reference to the DBE's 20-year plan in terms of the development of full services/inclusive schools, the teachers' basic question remains: "What can we use to resolve the barrier(s) facing a specific learner?" While teachers might be seeking solutions from the plethora of existing ICTs the sheer number of possible solutions can be daunting for some. Furthermore, the complexities and costs associated with certain ATs prove to hamper their implementation. For this reason Conway (2017) posits that "[t]teachers must be trained in how to assess and recommend devices according to learners' disabilities" (p. 32).

In this chapter, it is argued that teachers' choices of ATs are underpinned by their attitudes, values, skills, techniques, beliefs, and knowledge about teaching and learning generally and ICTs specifically (Daya, 2017). The same can be said of student teachers who are in the process of being educated in the use of ICTs (Sang et al., 2010). For a clearer understanding of both student teachers and teachers' integration of ICTs in their teaching Mishra and Koehler's technological pedagogical content knowledge framework (TPACK) offers a workable model (Mishra & Koehler, 2006). The TPACK framework entails different knowledge domains upon which a teacher relies. This supports the notion that a close link exists between teachers' specific and generic pedagogic competencies and their understanding of learners' unique educational needs (Tchombe, 2017). As hinted at the outset of this chapter, by applying the TPACK framework, teachers' generic pedagogic competencies thus include technological knowledge, technological pedagogical knowledge, and technological pedagogical content knowledge. Al-Azawei, Parslow, and Lundqvist (2017) cite Benton-Borghi (2013) who argue that TPACK in combination with UDL principles can promote the use of technology in teaching and learning.

A point raised earlier is that selecting ATs and developing a working knowledge of applications and devices are time-consuming and require on-going training. However, a good starting point for student teachers would be to ensure that the digital content they create during the course of their education, especially during their teaching practice, adheres to the W3C and IMS LIP specifications (IMS, n.d.; W3C, 2019; Webb et al., 2011). Software applications like Microsoft365 (formerly known as Office365), Google's G-Suite, and open source suites such as LibreOffice all have features that allow for meta-data to be added to digital objects. This is a requirement to ensure accessible digital content. For example, ALT-text options for images in digital documents are necessary to enable screen readers to describe the image. Without the required alternative text screen readers cannot describe images, which results in a barrier for those learners who rely solely on their screen readers to access all content.

Screen readers have become common features for operating systems such as Microsoft Windows and web browsers such as Microsoft Edge. While screen readers provide audio output which is a solution for learners with visual impairment, attention has to be given to captioning and text transcripts for video (Morris et al., 2016; Parton, 2016). In the case of video, a distinction is made between open and closed captioning: open captioning is embedded in the video and cannot be turned off or manipulated by the user; closed captioning can be turned on or off, since the descriptive text is produced by the media player. A range of applications, some are free, mitigate the high costs that are often associated with outsourcing. Apart from being expensive, outsourcing also requires some lead-time which requires advanced planning. As content producers, teachers often want to retain control over the process of lesson planning and content preparation. This includes creating transcripts and captioning for video material. Fortunately, a wide range of applications exists (Louder et al., 2016). Learning to use some of these, like PowerPoint and Microsoft's Picture and Video editor, the learning curve should not be particularly steep. YouTube's captioning tool, for example, is a much-welcomed feature; the auto-captioning feature, however, has raised concerns over accuracy (Louder et al., 2016; Parton, 2016).

Given the central place e-learning has managed to attain, especially in recent times during the COVID-19 pandemic, attention has to be given to learning management systems (LMS) such as Moodle, Blackboard, and Sakai; these are widely used at tertiary institutions for blended learning and/or independent online learning. Note that Microsoft Teams is not considered an LMS although it has features that allow for online learning. Fully-fledged LMSe require scrutiny of their levels of accessibility and ease of use, not only for learners with special educational needs. As part of all student teachers' education, it is thus necessary to learn how to review LMSe by using the principles of UDL, the W3C's specifications, and the IMS LIP's specifications. Each LMS's short-comings have to be identified, since a platforms' limitations would cause a barrier for certain learners depending on their impairment. In an online environment, accessibility hinges on two aspects: the LMS platform itself and the content that gets uploaded. Therefore, the content that teachers produce and upload has to be accessible as explained earlier in this chapter. Assessment must also be accessible (Aitken et al., 2012; Winter & O'Raw, 2010).

Learners with special educational needs can often go unnoticed in online environments. Kent (2015) states that "[s]tudents with disabilities can become invisible online" (n.p.). It is therefore notable that Blackboard, a widely used LMS that was launched in 1997, was awarded the Nonvisual Accessibility Gold Certification by the National Federation of the Blind in the United States in July 2010, a considerable feat that took a long time to achieve (Kent, 2015). Despite efforts to ensure overall accessibility, in the case of Moodle a number of limitations have been pointed out (Calvo et al., 2014). However, being an open source platform its extensive user community is continuously seeking solutions to overcome specific barriers. While Google attempts to ensure high levels of accessibility with their G-Suite (Accessibility for Every Student, n.d.), it is not uncommon for end-users to experience accessibility issues (U-M Google Accessibility/U-M Information and Technology Services, n.d.).

Across the world, as well as in South Africa, a number of companies and/or resellers exist that specialise in products and services aimed at education. It is noteworthy that representatives of suppliers and/or their resellers aim to assist individual learners who experience barriers, as well as teachers and caregivers who will be assisting the learners. One of the world's largest independent AT companies, Microlink PC, has its head office in the UK, but does have a reseller in South Africa, namely Microlink PC South Africa (Microlink PC South Africa Assistive Technologies, n.d.). Other South African companies include Edit Microsystems ('Edit Microsystems', 2014) and Inclusive Solutions, the latter offers SACE and PHCSA accredited courses, apart from a wide range of ATS (Inclusive Solutions, South Africa, n.d.). Numerous NGOs and nonprofit organisations (NPOs) are also able to assist. Disability info South Africa is an example of a nonprofit organisation that offers a host of useful information (Disability Info South Africa. Info on Disabilities, 2016).

Earlier reference was made to difficulties teachers face when having to select appropriate ATs, which underscores the importance of professionals' assistance. Lewis (1998) proposed a model with three pervasive facets for conceptualising AT in terms of its usefulness in classrooms. Other frameworks have been developed as well, e.g. the Matching Persons and Technology (MPT) Model. This model can be applied to both adults and children in the Matching Assistive Technology and Child (MATCH) version. This approach draws on the medical model of disability; it aims to determine the extent and nature of the learners' limitations in terms of functioning. Subsequently, upon identifying goals and outcomes with the learner in question, technological solutions are sought that could be used to enable the learner to achieve a set of desired outcomes (Rowlands, 2015).

The Consortium for Assistive Technology Outcomes Research (CATOR) encompasses three descriptors: effectiveness, social significance, and subjective well-being. This framework aligns with the World Health Organisation's International Classification of Functioning Disability and Health (ICF) (WHO, 2001). These models and frameworks help to provide guidance for engaging in the systematic evaluation of how available ATs are being used. Lastly, Rowlands (2015) cites the work of Cook and Polgar (2014) in as far as it draws on the Human Activity Assistive Technology (HAAT) model.

Kent (2015) emphasises the benefits of ensuring that all digital content be made accessible from the outset of the creation process, since "[a]ll people should be seen as only temporarily 'able-bodied'" (n.p.). This premise rests upon the stark reality that apart from the effects of aging, people can and do experience life changing events during their live time. In the subsections below, AT solutions for specific barriers are provided.

5.1   *Technology for the Deaf*

Conway (2017) maintains that deafness is one of the most prevalent disabilities. It is, however, difficult to recognise and to appreciate the extent of the barrier to learning because it is invisible. For assistance, it is advisable to contact the South African National Deaf Association (SANDA), DeafSA, which represents a medical diagnostic group. Universities are also worth noting for their work in the field of speech-language pathology and audiology, e.g. the University of Pretoria's (UP), the Sefako Makgatho Health Sciences University (SMU) and the University of the Witwatersrand, among others, that host Departments of Speech-Language Pathology and Departments of Audiology.

Storbeck (2019) provides an overview of the effects of hearing loss and total deafness on the development and education of learners. A sombre picture, however, is sketched in terms of policy implementation in South Africa to ensure that learners with deafness receive the necessary support at school level (Magongwa, 2010). Ideally, learners with hearing impairments should be viewed as any other learner with the potential of achieving the same outcomes as their hearing peers (Batchelor, 2010).

A summary is provided in Table 6.1 along broad categories of ATs that are relevant to learners with hearing impairments. Choices will depend on four categories of information, i.e. level of hearing loss, type of hearing loss, cause of hearing loss, and the age of onset of the hearing loss. For the purposes of this chapter, emphasis is placed on the two broad categories of ATs, namely augmenting devices/systems and transforming devices/systems.

TABLE 6.1   Summary of AT available to Deaf and hard-of-hearing learners

Augmenting devices/systems	Transforming devices/systems
Personal FM systems (microphone, transmitted, receiver system)	Translation services: provide word-for-word or condensed meaning-for-meaning translation of spoken words into text; e.g. C-Print, TypeWell, Communication Access Real-time (CART). According to the American Speech-Language-Hearing Association (ASHA), FM systems are the best choice for children with sensorineural hearing loss (TeachTought Staff, 2019)
Sound-field systems (microphone, transmitter, speakers around the room at strategic places)	Captioning services for video/audio
Other assistive listening devices (ALD) Includes infrared systems through which sound is transmitted using infrared light waves	Face-to-face communication systems
Audiovisual FM systems Facilitate speech-reading for learners who are oral-deaf or hard of hearing; devices for both the teacher and learner allow the learner to hear the teacher (if possible), but also see the teacher's face	TTY: Text and other adaptive telephones

Apart from the list of ATs provided in Table 6.1, an add-in worth mentioning is available for Microsoft PowerPoint, namely the PowerPoint Translator. Key features include live subtitling, customised speech recognition, personal translations that users can follow on their own devices in their chosen language, and multi-language questions and answers, which users can use from their own devices. For learners with hearing impairments, inclusivity can thus be achieved by providing text presentations, making it possible for them to participate fully in synchronous discussions, i.e. in real time (Microsoft, n.d.).

5.2   *Technology for Learners with Visual Impairments*

The nature and range of visual impairment (VI) among learners varies considerably, as explored by Mulloy et al. (2014). Visual impairment not only inhibits direct access to information that is meant to be observed visually, it also inhibits incidental learning, which takes place by observing others and the environment. Depending on the age at which VI becomes a factor, it affects a learner's physical, cognitive, linguistic, social, and academic development. As could be expected, behavioural problems are not unusual.

Visual impairment, although regarded as a barrier with low incidence, impacts teachers who themselves need special support to assist learners with VI in their classrooms (Conway, 2017). However, advances in our understanding of VI aid teachers and caregivers in their efforts to provide solutions to learners with VI. Consequently, it is necessary for student teachers, and in-service teachers alike, to attain knowledge about the manner in which VI affects a learner. A learner's visual acuity, visual field, and extent of light perception determine this. The assessment of learners who present with visual impairment also needs to ascertain their skills and abilities, functional limitations, and learning needs. Various task analyses of different activities are also undertaken to determine what type of support would be required. All of this information about a learner is also used to aid with the selection of solutions to ensure inclusion during teaching and learning. These solutions could include augmenting the existing visual sense or drawing on other senses as a means to compensate for the type of VI. The latter would depend also on the learner's preferred sensory channel(s), be it vision, touch, or hearing.

In the previous section, options to produce digital content that can be managed by screen readers using widely available applications such as applications from the Microsoft365 Suite were explored. Given the prevalence of e-learning reference was also made to the importance of reviewing different LMSe for their accessibility. Table 6.2, however, provides a summary of specific ATs along very broad categories that are age-relevant and subject-specific. These categories have been derived from the work of Mulloy (2014) and Landsberg (2019), among others.

TABLE 6.2   Summary of solutions related to learners with visual impairment

Age group	Technologies to enhance sight capabilities	Technology to engage sense other than sight
Infants to pre-school	Toys and adapted play areas: toys that give off light, bright colours, or produce a sound	Textured objects
	Facial treatments: especially young infants—make-up, lighting—improve ability to perceive lips and tongue movement	Audio
	Electronic vision enhancement systems (EVES)—danger of breaking up images into segments which inhibits the ability to see the whole—CCTV	
School Going: Reading	Large print text	Oral/audio text readers
	Typoscopes—writing guides—non-optical devices—reduce glare—support scanning	Braille—paper-based
	Reading stands	Braille translation software, computer printers
	Lamps Provide additional lighting	Refreshable Braille display
	Lens-based magnification aids—close up reading; distant-viewing optical aids	Audio format materials
	Electronic magnification aids	Screen and document reading software
AT for writing	Paper and writing utensils that provide visual and tactile cues	Braille making devices—software—hardware requirements—be able to produce Braille
	Typoscopes—not only for reading—also used during writing—guide	Voice recorders

(cont.)

USING INFORMATION COMMUNICATION TECHNOLOGIES 105

TABLE 6.2   Summary of solutions related to learners with visual impairment (*cont.*)

Age group	Technologies to enhance sight capabilities	Technology to engage sense other than sight
		Speech-to-text software
		Text-to-speech software
		Spelling and grammar checking software
AT for Visually Impaired: Mathematics	Interactive whiteboards > Project onto learner's desk; can enhance vision if working on the board directly	Adapted calculators
	Adapted graph paper	Abacus
		Maths manipulatives
		Tactile graphics
		Braille translation software for mathematics
AT for Science	Data collection aids	Three-dimensional models
	Personal computer-based laboratory equipment	Tactile graphics

However, before selecting specific ATs, it is worth doing an online search for the latest available products and applications. Two specific sources include the South African National Council for the Blind[1] and Blind SA.[2] As is the case with speech and audiology, those universities that host faculties of health sciences and specialise in sight include the University of the Witwatersrand (Wits), the University of Cape Town (UCT), the University of South Africa (Unisa), and the University of Pretoria (UP).

5.3   *Technology for Learners with Learning Impairments*

In a concise chapter like this one, it is impossible to do justice to the myriad of impairments that affect countless learners on a daily basis across the world, including South Africa. Table 6.3 lists some solutions for some of the more common impairments. It is advisable for teachers, parents, and caregivers to connect with others by joining support groups such as professional learning communities (PLCs) where they can share their approaches to problems and solutions. Nowadays support groups abound, which means that finding information and sourcing solutions are close at hand.

TABLE 6.3   Some learning impairments and examples of assistive technologies

Disorder/learning impairment	Assistive technological solutions
IADHD	Affecting abilities in a wide range of ways: reading, speaking, writing, hearing, sleeping, walking, getting things done, focusing, remaining on task
	DropTask; Wunderlist; MindX; Learning Ally; Ghotit Real Writer and Reader; Notability; Isolator; Time Timer; Wizcom Tech Pen; wordQ
Auditory Processing Disorder	Personal listening devices (PLD); Sound-field systems; Noise-cancelling headphones; Audio recorders; Captioning to audiovisual material; Text-to-speech software; Kurzweil 3000 Software
Dyslexia and other disorders affecting reading and writing	Integrating Text-to-Speech (TTS) to Writing assistive technologies, e.g. Ghotit; Word prediction and abbreviation expansion Ginger: offers several features that can help students with dyslexia and other learning disorders with writing Ghotit: designed for students with dyslexia and other learning disorders who have difficulties with writing
Dyscalculia	Talking calculator; MathTalk: speech recognition software program for math—help learners with a range of disabilities
Dysgraphia	Letter tracing apps, e.g. Little Writer

5.4   *Technological Solutions for Learners with Severe Disabilities*

Severe physical disabilities call for an individualised set of solutions that are tailor-made for the learner with special needs. The International Classification of Functioning, Disability and Health (ICF) helps with determining the nature and extent of the disability. Considerable emphasis is placed on autonomy and individual choice. However, the addition of a layer of technology to the relationship between learners and the world around them often complicates matters. For example, some applications might aid with communicating a user's inner psychological state to others; a potential drawback is a risk of misrepresentation (O'Brolcháin, 2018). For paralysis and fine motor skill disabilities, so-called sip-and-puff systems are on offer. For example, the Jouse3 is a sip-and-puff system that allows users to control a device using any part of their mouths, cheeks, chins, or tongues. In other cases, pointer devices can be tailor-made to control other devices, such as a computer and its applications, by using any range of possible movements of any body part (e.g. eye movement). With endless possibilities offered by modern day technology, a myriad of solutions can in fact be devised. One development that has transformed countless lives is 3D printing. However, such solutions can be very costly, which places them out of reach of the poor, unless funding can be sourced.

6   Conclusion

Ensuring that schools are inclusive remains a management function, based on the legal framework that governs South African society (SAHRC, 2015) and educational polices (DoE, 1995, 2001). However, student teachers need to be clear about their future responsibilities as teachers, since they will be responsible for ensuring that all teaching and learning is accessible to all learners. However, in South Africa, a myriad of factors hampers the implementation of policies to achieve the goals of attaining inclusive education. Many of these factors also hamper the implementation of other policies, such as e-learning, which relies on sensible ICT integration. One of the main inhibitors remains cost. Notably, the cost-factor is not limited to initial procurement, but extends to maintenance and servicing, and upgrades (e.g. software). Insurance is another cost-related factor that must be considered. Overall, these and other inhibiting factors affect the quality of education across a broad spectrum.

A key factor in achieving quality, inclusive education therefore hinges on policy implementation, but above all, adequately resourced institutions and well-trained teachers who would be willing to support an inclusive model through the effective use of ICTs, amongst other technologies. Despite the need for broad-based ICT integration in all education, teachers also have to employ tailor-made ATs as a means to help certain learners overcome specific barriers. This chapter provided detail about such solutions for specific types of impairments. However, student teachers need to be aware that technological solutions on their own are not enough. Instead, human support and care form the basis for the inclusion of all learners, especially those with special educational needs.

Notes

1   See http://sancb.org.za/
2   See https://blindsa.org.za/

References

Afshari, M., Bakar, K. A., Luan, W. S., Samah, B. A., & Fooi, F. S. (2009). Factors affecting teachers' use of Information and Communication Technology. *Online Submission*, *2*(1), 77–104.

Akbaba-Altun, S. (2006). Complexity of integrating computer technologies into education in Turkey. *Educational Technology & Society*, *9*(1), 176–187.

Al-Azawei, A., Parslow, P., & Lundqvist, K. (2017). The effect of Universal Design for Learning (UDL) application on e-learning acceptance: A structural equation model. *International Review of Research in Open and Distributed Learning*, *18*(6), 54–87.

Albion, P. R., Tondeur, J., Forkosh-Baruch, A., & Peeraer, J. (2015). Teachers' professional development for ICT integration: Towards a reciprocal relationship between research and practice. *Education and Information Technologies*, *20*, 655–673.

Anderson, T. (2016). Theories for learning with emerging technologies. In G. Veletsianos (Ed.), *Emerging technologies in distance education* (pp. 35–50). Athabasca University Press.

Badat, S., & Sayed, Y. (2014). Post-1994 South African education: The challenge of social justice. *The Annals of the American Academy of Political and Social Science*, *652*(1), 127–148.

Batchelor, M. (2010). The teacher experience: Deaf education at Sizwile school: Challenges and strengths. *American Annals of the Deaf*, *155*(4), 488–518.

Beckmann, J. (2011). Onderwys in Suid-Afrika van 1961 tot 2011. *Tussen twee paradigmas en ontwykende ideale. Tydskrif Vir Geesteswetenskappe*, *51*(4), 507–532.

Benton-Borghi. (2013). A Universally Designed for Learning (UDL) infused Technological Pedagogical Content Knowledge (TPACK) practitioners' model essential for teacher preparation in the 21st century. *Journal of Educational Computing Research*, *48*(2), 245–265.

Bronfenbrenner, U. (1979). *The ecology of human development*. Harvard University Press.

Calvo, R., Iglesias, A., & Moreno, L. (2014). Accessibility barriers for users of screen readers in the Moodle learning content management system. *Universal Access in the Information Society*, *13*(3), 315–327.

Carrington, A. (2020, February 17). The pedagogy wheel—It's not about the apps, it's about the pedagogy [Blog]. TeachThought. https://www.teachthought.com/technology/the-padagogy-wheel/

Castells, M. (2011). *The rise of the network society* (2nd ed.). John Wiley & Sons.

CHE. (2010). *Access and throughput in South African higher education: Three case studies*. Council on Higher Education.

Chisholm, L. (2011). The challenge of South African schooling: Dimensions, targets and initiatives. In J. Hofmeyer (Ed.), *Transformation audit 2011. From inequality to inclusive growth. South Africa's pursuit of prosperity in extraordinary times* (pp. 50–57). Institute for Justice and Reconciliation.

USING INFORMATION COMMUNICATION TECHNOLOGIES 109

Conway, C. (2017). *Teachers' perspectives of learner support in a Full-service school – A case study* (Med, Educational Psychology). University of Stellenbosch, Stellenbosch.

Cook, A. M., & Polgar, J. M. (2014). *Assistive technologies: Principles and practices* (3rd ed.). Mosby.

Curry, C. (2003). Universal design: Accessibility for all learners. *Educational Leadership, 61*(2), 55–60.

Dalton, E. M., Mckenzie, J. A., & Kahonde, C. (2012). The implementation of inclusive education in South Africa: Reflections arising from a workshop for teachers and therapists to introduce Universal Design for Learning. *African Journal of Disability, 1*(1), 1–7.

Davis, N. (2016, January 19). *What is the fourth industrial revolution?* https://www.weforum.org/agenda/2016/01/what-is-the-fourth-industrial-revolution/

De Macedo, C. M. S., & Ulbricht, V. R. (2013). Universal design and accessibility standards in online learning objects. In C. Stephanidis & M. Antona (Eds.), *Universal access in human-computer interaction. Applications and services for quality of life* (pp. 179–186). Springer.

Department of Basic Education (DBE). (2005). *Guidelines for inclusive learning programmes*. Department of Basic Education.

Department of Basic Education (DBE). (2010). *Guidelines for full service/inclusive schools*. Department of Basic Education.

Department of Basic Education (DBE), & Department of Higher Education and Training (DHET). (2011). *Integrated strategic planning framework for teacher education and development in South Africa 2011–2025*. Departments of Basic Education and Higher Education and Training.

Department of Education (DoE). (1995). *White paper on education and training, notice 196 of 1995*. Parliament of the Republic of South Africa.

Department of Education (DoE). (2001a). *Building integrated classrooms: An educator's workbook. Integration guide book for principals and teachers*. Department of Education.

Department of Education (DoE). (2001b). *Education White paper 6. Special needs education: Building an inclusive education and training system*. Department of Education.

Department of Education (DoE). (2002). *Curriculum 2005 assessment guidelines for inclusion.* Department of Education.

Du Plessis, A., & Webb, P. (2012). Teachers' perceptions about their own and their schools' readiness for computer implementation: A South African case study. *Turkish Online Journal of Educational Technology, 11*(3), 312–325.

Engelbrecht, P. (1999). A theoretical framework for inclusive education. In P. Engelbrecht, L. Green, S. Naicker, & L. Engelbrecht (Eds.), *Inclusive education in action in South Africa* (pp. 3–11). Van Schaik Publishers.

Ezziane, Z. (2007). Information technology literacy: Implications on teaching and learning. *Educational Technology & Society, 10*(3), 175–191.

Fee, K. (2009). *Delivering e-learning: A complete strategy for design application and assessment.* Kogan Page Publishers.

Florian, L. (2014). What counts as evidence in inclusive education? *European Journal of Special Needs Education, 29*(3), 286–294.

Fu, J. S. (2013). ICT in education: A critical literature review and its implications. *International Journal of Education and Development Using Information and Communication Technology, 9*(1), 112–125.

Goosen, L. (2016). Policy issues in ICT education towards effective teaching and meaningful learning. In *Proceedings of the Institute of Science and Technology Education (ISTE) conference on mathematics, science and technology education* (pp. 660–672). Unisa Press.

Hodgkinson-Williams, C., Sieborger, I., & Terzoli, A. (2007). Enabling and constraining ICT practice in secondary schools: Case studies in South Africa. *International Journal of Knowledge and Learning, 3*(2–3), 171–190.

Holmes, W., Bialik, M., & Fadel, C. (2019). *Artificial intelligence in education: Promises and implications for teaching and learning.* Center for Curriculum Redesign.

Instructional Management Systems (IMS). (n.d.). *Accessibility: IMS global learning consortium* [Website]. http://www.imsglobal.org/activity/accessibility

Jang, S.-J., & Chen, K.-C. (2010). From PCK to TPACK: Developing a transformative model for pre-service science teachers. *Journal of Science Education and Technology, 19*(6), 553–564.

Kent, M. (2015). Disability and e-learning: Opportunities and barriers. *Disability Studies, 35*(1).

Lai, K.-W. (2010). *School readiness for using ICT adapted to student needs.* In D. Gibson & B. Gibson (Eds.), *Proceedings of the society for information technology & teacher education international conference* (pp. 1487–1490). Association for the Advancement of Computing in Education (AACE).

Lee, C.-Y., & Cherner, T. (2015). A comprehensive evaluation rubric for assessing instructional apps. *Journal of Information Technology Education, 14*, 21–53.

Lewis, R. (1998). Assistive technology and learning disabilities: Today's realities and tomorrow's promises. *Journal of Learning Disabilities, 31*, 16–26.

Lewis, R. B., & Doorlag, D. (2006). *Teaching students with special needs in general education classrooms* (7th ed.). Pearson.

Loopoo, V., & Singh, P. (2010). *Barriers to learning within a South African context.* ICERI 2010 Proceedings, 3627–3634, IATED.

Louder, J. R., Tapp, S., Phillippe, L. K., & Luft, J. (2016). Video captioning software to help comply with ADA accessibility requirements. *Community College Enterprise, 22*(1), 71–76.

Magongwa, L. (2010). Deaf education in South Africa. *American Annals of the Deaf, 155*(4), 488–518.

McGhie-Richmond, D. R., & de Bruin, C. (2015). Tablets, tweets and talking text: The role of technology in inclusive pedagogy. In J. M. Deppeler, T. Loreman, & R. A. L. Smith (Eds.), *Inclusive pedagogy across the curriculum. International perspectives on inclusive education* (Vol. 7, pp. 211–234). Emerald Group Publishing Limited.

Mishra, P., & Koehler, M. (2006). Technological pedagogical content knowledge: A framework for teacher knowledge. *The Teachers College Record, 108*(6), 1017–1054.

Morris, K. K., Frechette, C., Dukes III, L., Stowell, N., Topping, N. E., & Brodosi, D. (2016). Closed captioning matters: Examining the value of closed captions for 'all' students. *Journal of Postsecondary Education and Disability, 29*(3), 231–238.

Motitswe, J. M. C. (2012). *Teaching and learning methods in inclusive classrooms in the foundation phase* (M.Ed. thesis). Unisa.

Mulloy, A. M., Gevarter, C., Hopkins, M., Sutherland, K. S., & Ramdoss, S. T. (2014). Assistive technology for students with visual impairments and blindness. In G. E. Lancioni & N. N. Singh (Eds.), *Assistive technologies for people with diverse abilities* (pp. 113–156). Springer.

Naidoo, P. (2005). *A study of the academic needs of students with visual impairments at the University of Kwazulu-Natal* (Masters in Social Work). Westville Campus, University of Kwa-Zulu Natal.

Ndlovu, N. S., & Lawrence, D. (2012). *The quality of ICT use in South Africa classrooms.* Paper presented at Towards Carnegie III, Strategies to Overcome Poverty and Inequality, Cape Town, South Africa.

Nepo, K. (2017). The use of technology to improve education. *Child & Youth Care Forum, 46*(2), 207–221.

Newhouse, P. (2002). *The impact of ICT on learning and teaching.* Specialist Educational Services.

Nkula, K., & Krauss, K. E. (2014). The integration of ICTs in marginalized schools in South Africa: Considerations for understanding the perceptions of in-service teachers and the role of training. In J. Steyn & D. Van Greunen (Eds.), *Proceedings of the 8th International Development Informatics Association (IDIA) Conference* (pp. 241–261). Cambridge Scholars Publishing.

Nyamnjoh, F. B. (Ed.). (2011). A relevant education for African development-Some epistemological considerations. *Africa Development, XXIX*(1), 161–184.

O'Brolcháin, F. (2018). Autonomy benefits and risks of assistive technologies for persons with intellectual and developmental disabilities. *Frontiers in Public Health, 6*, 1–7.

Oyeshile, O. A. (2008). On defining African philosophy: History, challenges and perspectives. *Humanity & Social Sciences Journal, 3*(1), 57–64.

Parton, B. (2016). Video captions for online courses: Do YouTube's auto-generated captions meet Deaf students' needs? *Journal of Open, Flexible, and Distance Learning, 20*(1), 8–18.

Phasha, N. (2018). Inclusive education in the South African context. In E. Lemmer & N. Van Wyk (Eds.), *Themes in South African education. For the comparative educationist* (pp. 163–182). Pearson Education South Africa.

Reisier, R. (2002). A history of instructional design and technology. In R. Reiser & J. Dempsey (Eds.), *Trends and issues in instructional design and technology* (pp. 17–34). Prentice Hall.

Republic of South Africa. (1996). The Constitution of the Republic of South Africa, 1996: As adopted on 8 May 1996 and amended on 11 October 1996 by the constituent assembly. Government Printers.

Rowlands, T. (2015). *The utilization of assistive technology to enhance educational support for all learners in a mainstream school* (D.Ed.). Inclusive Education, Unisa.

SAHRC. (2015). *South African Human Rights Commission (SAHRC) disability toolkit. A quick reference guide and monitoring framework for employers.* South African Human Rights Commission.

Sang, G., Valcke, M., van Braak, J., & Tondeur, J. (2010). Student teachers' thinking processes and ICT integration: Predictors of prospective teaching behaviors with educational technology. *Computers & Education, 54*(1), 103–112.

Sideeg, A. (2016). Bloom's taxonomy, backward design, and Vygotsky's zone of proximal development in crafting learning outcomes. *International Journal of Linguistics, 8*(2), 158–186.

Singh, S. (2010). The South African 'information society', 1994–2008: Problems with policy, legislation, rhetoric and implementation. *Journal of Southern African Studies, 36*(1), 209–227.

Solomon, G., & Schrum, L. (2007). *Web 2.0: New tools, new schools.* International Society for Technology in Education.

Spaull, N. (2015). Schooling in South Africa: How low-quality education becomes a poverty trap. *South African Child Gauge, 12*, 34–41.

Spencer, S. A. (2011). Universal design for learning: Assistance for teachers in today's inclusive classrooms. *Interdisciplinary Journal of Teaching and Learning, 1*(1), 10–22.

Starcic, A. I., & Bagon, S. (2014). ICT-supported learning for inclusion of people with special needs: Review of seven educational technology journals, 1970–2011. *British Journal of Educational Technology, 45*(2), 202–230.

Storbeck, C. (2019). Educating the Deaf and hard-of-hearing learner. In E. Landsberg, E. Swart, & D. Krüger (Eds.), *Addressing barriers to learning. A South African perspective* (4th ed.). Van Schaik Publishers.

Svetsky, S., Moravcik, O., Sobrino, D. R., & Stefankova, J. (2010). The implementation of the personalised approach for technology enhanced learning. In *Proceedings of the World Congress on engineering and computer science* (pp. 321–323). International Association of Engineers.

Swart, E., & Pettipher, R. (2019). A framework for understanding inclusion. In E. Landsberg, E. Swart, & D. Krüger (Eds.), *Addressing barriers to learning. A South African perspective* (4th ed.). Van Schaik Publishers.

Tchombe, T. M. S. (2017). Epistemologies of inclusive education and critical reflexivity for pedagogic practices in primary years (4–11). In N. Phasha, D. Mahlo, & G. J. S. Dei (Eds.), *Inclusive education in African contexts. A critical reader* (pp. 19–36). Brill | Sense.

TeachTought Staff. (2019, February 4). 15 assistive technology tools for students with disabilities [Blog]. *TeachThought.* https://www.teachthought.com/technology/15-assistive-technology-tools-resources-for-students-with-disabilities/

United Nations. (2008). Universal Declaration of Human Rights: Adopted and proclaimed by UN General Assembly Resolution 217 A (III) of 10 December 1948 Text: UN Document A/810, p. 71 (1948). *Refugee Survey, 27*(3), 149–182.

WHO. (2001). *International classification of functioning, disability and health* (ICF). World Health Organisation.

World Wide Web Consortium. (2019, March 6). How people with disabilities use the web [Website]. Web Accessibility Initiative (WAI) website. https://www.w3.org/WAI/people-use-web/

CHAPTER 7

The Role of ICT in Supporting Students Experiencing Barriers to Learning in the ODeL

Anniah Mupawose, Sharon Moonsamy and Skye Nandi Adams

Abstract

Given the colonial history of Southern Africa, with specific focus on South Africa, information and communication technologies (ICT) can no longer be used as an appendage to teaching and learning in open distance and e-learning (ODeL). ICT must be the vehicle used to drive transformation and decolonisation of educational programs. There is a dearth of information on how ICT has enriched and improved the quality of teaching and learning; however, there have also been unintended barriers to learning for students. We argue that instructors need to have the necessary skills and knowledge to mitigate the unintended barriers to learning when using ICT in ODeL. These barriers to learning if not addressed serve to exclude and prevent epistemological access to the marginalised students ODeL serves. As instructors, if we are committed to the transformation, Africanisation, and decolonisation agenda, then transformation needs to start with us. We can no longer afford to sit on the side benches and constantly cite the barriers to student learning as reasons to not embrace pedagogical change. It is therefore important that instructors be innovative and put in the work that is required to make sure learning via ICT in ODeL is accessible and inclusive of all students.

Keywords

higher education – ICT – open distance learning – South Africa – student learning

1 Introduction

Learning is generally an obstacle course that students have to navigate. For some students these obstacles are exciting, while for others they may be insurmountable. Thus, the question we may ponder as instructors is, "What factors are contributing to students not learning or performing at their best? Are there

© KONINKLIJKE BRILL NV, LEIDEN, 2021 | DOI: 10.1163/9789004447226_008

strategies we can employ to assist students to learn? What can we do to ensure that students can and do navigate this obstacle course when enrolled in Open Distance and e-Learning (ODeL) education programs?" (Boles, 2010, p. 1). With the advent of the Fourth Industrial Revolution, the manner in which teaching and learning is conducted has to change. Information and communication technologies (ICT) by their very nature serve to support and undergird independent learning (Amin, 2013). ICT in ODeL lends itself to student-centered approaches of learning, whereby students, whether collaboratively or independently, can construct their knowledge based upon their interactions within their learning environment(s) (Vasudevaiah, 2016). ICT can be used to facilitate multimedia learning that targets students with different learning styles and learning disabilities. The use of multimedia for learning has moved learning to mobile devices and smart phones as most of these have internet browsing capabilities and social networking applications (Serote, Mathimbi, & Mbodila, 2013). In this chapter we use ICTs to refer to computers, the internet, email, cellular telephones, tablets, and learning management systems. ICT has made it possible for students to access knowledge anywhere and anytime (Rahman, 2014).

Gone are the days where teaching is the transmission of information and learning is a passive engagement for acquiring knowledge. With the advances being made in the 21st Century with regards to information and communication technologies (ICT), instructors are being pressured to transform their teaching and learning practices. ICT is the modern method of gathering, storing, manipulating, processing, and communicating desired types of information in a specific environment (Vasudevaiah, 2016). ICT helps distance learners to communicate—learner with instructor, learner with learner, and learner with the learning materials (Rahman, 2014). We argue that ICT in ODeL can undergird both asynchronous and synchronous learning while serving as teaching and learning tools. As a teaching tool, it can provide varied models of instruction that are both inclusive and interactive but allow for individually paced learning. As a learning tool, it can serve to provide not only summative but also continuous formative assessment on student learning. This chapter provides background and context in order to provide an elaboration on ICT in ODeL and the instructor's role. The next section will discuss barriers to learning. The final section will discuss support to students and recommendations that instructors may utilise to mitigate the barriers to learning. The sections pertaining to barriers and support of students will be infused with theory. It is the belief of the authors that barriers and support for students are heavily reliant on the pedagogy of the instructor(s). Pedagogy needs to be undergirded by theory.

2 Background

Instructors within higher education contexts play a key role in bridging the gap(s) for students who experience barriers to learning in the ODeL and online educational contexts. Bridging the gap(s) means transformation of the curriculum so as to decolonise content, learning, and assessment. Given the history of South Africa, approximately 70% of students enrolled in South African tertiary institutions come from marginalised backgrounds created as a result of coloniality (Letseka, Cosser, Breier, & Visser, 2010). Coloniality is a system that perpetuates "the cultural, political, sexual and economic oppression/exploitation of subordinate racialised/ethnic groups by dominant racial/ethnic groups with or without the existence of colonial administrations" (Grosfoguel, 2011, p. 15). With the advent of independence, higher education systems were given the mandate to transform and promote a more equitable education system, providing access to those who had been previously excluded and discriminated against (DoE, 2008). Transformation was witnessed through change in the demographics of students entering tertiary institutions to majority black and the inclusion of students with disabilities who were previously denied access (Maboe et al., 2018; Mbembe, 2016). However, despite this increase of black and marginalised students, Eurocentric institutional cultures and epistemological traditions have not changed (Heleta, 2016). We align with McDougall et al.'s (2018) claim that ICT, if used innovatively by instructors, can address marginality and exclusion perpetuated by coloniality.

Many of the students in South Africa, like other students in Southern Africa, chose to study via ODeL because of the reduced cost, accessibility to education, and flexibility. The flexibility includes the ability to study part-time whilst continuing to work. Working allows students to still receive an income while completing their education (Mtebe & Raisamo, 2014). However, despite the accessibility of ODeL the through-put remains poor and is not at the expected levels (Assareh & Hosseini Bidokht, 2011; Prinsloo & van Rooyen, 2007). Some students enrolled in ODeL come from peri urban and/or rural lower socio-economic backgrounds, with limited infrastructure and sustained electricity supply (Sedimo, Bwalya & Du Plessis, 2011; Vasudevaiah, 2016). Other students lack the digital competency required to engage in online learning (Kanwar, 2017).

2.1 Information Communication Technologies in Open Distance and e-Learning

ICT by its very nature serves to support and undergird independent learning (Amin, 2013). ICT in ODeL lends itself to student-centered approaches to learning, whereby students, whether collaboratively or independently, can construct their knowledge based upon their interactions within their learning environment(s). ICT can be used to transform learning experiences to higher levels of achievement for students by engaging their metacognitive abilities (Maphosa & Bhebhe, 2019; Roberts & Gous, 2014). ICT has also made it feasible for students to access knowledge anywhere and anytime. This accessibility has made it possible for instructors to generate meaningful and engaging learning activities (Amin, 2013) that can allow for learning to be assessed continuously, and not at the end of teaching module/course.

ICT in ODeL by its very nature incorporates asynchronous and synchronous learning. The asynchronous aspect of learning in ODeL is appealing to students who want to receive an education that is centered around their schedule, and where distance does not impede learning (Al-Asfour, 2012). As a teaching tool, ICT can provide varied models of instruction that are both inclusive and interactive but allow for individually paced learning (Al-Asfour, 2012). Furthermore, ICT can serve as an effective tool to encourage and support independent learning and inform teaching methods. Unfortunately, in some cases asynchronous can facilitate surface learning whereby the student only engages with the content material to pass assignments or exams (Prinsloo & van Rooyen, 2007). Alternatively, synchronous learning via ICT enables collaborative learning since learning is a social process (Vygotsky, 1978). Collaborative learning occurs through critical dialogue with other students. When one appreciates or interrogates a different point of view, disruptions in frames of reference can occur (Mezirow, 1997). When disruptions in frames of reference or unease occurs, learning happens (Mezirow, 1997).

Disabilities can be classified as medical or mental illness, physical impairment, hearing or visual disability, learning disability as well as intellectual impairment. Research has indicated that more students with disabilities are enrolling in ODeL courses, as are all other students (Maboe et al., 2018). This is because it allows students to go through the material at their own pace, in their own space and time. For example, In South Africa, the number of students with disability attending the University of South Africa (UNISA), an ODeL institution, has grown to 59% from 2007 to 2011 (Rahman, 2014). These numbers continue to increase although there is no exact number.

A variety of assistive and augmentative technological devices are available to make computers use easier for learning and communication for students with disabilities. These devices include any item, piece of equipment or product system, whether acquired commercially off the shelf, modified, or customised, that is used to increase, maintain, or improve the functional capabilities of people with disabilities (Maboe et al., 2018). An illustration of this is how UNISA has set up a Resource Centre which provides personalised services to students including texts in braille, and providing services in sign language (Rahman, 2014). However, due to the digital divide, there is a lack of certain digital infrastructure and government services (especially in developing nations) to provide the practical and financial means needed to guarantee access to information and communication technologies to all citizens (Sedimo, Bwalya, & Du Plessis, 2011). The context students come from has profound influence on the ICT methods that can be employed to address their diverse learning needs. However, despite the context we believe that the use of ICT in higher educational settings can serve as a catalyst for transforming and decolonising the curriculum so that it becomes relevant and accessible to students who experience barriers to learning.

Having said that, with the move of education into the digitalised world, students need to transition into a knowledge-based economy, grounded on digital literacy so that they do not lag (Sedimo, Bwalya, & Du Plessis, 2011). Any aspiration to move towards a knowledge based economy cannot be achieved without the efficient use of ICTs.

2.2 *Barriers to Learning*

According to Assareh and Bidokht (2011) there are four kinds of barriers to learning: students, instructors, curriculum, and the institution. We discuss various aspects of these barriers below.

2.2.1 Students Confidence and Expertise in ICT

Meeting the needs of today's learners requires instructors to rethink delivery strategies and instructional methods. Student's confidence and expertise in using computers is related to their age and educational background (Assareh & Hosseini Bidokht, 2011). Students growing up in the fourth industrial revolution are more adept at using ICT, however this does not always translate to computer or digital literacy. Digital literacy is a step further than reading and writing, it is ability to utilise information and communication technologies in learning (Maphosa & Bhebhe, 2019). Digital literacy entails the use of devices, such as, smartphones, tablets, laptops, and desktop PCs. Thus, digital literacy refers to an individual's ability to find, evaluate, produce, and communicate clear information through writing and other forms of communication on various digital platforms (Maphosa & Bhebhe, 2019). Digital literacy does not replace traditional forms of literacy, instead it builds upon the skills that form the foundation of traditional forms of literacy (Common sense media, 2018).

As far as South Africa is concerned there are many students studying at tertiary level whose levels of literacy, including language literacy, are not in line with the academic demands required by their studies (Hugo, 2003). The afore mentioned literacy levels provide a shaky foundation for digital literacy. ODeL students need digital literacy so that they can navigate in a knowledge based economy.

2.2.2 Student Access to ICT Facilities at Home

In South Africa there exists a digital divide, as in most Southern African countries. Researchers agree that digital divid' is the metaphor used to "describe the perceived disadvantage of those who either are unable or do not choose to make use of information technologies in their daily life" (Cullen, 2003, p. 247, cited in Maphosa & Bhebhe, 2019). Because of coloniality, the majority of marginalised populations of Southern Africa live in poverty (Ndlovu-Gatsheni, 2015). As a consequence, most marginalised students are more predisposed to not owning tablets, laptops, or desktop PCs and few have connectivity at home except via data purchasing (Vasudevaiah, 2016). In instances where students do not have access to technology and technological skills, it becomes a serious challenge to expect effective utilisation of technologies in teaching and learning (Cloete, 2015). This reality has been demonstrated with the outbreak of the COVID-19 pandemic, where higher education's expectations to transition to online learning confirmed the digital divide between the 'haves' and the 'have nots' (personal communication, 2020).

All of these will impact the throughput of students with disabilities, instructors may not be equipped in working with students with disabilities nor know who these students are in their class while, at the same time, the course needs to be designed to support these students. There are a number of ways to support students with disability as well as those from diverse backgrounds and can improve student throughput rates with the use of relevant and appropriate assessment methods. However, these issues are universal and cannot be improved solely by the lecturer or even the institution, but require government policy in order to make effective change. An example of effecting change has been in Pakistan, where free education has been offered to all disabled students up to PhD level attending an open distance institution (Ahmed & Yousaf, 2011). However, in order for this to work, greater government involvement was required, and the government secured additional resources and funds to support this policy.

2.2.3 Student Behaviors in Asynchronous Learning

When using ICT, it is important to understand that the lecturer and the students are all in different geographical locations (Kanwar-Cheng, 2017). Several students have reported that they generally work in the evenings or on the weekend due to work or family commitments that may take precedent (Ferreira &

Venter, 2011). This requires students to be more active in their learning as they need to be independent in their reading and writing in comparison to those students on campus at traditional universities (Kanwar-Cheng, 2017). Thus, students attending ODeL are required to take greater responsibility for their learning; however, they themselves also need to be in an appropriate learning environment outside of the classroom setting in order to optimise their understanding.

2.2.4   Student Behavior in Synchronous Learning—Peer Learning

Level of engagement is not solely based on how a student interrogates the content for themselves, but also how they engage with peer learning. Research has indicated that the greater the transactional distance, the more socially isolated students are. Social isolation tends to contribute to students not completing their ODeL or online courses. Thus, creating collaborative activities can go a long way in establishing online learning communities and fostering a sense of "belonging" or "presence" (Boles, 2010; Roberts & Gous, 2014). Peer learning and assessment also provides an avenue to reduce the transactional distance students experience with ODeL and online courses (Rahman, 2014). Students learn from critical reflection and critical discussions from each other (Mezirow, 1997). Too often the students' performance is based on the assessment of the instructor, but according to programmatic assessment student performance should be based on several sources other than the instructor, including self, peers, instructor, and field supervisors (Van der Vleuten, 2015). Assessment from multiple sources provides a richer description of student performance.

2.2.5   Student Self-Regulation

Studying via ODeL requires students to be self-regulated and self-determined. ODeL students are usually prepared to develop an independent learning capability, motivate themselves to learn, and engage in learning activities that make them persistent and successful in learning. However, contextual factors such as work and/or family commitments, academic and digital literacy, and institutional and instructor support can greatly influence one's desire to want to put the time and effort to engage in learning.

2.2.6   Student Attributes—Learning Style

A student's learning style can either promote or impede learning of the content. Biggs (1989) describes two types of students: surface students and deep students. Surface learning is associated with more rote learning and understanding and a goal to only pass the class. Deep learning involves higher order thinking and cognitive processing such as synthesis, evaluation, and analysis.

When teaching it is important to try and engage students to be deep students in order to better understand and integrate knowledge. Reports on the use of ODeL have indicated that students tend to be active students who engage with information given to them and are no longer just passive recipients of knowledge (Ferriera & Venter, 2011; MacKeogh & Fox, 2009). However, this proactive scenario is not always reflected in graduation throughput rates. Furthermore, students who engage in surface learning are not building the relevant schemas required to gain subject knowledge. Hence, students may not be making appropriate links between concepts and this then impacts their comprehension of the material.

2.2.7 Student Attributes—Self-Efficacy

According to Bandura's Social Cognitive Theory (1997), academic self-efficacy beliefs refer to pupils' judgments concerning their capability of accomplishing a task or succeeding in an activity. Bandura (1977) states that knowledge acquisition is product of an individual's interaction with cognitive, behavioural and environmental influences surrounding him/her. Self-efficacy beliefs determine students' choices, their efforts, their persistence, and their perseverance when facing difficult challenges. If a student has positive beliefs about their capabilities, they are more likely to be self-determined and own the responsibility for their learning. Self-determination is critical for academic success at ODeL institutions. Most of the e-learning occurs asynchronously, so if a student is not a self-starter, he/she is more likely to become demotivated and disengage from the learning process. One needs to note that one can be a self-starter who engages in surface learning. A student who is a self-starter and engages in surface learning is a student who learns just to pass and do the minimum to obtain a qualification.

2.2.8 Instructor Digital Literacy

The capacity of instructors to manage e-learning programs remains low (Vasudevaiah, 2016). While some do not have the adequate skills, others are averse to using ICT. Instructors need to be digitally literate too, it is not sufficient for instructors to devise lesson plans that require students engage in lower order thinking skills (LOTs) such as accessing or describing information. Instructors need to devise activities where students learn how to apply and evaluate accessed information, and synthesise information as per Bloom's Taxonomy. One of the most important components of digital literacy is the ability to not just find, but also to evaluate, information.

If an instructor is not digitally literate, they can hamper the learning of students, in that learning platforms and ICTs are not used to their optimum functionality. Greenhow et al. (2009) suggest that it is no longer feasible for anyone to be literate in every available online technology. They further point out that digital literacy includes knowing which technologies are fit for the user's intended purpose, knowing when to use these technologies, and how and which functions to use (Greenhow et al., 2009, cited in Serote, Mathimbi, & Mbodila, 2013) Knowing the intended uses of technology can be overwhelming, but it behooves instructors to go for continual professional development so that they are abreast of technological developments.

2.2.9 Instructor Pedagogy

As alluded to before, the instructor's role needs to change from didactic (teacher-centered) to being student-centered. The teacher-centered instructor controls the learning situation and does not see the student as an active participant in the learning process. Many instructors may have a good understanding of using the ODeL system but not how to adapt it for the needs and diversity of the students enrolled for the course (Kop et al., 2011). Therefore, it is important for instructors to understand their capabilities and the need for institutional support and training. Many instructors have complained about the constant system upgrades and the difficulty in having to adapt to new servers (Kop et al., 2011). Self-evaluation by instructors becomes even more important with the fast pace at which technology on different platforms and systems change as the ability to identify when additional support may be required. In addition, careful planning needs to take place to ensure that instructors are equipped to deal with any problems that may arise. Planning should start with having a good grasp on what theory of learning is undergirding their teaching, namely constructivism and social constructivism.

2.2.10 Curriculum Content Barriers

Curriculum includes the design of the program/course and the extent to which students can see relationships between courses and their real lives. It also relates to the way in which the course is organised (Boles, 2010).

Another obstacle several students' face is related to content. Content barriers could relate to language competency as well as the material being used in the courses (Kanwar-Cheng, 2017). Students may have difficulty understanding what is being said and/or the information may not be in a format that is accessible, whether it is in .doc or .pdf, and they may have trouble accessing the platform it is being uploaded to. This can cause a lot of confusion as well as frustration for both the instructor and the students. Another key factor related to content is that learning material is presented in a language that may not be the student's first language. The students' competency in their language of learning and teaching (LOLT) may not be enough to comprehend content at a deeper level as academic language skills are different from those required for conversation. Academic language competency is foundational to academic success. Again, this is a universal challenge and requires additional resources and support, although it is still important to understand how this can influence teaching and learning.

The final comment on content barriers relates to coloniality. There is something inherently amiss when courses are designed in a manner that meets the needs of colonialism and apartheid well after independence (Mbembe, 2016). Courses are being taught in a manner that espouses Eurocentric epistemologies to the detriment of indigenous knowledge (Heleta, 2016; Mbembe, 2016). 'While Tertiary institutions have mandated policies and frameworks that speak about equality, equity, transformation and change, institutional cultures and epistemological traditions have not considerably changed' (Heleta, 2016, p. 2). The 'spirit' is willing but the 'will to do is weak' (DoE, 2008). Sometimes it is difficult to engage with course material as a student, when you cannot relate or 'see yourself' in the content.

2.2.11 Digital Divide's Impact on Curriculum

As mentioned, a digital divide exists in most developing countries and one's exposure to ICT impacts how one accesses and integrates the curriculum (the content). Accessibility for all to ICT infrastructure is a means of bridging the digital divide (Maboe, 2018). The digital divide can be viewed as a function of coloniality and/or poor governance. Some might see the use of ICT as bridging the digital divide, because it is cost effective and inclusionary.

> Universal accessibility appears to repeatedly take for granted certain socioeconomic situations, such as the availability of advanced technological infrastructure, end-user computer training and literacy and use of an unofficial language. (Abascal et al., 2016, cited in Maboe et al., 2018, p. 222)

However, many students may be unable to afford data new hardware, software and or equipment (Sedimo et al., 2011). This can result in reduced access to content and materials as well as student participation and interaction.

2.2.12 Institutional Barriers

The institution deals with the infrastructure that is in place to support students, academics, and administrative staff in the business of teaching and learning. If there cracks in the infrastructure and mismanagement of resources, barriers to learning can occur. Barriers to learning can greatly impact throughput. Mismanagement at the level of the institution can lead to a lack of academic integration and social integration or, conversely, can contribute to academic isolation (Boles, 2010).

According to Assareha and Hosseini Bidokht (2010), the institution is responsible for the following:

– Refining and implementing a vision for strengthening the OeDL program and the use of technology in education;
– Providing a range of consultative and advisory supports such as counselling, financial advice, technical support, and academic support;
– Co-ordination of systems of people, processes, and infrastructure to provide access, deliver programs, manage projects, and ensure accountability;
– Promoting an innovative learning environment through strategic professional development using a variety of methods and technologies;
– Developing and implementing decolonised and Africanised curricula and exemplary curricula/courses for the guidance of teachers and learners;
– Identifying, evaluating, developing, recommending, and distributing resources to support teaching and the achievement of learning outcomes.

All of these barriers effect all students, including those with disabilities, in different ways. There is not a one-to-one relationship between barriers and strategies because often one strategy addresses a number of barriers. There are also barriers that cannot be overcome through teaching alone (Boles, 2010).

2.3   *Supports and Recommendations for Barriers to Learning*
The following are possible solutions and supports that can be employed by an instructor to address some of the barriers identified.

2.3.1   Assessment for Learning
One cannot talk about learning without assessment. Gone are the days when retention and knowledge is assumed without finding out via assessment whether learning has occurred. Today's students demand more control of the learning environment in terms of when they need it and how they need it. As result this has put more pressure on instructors to change from "assessment for learning" to "assessment of learning". Assessment of learning or "summative assessment" means the same as "assessment of learning". Summative assessment sums up the learning of students at the end of periods of learning, for example, once a school term or a course has finished. As it sums up what the students have achieved, it looks back and indicates what the students have learned, sometimes measured against clearly defined standards. Some

summative assessment is high stakes pass or fail of a module or course. Assessment for learning is formative assessment, where a student is given feedback on the process of learning. This feedback allows the student to gauge their learning because the student gets feedback on where the student is going (clarify aims), how to get there (provide feedback), and where the student is now (check progress). Formative assessment is usually for low stakes.

Assessment for learning is usually associated with the socio-constructivist model of learning. Socio-constructivism proposes that learning does not occur in a vacuum but is socially constructed through interacting with others. Mezirow's (1997) transformative theory states that learning occurs when frames of references are disrupted by interacting with others and hearing different perspectives. These perspectives cause an individual to rethink their assumptions or frames of reference. When assumptions are disrupted via cognitive dissonance learning is taking place. According to Mezirow (1997) learning can also occur through assimilation. Assimilation occurs when an individual interacts with others and from that interaction one is able to add this new information to knowledge that already exists. Mezirow (1997) states that cognitive dissonance occurs through critical reflection and discourse. So, students in ODeL need to be given the opportunity to engage in critical discourse over the content with other students.

In order to improve student participation in different activities, it is important to have both high and low stake assessment tasks. High stakes are your summative tasks that are usually assigned a grade or mark. Examples of high stakes activities include assignments, peer assessments, tests, and exams. Low stake tasks are generally not for marks or grades. Many students generally will only participate in low stake assessment tasks if they know that marks will be assigned. Examples of low stakes include self-assessment (reflections), discussion forums, writing and reading activities. Low stakes activities are very important in that they provide qualitative feedback on student performance. Qualitative feedback is very important for continuous assessment (van der Vleuten, 2015). Students have been shown to value qualitative feedback because it allows them to assess and reflect on their learning. It motivates them to become self-determined and take responsibility for their learning.

2.3.2 Constructive Alignment

Constructive alignment ensures that students are not engaging in surface learning. Surface learning occurs when students are learning for the sake of learning, i.e. to pass. Students are not interrogating the subject/topic matter. Instructors should not be the main source of teaching; instead, the source of information and direction of learning should be that of the student. Therefore, using a lesson plan allows for you to be both structured and flexible in your teaching. Furthermore, the use of a lesson plan ensures the constructive alignment of outcomes, teaching, and learning activities (Biggs, 1989). If lesson plans are constructively aligned the chances of the students engaging as deep students with the topic matter is greatly increased by engaging students in critical thinking tasks, such as analysis, synthesis and making. Our aim is to have students who become self-determined and lifelong learners.

Lesson plans can help both instructor and the students structure their learning. Study guides serve to assist the student in terms of learning information pertaining to course/topic, expectations, and assessment criterion. Whereas lesson plans serve to guide the instructor in relation to teaching and learning methods being applied and their effectiveness.

We argue that if an instructor is adhering to a curriculum design, lesson plans need to be developed for every topic of instruction. Without a lesson plan how does one determine if learning is occurring? We further argue that self-evaluation of teaching and learning methods needs to be continuous and dynamic. One must be continuously evaluating the effectiveness of teaching and learning methods. One way of achieving this is through a lesson plan.

Practical tips:

- Instructors should rely more on formative assessments than summative.
- It is important to gauge the learning of the students via self-reflections, quizzes, discussion forums or Classroom Assessment Techniques (CATS). CATS are generally simple, non-graded, anonymous, in-class activities designed to give the instructor and students useful feedback on the teaching-learning process as it is happening, e.g. one-minute paper, one sentence summary.

2.3.3 Self-Efficacy

Bandura's (1977) social learning theory also suggests that students learn from observation and modelling behaviours. Asynchronous ODeL courses offer limited exposure to expert performance but some modelling of processes. Exposure to expert performance shows students' real-world practices. When a student observes experts demonstrating practical reasoning skills to solve a problem, this informs their learning in terms of how to engage in higher thinking skills. An example of modelling of processes can be provided via case-based learning. Case studies are helpful as students engage in higher level cognitive thinking and processing.

As instructors we can sometimes get driven to cover content rather than what is relevant for the student to grasp. In most cases, if a student can grasp a key element(s) of a topic, that student through self-determination can generate solutions to discipline related problems. Hence, the use of case studies is a great way to focus on relevance while covering the content. The use of case studies allows instructors to engage students in lower order and high order thinking skills as per Bloom's Taxonomy. The use of case studies also provides opportunities for students to give views and perspectives on how they are interrogating the content matter. An illustration of this could be to ask students to generate their questions based on the content and theory, to allow them to bring in their own opinions and views. If these questions are appropriate, they can even be used in an assignment or assessment.

2.3.4 Peer Mediated Learning

Through synchronous course activities, communication tools e.g. chat groups/rooms and discussion forums, peers can rehearse presentations, provide instant feedback, clarify misunderstandings, and share knowledge. However, this type of learning would need to be mediated through an instructor (known as the knowledgeable other) (Vygotsky, 1978). Vygotsky (1978) argues that learning is a social process that requires mediation. Mediation from the instructor allows for the creation of communities of practice (Lave & Wenger, 1991). As students collaborate and contribute to each other's knowledge through mediation they are preparing to become experts in a community of practice. Peer learning also creates a thinking environment that enables students to reflect socially and engage in meaningful discussions (Boles, 2010; Kline, 2017). The opportunity to provide students with meaningful interactions in the context of structured learning activities has been shown to enhance learning and well as increase throughput rates (Andersen, Annand, & Wark, 2005).

2.3.5 Writing Intensiveness

Writing is a major challenge for most students entering university, especially in the South African context (Hugo, 2003). The language of learning and teaching in most South African universities is English. This puts many South African students at a disadvantage because they are having to learn in either their second or third language which has major implication for academic success. Academic writing is the "key assessment tool" in most programmes, and therefore a common cause of failure. Students who are generally identified at risk for failure are referred to generic writing skills course. These courses generally do not provide the necessary foundational skills needed for reading and writing within their disciplines. When writing is taught within the confines of the discipline then students can make the necessary connections between writing and knowledge construction (Somerville & Creme, 2005, cited in Wingate & Driess, 2009). The strategies of reading and writing need to be taught explicitly. Therefore, the need to incorporate reading and writing activities cannot be stressed enough in each program of study. ICT in ODeL with careful thought can be effectively used to support reading and writing activities. Some practical tips:

- Students need to be allowed to write their assignments and take photos of written work, which can be emailed to the instructor if possible.
- Students need to be allowed to demonstrate understanding via different modalities; instead of writing, students can produce mind maps, or other forms of graphics to indicate learning.

2.3.6 Coaching and Scaffolding

Traditional methods of teaching have focused predominantly on direct instruction. Direct instruction goes hand in hand with teacher-centered approaches. From the social constructivist viewpoint, knowledge is acquired via social interaction. Lynch (2002) suggests there are four levels of interactions that need to be considered for when using ICT in ODeL. The levels of interactions include: (a) interaction with the content, (b) interaction with the instructor, (c) interaction with peers, and (d) interaction with self. All are critical for effective instruction and difficult to replicate using ICT in any online format. These four levels of interaction are fluid because the instructor can move from one state of interaction to another to assist and meet the student's needs. Strategies determine the approach a teacher may take to achieve learning objectives. Depending on the student, the instructor has to change the manner in which she/he interacts with the student(s). The instructor can either serve in the capacity of an instructor, coach, or mentor.

A student who is struggling to understand the content may need direct instruction that is more telling and guiding. A student who is more self-determined and an independent thinker may require a more non-direct approach. An instructor as mentor serves to guide, support, and provide feedback students need to succeed and scaffolds the learning more. Being an instructor requires you to know your student's context and background so that you can effectively interact with one other for academic success. Using coaching and scaffolding as an instructor can go a long way towards helping a student who may be experiencing difficulties with epistemological access feel safe. Providing a safe environment for learning allows students to be vulnerable and ask questions that are important for 'knowing how'. Students from disadvantaged backgrounds flourish in safe learning environments.

The quickest way to shut down discussion is for someone to feel attacked. Students need (and deserve) to feel safe in class discussion (Doyle, Sammon, & Neville, 2015; Kline, 2017), and this is perhaps more challenging in the online environment, where typed messages are easily misinterpreted. Students report the need for an honest, open, and respectful environment. The instructor has the responsibility of setting the tone from the beginning. The instructor needs to model appropriate responses and challenges through additional questions.

There is a tendency among instructors to objectify students and not relate to the student as part of a system or see the role of student as only one role of many in a student's life (Bronfenbrenner, 2005). Interaction with students should be paramount for any student, cognitive, economic and psychosocial factors can create barriers to learning for students. For instance, instructors have several ways to support students with disability as well as those from diverse backgrounds. Strategies employed can improve student throughput rates with the use of relevant and appropriate assessment methods. Some of these methods can include:

- Supplementing lecture notes with text outlines of all content, readings, and other print resources.
- The telephone is also an option for personalizing communications with student (Serote, Mathimbi & Mbodila, 2013)
- Lectures can be presented visually with key points and graphics.
- Any audio streamed information can be captioned if necessary.

Some practical tips:
- Increase instructor presence online: Schedule times when students can meet or ask questions of you online.
- The ratio of synchronous to asynchronous activities should be 20% to 80% per week if possible.
- Due to the costs of synchronous activities, real time instructors should use live sessions sparingly and limit the time of live sessions to reduce the data students require to participate in a live session in Teams or Zoom. Ensure all participants switch off their video feeds. Always record your live sessions for students who cannot attend.
- Before uploading onto a learning management system/platform (LMS), instructors should compress videos to a smaller file size (tools such as ClipChamp, Handbrake or VLC Media Player can be used). This costs less for the students to download.
- Instructors should avoid embedding videos from other sites (e.g. embedding a YouTube video into the LMS but rather provide a link or URL). Students will be charged more for data usage
- Instructors should avoid uploading videos longer than fifteen minutes. Screencast-O-Matic can assist in creating videos for free.

The solutions and recommendations highlighted indicate the importance of instructors in ODeL using ICT as an innovation to change pedagogies. Instructors have a major role to play in helping students mitigate learning barriers they experience. Finally, student-centred approaches to teaching are labour intensive and require a lot of preparation and constant self-evaluation of teaching and learning methods. As instructors, if we are committed to the transformation agenda then transformation needs to start with us. Progressive instructors must take the lead and not wait until the institutional cultures and environments transform. "They need to decolonize their curriculum and democratize the learning space in which they operate. As academics we have an opportunity to involve students in the process of transformation of the curriculum, teaching and learning" (Heleta, 2016, p. 7).

References

Ahmad, S., & Yousaf, M. (2011). Special education in Pakistan: In the perspectives of educational policies and plans. *Academic research international, 1*(2), 228–231.

Al-Asfour, A. (2012). Online teaching: Navigating its advantages, disadvantages and best practices. *Tribal College, 23*(3). https://www.learntechlib.org/p/86959/

Amin, S. (2013). An effective use of ICT for education and learning by drawing on worldwide knowledge, research and experience: ICT as a change agent for education (a literature review). *Scholarly Journal of Education, 2*(4), 38–45.

Andersen, T., Annand, D., & Wark, N. (2005). The search for learning community in student-paced distance education: Or having your cake and eating it too. *Australian Journal of Educational Technology, 21*(2), 222–241.

Assareh, M., & Hosseini Bidokht, M. (2011). Barriers to e-teaching and e-learning. *Procedia Computer Science, 3*, 791–795.

Bandura, A. (1977). *Social learning theory.* Prentice-Hall.

Bates, A. W. (1997). The impact of technological change on open and distance learning. *Distance Education, 18*(1), 93–109.

Biggs, J. B. (1989). Approaches to the enhancement of tertiary teaching. *Higher Education Research and Development, 8*(1), 7–25.

Boles, W. (2010). *Overcoming barriers to learning: A guide for academics.* Queensland University of Technology, Department of eLearning Services.

Bronfenbrenner, U. (2005). Ecological systems theory (1992). In U. Bronfenbrenner (Ed.), *Making human beings human: Bioecological perspectives on human development* (pp. 106–173). Sage Publications.

Cloete, A. L. (2015). Living in a digital culture: The need for theological reflection'. *HTS Teologiese Studies/Theological Studies, 71*, 1–7. http://dx.doi.org/10.4102/hts.v71i2.2073

Common Sense Media. (2018). *What is media literacy and why is it important?* https://www.commonsensemedia.org/news-and-media-literacy/what-is-media-literacy-and-why-is-it-important

Department of Education. (2008). *Report of the ministerial committee on transformation and social cohesion and the elimination of discrimination in public higher education institutions* (Final report). Department of Education.

Downey, M. (2014). *Effective modern coaching: The principles and art of successful business coaching.* LID Publishing Ltd.

Doyle, C., Sammon, D., & Neville, K. (2015). Building an evaluation framework for Social Media-Enabled Collaborative Learning Environments (SMECLEs) *Journal of Decision Systems, 24*(3), 298–317.

Ferreira, J. G., & Venter, E. (2011). Barriers to learning at an ODL institution. *Progression, 33*(1), 80–93.

Greenhow, C., Robelia, B., & Hughes, J. E. (2009). Learning, teaching, and scholarship in a digital age: Web 2.0 and classroom research: What path should we take now? *Educational Researcher, 38*(4), 246–259. doi:10.3102/0013189X09336671

Grosfoguel, R. (2011). Decolonizing post-colonial studies and paradigms of political-economy: Transmodernity, decolonial thinking, and global coloniality. *Transmodernity: Journal of Peripheral Cultural Production of the Luso-Hispanic World, 1*(1), 1–38.

Heleta, S. (2016). 'Decolonisation of higher education: Dismantling epistemic violence and Eurocentrism in South Africa. *Transformation in Higher Education, 1*(1), 1–8.

Hugo, A. (2003). From literacy to literacies: Preparing higher education in South Africa for the future. *South African Journal of higher Education, 17*(2), 46–53.

Kanwar, A., & Cheng, R. Z. (2017). *Making open and distance learning inclusive: The role of technology.* Keynote address at the 6th International Conference on Information and Communication Technology and Accessibility.

Kline, N. (2017). *Time to think: Listening to ignite the human mind.* Casell Illustrated.

Kop, R., Fournier, H., & Mak, J. S. F. (2011). A pedagogy of abundance or a pedagogy to support human beings? Participant support on massive open online courses. *The International Review of Research in Open and Distributed Learning, 12*(7), 74–93.

Lave, J., & Wenger, E. (1991). *Situated learning: Legitimate peripheral participation.* Cambridge University Press.

Letseka, M., Cosser, M., Breier, M., & Visser, M. (Eds.). (2010). *Student retention and graduate destinations: Higher education and labour market access and success.* HSRC Press.

Lynch, M. M. (2002). *The online educator: A guide to creating the virtual classroom.* Routledge.

MacKeogh, K., & Fox, S. (2009). Strategies for embedding e-learning in traditional universities: Drivers and barriers. *Electronic Journal of E-Learning, 7*(2), 147–154.

Maphosa, C., & Bhebhe, S. (2019). Digital literacy: A must for Open Distance and e-Learning (ODeL) students. *European Journal of Education Studies, 5*(10), 186–199.

Maboe, M. J., Eloff, M., Schoeman, M., & Kayode, O. (2018). The experience of students with disabilities at an open distance e-learning institution. In *Proceedings of the 13th*

International Conference on e-Learning (ICEL 2018) (p. 220). Academic Conferences and Publishing Limited.

Mbembe, A. J. (2016). Decolonizing the university: New directions. *Arts & Humanities in Higher Education, 15,* 29–45.

McDougall, J., Readman, M., & Wilkinson, P. (2018). The uses of (digital) literacy. *Learning Media and Technology, 43*(3), 263–279. https://doi.org/10.1080/17439884.2018.1462206

Mezirow, J. (1997). Transformative learning: Theory to practice. *New Directions for Adult and Continuing Education, 74,* 5–12.

Mtebe, J. S., & Raisamo, R. (2014). Investigating perceived barriers to the use of open educational resources in higher education in Tanzania. *International Review of Research in Open and Distributed Learning, 15*(2), 43–66.

Ndlovu-Gatsheni, S. (2015). Decoloniality as the future of Africa. *History Compass, 13,* 485–496.

Prinsloo, P., & van Rooyen, A. A. (2007). Exploring a blended learning approach to improving student success in the teaching of second year accounting. *Meditari Accountancy Research, 15*(1), 51–69.

Rahman, H. (2014). The Role of ICT open and distance education. *Turkish Online Journal of Distance Education, 15*(4), 161–168.

Roberts, J. J., & Gous, I. G. (2014). ODeL – Open and Distance Education and Listening: The need for metacognitive listening strategies. *Journal of Educational and Social Research, 4*(3), 63–70.

Sedimo, N. C., Bwalya, K. J., & Du Plessis, T. (2011). Conquering the digital divide: Botswana and South Korea digita l divide status and interventions. *SA Journal of Information Management, 13*(1), Article 471. http://dx.doi.org/10.4102/sajim.v13il.471

Segoe, B. A., & Dreyer, J. M. (2015). The reliability of mentor assessments in teaching practice in an Open Distance e-Learning (ODeL) context. *International Journal of Educational Sciences, 8*(1), 15–22 doi:10.1080/09751122.2015.11917588

Serote, M., Mathimbi, M., & Mbodila, M. (2013). Towards Open Distance and Electronic Learning (OdeL). In *Proceedings of the International Conference on e-Learning, e-Business, Enterprise Information Systems, and e-Government (EEE)* (p. 325). The Steering Committee of The World Congress in Computer Science, Computer Engineering and Applied Computing (WorldComp).

Snow, E., & Sampson, P. (2010). *Course platforms for teaching online, teaching geoscience online – A workshop for digital faculty.* University of South Florida, University of Texas, University of Michigan [Online]. http://serc.carleton.edu/NAGTWorkshops/online/platforms.html

Van Der Vleuten, C. P. M., Schuwirth, L. W. T., Driessen, E. W., Govaerts, M. J. B., & Heeneman, S. (2015). Twelve tips for programmatic assessment. *Medical Teacher, 37*(7), 641–646. https://doi.org/10.3109/0142159X.2014.973388

Vasudevaiah, G. (2016). Promoting usage of ICT in open and distance education pro-grams. *International Journal of Indian Psychology, 3*(3), 77–80.

Vygotsky, L. S. (1978). *Mind in society, the development of higher psychological processes.* Harvard University Press.

Wingate, U., & Dreiss, C. (2009). Developing students' academic literacy: An online approach. *Journal of Academic Language and Learning, 3*(3), 14–25.

CHAPTER 8

Using ICT in Higher Education for Student Empowerment: An Academic Perspective Using Critical Pedagogies

Nazira Hoosen and Andrew Crouch

Abstract

Many academics within higher education institutions (HEIS) are impeded when developing and thinking about content and learning interaction design for critical pedagogies using ICT. Professional learning seems insufficient as academics focus on being teacher centered. When exposed to incorporating ICTs in learning and teaching (L&T), academics often concentrate on the technology and neglect the student-centered pedagogy that should cater to student agency, inclusiveness, and equality. Academics regard the online space as a third space which alienates them from the human aspect of thinking about how to develop skills in students.

Learning activities are not grafted to the learning process to ensure student centered learning which is inclusive and equal. ICTs as tools are good only insofar as they are used. The tools dictate vigorously how they can be utilised as material affordances; if not, academic agency is eliminated by covertly reducing what and how is facilitated as commodified data. Ideally, this can be mitigated by engaging in critical pedagogy when using ICTs. Much of our thinking about learning and teaching (L&T) in the online space starts with us focusing on the tools (technical aspect) when, instead, we need to start with the human aspect to attain learning outcomes (sociological aspect). This chapter explores this challenge and the nuances that surround it. It approaches learning and teaching using ICTs through the lenses of structure, culture and agency as espoused by Archer (1995) in order to refine and condense the focus on critical pedagogy using ICTs.

Keywords

access – critical pedagogy – educational systems – Information and Communication Technologies

© KONINKLIJKE BRILL NV, LEIDEN, 2021 | DOI: 10.1163/9789004447226_009

1 Introduction

This chapter provides a theoretical exploration of critical pedagogies through the integration of information communication technologies (ICTs) in the context of universities going through a transformation and transition phase in a post-colonial context. In doing so, the chapter focuses on student empowerment through the pedagogical practice of the academic. The higher education (HE) landscape in South Africa has undergone significant changes since attaining democracy in 1994. Marwala (2015) has demonstrated that a new model of university has emerged that engages in teaching, research, and service delivery through the use of ICTs. Globally, ICT integration within higher education is viewed to effectively and efficiently transform HE institutions and their associated outputs (Porter et al., 2014; Kiviniemi, 2014).

Using ICTs has, in part, revolutionised HE in a way that could reposition the process and structure of L&T models. HE serves the public interest by empowering students to improve societies and attain developmental goals. However, ICTs are a human endeavor and "humans are not neutral" (Bradshaw, 2017, p. 8). The professional learning initiatives of academics reflect priorities and positionalities that have in the past neglected the praxis of culture and ICTs. For academics to use ICTs effectively they need to foreground issues around relevance, equity, access, student agency and ethics in L&T. Incorporating ICTs in the process is a challenge that forces academics to rethink their pedagogy. Critical pedagogy offers an ethical lens to consider practices and perspectives in L&T. It involves educational approaches that are aligned to the lived experience of students, addressing direct and immediate issues relevant to their communities that focus on student empowerment forcing them to be participants in a democratic society (Bradshaw, 2017). Together with critical theory, ethics, liberation and progressive education, critical pedagogy is grounded in manifestations of social justice, equity and fairness.

One of the barriers to L&T when using ICTs is the non-embodiment of critical pedagogies from the academic perspective (Bladergroen et al., 2012). Academics should consider incorporating sound critical pedagogical foundations like, student needs, their lived experiences, and student-centred designs into their L&T practices. This consideration would provide the relevant springboard needed to maximise participation. It would also create critically minded students who are not only prepared for employment but also to handle social justice challenges in their communities and societies as a whole. However, the design and development of ICTs may, in new ways, covertly favour "social exclusion" in the academic context; it remains the academics' endeavor to show how such technology plays a material affordance role. This can be done through technology integration and transitioning of mindsets in individuals based on how they choose to pedagogically reason while integrating ICTs into L&T practices. It is this aim that this specific chapter brings into the overall theme of the book, especially to audiences that are seated in positions of educational leadership and L&T practices, be it developed or developing contexts. This chapter weaves securely through the notion of barriers to L&T when using ICTs as one of the key themes in this book. Therefore, as critical pedagogues (academics who enact critical practice in L&T), the authors seek to understand what works and what does not when integrating ICTs into L&T.

2 Background

Universities in South Africa, like other institutions globally, have been plagued by various challenges, such as: massification, poverty and inequality, diverse student bodies, cost efficiency, and attaining measurable outcomes. Aligned with these challenges is the need to investigate the potential of advancing technologies to provide personalised learning whilst still adhering to the fundamental ideas of the purpose of education (Nel & Wilkinson, 2006). Recently, South African (and global) HE institutions experienced a challenge that was not encountered before. While the 2015 "Fees Must Fall Movement" that saw rampant student protests across the country brought many institutions to a standstill, the scramble in 2020 to move to online L&T due to the global outbreak of the COVID-19 virus has created other unexpected challenges.

During the student protests in 2016, and more recently the global outbreak of COVID-19 in 2020, the authors observed that many academics found themselves scrambling to transition their traditional contact classrooms into online learning environments to engage students via alternative teaching and learning platforms Many academics struggled in the process due to not possessing enough experience in online learning environments. Many academics lack the confidence to use ICTs for teaching and learning purposes (Yuen & Ma, 2008). This is substantiated by Xu and Jaggars, (2013) who claim that academics teach the way they were taught and therefore struggle to transcend to using ICTs in learning interaction design. Scheepers (2015) argues that most academics are insufficiently prepared for their teaching careers and base their understanding of effective teaching on their experiences as a student. Clearly academics are under prepared to facilitate 21st century skills and it is, therefore, fitting that they receive continuous professional learning activities to support them in delivering meaningful learning activities (Lipinge, 2013).

It is argued that academics are under tremendous pressure to incorporate ICTs for innovative critical pedagogy, curriculum and assessment practices that ultimately affect student learning (Yuen, 2011). In the context of Wits University, the wide range of diversity in terms of age distribution, with the majority of academics on average above the age of 50, makes this an even bigger challenge. The group of academics have themselves not had a history of extensive exposure to technology since most have received their formal training prior to the advent of the internet (Prensky, 2009). Many have kept pace with technological developments, but the majority have not, leading to them continuing with practices where limited technology use is part of their day-to-day teaching practice. They are the group who feel the pressure both from within institutions, as well as from the new generation of students who enter the learning spaces on traditional campuses (Yuen, 2011).

3 Clarification of the Use of the Term ICTs

There seems to be an inconsistent use of the term "digital technologies" by various authors. While they use the term as it stands, others refer to it as information communication technology (ICT), computing, educational technology, or instructional technology. In a similar vein, the concept of assistive technology as an extension of ICTs is also employed. Assistive technologies include any technology such as those that "facilitate access to a standard computer, to a network, access to and manipulation of written and spoken words or any technology that may assist in compensating for cognitive deficits" (Alnahdi, 2014, p. 18). In sum then, these technologies enable disabled people to use a computer while also making their use of that computer more efficient to allow them access to online information. Assistive technologies tend to facilitate access to learning and teaching material, with a focus on promoting access to technologies that can bridge the gap between the material and the student. If the correct assistive technologies are used, then the material itself need not be altered. Selwyn (2011) provides an umbrella term that includes various aspects of contemporary technologies discussed above as follows:

- Computing hardware, systems, and devices (such as desktop PCs, laptop computers, tablet computers, interactive whiteboards, simulation systems and immersive environments);

- personal computing devices (such as mobile phones, smart phones, personal digital assistants, mp3 players);
- audiovisual devices (such as digital radio, digital television, digital photography, digital video);
- games consoles and hand-held games machines;
- content-free computer software packages (such as word processors, spreadsheets);
- content-related computer software packages (such as simulation programmes, tutorial packages);
- worldwide web content, services and applications (not least webpages and web based services);
- other internet applications such as email and voice over internet protocol (such as Skype and other web-based telephone services). (Selwyn, 2011, p. 14)

While some technologies are particularly designed for educational purposes, others may be repurposed for use in educational settings (Mishra & Koehler, 2006). Therefore, in this chapter the term ICTs will be used to refer to all the above.

4   Critical Pedagogies

Critical pedagogy remains a crucial L&T approach in the transformation of education through emancipatory practices, especially those aimed at marginalised students. One of its major approaches focuses on criticizing the L&T practices in capitalistic societies. Critical pedagogy is mainly associated with Brazilian activist and educator, Paulo Freire (1972) who used it as a response to oppressive power relations and inequalities that exist in educational institutions. The aim of the critical pedagogical approach is to enable students to become critically conscious individuals in society, in order to attain the prerequisite skills, resources, and knowledge to create change. One of the major concerns of critical pedagogy is the transformative nature of the teacher as facilitator (Darder, 2017). The facilitator's aim is to liberate students through open curriculum design methods and pedagogical practices that consider the vision and lived experiences of students. If teachers or academics used this approach it would mean that students would eventually become empowered to attain a certain amount of control in their education. In this way, students engage seriously on various aspects of their lives because of influence from their liberatory education (Darder, 2017).

5 Student Learning through Co-Creation

The introduction of the online modality in HEIs has encouraged technological innovation such as, digital teaching aids, online teaching, and virtual learning environments (Kiviniemi, 2014). Engaging in these modalities provides certain material affordances to the academic and the student in various ways. Students can make new connections between the pockets of information to create new meaning, while sound, text, media, and data sources become easy to create, and differentiated learning becomes more possible (Arenas, 2015). When likened to partnerships, students are increasingly being viewed as partners and co-creators of knowledge in L&T practices (Cook-Sather et al., 2014; Dunne, 2016; Mercer-Mapstone et al., 2017). However, this practice is not so prominent in the global south as it occurs more so in the global north.

A reason for this might be the perceived technological advantage that the global north has over the south, but in reality, it is the access to more resources and better schooling systems that provides this advantage. Students from developing countries, the majority sitting in the African continent, have, however, caught up in the practices of co-creation through access to better networks and mobile devices. In Central and West Africa, there has been explosive growth in the uptake of technology amongst the 18 to 25 age group, leading to knowledge creation in very innovative ways. The authors noticed key projects at the e-Learning Africa conferences in 2018 and 2019 which they attended. This included innovation around drone technology in L&T, cyber security using ICTs as a facilitator of justice and human rights, applications and software made in Africa to address African needs and markets, among others. However, in our context, we align and view co-creation as a pedagogical practice that emphasises student empowerment through student learning.

One of the ways to conceptualise co-creation is to occupy the space between student engagement and partnership, so that a meaningful collaboration between students and academics occurs, with students becoming more active participants in the L&T process. This happens through constructing understanding and resources with the facilitator. Another way is to engage in a participatory design process where there is collaboration between stakeholders (academics and students) in the design and development of the curriculum and L&T practice. Everyone's input is valued as there is emphasis on the development of ICTs in the design phase. However, Martens et al. (2019) is of the view that students often remain as participants or testers instead of partners who have some form of autonomy. There are four roles that students occupy in co-creation, namely: representative, consultant, co-researcher, and pedagogical co-designer (Bovill et al., 2016). Buckley (2014) states that work which entails a partnership can be divided into the pedagogical and political areas of focus, with the former focused on L&T practices while the latter on institutional governance.

There are differences in types of co-creation with students. This could mean that students learn through "co-researching university-wide projects and acting as change agents, undertaking research and scholarship projects with staff, collaborating with university staff on committees for quality assurance and enhancement purposes providing feedback on teaching observations, designing their essay titles co-evaluating courses" (Buckely, 2014, p. 4). This particular move embraces diversity, can help to motivate students, and can serve to focus values, methods, and outcomes.

6   The Challenge

The introduction of ICTs at HE institutions encourages technological innovation such as digital teaching aids, online teaching, and virtual learning environments. Engaging ICTs provides various e-affordances such as ubiquitous learning that makes it easier for students to access content from a plethora of devices anywhere and anytime. Students can make new connections among the pockets of information to create new meaning. While sound, text, media, and data sources become easy to create, differentiated learning becomes more possible (Arenas, 2015). However, how content is transformed and how pedagogies are reasoned with, changed, and elaborated proves to be a challenge. The main challenge faced by HE is an over reliance on traditional pedagogies by academic staff. Global research on pedagogic change suggests that critical pedagogies using ICTs could transform HE as established practices are difficult to change and that more professional development interventions are required (Gast, Schildkamp, & Van der Veen, 2017).

Academics now need to identify, orchestrate, and manage learning activities within specific content areas in a way that will support students and guide them in attaining critical learning skills whilst taking advantage of ICTs. At this point the need to understand the duality of facilitation and teaching is crucial as any programme that is structured with a healthy blend of facilitation and teaching could be advantageous for learning and teaching with ICTs. Engaging in critical pedagogy could be a challenge to many academics as it is more than merely having an understanding of content; it challenges their pedagogical reasoning and modes of facilitation whilst concomitantly paying attention to ongoing struggles, realities, and experiences of students. The students' experience is to a large extent influenced by the culture within the country, the region, and the institution. Country culture could be diverse, sometimes influenced by sectarianism and even tribalism like in South Africa and many parts of Africa. This could flow into the institutional culture of individual educational institutions. In the global north, higher education formed by religious groups and sectors have always played a fundamental role in how the educational experience has been shaped.

7   Agency

Archer (1995, 2000) posits that the social world is comprised of the parts (structure and culture) and people within institutions (agents). Structural and cultural contexts in which agents reside shape the situations which they are confronted with, and the way they respond to, the enablement and constraints in these contexts which is dependent on the agents' concerns. For something to be an enablement or constraint, it has to stand in a position showing so (Archer, 2003). The ability which individuals possess to make differences through their actions is defined as agency (Chamber, 2005). Agency, within the context of this chapter, is employed in a dual fashion. First, it refers to academics who engage in "open [autonomous] educational practices that use technology, but which are rich because of the social interaction and open attitudes underlying the practices rather than the particular technologies involved" (Bali & Caines, 2018, p. 22). Agency also refers to the notion of student-centredness, whereby students are co-creators of knowledge and partners in the knowledge production practice. So, in as much as the academic possesses agency, it needs to be fostered in students.

8   Institutional Culture

Culture is conceptualised as "description of the ideas, beliefs, theories, concepts, values and ideologies that manifest through discourses used by agents at specific times and places" (Archer, cited in Quinn, 2012, p. 29). Therefore, the connection between agency, culture, and HEIs refers to discourses from a social realist position and being part of the cultural system that enables or constrains factors, particularly in HEIs. Institutional culture has the tendency to change depending on the leadership and dispensation within institutions. The dynamic drivers that determine institutional culture are the staff, students, processes, and regulations of the institution. Whilst the student body may have transformed and moved through the university, the biggest impact on institutional culture is its staff, rules, and processes (Tierney & Lanford, 2018). Generally, the transformation in the staffing environment has been slow due to the longer residence of staff in any educational environment. To a large extent this influences the culture of the organisation much more than the cohort which has a shorter residency, i.e. the student body.

The decolonisation of the curriculum debate in the last few years is a recognition that institutional culture change is best addressed by a fundamental change in the core business of the institution and something that speaks to the heart of its operations. Decolonisation of the curriculum emerges from calls by students for university curricula to be decolonised. The concept decolonisation is a nuanced, yet layered, concept that cannot be unlocked through the use of specific formulae or definitions. This means that to understand the ways to decolonise, we need to look beyond its definition by focusing on its detail. A suitable example of detail would be the ways that HEIS continue to mimic colonial methodologies and practices that may not be as relevant in South African HEIS today. The "de-" in decolonisation refers to is an offer to be active in making a "gesture" that breaks with colonial ways of doing things, especially those that continue to alienate, marginalise, and silence people and their experiences. We argue that things should be done differently, in terms of interacting, drawing on backgrounds, contexts, dispositions and change in meaningful ways. The aim is for individuals to be able to find their voices, contribute meaningfully to discussions and feel valued through the personal and professional narratives and expertise they bring to innovative L&T practices.

This debate on curriculum transformation could not be addressed in its entirety without considering the impact technology would have on the modes of delivery. "Technology should not merely be viewed as a tool, but rather as a medium that shapes culture" (Tierney & Lanford, 2018, p. 4). The view here is that the medium itself controls and shapes human action. Academics tend to focus more on content in transmission but in the process omit the structural changes that take place over a period of time. As values and norms change due to ICTs, the social implications of the medium are realised. These structural changes contribute to and sometimes determine culture within the institution. Due to the rapid pace of change of technology in the last 20 years, there has been a fundamental time lag in culture adjustment within institutions due to the slow alignment towards technological changes. Where we have seen rapid cultural change was in the use of mobile technologies, which fundamentally changed the way society communicates, handles financial transactions, logistics and even changing the political directions of countries (the Arab Spring). The generation Z or X who grew up with this technological advance has embraced it, used it in their daily interactions and practices, but this has not entirely infiltrated the HE spaces to the same extent in influencing curriculum change. There are some pockets where it is happening, but due to the large inequalities, in particularly South African society, it is not an equally distributed practice (the current debates around rolling out online learning in the midst of the COVID-19 crisis is a clear example of the digital divide in our country and the developing world).

9 Affordability and Access

Many researchers advocating for the use of ICTs in learning and teaching view it as a more cost-effective means to facilitate education to remote audiences (access) as well as offering the possibility of generating additional revenue through increased enrolments (Allen & Seaman, 2013; Dibiase, 2000; Di Rienzo & Lilly, 2014; Yamagata-Lynch, 2014). The introduction of free open online resources (MOOCS) and open platforms such as EdX has provided further impetus to activity in the online world. The proliferation of virtual universities and introduction of micro-credentials are all attempts to widen access and to increase affordability. In addition, it provides the added benefit of savings in classroom space (Chao & Chen, 2009). Yamagata-Lynch (2014) propose that the use of ICT is now being touted as a method to make educational opportunities accessible to a wide range of audiences. It has also been gaining attention as a vehicle for improving pedagogy through introducing flexibility in student access to facilitation and lower costs associated with education. In the last few years, there has also been a trend in leveraging online education in giving access to the adult education market.

In a similar vein, other aspects such as approachability, reachability, and usability are related to access in a manner that looks at the critical pedagogical aspects of how courses and materials are designed and developed to reduce frustration yet maintain student motivation to support student success and student-centeredness. Hence, in as much as a certain tone is set in the face-to-face classroom to support student learning, so too should the online classroom set a similar tone. The usability aspect should ideally enhance student navigation and learning throughout the online course environment. Additionally, the authors also suggest that access encases the concepts of locating, retrieving, understanding, and using of information in a manner that is participative and assists knowledge and skills development within the learning and teaching landscape.

10 Educational Structures and Systems

Education systems are embedded in their specific environment. "The HE sectors in South Africa currently is in many ways profoundly different from its fragmented, insular, elite and uneven apartheid inheritance" (Webbstock, 2016, p. 23). The shape of the sector is different from the stratified and fragmented 36 public institutions of different types that had been governed by a range of regimes prior to 1994 and the more than 300 private institutions that in most cases had been unregulated, leading to many levels of public confidence in their quality (Webbstock, 2016). Within this shifting field, individual institutions in the form of traditional universities, universities of technology, and the new comprehensive universities have actively attempted to reposition themselves, providing a further, and sometimes insufficiently acknowledged dimension, to the processes of system change and transformation.

South African HE systems have followed the traditional model of a contact university for many years. One exception has been UNISA, which follows the distance education model. With the change in legislation six years ago (South African Department of Higher Education and Training, 2014) all universities in SA were afforded the opportunity to rethink their mode of delivery to widen access. This also brings with it the opportunity to think critically about how institutions need to engage around critical pedagogy and technology. A rethinking of strategies, resource models, and structures is required as they could influence how pedagogies are expressed.

11 The Political Inherence of Educational Systems and Structures

The HE discourses in South Africa, as elsewhere, takes for granted a shared set of assumptions about decision-making, modes of participation, and representation with associated outcomes (Feinstein et al., 2013). Reform efforts focus more on the fidelity of implementation and tend to ignore the reality of process and variability across the South African HE system. There are institutions and units within these institutions with distinctive organisational characteristics and challenges, unique student dynamics, diverse communities, and institutional histories (Feinstein et al., 2013).

In the South African context, the government has introduced an E-education bill because of the importance of ICTs in education for social and economic development. This may be aimed primarily at basic education level. It is critical for institutions wishing to survive in the global marketplace to understand that learning is crucial for improved economic conditions as it lays the foundation for knowledge construction. Theoretically, there is no direct policy at the HE level, yet. However, there is a supervisory approval process currently taking place.

The Department of Higher Education and Training (DHET) and Council for Higher Education (CHE) engage in the supervisory and approval process (mainly quality control) for distance learning; however, there is no strategic national plan from the government to date. In hindsight, if there was a policy, the question is: What would its focus be? SA must meet its national development goals and must prioritise its spending based on the acuteness of the problem as the funding will be directed towards high impact projects to reduce inequality and poverty. Unfortunately, spending on ICT would then not enjoy as high a priority as one would think. Throughout this process effective governance and management is required to control the change, albeit in a participatory manner. Central to this argument is that legislation as a solution to the institutions' challenge of access, value, and greater participation does not amount to greater representation of the diverse needs and interests of a diverse body of students.

12 Pedagogic Discourse within the African Lens

Research on pedagogy advances the argument that HEIs have always assumed an international character. Knight (2014) states that it is now more crucial than ever that academics increase their awareness of theories and philosophies of L&T as a foundation to a more precise understanding of how individuals learn in their context. Globalisation imposes western episteme through the guise of opportunities that it offers and then dictates to keep abreast of international patterns in the field of HE pedagogy. The authors' conceptualisation of "western episteme" refers to the dominant mode of knowing in relation to knowledge production. Many HEIs globally, tend to follow the western model and place European ways of knowing above all that is local. In doing so, a situation is created whereby the way knowledge is produced and organised follows a historical pattern from the colonial era. Hence, in part, our world view as national citizens, the types of institutions we accept, the discourses and kinds of knowledge that we experience and embody, all point (to a large extent) to western influence. Therefore, we think that it is fair to state that, currently, the world operates largely through western thinking. The implication of these ready-made ideas in the African context is that it assumes a subtle perpetuation of western epistemological ideas in pedagogical transformation (Angu, 2018).

This pseudo transformation contributes very little to the promotion of critical pedagogies (Maringe, 2017) in African education, especially one that considers the use of ICTs in learning and teaching. African education in the post-colonial era has primarily focused on educational reform with a focus away from the bonds they experienced during colonialism. The colonial experience of assimilation of western content and the disregard for local knowledge systems formed the basis for African countries to immediately develop a policy domain in the post-colonial era which promoted Africanisation (Mosweunyane, 2013). Whether this strategy succeeded is a question that must still be answered. Whilst some countries have made headway in including local knowledge into the curricula, most have defaulted to a pre-colonial style of education, primarily due to the education systems framed by civil strife, corruption, and poverty (Mosweunyane, 2013). Where African countries have progressed is in changing who delivers the curriculum. Whilst the pre-colonial era was dominated by European educators, the Africa of today has almost completely transformed in certain countries like Zimbabwe and Kenya (mainly East, West, and Central Africa). In many cases, these educators have developed the first locally based curricula (Ndille, 2018).

In this respect the developments in ICT have flattened the curve in providing a basis of more international access to content, more locally based content being more readily available, and more power and agency being placed in the hands of the educator. Some challenges still exist, especially where educational policy is centrally driven and highly prescriptive. It could be argued that ICT has significantly enhanced the Africanisation project which many of the founding fathers of post-colonial education envisaged. The fact that ICT in education features prominently in the Africa 2063 strategy shows that technology as a tool has been embedded in the policy frameworks of the further African paradigm. Earlier reference was made to the fast and high penetration of mobile devices on the African continent. This must surely be a factor in assisting Africans to develop their content, share their own stories, spread their own culture, and thereby change the narrative that only the Western episteme should be valued. A major drawback, however, is the failure in some quarters to provide sustainable power, which might slow down this development. Technology has definitely enhanced the African agenda, and will continue to do so amidst all the other challenges (African Union, Agenda 2063).

Of equal importance and in relation to African education is the creation of critical pedagogical links to the decolonisation discourse and its implications for higher education. Critical pedagogies advance the relationship of the institution and professional knowledge, democracy in powerful times and the manner in which knowledge is accessed with a type of knowledge that fosters democracy, equity, and equality. In a democratic context, social injustices are erased through the creation of structures and legislation that provides integration and equality in society. One aspect of defining critical pedagogies could be to view the concept in the opposite—to understand it.

If one looks at a context that places groups of people above others that is socially unjust with the aim of becoming socially just, then contextual dimensions are the crucial lenses through which critical pedagogies may be enhanced (Maringe, 2017). Therefore, engaging in critical pedagogies levels the educational field by equalizing opportunities to society and providing a springboard to access, knowledge, success, and progress beyond. Hence, this advance in promoting agency allows the expansion of human capital as well as deals with local challenges and lived realities through education. HE institutions should focus on developing critical pedagogies that are relevant to the manner in which knowledge is accessed, co-created, and shared. Critical pedagogy promotes dialogical teaching and learning. Brown and Renshaw (2006) posit "books and teachers and ICTs and books are the common binaries" that enhance the teaching and learning encounter. Hence, dialogical learning should just not be an abdication of responsibility for teaching with the assumption that students are indeed learning.

Patel and Lynch (2013) are of the view that learning involves reconstruction that occurs in the personal, disciplinary, and social space. The authors state further that internationalisation ignores the personal space of students whilst placing credence on their disciplinary space. We suspect that students are introduced into the social space only because their personal spaces could have been undermined. Hence, the social space then becomes an environment and opportunity for personal relevance, knowledge creation, and recreation, generation, and regeneration due to the ideas and values being transmitted in the social groups and networks. Therefore, critical pedagogies liberate the mind in the process of co-creating and sharing new knowledge that defines and creates identities and self-worth for those who are marginalised. Hence, teaching is viewed as a profession and recognises that the teacher possesses a set of skills (a knowledge base) that is in itself further developed through co-creation during the process of learning and teaching.

13 Critical Pedagogy and the Development of a Knowledge Base

In the context of teaching, a central issue that emerges often is a definition of the skills that a teacher needs to know how to teach (knowledge base). It was common belief for a long time that a teacher needed to know specific content in order to teach (Fernandez, 2014, p. 80). If one looks at the practice of a teacher, one can conclude that this is not the case as knowing specific content is not the only construct that characterises a good teacher. If this were the case then all teachers (school, university, researchers, and content experts) would be excellent teachers. Fenstermacher (1994) posits that two forms of teaching practice co-exist that give rise to two conceptualisations about teachers' knowledge. The first type is formal knowledge which refers to knowledge obtained by expert researchers and provided to teachers through professional development. The second type involves practical knowledge, what teachers know from their professional expertise (Fenstermacher, 2014).

There is consensus in the literature that practical knowledge stems from the teacher's professional knowledge. The authors' assumption is that the teacher builds knowledge because of their collaboration with the student and this is different to the knowledge attained in academia. Over time, many propositions about the composition of practical knowledge have been formed. The propositions include "personal knowledge" (Connelly & Clandinin, 1985); situated knowledge (Brown, Collins, & Duguid, 1989); action-oriented knowledge (Carter, 1990); and tacit knowledge (Eraut, 1994). In this regard, Verloop, van Driel, and Meijer (2001) state that these conceptions indicate that knowledge and beliefs could influence teachers in their practice. At the same time, the components of the characteristics of teacher's professional practice require situational and intuitive knowledge of one's rationality (Carter, 1990). More recently, Ball, Thames, and Phelps (2008) devised five components representing teacher knowledge: "common content knowledge, specialized content knowledge, knowledge of content and students, knowledge of content and teaching, knowledge of content and curriculum horizon" (p. 399). Ball et al. (2008) seem to align their domains of educator knowledge by expanding on Shulman's (1987) pedagogical content knowledge (PCK).

To attain a knowledge base of teaching, Shulman (1987) asserts that the knowledge base consists of content knowledge (CK), general pedagogical knowledge, curriculum knowledge, and pedagogical content knowledge (PCK). He also states that it is important to have knowledge of students and associated characteristics, educational context, ends, purposes, and values. PCK appears to be very important as it intersects content and pedagogy. Shulman's view is that possessing CK (having knowledge about a specific topic) and general pedagogic knowledge remained insufficient for good quality teaching. A combination of PCK (having knowledge about knowing how to teach a specific topic) is required, which enables improved pedagogical representations (Smart, 2016).

The representations refer to "taught topics in one subject, forms of representation of ideas, powerful analogies, illustrations and examples which lend it to the ways of representing and formulating the subject that make it comprehensible to others" (Shulman, 1987, p. 9). In the same year that Shulman (1987) refined the construct of PCK, he presented the model of pedagogical reasoning and action (MPRA) to represent how a teachers' practical knowledge can be developed to include the process of reflection and reasoning. The authors are of the view that Shulman presented these two constructs in the same year as this may be his proposition that PCK may be developed through the process of pedagogic reasoning.

The technological, pedagogical, and content knowledge (TPACK) framework by Mishra and Koehler (2006) specifies what knowledge is required to teach within contemporary times. In further developing the model, Mishra and Koehler (2006) attached the concept of technological knowledge (TK) which refers to the knowledge of how one can work with and apply technological recourses (Willermark, 2018). Hence, the framework, apart from emphasizing each construct independently also stresses a complex interplay of technology, pedagogy, and content knowledge and how to apply this knowledge in various contexts. The TPACK framework has been adapted for use in over 600 journal articles (Koehler, Mishra, Kereluik, Shin, & Graham, 2014) due to its conceptualisation of how ICTs can be integrated in teaching. This implies a rounded view of the entire knowledge base that teachers need to master so that that they can effectively apply technology in their teaching. Much criticism of the framework has been cited due to the framework not being practically useful and its insufficiency in terms of the definitions of the various knowledge domains (Anderson, Krathwohl, & Bloom, 2001; Cox & Graham, 2009; Graham, 2011). Such scholarly debate and criticism of the TPACK framework illuminates the challenge of the identifying complex knowledge that the framework attempts to capture as well as the need to engage students in co-creation.

It is argued that there is a challenge when considering the usefulness of the framework in social research as it lacks strategies to deal with the lived realities of students and operational challenges, such as the availability of hardware and bandwidth (Angeli & Valanides, 2009; Brantley-Dias & Ertmer, 2013). Additionally, the criticism highlights the challenge of defining the point of intersection of technology, pedagogy and content in relation to distinguishing the various knowledge domains (which appear entangled) in practice. Based on the above overview of the TPACK and its development towards empowering students through ICTs, its importance is overtly presented in research terms to understand pedagogy from various viewpoints.

14   Change and Transformation as an Approach

A theoretical explanation of HEIs undergoing transformation brings a range of conceptual ideas that compete for space in discourses relating to transformation of HE pedagogies.

> Afro-political theorists with a post-colonial philosophy like Julius Nyere (1967), Kwame Nkrumah (1970), Chinua Achebe (1966), Ngugi Wa Thiongo (1986), Achille Mbembe (1992) advance the distinction between change and transformation that are conflated yet used interchangeably. (Maringe, 2017, p. 103)

Although change means different things in various contexts, in the context of education it is fundamental due to the alteration of human attitude, behaviors, and thinking due to institutional intervention. On the other hand, transformation as a term "implies a complete change in structure, purpose and method relating to social processes in communities and societies" (Maringe, 2017, p. 103). Perhaps transformation characterises a rejection of the status quo and establishing new prospects that may be urgent. While change relates to movement or transitioning, transformation may be all things necessary from slow to incremental that may not change the focus of the institution in the context of HE L&T.

Transformation takes place when the actors managing a system focus to co-create new ways of learning and teaching through critical mind-sets, irrespective of the modality being used (Daskzko & Sheinberg, 2005). Hence, change and transformation in this narrative include the purpose and means of critical pedagogy as transformative in formal learning contexts. These contexts then progress from being authoritative and transactional to being dialogical, collaborative, engaged, and co-created within transformed educational spaces as "locations of possibilities" (hooks, 1994).

The suggested analytical approach used in this narrative at a cursory level aligns to thinking around social change as espoused by Archer (1995, 2000). This approach considers how people and systems either promote or impede opportunities for social transformation. For social change to take place, Archer (1995) uses the morphogenetic account of change and constructs the social domain to comprise of structure, culture, and human agency. Structure is conceptualised as the "roles, organizations, institutions and systems" (Archer, 1995, p. 1). Culture is viewed as the dominant register of propositions in society. The assertion is that people find themselves in structural and cultural contexts that shape and tailor situations which they confront as well as how they respond (agency) to objective constraints or enablement (Archer, 1995). This translates to students enabling the space and the space enabling them. In terms of the learning space, what kind of learning space do we need to make, to create a learner identity? Thinking around critical pedagogy is necessary at this stage as the idea is to co-create knowledge with the student and pedagogy must take this into account.

It is crucial to note that the nature of subjective concerns, powers that people possess, and their personal properties determine how they respond in these contexts. Therefore, causative powers that structural and cultural contexts generate may be exercised as constraints or enablement, subject to the take up by human agency. However, it may not be possible to ascertain how change occurs in any situation because the powers of arrangement are activated by people and their sense of agency. The notion is that people may not possess absolute free will, nor can free will be determined by cultural and structural arrangements. Due to human agency, people interact with arrangements that eventually lead to new social arrangements or arrangements that remain the same. The crucial link to understanding how we behave as humans, relative to the given or reality, lies in our sense of agency as this influences how we respond to the causal powers as constraints or enablement's posed by social arrangements. Archer (2000) asserts that agency is partially dependent on our skill, knowledge, concerns, and commitments in understanding how we deal with the causal powers.

15   The Embodiment of Social Change

Change in the broad sense refers to the activity of attaining an outcome from a change process (Parlakkihc, 2014). Due to movement from one modality to the other, change is constructed around the social acceptance and execution of change because of the use of ICTs in the thinking and behavior of the users of such technology. In this narrative, the authors view L&T as a social activity with social structures imbued with community, which is further imbued with values, rules, and discourses. The link between student-centeredness and university culture renders it pointless to talk about learning without looking at social structures and university structures. Structures could mean policies, physical spaces, and so on. Academics need to understand that students learn in different ways and in different spaces. In addition to formal university structures and spaces, there are informal university spaces like the LinkedIn network; hence, students create different communities and networks in both physical and virtual spaces. These learning networks are equally valid. There are students whose learning may not be their strong point, but they have networks through which they do learn. Academics need to become sensitive and aware of how the student's culture of learning in their communities can be incorporated using critical pedagogy. The relationship among the groups of information summarises the extent to which academics and students may be constrained or determined by social structures in Table 8.1.

TABLE 8.1   The interplay between structure, culture and agency

Structure	Agency	Culture
Policies	Actions, behaviors and	Beliefs & practices
Procedures	perceptions	Expectations
Rules	Pedagogy	Relationships
Classroom & spaces	Facilitator agency	Community participation
F2F and online	Student agency	Civic engagement
ICTs	Learning interaction design	connected learning
Institutional support	Knowledge creation through	Knowledge sharing,
structures	student agency & facilitator	learning networks
OER	agency	F2F and online
Technical affordances		Philosophy of openness

The integration of ICTs is inherently a social activity shaped within social practices (Pratt, 2014). In the case of universities, academics who integrate ICTs into practice may be influenced by their university's institutional culture and structure. Equally so, those academics that are in the habit of using ICTs in their L&T practices are participating in social practices that emerge due to global, local, institutional, and individual factors. These interactions are separated into structural, cultural, and agential views because of Archer's (1995) analytical dualism to bring about a clearer understanding of those mechanism that are generative in nature and that we cannot see. The implication is that practices occur, irrespective of whether we can view it or not.

16   Recommendation

One recommendation is to provide as much agency as possible to the student, therefore academics need to think of designing both virtual and face-to-face spaces in ways that are generative and which allow slippage from one space to another. There is a need to consider students who learn effectively and those that use learning networks when designing and developing content and learning interaction design. This approach gives credence and has some imbuement to critical pedagogies. Equally of importance is the notion of co-creating knowledge so that students do not only consume media, they create it as well when they are given the agency to partly co-create a course. In this manner students have the ability to create part of the learning environment themselves. Students may not necessarily attend university with a learning culture. Through using critical pedagogies and ICTs, academics should in a way model and create a culture by designing in ways that are sensitive to agency, co-creation of and within the space, and to students as producers and not only as consumers of knowledge.

Another recommendation is the urgent (in full force) orchestration of a single unifying online L&T policy for the African continent. In its bid to reposition the African citizen as an effective change agent for sustainable development as envisioned by the African Union (AU) and its 2063 Agenda, the continents' leaders developed a continental education strategy (CES). One relevant aspect of this strategy is to re-orient the education and training systems within Africa to meet the "knowledge, competencies, skills, innovation and creativity required to nurture African core values and promote sustainable development at the national, sub-regional and continental levels" (African Union, 2016b, p. 8). In a similar vein, with specific reference to the strategic objectives of this coalition is SO2 which is to "build, rehabilitate, preserve education infrastructure and develop policies that ensure a permanent, healthy and conducive learning environment in all sub-sectors and for all, so as to expand access to quality education" (African Union, 2016b, p. 22) and SO3 focuses on "harnessing the capacity of ICT to improve access, quality and management of education and training systems" (African Union, 2016b, p. 23). In considering the above strategy, it is crucial to note that to fully evoke these strategic objectives, a unifying policy needs to be urgently devised, aligned, and implemented.

17 Conclusion

There is no question about the disruptive nature ICTs can play. In the South African context, they can be used as a facilitator to create access to students, thereby addressing the National Development Goals of the country. However, when using ICTs as transformative tools, academics should engage with pedagogies that will help them keep in focus how the structure of the institutions could be affected and modified, and how ICTs could fundamentally change the way in which the institution plays a role in the higher education project, through effective policy implementation. Academics should engage in this transformative project by using critical pedagogies and fomenting a culture of co-creation of knowledge.

References

Allen, I. E., & Seaman, J. (2013). *Changing course: Ten years of tracking online education in the United States*. Babson College/Quahog Research Group.

Alnahdi, G. (2014). Assistive technology in special education and the universal design for learning. *TOJET: The Turkish Online Journal of Educational Technology, 13*(2), 18–23.

Anderson, L. W., Krathwohl, D. R., & Bloom, B. S. (2001). *Taxonomy for learning, teaching, and assessing: A revision of Bloom's taxonomy of educational objectives*. Pearson.

Angeli, C., & Valanides, N. (2009). Epistemological and methodological issues for the conceptualization, development, and assessment of ICT-TPCK: Advances in Technological Pedagogical Content Knowledge (TPCK). *Computers & Education, 52*(1), 154–168.

Angu, P. E. (2018). Disrupting western epistemic hegemony in South African universities: Curriculum decolonisation, social justice, and agency in post-apartheid South Africa. *International Journal of Learner Diversity and Identities, 25*(1), 9–22. http://doi.org/10.18848/2327-0128/CGP/v25i01/9-22

Archer, M. (1995). *Realist social theory*. Cambridge University Press.

Archer, M. (2000). *Being human: The problem of agency*. Cambridge University Press.

Arenas, E. (2015). Affordances of learning technologies in higher education multicultural environments. *The Electronic Journal of e-Learning, 13*(4), 217–222. https://academic-publishing.org/index.php/ejel

Bali, M., & Caines, A. (2018). A call for promoting ownership, equity, and agency in faculty development via connected learning. *International Journal of Educational Technology in Higher Education, 15*(1), 46. https://doi.org/10.1186/s41239-018-0128-8

Ball, D. L., Thames, M. H., & Phelps, G. (2008). Content knowledge: What makes it special? *Journal of Teacher Education, 59*(5), 389–407.

Bladergroen, M., Chigona, W., Bytheway, A., Cox, S., Dumas, C., & Van Zyl, I. (2012). Educator discourses on ICT in education: A critical analysis. *International Journal of Education and Development using ICT, 8*(2), 107–119. https://www.learntechlib.org/p/188046/

Bovill, C., Cook-Sather, A., Felten, P., Millard, L., & Moore-Cherry, N. (2016). Addressing potential challenges in co-creating learning and teaching: Overcoming resistance, navigating institutional norms and ensuring inclusivity in student-staff partnerships. *Higher Education, 71*(2), 195–208.

Bradshaw, A. C. (2017). Critical pedagogy and educational technology. In A. D. Benson, R. Joseph, & J. L. Moore (Eds.), *Culture, learning and technology: Research and practice* (pp. 8–27). Routledge.

Brodie, K., & Sanni, R. (2014). "We won't know it since we don't teach it": Interactions between teachers' knowledge and practice. *African Journal of Research in Mathematics, Science and Technology Education, 18*(2), 188–197.

Brown, J. S., Collins, A., & Duguid, P. (1989). Situated cognition and the culture of learning. *Educational Researcher, 18*(1), 32–41.

Brown, R., & Renshaw, P. (2006). Positioning students and actors and authors, a chronotropic analysis of collaborative learning activities. *Mind, Culture and Activity, 13*(3), 247–259.

Buckley, A. (2014). How radical is student engagement? (And what is it for?). *Student Engagement and Experience Journal, 3*(2). https://doi.org/10.7190/seej.v3i2.95

Cook-Sather, A., Bovill, C., & Felten, P. (2014). *Engaging students as partners in learning and teaching: A guide for faculty.* Jossey Bass.

Darder, A. (2017). *Reinventing Paulo Freire.* Routledge. https://doi.org/10.4324/9781315560779

Daszko, M., & Steinberg, S. (2005). Survival is optional: Only leaders with new knowledge can lead the transformation. *Transformation, 408*, 247–7757. http://cflcs.com/docs/Survival%20is%20Optional_Daszko_Sheinberg.pdf

Department of Education. (2014). *Policy for the provision of distance education in South African universities in the context of an integrated post-school system.* South Africa.

Dunne, E. (2016). Design thinking: A framework for student engagement? A personal view. *Journal of Educational Innovation, Partnership and Change, 2*(1), 1–8.

Education, S. A. D. of B. (2011). *Integrated strategic planning framework for teacher education and development in South Africa, 2011–2025: Technical report.* Department of Basic Education.

Feinstein, N. W., Jacobi, P. R., & Lotz-Sisitka, H. (2013). When does a nation-level analysis make sense? ESD and educational governance in Brazil, South Africa, and the USA. *Environmental Education Research, 19*(2), 218–230. https://doi.org/10.1080/13504622.2013.767321

Fenstermacher, G. D. (1994). Chapter 1: The knower and the known: The nature of knowledge in research on teaching. *Review of Research in Education, 20*(1), 3–56.

Fernandez, C. (2014). Knowledge base for teaching and Pedagogical Content Knowledge (PCK): Some useful models and implications for teachers' training. *Problems of Education in the 21st Century, 60*, 79.

Gast, I., Schildkamp, K., & van der Veen, J. T. (2017). Team-based professional development interventions in higher education: A systematic review. *Review of Educational Research, 87*(4), 736–767.

hooks, b. (1994). *Teaching to transgress: Education as the practice of freedom.* Routledge.

Iipinge, S. M. (2013). Challenges of large class teaching at the university: Implications for continuous staff development activities. *The Nambia CPD Journal for Educators, 1*(3). (Published online February 2018) http://journals.unam.edu.na/index.php/NCPDJE/article/view/1263

Kiviniemi M. (2014). Effects of a blended learning approach on student outcomes in a graduate-level public health course. *BMC Medical Education, 14*(47), 1–7.

Knight, J. (2014). *Higher education and diplomacy.* Canadian Bureau for International Education (CBIE).

Koehler, M. J., Mishra, P., Kereluik, K., Shin, T. S., & Graham, C. R. (2014). The technological pedagogical content knowledge framework. In J. M. Spector (Ed.), *Handbook of research on educational communications and technology* (pp. 101–111). Springer.

Maringe, F. (2017). Creating opportunities for a socially just pedagogy: The imperatives of transformation in post-colonial HE spaces. In R. Osman & D. Hornsby (Eds.), *Transforming teaching and learning in higher education* (pp. 59–78). Springer.

Martens, S. E., Meeuwissen, S. N. E., Dolmans, D., Bovill, C., & Könings, K. D. (2019). Student participation in the design of learning and teaching: Disentangling the terminology and approaches. *Medical Teacher, 41*(10), 1203–1205.

Marwala, T. (2015). *Causality, correlation and artificial intelligence for rational decision making.* World Scientific.

Mercer-Mapstone, L., Dvorakova, S. L., Matthews, K. E., Abbot, S., Cheng, B., Felten, P., Knorr, C., Marquis, E., Shammas, R., & Swaim, K. (2017). A systematic literature review of students as partners in higher education. *International Journal for Students as Partners, 1*(1), 1–23. Retrieved January 21, 2002, from https://www.researchgate.Higher Educationnet/publication/316764140_A_Systematic_Literature_Review_of_Students_as_Partners_in_Higher_Education

Mishra, P., & Koehler, M. J. (2006). Technological pedagogical content knowledge: A framework for teacher knowledge. *Teachers College Record, 108*(6), 1017–1054.

Mosweunyane, D. (2013). The African educational evolution: From traditional training to formal education. *Higher Education Studies, 3*(4), 50–59. doi:10.5539/hes.v3n4p50

Ndille, R. N. (2018). *Educational transformation in post-independence Africa: A historical assessment of the Africanization project.* https://www.preprints.org/manuscript/201808.0062/v1

Nel, L., & Wilkinson, A. (2007, June 13–16). *Blended learning, collaboration and cultural diversity: South African perspectives.* Paper presented at the Annual Conference of the European Distance and E-Learning Network Secretariat (EDEN 2007).

Patel, F., & Lynch, H. (2013). Globalisation as an alternative to internationalization in higher education: Embedding positive global learning perspectives. *International Journal of Teaching and Learning in Higher Education, 25*(2), 223–230.

Porter, W., Graham, C., Spring, K., & Welch, K. (2014). Blended learning in higher education: Institutional adoption and implementation. *Computers and Education, 75*(3), 185–195.

Prensky, M. (2009). H. sapiens digital: From digital immigrants and digital natives to digital wisdom. *Journal of Online Education, 5*(3), 1–9.

Scheepers, D. (2015). Professional development for teaching with technology. In W. R. Kilfoil (Eds.), *Moving beyond the hype: A contextualised view of learning with technology in higher education* (pp. 50–52). Universities South Africa.

Selwyn, N. (2011). *Education and technology: Key issues and debates.* Continuum International Publishing Group.

Shulman, L. S. (1987a). Knowledge and teaching: Foundations of the new reform. *Harvard Educational Review, 57*(1), 1–22.

Tierney, W. G., & Lanford, M. (2018). Institutional culture in higher education. In J. C. Shin & P. N. Teixeira (Eds.), *Encyclopedia of international higher education systems and institutions.* Springer. doi:10.1007/978-94-017-9553-1_544-1

Union, A. (2015). *Agenda 2063: The Africa we want, popular version.* Addis Ababa.

Verloop, N., Van Driel, J., & Meijer, P. (2001). Teacher knowledge and the knowledge base of teaching. *International Journal of Educational Research, 35*, 441–461.

Webbstock, D. (2016). *Overview in South African higher education reviewed: Two decades of democracy.* Council on Higher Education.

Xu, D., & Jaggars, S. (2013). The impact of online learning on students' course outcomes: Evidence from a large community and technical college system. *Economics of Education Review, 37*, 46–57.

Yamagata-Lynch, L. C. (2014). Understanding and examining design activities with cultural historical activity theory. In B. Hokanson & A. Gibbons (Eds.), *Design in educational technology: Design thinking, design process, and the design studio* (pp. 89–106). Springer.

Yuen, A. H., & Ma, W. W. (2008). Exploring teacher acceptance of e-learning technology. *Asia-Pacific Journal of Teacher Education, 36*(3), 229–243.

PART 2

The Use of ICT to Empower Students in Different Areas

∵

CHAPTER 9

The Role Played by ICT in Mathematics and Science Teaching and Learning Mediation

Mapula Gertrude Ngoepe

Abstract

This chapter examines the role played by Information communication technology (ICT) in mathematics and science teaching and learning mediation towards empowering students. The chapter is anchored to three main aims: (1) to show that effective ICT integration into mathematics and science teaching and learning can be enhanced by identifying and lowering of barriers to teaching and learning in the 21st century, (2) to argue for the importance of integrating ICT into instruction in order to promote inclusiveness and equality for students experiencing barriers to learning, including learners with disabilities, and (3) to offer a resource for educators on integrating ICT in teaching mathematics and science with an aim of maximizing access and student participation. It is recommended that more mediation initiatives and innovation are required to work towards effective and inclusive ICT integration into mathematics and science teaching and learning. Some recommendations on how to do this are provided.

Keywords

barriers to teaching and learning – empowerment of students – inclusiveness – ICT integration – learners with disability – Mathematics and Science teachers – teaching and learning mediation

1   Introduction

The present chapter considers the role played by ICT in mathematics and science teaching and learning mediation. ICT is used to refer to such new media technologies as the computers, software, networks, satellite links, and related systems that allow people to access, analyse, create, exchange, and use data, information, and knowledge in ways that were almost unimaginable. Teachers and university lecturers, including those in ODeL spaces, are expected to

© KONINKLIJKE BRILL NV, LEIDEN, 2021 | DOI: 10.1163/9789004447226_010

enable citizens, workers, and communities to acquire practical ICT and critical thinking skills. Consequently, educators must be knowledgeable and competent in ICT so that they are able to integrate it into mathematics and science teaching and learning. ICT integration should also consider the barriers to teaching and learning in view of the needs of students with disabilities. In this way, teachers will be better prepared to provide their mathematics and science students with technology-supported learning opportunities which can also impact inclusion (United Nations Educational, 2011). Innovative teaching is necessary for all teachers to meet the educational needs of new generations. Zhu et al. (2013) found that teachers' technological competency is positively related to their innovative teaching performance. Thus, teachers have to be proficient in using ICT in their classrooms in order to mediate the teaching and learning process of mathematics and science. It is important to understand how ICT is used in educational contexts, what educational goals it caters to, and what role it plays in the success of learning and teaching processes, specifically as they related to mathematics and science.

This chapter has adopted constructivism as its framework because it promotes active learning through knowledge construction (Gagné, Briggs, & Wager, 1992). Consequently, Woolfolk (1993) appropriately stated that, "The key idea is that students actively construct their knowledge: the mind of the student mediates input from the outside world to determine what the student will learn. Learning is active mental work, not passive reception of teaching" (p. 485). By adopting constructivism, the practical approach to teaching and learning mathematics and science in view of ICT would be applicable.

To explore this issue, a secondary data analysis was conducted of a wide range of texts, including: book chapters, journal articles, dissertations or theses, periodicals and government records. Data was also collected from previous research that explored themes such as: the importance of technology in instruction; the digital tools and their application and selection for teaching; the strategies of integrating ICT tools in teaching and learning; professional development and training opportunities for ICT integration; the role of pedagogical content knowledge (PCK) as the specific strategy and application that teachers' use to deliver content to students; and the infusion of technology in the Technological Pedagogical Content knowledge (TPACK) framework (see Shulman, 1986; Mishra & Koehler, 2006).

2 Background

Bingimlas (2009) acknowledges that ICT is an important tool for learning mathematics and science in the 21st century. It is believed that rapid global

THE ROLE PLAYED BY ICT IN MATHEMATICS AND SCIENCE TEACHING 163

technological advancement and economic development places a great investment in education (Tedla, 2012, p. 199). Muhammad (2008) explains that, "ICT is the study, design, development, implementation, support or management of computer-based information systems, particularly software applications and computer hardware" (p. 3). Muhammad (2008) further admits that, "ICT deals with the use of electronic devices and software to convert, store, protect process, transmit, and securely retrieve information" (p. 3).

Prior to discussing the role of technology in mathematics and science education, this chapter first foregrounds some important aspects that comprise the milieu underpinning the book. These include, but are not limited to, inclusiveness and equality in teaching and learning ICT, barriers to teaching and learning ICT, challenges for access and participation for people with disabilities, ICT and support mechanisms supporting the empowerment of students.

2.1 Awareness of Inclusiveness and Equality in Teaching and Learning ICT

Any effective effort towards ICT integration in mathematics and science teaching and learning must account for the importance of inclusiveness and equality. In Bergh's (1993) discussion of "multicultural education" (p. 45), reference is made to an education system that stresses inclusiveness and equality in both theory and practice. Integration of ICT in mathematics and science teaching and learning constitutes an educational reform. Socio-cultural factors cannot be neglected if meaningful educational reform is to be implemented (Gretta, 2001). Furthermore, Gretta (2001) reaffirms that, "In multicultural education all learners should enjoy an equal chance to maximise their potential" (p. 66). In numerous places, societies and learning institutions have been accused of exclusivism and/or racial inequality against learners, either as new entrants into the system or those already in the system.

South Africa is a pluralistic society; the country comprises various ethnic groups and multicultural societies. Gretta (2001) states that "in pluralistic and democratic societies, justice, access, quality, equity, equality and respect for other human rights are important elements" (p. 56). That is why the integration of ICT into the education system must be done with an awareness of the way that racial inequality creates impediments to an effective and inclusive teaching and learning environment. For example, during the apartheid era, the education system was extremely exclusive which led Cross (1992) to write that, "The Christian National Education (CNE) glorified traditional Afrikaner values and promoted Afrikaner nationalism, thus developing an extensively 'white-centred' view of the history of education in South Africa" (p. 9). In my view, this exclusiveness as Cross (1992) alluded to, could have led to unequal attainment of both ICT skills and knowledge of mathematics and science between whites and Blacks. In post-apartheid South Africa, questions of racial discrimination and exclusivism on the basis of cultural and/or ethnic belonging are not wholly non-existent, but efforts to eliminate such practices are being appreciated by both white and Black South Africans.

2.2 *ICT Integration and Barriers to Teaching and Learning Mathematics and Science*

A barrier is any constraint or challenge that stands in the way of student learning. Lack of adequate training and knowledge of ICT by the teaching practitioner may be an impediment to the learning process. Conventionally, research has classified all factors impeding teachers' use of ICT either as barriers extrinsic to the teacher; these are often related to the school as an institution and can include such things logistics, lack of time, or appropriate training, the school's ICT policy, etc. On the other hand, intrinsic barriers are those associated with teachers' beliefs, which can include their perspectives about the role of technology, their competence when using ICT, and their capacities with these tools (De Koster, Kuiper, & Volman, 2012). To minimise the intrinsic barriers to the integration of technology it will require an elongated process of targeted professional development. However, implementing the use of some tools as measures to work towards ICT integration will assist in dealing with the aforementioned intrinsic barriers. For example, continuous teacher training, workshops, seminars, conferences, paper presentations, and/or encouraging accessibility of online ICT packages may function as critical and important tools to help eliminate these barriers. Hiring of teaching staff is also another critical component towards minimizing these barriers.

The country's Department of Higher Education must ensure that policies in terms of the hiring of teaching staff are revised, realigned, and reinforced so that prior to engaging an ICT teaching practitioner, ICT training and expertise must be one of the key criteria for both employment and deployment. Poverty in Africa in general, and sub-Saharan Africa in particular, has been cited as one of the outstanding barriers of ICT integration. Hence, Banks and Chikasanda (2015) have alleged that preoccupation with democratisation within sub-Saharan African countries has exacerbated poverty at the expense of ICT integration and socio-economic development. Because of this, intergovernmental organisations such as UNESCO (2011) recommended that, to eradicate poverty, developing countries must see technology not as something external to them. However, South Africa and Botswana have incorporated TE and design as learning areas in their curricula because they have a much larger and better developed capacity for investment in education (Du Toit & Gaotlhobogwe, 2017).

2.3 Challenges to Participation and Access to ICT of People Living with Disabilities

The barriers to teaching and learning with ICT and the inclusion of people with disabilities need not be taken for granted. Muhammad (2008) noted that over 10% of the world's population suffers from a variety of disabilities. An ICT instructor will need to be mindful of the consequences of these barriers on the integration of ICT in mathematics and science teaching and learning. Muhammad (2008) identifies six barriers to teaching and learning which stand in the way of students with disabilities: lack of interest, lack of awareness, difficulty of access, high cost of ICT, lack of training, and lack of on-going support.

It appears some learners with disabilities may not be interested in learning ICT. Some of the reasons for lack of interest are not explicit. However, one could surmise that lack of interest could be attributed to the unavailability of information concerning ICT integration in regards to learners with disabilities in the absence of the participation of individuals facing challenges to accessing education. In my view, any initiative towards ICT integration into mathematics and science teaching and learning must involve the participation of people with different forms of challenges. It was established that lack of awareness also stands as a barrier for learners with disabilities in accessing ICT in mathematics and science teaching and learning. For most learners with disabilities, awareness of the benefits of integrating ICT in mathematics and science teaching and learning is scanty. Lack of this awareness, its difficulty of access, the high cost of ICT, the lack of training as well as lack of on-going support have collectively been cited as causes of lack of appreciation for ICT integration in mathematics and science teaching and learning.

Thus, Sofowora and Adekomi (2012) noted that when clarifying the inseparability of science, mathematics and technology, mathematics and science education are important to the understanding of the processes and meaning of technology and their integration with TE. For example, it is acknowledged that while many developed countries like Japan, China, Russia, and the USA have made remarkable progress in the areas of STEM (science, technology, and mathematics) education, developing nations, especially sub-Saharan African nations, are just beginning to wake up to their responsibility of providing quality STEM education (Sofowora & Adekomi, 2012). The challenges (or barriers) faced by people with disabilities are not only related to exclusivity in terms of entrance into ICT skills learning centres and/or neglect of their physical and special needs by society. The employment market itself cannot be exonerated from the accusation of inequality because it has been established that not many companies are prepared to employ qualified individuals with disabilities. Wood (2000), Murray (2001) and Bracking (2003) describe such practices as "social exclusion".

2.4 *ICT and Support Mechanisms towards Empowerment of Students*

ICT integration should aim at preparing and empowering students in their careers to face the challenges in a real and physical postmodern world. Yearwood, Cox, and Cassidy (2016) posit that empowered students take responsibility for their learning, and leave a course or program feeling confident of their abilities. The mathematics and science educator will need to employ the mechanism of constructivism in order to empower students. The above opinion by Yearwood, Cox, and Cassidy (2016) is suggestive of constructivism (see Fosnot, 1996; Fox, 2001). Fry, Ketteridge, and Marshall (2009) maintained that constructivism tells us that we learn by fitting new understandings and knowledge into, and with, old understanding and knowledge, often extending and supplanting what we once knew.

A constructivist approach stresses the independence of mathematics and science students to be self-actualised. The question of resource allocation is also critical in developing the students to be empowered. Of resource allocation we are referring to the availability and accessibility of gadgets such as, phones, computers, and software. The education system and curricula should be revised and developed taking into consideration the technological advancement in our postmodern life realities. Teacher professional development (TPD) needs to be emphasised in terms of refresher courses, training workshops, and seminars to continue empowering the educator who will subsequently empower students under their instruction.

3 The Role of ICT in Mathematics and Science Education

As a tool for empowering students, researchers have asserted that ICT should be incorporated as an integral resource for deepening learners' understanding. It can enlarge the scope of the content and broaden a range of the problems that students are able to tackle. This next part of the chapter attempts to grapple with aspects developed by Shulman (1986) and Mishra and Koehler (2006), respectively, which I perceive to be supportive of and informative to the present discussion on the role of ICT in mathematics and science education. By borrowing and incorporating Shulman's (1986) and Mishra and Koehler's (2006) ideas, I am acknowledging several aspects associated with the role of ICT in teaching and learning of mathematics and science which are discussed as strategies for empowering students. Ten aspects are examined (see Shulman, 1986; Mishra & Koehler, 2006). Discussions of the ten aspects by Shulman

(1986) and Mishra and Koehler (2006), have been chosen because they inform in detail the present chapter and the theme of the book.

3.1 The Importance of ICT in Instruction

ICT has gained increased importance in globally because it can be used to potentially make teaching and learning more efficient, more engaging, more personalised, more adaptive, and more widespread. Reviews of computer assisted systems (CAS) in the literature show that CAS enable:

- Students to learn mathematics better and with deeper comprehension.
- An increase in students' motivation and makes them deal with the harder and realistic mathematical structures earlier by making them easier.

Many countries have reformed their school curricula to establish technology as a key learning area for reasons that include the technological nature of society; technology being a driver of the global economy; technology enhancing the opportunities of the disadvantaged; and technology opening possibilities for developing higher cognitive skills, including creative thinking and problem solving (Banks & Chikasanda, 2015). Furthermore, in most developed countries, technology education (TE) is incorporated into the scope of other subjects such as physics, chemistry, biology, home economics, and craft education.

Given the fact that both Botswana and South Africa have the capacity for investment as noted above, it would be appropriate for the DoE of the two respective countries to package their investment in education with ICT. They could respectively do so in two ways: (1) by recruiting and appointing qualified personnel who have the curriculum development expertise as well as ICT training from a recognised institution, and (2) through the exchange and transfer of technology expertise. For example, Jenkins (2001) has revealed that, "Outward investment from South Africa will both increase resources (access to savings and foreign exchange) and provide opportunities for technology transfers and better integration with South Africa's more sophisticated financial markets" (p. 26). South African government efforts include its "... initiatives to build research and development capacity have been the creation of the Department of Arts, Culture, Science and Technology (DACST) and the establishment of a National Plan of Innovation for the country" (Brown, 2003, p. 5). However, such initiatives need to be revisited and practically implemented.

3.2 The Use of Digital Tools in Schools

The digital tools that are in the school environment include, among others, interactive whiteboards (IWBs), laptops, and digital textbooks (DTs). One of the most popular and most widely used dynamic mathematical software packages is GeoGebra, a free and multi-platform software for all levels of education that brings together geometry, algebra, calculus, and statistics in one user-friendly interactive application. The programs Cabri II Plus and Geometer's Sketchpad have been the most widely used programs in Europe and the USA (Dockendorff & Solar, 2018). The use of GeoGebra appears to be fundamental because it both builds on the human sense of perception and action and links this to "making sense" of the symbolic operations.

The focus of the use of technology in schools can be categorised in a variety of ways, including productivity, instruction, and creation (Hughes, 2013). Productivity technology, such as word processors, spreadsheets, presentations, database and graphing tools, typically are void of built-in content and require the teacher or the learner to build or engage with content using these tools. For example, students might analyse class-collected or publicly available weather data in spreadsheets to identify local trends. Instructional software, such as drill and practice, tutorials, simulations, games, problem-solving, and personalised learning, include sequenced curricular content that allows students to practice specific skills. Creation technologies are devices and software that allow students to create multi-modal representations such as digital art and images, video, audio, and websites often leading to book making, digital storytelling, and/or digital publishing with frequent use of web 2.0 technologies including wikis, blogs, and websites. Web 2.0 technology allows students to share their creations with others and communicate and collaborate with topic experts and peers both within and outside their school to learn deeply about their topic. The opportunities that are available in the class give the students opportunities to do a project which can involve data from weather in newspapers or media that could be displayed to show weekly or monthly trends in their geographical areas.

Research focusing on best practices for the integration of technology in early childhood education (ECE) has shown that the use of ICT can lead to improvements in engagement, motivation, insistence, curiosity, and attention of preschool children in mathematics and science (Schacter & Jo, 2017). Other studies which used tablets with primary school children found that preschool children learn to use the devices quickly, independently, and confidently and explore freely (Schacter & Jo, 2017). Also, tablets have three new features with the ability to make a positive difference in the initial training of technology use, namely that: they are portable and lightweight; they eliminate the need for separate input devices, such as the mouse and keyboard; and they host a series of apps, many of which have a child-friendly intuitive design (Schacter & Jo, 2017). If teachers could tap into this attribute, a good foundation for technology use and integration would be built into the curriculum for pre-school children, and those with barriers to developing their cognitive abilities in maths and science specifically. For in-service teachers, professional development can be designed to meet the needs of teachers, and to address and overcome obstacles that they face when considering technology integration.

3.3   *Studies on the Use of Technology*

Studies examining the use of technology from the students' perspectives tend to reveal the predominant use of technology for productivity, whereas students yearned for more creative uses. Steinberg and McCray's (2012) interviews of middle school students showed that they wanted more teacher modelling of student-centred, active learning with technology. Likewise, yet another study by Zhu (2013) of middle school science classrooms found that students reported using word processing, spreadsheets, presentation tools, and web searches most frequently in class. At the same time, Hughes (2013) found that teachers maintained traditional approaches with lectures and pencil/paper. The trend revealed in the studies of the use of technology in schools shows that whereas the students yearned for student-centred constructivist ICT use, the teachers were more comfortable with teacher-centred approaches.

Other studies of teachers' use of ICT have shown that, even when recognizing some possible benefits of using ICT in their lessons, teachers are unlikely to develop their understanding of how technology can improve the teaching and learning process through professional development platforms (Aflalo, Zana, & Huri, 2018). Instead, the majority of teachers used ICT to design general activities pursuing only motivational and work-enhancing purposes. From the perspective of science education, ICT offers a much wider range of benefits for improving teaching and learning: teachers can easily display abstract scientific ideas through images, graphs, animations, or simulations; represent natural events that occur very fast/slowly or on a very big/small scale; summarise experimental results or ideas to identify patterns or draw conclusions. All these affordances can help students to better express their previous understandings of natural phenomena, to design experiments, establishing connections between scientific concepts, or draw conclusions about certain experimental results, with ICT playing an important role in improving the quality of science education (Simo, Grimalt-Alvaro, & Lagaron, 2018). Thus, considering the gap between the multiple benefits of ICT for science education and its real use in class, it is necessary to understand how teachers' pedagogies can be changed to make the most of these tools and how they can be adapted for students experiencing barriers to learning.

3.4 Integration of ICT in Teaching and Learning

Integration of ICT into education (mathematics and science) plays an important role in facilitating and enhancing student learning. However, Aslan and Zhu (2015) have pointed out that teachers' integration of ICT into their teaching practices is a complex and challenging issue. The research of Inan and Lowther (2010) showed that teachers integrate ICT into teaching and learning at a low level or a basic level. This will weaken the claim that access to technology results in an improvement in the quality of instruction to support student learning. Furthermore, other researchers such as Afshari et al. (2009) suggest that most teachers do not use technology for delivering instruction and they do not integrate it into their curriculum. There are several factors that can account for this. It is acknowledged that many mathematics and science teachers (and their students) predominantly use technology as a simple calculation tool, or for data storage, or for the display of static materials, methods which are unlikely to develop student understanding, stimulate their interests, or increase their proficiency in mathematics or science (Ertmer et al., 2012). Having said that, a good teacher will always have a reason for every activity they do in a classroom. Implementing ICT is no different. Regardless of curriculum, pedagogy, culture, socio-economic status, or any other factors influencing the classroom, ICT should be used as a tool to reach an outcome, "not as a gimmick or to fill quotas" (Ertmer & Ottenbreit-Leftwich, 2013).

3.5 Factors Affecting the Integration of Technologies

There are numerous factors that create a barrier for implementing technology in mathematics and science classrooms. Keong, Horani, and Daniel, (2005) have found that there is no doubt that effective integration of technology in teaching and learning can enhance students' understanding of basic concepts in science and Mathematics. Keong et al. (2005) remarked that when ICT is appropriately integrated in science and mathematics classrooms, it can help improve learning through increased collaboration and a high level of communication and sharing of knowledge among students. Furthermore, teachers can also provide rapid and accurate feedback to students and allow them to focus on strategies and the interpretation of answers rather than spend time on tedious computational calculations. Collis and Moonen (2012) assert that the constructivist learning approach is enhanced when technology is used in teaching.

Several elements that are involved in, or that can hinder the process of, adopting technology in science classes have been identified in the literature. Some of them are obviously related to teachers having to contend with "technical" issues due to missing or inadequately provided equipment, and the lack of time or support available to implement the technology in teachers' environments (Baydas & Goktas, 2016). However, even when teachers are not confronted with technical difficulties, the use of ICT in the classroom does not necessarily lead to a shift in teaching methods (Cook et al., 2013). Research shows that the use of ICT tools in classrooms, particularly for science lessons, are at the service of the teachers' pedagogical purposes. In view of this, teachers need to be actively involved in changing their methodological paradigm to make the most of ICT. This implies that teachers will need to change their pedagogies in favour of active and engaged students activities.

To reduce the effect of, or remove, internal factors (beliefs, attitudes, self-confidence, etc.) standing in the way of ICT adoption requires a more significant, difficult, and longer process compared to dealing with external factors. Research has shown that insufficient levels of support for teachers in terms of information, attitudes, and beliefs about technology negatively affect the process of combining it with learning and teaching (Baki, 2000). The existing beliefs of teachers may be determinants of how they work to integrate technological applications into teaching (Ertmer & Ottenbreit, 2012).

In order for teachers to help prepare students for life in an information society and to create social learning environments with active participation, they need to have effective skills in using different types of technologies (Baydas & Goktas, 2016). However, teachers have not reached sufficient levels in terms of integrating new technologies with teaching in the classroom (Yilmaz, 2013). Also, as Bingimlas (2009) observed, it appears that teachers have not received the necessary professional development to be able to use these tools effectively in teaching. In addition, newly graduated pre-service teachers indicated that they do not have sufficient levels of experience in using computer technologies in mathematics education (Kurz & Middleton, 2006). They furthermore stated that they did not feel ready to use these technologies well in teaching after graduation (Kurz & Middleton, 2006).

One of the main elements necessary for successful technology integration are teachers' intentions and personal beliefs (Ertmer, 2005). Ertmer and Ottenbreit (2012) suggest that it is necessary to prepare teacher development programs to target these beliefs for pre-service teachers to successfully use technologies in their future classrooms. Thus, teachers and pre-service teachers should be aware of the benefits of technological tools, and at the same time believe in them, before applying these teaching technologies in their classrooms (Baki, 2000). The success of technology integration depends, at least in part, on the type of software selected (Bauer, & Kenton, 2005) and the type of tasks implemented (Sherman, Cayton, & Chandler, 2017). Perhaps more important, however, than type of software used, is the role the teacher plays in its implementation. The teacher and the decisions he or she makes when integrating technology is critical to its successful implementation (Ertmer, 2005).

Teachers make decisions about whether to include technology in their instruction based on their comfort or confidence with the tool, their perceptions of whether students would be able to use it, and their confidence in the technology working. Teachers who use technology should also be aware of the different roles it can force them to take one, including: allocator of time, catalyst and facilitator, collaborator, counsellor, evaluator, explainer, manager, planner and conductor, resource, task setter, and technical assistant. It is likely that these roles are influenced by teachers' beliefs and affected teachers' instructional practices.

3.6   *Teacher Beliefs*

Ertmer (2005) reports that "although many teachers are using technology for numerous low-level tasks such as (word processing, Internet research), higher level uses are still very much in the minority" (p. 26). Teacher beliefs are often suggested as a factor in why teachers are not integrating technology; specifically, beliefs about teachers' technological skills (Wachira & Keengwe, 2011), beliefs about the nature of teaching and learning (Becker, 2000), beliefs about the nature of mathematical knowledge (Goos, 2005), beliefs about the role of computers in the classroom and their possible effects on student outcomes (Hall & Hord, 2011), beliefs about the role of the teacher, and beliefs about their students' capabilities (Beyerbach, Walsh, & Vannatta, 2001). Teacher knowledge is another commonly suggested factor: technological knowledge (Koehler & Mishra, 2014), pedagogical knowledge and content knowledge (Mishra, Koehler, & Kereluik, 2009), as well as the intersection of these areas of knowledge (Goos, 2005; Mishra, Koehler, & Henriksen, 2011). Additional factors suggested by other authors included the amount of curricular freedom afforded to the teacher (Becker, 2000), previous teaching experiences with technology, adequate training and preparation of teachers, adequate planning time, preferred style of teaching, lack of appropriate software (Bauer & Kenton, 2005), and time since the adoption of the software (Ertmer, 2005). These various beliefs will affect how teachers integrate technology in the classroom for the mediation of teaching and learning in mathematics and science.

3.7   *Teacher Education and ICT*

It is believed that teacher education plays a critical role in helping prospective mathematics and science teachers develop the knowledge and confidence to teach in general, and to promote appropriate integration of technologies in classrooms. According to Sherman, Cayton, and Chandler (2017), the technological tools that mathematics educators noted as important to for their courses included graphing calculators, dynamic geometry software, spreadsheets, and access to information on the web.

Schwarz (2015) opined that the influence of the predominant teacher education accreditation organisation in the United States of America (USA) and the technology to be present throughout a teacher education program marks a trend in teacher education policies and practices towards programmatic models that prepare teachers to regularly and effectively use technology to support student learning. Nevertheless, comprehensive approaches to technology integration instruction are frequently lacking in teacher preparation programs. New teachers interviewed by Chesley and Jordan (2012) representing 12 different universities reported that instruction on technology integration was "virtually non-existent", explaining that there was also almost no mention of technology standards or digital citizenship in pre-service teacher training.

3.8   *Professional Development for Mathematics and Science Teachers*
Research informs us that there is a relationship between teachers' digital competence and their use of ICT in the classroom. Consequently, it is reasonable to assume that professional development will be an important factor to support maths and science teachers' use of ICT. However, although there is much evidence that maths and science teachers have not been sufficiently trained to make the most of ICT tools for improving science education, there is still little research on how different types of professional development influences subsequent practices with these tools (Guzey & Roehrig, 2009). This is a gap in the literature for future investigation. Such information would be help shape our understanding of the training needs of science teachers with different profiles to enable them to make better use of ICT in their classrooms

Other factors affecting the impact of professional development on teachers' practices have been described as involving the length of the training. In order to appropriately support teachers in their process of technology integration at school, effective teacher professional training should be a long-term and continuous lifelong learning process (Faulder, 2011). Researchers such as Keong et al. (2009), and Mishra, Kohler, and Kereluik (2009) both indicated that it is not learning about how to use technology which improves an understanding of science and mathematics, but the manner in which technology is used to support learning that must be central professional development on the topic. They propose that when teachers decide to use technology, they need to consider the science or mathematics content they will teach with the technology and the pedagogical methods they will employ. Bingimlas (2009) sees the existing failure in science and mathematics teaching as resulting from teachers' poor knowledge of the subject content and instructional strategies and their poor representation of particular science or mathematical topics supported by digital technology to demonstrate and verify, drill, and practice (Mishra, Kohler, & Kereluik, 2009).

According to Niess (2005), access to technology without the necessary knowledge of related science and mathematics curricular materials does not have an impact on students' learning outcomes. As a result, Koehler and Mishra (2014) insist that teachers need to know not only the subject matter they teach or the technology, but also the manner in which the subject matter can be changed by the application of technology in a given pedagogical approach. Teachers, therefore, need to develop knowledge of various technologies in addition to an understanding of how science and mathematics teaching might change as the result of using particular technologies (Mishra, Koehler, & Henriksen, 2011). Studies by Beyerbach, Walsh, and Vannatta (2001) have shown that teachers' beliefs about how to teach science and mathematics are generally aligned with how teachers learned the subjects at the teacher training college. Teachers who learned to solve science and mathematics problems by using graphing calculators, spreadsheets, and some learning software are among the few who can embrace the use of those tools in teaching these subjects.

3.9   *Pre-Service Teachers and Integration of ICT*

In order for ICT to play a role in teaching and learning mediation, training needs to start at the level of teacher preparation. Studies by Aslan and Zhu (2015) and Dockendorff and Solar (2018) revealed that pre-service teachers are still learning about technology, pedagogy, and content as independent subjects, not as integrated knowledge. In this way, teachers have been prepared to teach technology as a discipline rather than use it as a tool to enhance students' learning (Beyerbach, Walsh, & Vannatta, 2001). According to Beyerbach et al. (2001), teachers should not only learn how to teach ICT but also how to apply it in teaching to enhance students' learning, particularly those with barriers to learning. In fact, teachers should be prepared to change their orientation from thinking they would teach technology to thinking they would use technology to support students' learning (Beyerbach et al., 2001). To develop this thinking among teachers, technology integration in teacher education should provide pre-service teachers with hands-on experiences as they explore how to use ICT and its applications in their teaching and learning. Educational courses should, therefore, model technology integration and field experiences in technology-rich classrooms.

Pre-service teachers may not easily realise the potential educational value of technology in education and may be reluctant to incorporate it into their teaching efforts, with research suggesting this is due to their limited teaching

THE ROLE PLAYED BY ICT IN MATHEMATICS AND SCIENCE TEACHING   175

experience and knowledge of both content and pedagogy (Albion, 2008; Hur et al., 2015). Existing research indicates that pre-service teachers' perception of the usefulness of technologies predicts their intention to incorporate them into their future teaching (Hur et al., 2015). This implies that discussions the usefulness of technology need to form part of teacher education curriculum.

3.10   *The Fusion of TPACK Framework into Teacher Education*

Effective teaching with technology requires that teachers understand the content they want to teach, the pedagogy which is concurrent with the content of the subject to be taught, and the technology that can support students' learning in different contexts. According to Mishra, Koehler, and Kereluik (2009), teachers' knowledge of content, pedagogy, and technology forms the heart of good teaching with technology, a process that has come to be known simply as TPACK, standing for Technological Pedagogical Content Knowledge. TPACK has been touted as

> the basis of effective teaching with technology, requiring an understanding of the representation of concepts using technologies; pedagogical techniques that use technologies in constructive ways to teach content; knowledge of what makes concepts difficult or easy to learn and how technology can help redress some of the problems that students face; knowledge of students' prior knowledge and theories of epistemology; and knowledge of how technologies can be used to build on existing knowledge to develop new epistemologies or strengthen old ones. (Mishra et al., 2009, p. 66)

TPACK, which was previously known as TPCK (Koehler & Mishra, 2005), provides the knowledge base needed by teachers to incorporate technology in their teaching (Guzey & Roehrig, 2009). According to Niess (2005), for technology to become an integral component in the teaching and learning process, pre-service teachers must develop an overarching understanding of their subject matter with respect to technology and teaching approaches (TPCK). The interplay between the various components of TPACK—technological knowledge (TK), pedagogical knowledge (PK), content knowledge (CK), technological content knowledge (TCK), technological pedagogical knowledge (TPK), and pedagogical content knowledge (PCK)—is what makes effective teaching with technology possible (Mishra, Koehler, & Kereluik, 2009). Teacher education curriculum should include the infusion of TPACK models in the training of pre-service teachers of mathematics and science to expose them to the integral nature of the components of the model before sending them into the field.

4 Recommendations

The present chapter explored several issues and problems associated with the role of ICT integration in mediating of the teaching and learning of mathematics and science. While acknowledging the complexities and challenges faced in ICT integration and the greater expectation to integrate ICT in classroom practice, recommendations on how the complexities and challenges can be solved are described below:

- *Focus on competency and proficiency.* Teachers are expected to assist citizens, workers, and communities in acquiring ICT skills; however, they must first be competent, proficient, and innovative in their use of ICT to be able to help develop high cognitive, creative thinking, and problem-solving skills in students.
- *Provide for technology resources.* Government departments (DoE & DHET) need to play a major role in the provision of technology resources in schools and in providing professional development for practicing mathematics and science teachers.
- *Budget towards promoting ICT.* Teacher training colleges on their own cannot sustain continuous professional development for teachers, especially with particular attention on ICT. Earlier on in this discussion, I alluded to the need for organizing conferences, training workshops, seminars, and symposiums focusing on ICT in teaching and learning. The invitees and attendees will be the mathematics and science teachers and students from teacher training colleges. Both teachers and student teachers at teacher training colleges should not be expected to fund their ICT training. When the allocation of the resources towards the development of ICT is made by both the DoE and DHET, each of the departments will also have to include a budget for conferences and symposiums as highlighted above. The budget will include costs for transportation, food, stationery, and/or bedding where necessary. Such a programme can be arranged at the district level on a regular basis, for example, during school holidays. Task force teams should be established for both efficiency and accountability so that the resources are not abused by being channeled into undesignated functions and or uses. The task force will report to the premier of the province.
- *Create a cohesive policy framework.* The DHET should develop a policy framework that stipulates that all training colleges should be ICT-oriented and reading materials on ICT, among other study resources, should be made available. The legislation will also make it mandatory that a mathematics and science student teacher will not graduate if a test of knowledge of ICT

THE ROLE PLAYED BY ICT IN MATHEMATICS AND SCIENCE TEACHING   177

is not successfully passed (by over 50%). DHET may also need to recognise a qualification in ICT as among the critical skills.

- *Make ICT use a compulsory requirement.* The DoE must also come up with a policy framework which makes it compulsory for Matric certificate to be incomplete when ICT as a subject is not passed. By so doing it will invigorate an ICT learning culture among mathematics and science learners. Equally important is that the policy will state that those willing to train as mathematics and science teachers will not be allowed to enroll when ICT has not been passed at high school.
- *Provide for continuous professional development.* Professional development in ICT integration should be continuous and lifelong. Mathematics and science teachers will certainly be aware of the critical need to integrate ICT in mathematics and science in teaching and learning. In addition, the TPACK framework needs to be part of the pre-service teacher education.
- *Emphasise the benefits of ICT.* Research has shown that most teachers do not use or integrate ICT in the curriculum. Teachers need to be aware of the benefits and role of ICT in teaching and learning mathematics and science.
- *Contextualise ICT.* One of the ways of sensitizing mathematics and science teachers to the benefits of ICT is through encouraging a contextually-brewed culture of writing about ICT. Certainly, one can appreciate the efforts foregrounded by western and European researchers who write on ICT. However, local resources are contextual and relevant, as much as they are anticipated to be cost-effective, cheaper, and accessible. Hence, Nakata et al. (2012) were already aware of such an initiative, proposing that, "... the development of learning dispositions in students that encourage openness to further inquiry and productive ways of thinking in and through complex and contested knowledge terrains" (p. 1).
- *Adopt of constructivism as an approach.* Teachers need to change their methodological paradigm to make it more student-centred. In the earlier conversation in this chapter, a constructivist method of teaching was recommended. Constructivism is more practical and encourages learners to engage and participate on matters related to mathematics and science.
- *Work to remove barriers to learning.* Teacher training colleges should not lose sight of the fact that a wrong approach in teaching and learning can be a barrier to the intended goal of learners achieving necessary skills. A call for the inclusion of the constructivism school of thought in the teacher training curriculum may need to get louder. It cannot be understated that the experiences of the underprivileged, persons with disabilities, excluded and marginalised persons, and orphans, among others can serve as barriers to

learning. This is also true of learning with ICT, though those same technologies can also help break barriers down.

With reference to professional development of both practicing and pre-service teachers, a special focus should be placed on:
– The various technologies, benefits of the suitability of the selected software, and knowledge about the availability of the technologies.
– How to select digital technologies for classroom practice.
– How to integrate the various technologies at different levels.
– Eliciting the teachers' classroom practice needs.
– Integration of technology needs to start at teacher training.
– Assessing the level of readiness to integrate technology.
– Preparing teacher development programs to target beliefs for pre-service teachers to successfully use technologies in their future classrooms.
– Creating a technology policy that makes it compulsory for any training college to only graduate students who pass some sort of ICT assessment. Such an approach prepares teachers who will regularly and effectively use technology to support student learning in a classroom.
– Emphasising learning ICT towards ODeL. ODeL is a system adopted by distance learning institutions all over the world. The University of South Africa (UNISA) is one of them. Integrating ICT in mathematics and science learning through ODeL is a grand opportunity for every learner. When an educator or a learner would like to familiarise themselves with online learning (ODeL), learning ICT becomes mandatory. Most learners who have managed to obtain their qualifications through ODeL would have learned ICT.

This chapter is informed by Resta's (2002) previous contribution on the findings of UNESCO. According to Resta (2002, cited in Rani & Kant, 2016), the UNESCO Planning Guide for ICT in teacher education mentions three key principles for effective ICT development in teacher education that were put forward by the Society for Information Technology and Teacher Education (SITE) as follows:
– Technology should be infused into the entire teacher education programme. This principle means that ICT should not be restricted to a single course but needs to permeate all courses in the programme.
– Technology should be introduced in context. According to this principle, particular ICT applications like word processing, databases, spreadsheets, and telecommunications should not be taught as separate topics but rather encountered as the need arises in all courses of the teacher education programme.

– Students should experience innovative technology-supported learning environments in their teacher education programme. This last principle requires that students should see their lecturers engaging in technology to present their subjects, for example, utilizing PowerPoint or simulations in lectures and demonstrations. Students should also have the opportunity to use such applications in practical classes, seminars and assignments. The application of these three principles will go a long way towards effectively integrating ICT in teacher education.

5 Conclusion

The main focus of this chapter was the role played by ICT in mathematics and science teaching and learning mediation. Of importance was the integration of ICT in instruction, the digital tools used in schools, and studies that have investigated the integration of technology in the classroom. Factors affecting the integration of technologies, teacher beliefs, integration of technology in teacher education and primary school, and the infusion of the concept of TPACK framework in teacher education were explored. Barriers to integrating ICT in mathematics and science teaching and learning were discussed. This chapter also examined the possibility of using ICTs to promote inclusiveness and equality as well as empower students, including learners with disabilities. However, further empirical research needs to be conducted involving practicing teachers at all levels: primary school, secondary/high school, and teacher education colleges. This chapter also noted that, although the integration of technologies needs to be accelerated at teacher training colleges, beginning with learners at both primary and secondary schools would be ideal. The supply of relevant technological resources in schools and teacher training colleges by both the DoE and DHET was highlighted. The final point of this chapter is that for students to benefit from hands-on experiences with ICT, teachers need to fully explore the use of ICT and its applications in teaching and learning.

References

ADB. (2009). *Good practice in information and communication technology for education*. ADB.

Aflalo, E., Zana, L., & Huri, T. (2018). The interactive whiteboard in primary school science and interaction. *Interactive Learning Environments, 26*(4), 525–538.

Albion, P. R. (2008). Web 2.0 in teacher education: Two imperatives for action. *Computers in the Schools, 25*(3–4), 181–198.

Aslan, A., & Zhu, C. (2015). Pre-service teachers perceptions of ICT integration in teacher education in Turkey. *Turkish Online Journal of Educational Technology, 14*(3), 97–110.

Baki, A. (2000). Preparing student teachers to use computers in mathematics classrooms through a long-term pre-service course in Turkey. *Journal of Information Technology for Teacher Education, 9*, 343–362.

Banks, F., & Chikasanda, V. K. M. (2015). Technology education and developing countries. In J. P. Williams, J. Alister, & C. Buntting (Eds.), *The future of technology education* (pp. 217–238). Springer.

Bauer, J., & Kenton, J. (2005). Toward technology integration in the schools: Why it isn't happening. *Journal of Technology and Teacher Education, 13*(4), 519–546.

Baydas, O., & Goktas, Y. (2016). Influential factors on pre-service teachers' intentions to use ICT in future lessons. *Computers in Human Behavior, 56*, 170–178.

Becker, H. J. (2000). Findings from the teaching, learning, and computing survey. *Education Policy Analysis Archives, 8*(51), 1–31.

Bergh, A. M. (1993). Curriculum reform and reconstruction in Africa and Latin America. In E. L. Bekker & E. M. Lemmer (Eds.), *Critical issues in modem education*. Butterworths.

Beyerbach, B. A., Walsh, C., & Vannatta, R. A. (2001). From teaching technology to using technology to enhance student learning: Pre-service teachers' changing perceptions of technology infusion. *Journal of Technology and Teacher Education, 9*(1), n.p.

Bingimlas, K. A. (2009). Barriers to the successful integration of ICT in Ttaching and learning environments: A teview of the Llterature. *Eurasia Journal of Mathematics, Science and Technology Education, 5*, 235–245.

Bracking, S. (2003). *The political economy of chronic poverty* (Chronic poverty research centre working paper 23). Institute for Development Policy and Management, University of Manchester. http://ssrn.com/abstract=1754446

Brown, M. (2003). The South African Network of Skills Abroad (SANSA): The South African experience of scientific diaspora networks. In R. Barré, V. Hernández, J.-B. Meyer, & D. Vink (Eds.), *Scientific diasporas* (pp. 1–22). IRD Editions Collection.

Chesley, G. M., & Jordan, J. (2012). What's missing from teacher prep. *Educational Leadership, 69*(8), 41–45.

Collis, B. (2012). *Flexible learning in a digital world: Experiences and expectations*. http://www.myilibrary.com?id=402385

Cross, M. (1992). *Resistance and transformation. Education, culture and reconstruction in South Africa*. Skotaville Publishers.

De Koster, S., Kuiper, E., & Volman, M. (2012). Concept-guided development of ICT use in 'traditional' and 'innovative' primary schools: What types of ICT use do schools develop? *Journal of Computer Assisted Learning, 28*(5), 454–464.

Dockendorff, M., & Solar, H. (2018). ICT ntegration in mathematics initial teacher training and its impact on visualization: The case of GeoGebra. *International Journal of Mathematical Education in Science and Technology, 49*(1), 66–84.

Du Toit, A., & Gaotlhobogwe, M. (2017). Benchmarking the intended technology curricula of Botswana and South Africa: What can we learn? *African Journal of Research in Mathematics, Science and Technology Education, 21*(2), 148–158.

Ertmer, P. A. (2005). Teacher pedagogical beliefs: The final frontier in our quest for technology integration? *Educational Technology Research and Development, 53*(4), 25–39.

Ertmer, P. A., & Ottenbreit, A. (2012). Teacher beliefs and technology integration practices: A critical relationship. *Computers & Education, 59*(2), 423–435.

Ertmer, P. A., & Ottenbreit-Leftwich, A. (2013). Removing obstacles to the pedagogical changes required by Jonassen's vision of authentic technology-enabled learning. *Computers & Education, 64*(1), 175–182.

Faulder, T. R. (2011). *Technology integration: A research-based professional development program* (MEd dissertation). Cedarville University.

Fosnot, C. T. (Ed.). (1996). *Constructivism: Theory, perspectives and practice*. Teachers College Press.

Fox, R. (2001). Constructivism examined. *Oxford Review of Education, 27*(1), 23–35.

Fry, H., Kitteridge, S., & Marshall, S. (2009). *A handbook for teaching and learning in higher education enhancing academic practice* (3rd ed.). Routledge.

Gagné, R., Briggs, L., & Wager, W. (1992). *Principles of instructional design* (4th ed.). Jovanovich College Publishers.

Goos, M. (2005). A sociocultural analysis of the development of pre-service and beginning teachers' pedagogical identities as users of technology. *Journal of Mathematics Teacher Education, 8*(1), 35–59.

Gretta, K. N. (2001). *A critical analysis of multicultural education with special reference to values issue in the South African context* (MPhil. Ed. dissertation). University of South Africa.

Guzey, S. S., & Roehrig, G. H. (2009). Teaching science with technology: Case studies of science teachers' development of Technological Pedagogical Content Knowledge (TPCK). *Contemporary Issues in Technology and Teacher Education, 9*(1), 25–45.

Hall, G. E., & Hord, S. M. (2011). Implementation: Learning builds the bridge between research and practice. *Journal of Staff Development, 32*(4), 52–57.

Hughes, J. E. (2013). Descriptive indicators of future teachers' technology integration in the PK-12 classroom: Trends from a laptop-infused teacher education program. *Journal of Educational Computing Research, 48*(4), 491–516.

Hur, J. W., Ying, W. S., Ugur, K., & Cullen, T. A. (2015). An exploration of pre-service teachers' intention to use mobile devices for teaching. *International Journal of Mobile and Blended Learning (IJMBL), 7*(3), 1–17.

Inan, F. A., & Deborah, L. L. (2010). Factors affecting technology integration in K-12 classrooms: A path model. *Educational Technology Research and Development, 58*(2), 137–154.

Jenkins, C. (2001). *Integration and co-operation in Southern Africa* (Working paper No. 172). OECD Development Centre.

Johnston, M. P. (2014). Secondary data analysis: A method of which the time has come. *Qualitative and Quantitative Methods in Libraries, 3,* 619–626.

Keong, C. C., Sharaf, H., & Daniel, J. (2005). A study of the use of ICT in mathematics teaching. *Malaysian Online Journal of Instructional Technology, 2*(3), 43–51.

Koehler, M. J., & Mishra, P. (2014). The technological pedagogical content knowledge framework. In M. J. Koehler, P. Mishra, K. Kereluik, & T. S. Seob (Eds.), *Handbook of research on educational communications and technology* (pp. 101–111). Springer.

Kurz, T. L., & Middleton, J. A. (2006). Using a functional approach to change pre-service teachers' understanding of mathematics software. *Journal of Research on Technology in Education, 39*(1), 45–65.

Mishra, P., Koehler, M. J., & Henriksen, D. (2011). The seven trans-disciplinary habits of mind: Extending the TPACK framework towards 21st century learning. *Educational Technology, 51*(2), 22–28.

Mishra, P., Matthew, J. K., & Kereluik, K. (2009). Looking back to the future of educational technology. *TechTrends, 53*(5), 48–53.

Muhammad, A. (2008). *Connecting people with disabilities: ICT opportunities for all* (MPRA paper No. 17204). https://mpra.ub.uni-muenchen.de/17204/

Murray, C. (2001). *Livelihoods research: Some conceptual and methodological issues* (CPRC working paper No. 5). http://ssrn.com/abstract=1754541

Nakata, N. M., Nakata, V., Keech, S., & Bolt, R. (2012). Decolonial goals and pedagogies for Indigenous studies. Decolonization: Indigeneity. *Education & Society, 1*(1), 120–140.

Niess, M. L. (2005). Preparing teachers to teach science and mathematics with technology: Developing a technology pedagogical content knowledge. *Teaching and Teacher Education, 21*(5), 509–523.

Rani, A., & Kant, K. (2016). Integrating ICT in teacher education: A step towards quality education. *Scholarly Research Journal for Humanity Science and English Language, 3*(14), 3328–3335.

Resta, P. (2002). *Information and communication technologies in teacher education.* UNESCO.

Schacter, J., & Jo, B. (2017). Improving pre-schoolers' mathematics achievement with tablets: A randomized controlled trial. *Mathematics Education Research Journal, 29*(3), 313–327.

Schwarz, G. E. (2015). CAEP advanced standards and the future of graduate programs: The false sense of "techne". *Teacher Education Quarterly, 42*(2), 105–117.

Sherman, M. F., Cayton, C., & Chandler, K. (2017). Supporting PSTs in using appropriate tools strategically: A learning sequence for developing technology tasks that support students' mathematical thinking. *Mathematics Teacher Educator, 5*(2), 122–157.

Sofowora, O. A., & Adekomi, B. (2012). Improving science, technology and mathematics education in Nigeria: A case study of Obafemi Awolowo University, Ile-Ife. *African Journal of Educational Studies in Mathematics and Sciences, 10*(1), 1–8.

Steinberg, M. A., & McCray, E. D. (2012). Listening to their voices: Middle schoolers' perspectives of life in middle school. *The Qualitative Report, 17*(34), 1–14.

Tedla, B. A. (2012). Understanding the importance, impacts and barriers of ICT on teaching and learning in East African countries. *International Journal for e-Learning Security (IJeLS), 2*(2), 199–207.

UNESCO. (2011). *UNESCO ICT competency framework for teachers*. UNESCO.

Wachira, P., & Jared, K. (2011). Technology integration barriers: Urban school mathematics teachers perspectives. *Journal of Science Education and Technology, 20*(1), 17–25.

Wood, G. (2000). *Concepts and themes: Landscaping social development* (Social development SCOPE paper 9). Department for International Development.

Woolfolk, A. E. (1993). *Educational psychology*. Allyn and Bacon.

Yearwood, D., Cox, R., & Cassidy, A. (2016). Connection-engagement-empowerment: A course design model. *Transformative Dialogues: Teaching & Learning Journal, 8*(3), 1–15.

Yilmaz, I. (2013). Pre-service physical education teachers preference for class management profiles and teachers self-efficacy beliefs. *Educational Research and Reviews, 8*(9), 539–545.

Zhu, C., Di, W., Yonghong, C., & Nadine, E. (2013). What core competencies are related to teachers' innovative teaching? *Asia-Pacific Journal of Teacher Education, 41*(1), 9–27.

CHAPTER 10

Conceptualising the Use of ICTs in ODL through Mathematical Participation Model for Community of Practice to Overcome Students' Barriers to Learning

Moshe Moses Phoshoko

Abstract

Community of practice (CoP) is one of the most cited social theories used to investigate a variety of topics, including those in the teaching and learning of mathematics. Noting that at the core of teaching is the facilitation of learning, it can be presumed that effective learning is informed by sound theories on learning. The theory of CoP situates the teaching and learning of mathematics in a participation framework where factors such as contexts and models such as information and communication technologies (ICTs) play a role. The current study presents the case of how e-tutors employed at one of the open and distance learning (ODL) institutions in the Southern African Development Community (SADC) region, are promoting the use of ICTs to enhance the teaching and learning of mathematics. Whereas the potential for the utilisation of ICTs in well-designed mathematics curricula has been explored, its successful usage was not reflected in the current study. The study suggests the need for learning approaches that are informed by the MP-model for full participation, aiming for inclusive education that promotes mathematical proficiency.

Keywords

communities of practice – content knowledge – mathematical proficiency – mathematics participation model – mathematics – teaching & learning – technological pedagogical & content knowledge

© KONINKLIJKE BRILL NV, LEIDEN, 2021 | DOI: 10.1163/9789004447226_011

1 Introduction

The digitisation of the STEM (science, technology, engineering and mathematics) subjects as envisioned by the plan to place South Africa (SA) in the position to respond to demands of 4IR (BusinessTech, 2018) is still be realised for the majority of education sectors in the country, most especially in institutions offering initial teacher education. According to Allen (2019) a developing country such as SA is lagging in terms of ICT infrastructure support and ICT resources, making it difficult for the county to face its challenges in terms of actualizing the envisioned plan. Mendoza and Mendoza (2018) consider information and communication technologies (ICTs) excellent didactic resources that may be applied in different subject areas and at different educational levels, making the most of the possibilities that they offer for student learning. Arguing that the introduction of ICTs in mathematics activities promotes the flexibility of students' thinking, the authors add that ICTs allow a wider deployment of students' cognitive resources for processing for meaningful learning.

The inevitable transformative demands of educational institutions with regards to the procurement of ICT resources for access, their management, and their governance is a something that may no longer be delayed. Concomitant to having to adjust to innovations brought about by the use of ICTs, SA is faced with mathematics education challenges in that it has been flagged for poor performance of learners in the subject when compared with other countries. In studies such as Trends in International Mathematics and Science Study (TIMSS, 2015) (Mullis, Martin, Foy, & Hooper, 2016) and Southern and Eastern Africa Consortium for Monitoring Educational Quality study (SACMEQ IV) (Department of Basic Education, 2017), SA mathematics learners were ranked amongst the lowest in terms of performance.

When faced with these kinds of challenges the implementation of ICT initiatives in higher education institutions tasked with the initial training of mathematics teachers is certainly not unproblematic. Hence, the current study pursued the following research question: To what extent does an ODL institution use ICTs to empower students in mathematical proficiency? Drawing on the mathematical participation model that is undergirded by the theory of communities of practice, the study focuses on the conduct of an ODL institution in terms of how it empowers its students by facilitating the teaching and learning of mathematics using ICTs in order to overcome barriers of learning in the subject.

2 Reflections on Open Distance and e-Learning

Reflecting on open and distance learning (ODL) in Africa, Oladejo, Abiodun, and Gesinde (2014) state that ODL has become a policy option for most African states because it has a very crucial role to play in the advancement of African development through the promotion of, participation in, and access to higher education. At a time when demand far exceeds resources and opportunities available in the conventional educational system are scarce, ODL seems to fit the bill to alleviate the crisis. Makoe (2018) notes that with institutions of higher learning in Africa having to reach large numbers of students who are in dire need of higher education qualifications, the method of delivering educational content within the confines of the classroom is no longer adequate. African countries are thus looking to the educational possibilities offered by ODL and ICTs as a way of expanding and improving education systems. In sub-Saharan Africa (SSA), ODL has been used primarily to widen access to basic education and to improve quality in the conventional school system through in-service training of teachers (Moore & Kearsley, 2005).

Jung and Latchem (2012) argue that as the demand for various levels and forms of education grow rapidly, ODL holds immense potential of meeting Africa's educational needs. Like many African higher education institutions, the University of Tshwane ya Mamelodi (UTYM) has deployed ODL to address to the growing need for higher education in South Africa and beyond. The cost-effective and efficient means by which ODL offers increased access to education to institutions such as UTYM has made it accessible to a diverse range of students, including those with learning barriers. UTYM thus enables more Africans in the SADC region to improve their qualifications without the high costs of building facilities and students leaving their communities, jobs, or other commitments (Jung & Latchem, 2012). However, the implementation of ODL policies and practices, influenced by inadequate ICT infrastructure (Masenya & Ngulube, 2019) as well as a shortage of qualified staff (Jung & Latchem, 2012; du Preez, 2018), is still a work in progress. The conceptualisation of a model that informs these policies in terms how ICTs may be used to enhance the teaching and learning of mathematics by drawing from theories of learning such as mathematical proficiency therefore becomes critical. Muyinda, Mayende, Maiga, and Oyo (2019) argued that an ICT-driven pedagogy in ODL has the potential to transform higher education in a way that ICTs have transformed other sectors. Highlighting the fourth sustainable development goal (SDG) alluding to use of ICTs, Muyinda et al. (2019) indicate that ICTs ensure inclusive and equitable quality education through promoting lifelong learning opportunities for all.

The Commonwealth of Learning (2003) denotes the importance of ODL as, (a) the mode with which physical distance may be overcome; (b) a tool for solving time or scheduling problems; (c) a way of expanding the limited number of places available at tertiary institutions; (d) the means of accommodating low or dispersed enrolments that are spread across vast geographic regions; (e) a resource that can make the best use of the limited number of teachers available at the institutions; and (f) a facility that makes it possible to deal with cultural, religious, and political differences and considerations. The preceding descriptions point to factors that are amenable to overcoming barriers to learning. Whilst Arnaiz Sánchez, de Haro-Rodríguez and Maldonado Martínez (2019) identify barriers to learning and participation as occurring at different levels such as the attitudinal, the organisational and the contextual, Dabaj (2011) in Aljaraideh and Al Bataineh (2019) categorised them mainly into two; (1) unhidden barriers, such as lack of expertise with technology, cost of communication and website access and (2) hidden barriers that include resistance to new technology, fear of technology, and rigid belief in traditional education. This chapter explores the extent to which UTYM as an ODL institution overcomes such barriers to students learning mathematics.

With UTYM enjoying its advantages as an ODL institution, it was positioned to help empower students who perform poorly in the subject of mathematics through the utilisation of ICTs. More importantly, the institution was positioned to include those who, through discriminatory systems of inequality such as apartheid, were deliberately kept from accessing quality education, such as was the case in South Africa (Boddy-Evans, 2020) and in a subject that was singled out for non-access to the marginalised majority in the country (Phoshoko, 2015).

The university under investigation offers mathematics education to students enrolled for the programme of initial teacher education. Considering the challenges that students are prepared for in the programme, namely to teach mathematics to learners, the expectation of addressing the latter's poor performance as reported in studies such as TIMSS (Mullis, Martin, & Jones, 2014), may be a daunting task. The question is: To what extent is the promotion of mathematical proficiency using ICT enacted under ODL conditions? Sedega, Mishiwo, Awuitor, and Nyamadi (2018) found that although the use of ICT could help to facilitate the teaching and learning of mathematics, the inability of college tutors to integrate ICT into the teaching and learning of mathematics was a hindrance. This matter is brought to the fore when considering how these teachers use such facilities to empower students who experience barriers to learning mathematics in terms of inclusion as suggested by Muyinda et al. (2019).

3 Mathematical Proficiency and the Mathematical Participation Model (MP-Model)

Mathematical proficiency is a term used by Kilpatrick, Swafford and Findell (2001) to capture aspects of expertise, competence, knowledge, and facility in mathematics. These authors consider the term as referring to what is necessary for "anyone to learn mathematics successfully" (Kilpatrick et al., 2001, p. 115). Mathematical proficiency is comprised of five interdependent and interwoven strands, namely, conceptual understanding, procedural fluency, strategic competence, adaptive reasoning, and productive disposition.

Kilpatrick et al. (2001) describe conceptual understanding as an integration of mathematical ideas in such a way that their functional grasp is formed. As a function that empowers students to know more than isolated facts and methods, conceptual understanding enables students to understand why a mathematical idea is important and the kinds of contexts in which it is useful, organizing their knowledge into a coherent whole that allows them to learn new ideas by connecting them with their prior knowledge (Kilpatrick et al., 2001).

The knowledge of procedures inclusive of when and how to use them refers to the second strand, which is called procedural fluency. In this strand, skills of flexibly, accuracy, and efficiency of performance are demonstrated (Kilpatrick et al., 2001). Students experiencing inadequacy in this strand struggle to develop a deep understanding of mathematical ideas or to solve mathematical problems, leaving them to rely on easily recallable and computable outcomes instead of focusing on the establishment of more important mathematical relationships. The use of ICTs in this regard may come in handy in addressing this aspect. Kilpatrick et al. (2000) argue that "students need well-timed practice of the skills they are learning so that they are not handicapped in developing the other strands of proficiency" (p. 122).

Strategic competence is the next strand identified by Kilpatrick et al. (2001) and it refers to modelling such that students are enabled to formulate, represent, and solve mathematical problems. This strand is particularly important as it is considered the first step in understanding mathematical representations, be they numerical, symbolic, verbal or graphical, acting as an entry point to what is considered to be at the core of doing mathematics, namely, modelling. The link to modelling is expressed more unequivocally by Kilpatrick et al. (2001) when stating that:

> ... a more proficient approach is to construct a problem model—that is, a mental model of the situation described in the problem. A problem model is not a visual picture per se; rather it is any form of mental representation that maintains the structural relations among the variables in the problem. (p. 125)

In this way, the maintenance of the relationship between the everyday life experiences as expressed in the problem to be solved and the mathematical representation in the form of the modelling is attained, enabling students, even those with learning barriers, to keep up with this important connection when doing mathematics. The current study proposes the mathematical participation model (MP-model) as the means by which this important link may be highlighted, maintained, and realised.

Phoshoko (2013) offers up the MP-model as a representation of the learning of mathematics that may fit the description of 'full participation' as envisioned by the theory of learning called communities of practice (CoP) (Lave & Wenger, 1991). In terms of CoP theory, Lave and Wenger (1991) maintain that learning is not in the heads of individuals as an acquired commodity, but is an interactive process of co-participation. They argue that as students gain increased access to participation, they perform various roles in the formation of their identities, a primary feature of what is referred to as learning and added:

> A community of practice is a set of relations among persons, activity, and world, over time and in relation with other tangential and overlapping communities of practice. A community of practice is an intrinsic condition for the existence of knowledge, not least because it provides the interpretive support necessary for making sense of its heritage. Thus, participation in the cultural practice in which any knowledge exists is an epistemological principle of learning. (Lave & Wenger, 1991, p. 98)

Therefore, the MP-model is informed by the inclusive nature of participation in CoP (Lave & Wenger, 1991), rendering it amenable to providing a description of participation for a variety of contexts, including that of students who may be faced with learning barriers when dealing with learning mathematics through the use of ICTs. The MP-model (Figure 10.1), composed of four nodes, namely, real-world data, CoP, mathematics, and model is representative of two-way processes linking each node with the others as participants draw from them (Phoshoko, 2013).

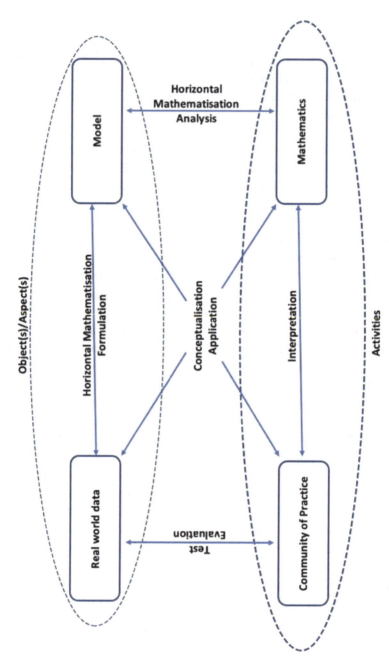

FIGURE 10.1 The Mathematical Participation Model (MP-model) (from Phoshoko, 2013, p. 86)

CONCEPTUALISING THE USE OF ICTS IN ODL

The linkages are in turn informed by Brodie's (2005) suggestion that knowledge is among people (in the CoP) and resources (real world data, models and mathematics). For enhanced and full participation, the participants in the CoP have to draw from all these resources (Phoshoko, 2018; Lave & Wenger, 1991). In accordance to the MP-model, the first process links real-life data with the mathematical model which either formulates a model or mathematises real-world data through horizontal mathematisation (Phoshoko, 2018). Mathematisation describes the step in which a model from real life experiences is encoded into mathematical representations in the form of a mathematical model (Kaiser, 2006).

In the second link, mathematical processes take prominence in connecting mathematics with the model in the form of analysis or vertical mathematisation, where the model formed will also be referred to as a mathematical one (Phoshoko, 2013). The interpretation process, Phoshoko (2013) added, is the third link where both the activities by members of the CoP as they engage with the mathematics shape the participants' learning while mathematical knowledge is constructed. Verification is done through the process of testing which links the CoP with real-world data for new understanding. The new understanding will inform future participation and will, in turn, be evaluated against the social, environmental, and cultural aspects (real world data) it sought to explain (Phoshoko, 2013). Cobb (1999) describes this modelling process as the reorganisation of both the activities (in the CoP) and the situation (in the real-world data). Phoshoko (2013) claims that these processes are structured in terms of mathematical concepts and relationships formed. Phoshoko (2013) further suggested that:

> Any link that does not include the CoP, say between real-world data, model and mathematics, may be described in terms of being outside the scope of participation or even going to the extent of being described in terms of "abstract". (p. 86)

Modelling invokes certain cognitive demands. It involves competencies such as, designing and applying problem solving strategies, arguing, and representing as well as involves the communication of knowledge that reflects real life experiences (Blum & Borromeo-Ferri, 2007; Kaiser, 2006). Phoshoko (2013) proposed that the cognitive demands, competencies, skills, and knowledge that entail modelling point to the strands of mathematical proficiency. Highlighting how the cognitive demands may be related to conceptual understanding, the competencies and skills to procedural fluency and strategic competency, and arguing to the adaptive reasoning strand whilst relating real life

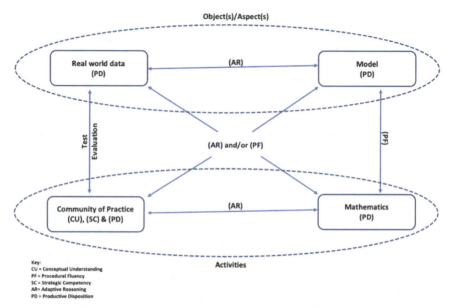

FIGURE 10.2   The MP-model and mathematical proficiency (from Phoshoko, 2013, p. 90)

knowledge to productive disposition, Phoshoko (2013) argued that mathematical proficiency is identifiable in the MP-model (refer to Figure 10.2).

In expanding on how mathematical proficiency relates to the MP-model (Phoshoko, 2013) adds:

> When participants are involved with processes that link the nodes of the MP-model with one another they will be engaging in one form or another with adaptive reasoning (AR) and/or procedural fluency (PD) of mathematical proficiency as shown in the figure above. Analysis, testing, interpretation, formulation, evaluation and mathematization require an element (if not a lot) of reasoning. As they are engaged in these processes the participants will develop conceptual understanding (CU) of the subject itself. This will in turn inform their engagement not only with these processes but with the components themselves and thus their strategic competency will be developed. When most and if not all of the first four strands of mathematical proficiency, namely, conceptual understanding, procedural fluency (PF), strategic competence, and adaptive reasoning are prevalent in participation, then productive disposition (PD) in the components of the MP-model is developed. Not only is the character and the nature of the CoP cultivated but the views that participants develop regarding the mathematics, the model and the real-world data informs and is informed by the participation. (pp. 91–92)

The current study sought to explore the extent to which the MP-model (Phoshoko, 2013) as informed by participation (leaning) in CoP (Lave & Wenger, 1991)—and undergirded by one of the most important theories in mathematics education, namely, mathematical proficiency (Kilpatrick et al., 2001)—may, through the use of ICTs, facilitate the learning of mathematics for students, particularly those with learning barriers. It was expected that for teaching that involved the use of ICTs to succeed, drawing from knowledge that informed technological pedagogy was important. The following section discusses in brief what is known as technological pedagogical and content knowledge (TPACK).

4 Technological Pedagogical and Content Knowledge (TPACK)

Mishra and Kohler (2006) argue that technological knowledge should be part of the content (what you teach) and pedagogy (how you teach) on which teachers base their plans for ICT use in classrooms in order to enhance learning. Using three circles, namely, content knowledge, pedagogical knowledge, and technical knowledge that intersect at a common place as representing what they refer as TPACK, the authors provide a description of a combination or integration of the different knowledges. Drawing on Shulman (1986), they refer to pedagogical content knowledge (PCK) as the combination of knowledge that teachers possess about the content with the knowledge they have about how to teach that specific content. With this kind of specialised knowledge, teachers are in a position to use the most effective methods for teaching specific content (Mishra & Kohler, 2006). The second combination of knowledge, called technological pedagogical knowledge (TPK), refers to a set of skills that teachers develop in order to identify and select for use the most appropriate technology to support a particular pedagogical approach. Technological content knowledge (TCK) is the last kind of knowledge they identified, and it combines that of technology and the content. TCK refers to a set of skills that teachers acquire as they identify the most appropriate technologies best suited to support the students as the latter learn the content (Mishra & Kohler, 2006).

This kind of description of knowledge, however, is idealistic in that it presupposes that knowledge is never formed outside other factors such the contexts. The expectation for the development of different kinds of TPACK, due to the level of availability of resources in different environments that students find themselves in, is not far-fetched. It was therefore likely for these kinds of differences to also play out in the institution of the current study. Koh (2019) reports that mathematics teachers face challenges when designing technology-integrated lessons to support mathematical inquiry with authentic problems and suggests the need for teachers to develop technological pedagogical knowledge (TPACK) or their professional knowledge for technology integration pedagogy. More importantly Muyinda et al. (2019) highlight that technology has the potential to promote authentic learning approaches which stimulate students' learning through simulating real-world problems in the classroom.

5 The Use of in ICTs through a Mathematical Participation Model

The MP-model as envisaged in the current study is considered a tool that may be used to explore the possibility of the use of ICT in the promotion of mathematical proficiency amongst students. The revised model is considered dynamic and not necessarily linear as depicted on a plane in the picture (see Figure 10.1) presented by Phoshoko (2013, 2018). The model may, in precision, take the form of a three-dimensional figure (Figure 10.3) such as tetrahedron. In this case, at the four vertices of the figure are the nodes of the MP-model, namely, real-world data (everyday experiences), CoP, mathematics (content), and modelling which are equidistant from one another, with the emphasis on the representation of participation that, ideally, depicts equal accessibility of one node to the other.

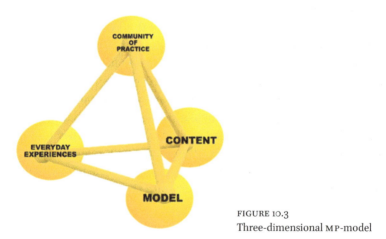

FIGURE 10.3
Three-dimensional MP-model

To avoid sounding repetitious, the revised MP-model which depicts the association with mathematical proficiency and was described in the previous section is presented in Figure 10.4. More importantly, there may be more than

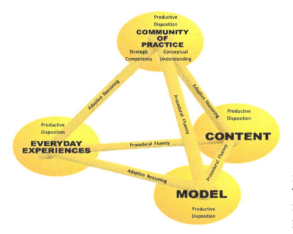

FIGURE 10.4
The relationship between the MP-model and mathematical proficiency

one strand linking the nodes as per the intertwining nature of mathematical proficiency.

All three kinds of knowledge found in the TPACK model are relatable to the processes of the MP-model (see Figure 10.5). With pedagogy being referred to as the act of teaching, it is imperative to note that the latter's inseparable association with learning is beyond doubt. The individuals identified in this association, teacher and student(s), are open to the descriptions of identities as captured in Lave and Wenger's (1991) CoP. Participants in CoP, just as in pedagogy, are involved in how knowledge and skills are exchanged. In this educational context, the interactions that take place during learning are considered participation. The content of what is taught is mathematics. The technology that facilitates the participation therefore represents the model in the MP-model. The processes that take place between the nodes of the MP-model thus generate kinds of knowledge mentioned in TPACK. The knowledge generated as a result of processes between the pedagogy (CoP) and content nodes is what is referred to as PCK (Shulman, 1986; Mishra & Kohler, 2006), the one between technology (model) and pedagogy nodes is called TPK (Mishra & Kohler, 2006), whilst the one between technology is known as TCK (Mishra & Kohler, 2006).

As argued in the preceding section, the TPACK model is idealistic in that it omits the fourth node identifiable in the MP-model, namely the important link with the real-world everyday experiences. The links that describe the association between the three nodes of the TPACK model, namely, pedagogical knowledge, content knowledge and technological knowledge with everyday experiences (contexts) are problem solving, interpretation, and modelling respectively. It is prudent to add here that the development of each node is

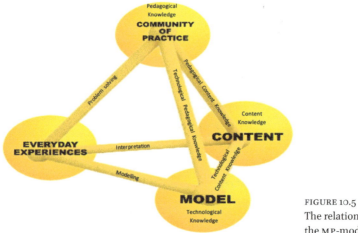

FIGURE 10.5
The relationship between the MP-model and TPACK

informed by participation that draws from more of these nodes. The inclusion of the context component, namely, the everyday experiences, in the TPACK model positions the latter to be able to highlight the descriptions of circumstances stated by Jung and Latchem (2012) as well as Sedega et al. (2018) in terms of hindrances to use of ICTs. The argument presented here is that pedagogy that is informed by CoP allows for a reflective participation that considers different social, political, and cultural contexts which have an impact on teaching and learning meant to empower students from different backgrounds, including those with learning barriers.

6   UTYM Response to Use of ICT

The study involved seven e-tutors employed at UTYM, which is one of the largest ODL institution in the SADC region. The participants were interviewed in terms of how they use ICTs to enhance the learning of the modules they teach. With qualifications that ranged from honours to masters level (one was registered for PhD), the e-tutors said they encountered students from diverse background through digital platforms. Highlighting the aspect of inclusiveness through the use of ICTs (Muyinda et al., 2019), one of the respondents, ET1, indicated:

> I find e-learning to be more effective, because we have different types of students in class, some students are shy to participate so e-learning helps them.

CONCEPTUALISING THE USE OF ICTS IN ODL

Weighing in on the accessibility of learning for different kinds of students offered by ICT platforms, another respondent said:

> Going online is easy and everybody can read the notes on the phone ... You can ask questions online at any time ...

It is apparent from above that the use of ICTs pointed to the facilitation of learning that may be of benefit to students with barriers to learning such as distance, where ICTs could be considered as bridging the gap in terms of the environment the students find themselves in.

The cost of setting up appropriate ICT infrastructure to support distance teaching online (Guri-Rosenblit, 2009; Simonson, Zvacek, & Smaldino, 2019), has often dictated how institutions adjust to the change. The participants indicated UTYM had resorted to a blended learning mode of course offerings in which the creation of a strategic mix of a variety of technologies, pedagogies, contexts, and delivery modes (such as online learning) are used to increase student success. According to the participants, every student registering with the institution was offered an email address by which online communication channels are opened and, in some cases, laptops are offered to students upon registration. They added that all the students had access to the institution's online facilities, most notably, the institution's website where students use their student number to log in. They also highlighted that there exists a website offering the students online study materials, contact details of the students per region as well as online discussion platforms between one another and their lecturer(s). The respondents however drew attention to the fact that due to the sizeable number of students not accessing the internet not all of them participated in the envisaged teaching and learning of mathematics. E-tutor ET2, in responding to the reason for lack of participation throughout the student population, captured the scenario:

> Maybe some of them are in rural areas, and that they are not aware that they can use their smartphones. But those in the urban areas can easily access internet, but I suspect most students are in the rural areas.

In order to cater to these kinds of students, the teaching and learning approach followed by the institution currently is called dual mode, such that online and paper-based tuition is prevalent. King (2012) defines dual-mode universities as those institutions that deliver the same programme in both face-to-face and distance mode. Makoe (2018) indicates in the era of technology, face-to-face and online delivery are also referred to as dual-mode, which is the case with UTYM. It is perhaps prudent to add the hindrance identified above is not captured by the TPACK model (Mishra & Kohler, 2006). The prevalent contexts in which students find themselves, such as having no access to internet, appear to be a hindrance to some students' learning. With the node of contexts noticeable in the MP-model, the possibility of the identification and consideration of this important aspect when using ICTs is enhanced.

In recognition of the contextual factors that may hamper full participation in CoP (Lave & Wenger, 1991) as per the MP-model (Phoshoko, 2018), such as no access to internet, the participants indicated that students are offered access to free WiFi at the UTYM regional centres through the use the computers in computer Labs or their computer or mobile devices. Additionally, free internet access is made available for all UTYM registered students at contracted telecentres around the country. This platform enables students, according to the respondents, to gather information, to complete as well as to submit assignments, and this points to participation that involves the link between the nodes of pedagogy (CoP) and content (mathematics) depicted in the MP-model.

When asked how they encourage their students to participate in the leaning of mathematics, the e-tutors lamented the apathy with which the majority of students enacted their participation in the e-tutor site as captured by the following quotes:

> I cannot say it is too large, because not all of them participate, because you find maybe 5–10 students are participating. (ET2)

> I will lay the blame on our students; we still have that type of students who will want to study at the last minute. I think we should encourage our students to have a timetable that help them to study throughout. (ET1)

> I do not know. It is one of the first things you as a researcher should be looking at. You should be interviewing students to find out what their thoughts (are). It is difficult for them to go online and organise themselves. (ET5)

In terms of participation that draws from subject content (mathematics) and the technological model, however, the e-tutors complained that the platform did not contain the software that are often used in mathematics such as Word's Math Equation and GeoGebra. The participation mentioned here points to the link in the MP-model (Phoshoko, 2013) between the two nodes, namely, subject content and model (ICT), where the latter is described as TCK

CONCEPTUALISING THE USE OF ICTS IN ODL

in the TPACK model (Mishra & Kohler, 2006). When asked about their familiarity with the online tools they use for assisting student, the following were some of their responses:

> Not very (well) would I say, other e-tutors emailed me on how you find how many students reviewed on (the) group site. I have not used it much. All I have done is post things, respond to students queries and post on the tutor site. (ET5)

> Yes, I am familiar with them, although there is some I do not touch, like statistics. (ET7)

The above quotes point to an element of inadequate training when it comes to the use of ICTS in mathematical instruction. Considering that statistics is one of the core contents in mathematics, it is apparent that the training on the use of ICTS that the e-tutors received may have been lacking in terms of modification as per specifications of the subject. The analysis of e-tutors' responses discussed above suggests, for the current study, that using the MP-model is amenable to providing a description of the type of participation that could be considered as adequate, subject to the participants in the CoP (inclusive of those faced with barriers to learning) being able to draw from all other nodes of the model.

7 Conclusion

The responses of HEIs seeking to employ ICTS to enhance the teaching and learning of subjects need to be informed by theories amendable to alleviating the challenges related to the implementation of such approaches. The MP-model undergirded by the theory of CoP was used in the current study to show how it related to mathematical proficiency as well as the TPACK model, where the latter incorporated the use of ICT, but more importantly, how it could be used for analysis of data that may be described as the full participation in CoP. With mathematics proficiency and TPACK considered very highly in education circles in terms of informing good practices when it comes to the teaching and learning of the subject, the fact that the MP-model incorporates both the theories in the description of participation is promising.

The MP-model was also used in the analysis of data sourced from e-tutors of one HEI using ICTS in the facilitation of mathematics teaching. The results emanating from the study suggest that policies that are formulated in HEI to inform practices that incorporate the use of ICTs and that cater to a variety of students in the promotion of equality, should be informed by frameworks such as the MP-model. Another matter for consideration by HEI involves offering mathematics teacher education so that the requisite ICT resources are made available to the students.

The study further highlights the prioritisation of, and the need for, subject specific ICT training for teachers if educators hope to ever successfully leverage technology to help students experiencing barriers to teaching overcome them.

The MP-model offers opportunities for those involved in mathematics education practices to integrate the use of ICTs with the teaching and learning of mathematics so that it is informed by appropriate learning theories. The current study makes a case for the use of the MP-model in terms of engaging the full participation (Lave & Wenger, 1991) of students such that the challenges they face with regard to learning barriers may not only be identified but addressed.

References

Aljaraideh, Y., & Al Bataineh, K. (2019). Jordanian students' barriers of utilizing online learning: A survey study. *International Education Studies, 12*(5). https://doi.org/10.5539/ies.v12n5p99

Allen, K. (2019). Africa should not be too quick to embrace the fourth industrial revolution. *The Guardian Weekly Mail.* https://www.theguardian.com/global-development/2019/sep/16/africa-should-not-be-too-quick-to-embrace -the-fourth-industrial-revolution

Arnaiz Sánchez, P., de Haro-Rodríguez, R., & Maldonado Martínez, R. (2019). Barriers to student learning and participation in an inclusive school as perceived by future education professionals. *Journal of New Approaches in Educational Research, 8*(1), 18–24.

Blum, W., & Borromeo-Ferri, R. (2009). Mathematical modelling: Can it be taught and learnt? *Journal of Mathematical Modelling and Application, 1*(1), 45–48.

Boddy-Evans, A. (2020). *Apartheid quotes about Bantu education.* ThoughtCo. www.thoughtco.com/apartheid-quotes-bantu-education-43436

BusinessTech. (2018). *By 2020 almost 80% of jobs will require STEM education.* https://businesstech.co.za/news/business/283516/by-2020-almost-80-of-jobs-will-require-stem-education/

Cobb, P. (1999). Individual and collective mathematical development: The case of statistical data analysis. *Mathematical Thinking and Learning, 1*(1), 5–43.

CONCEPTUALISING THE USE OF ICTS IN ODL

Department of Basic Education. (2017). *The SACMEQ IV project in South Africa: A study of the conditions of schooling and the quality of education.* Department of Basic Education. http://www.education.gov.za

du Preez, M. (2018). The factors influencing mathematics students to choose teaching as a career. *The South African Journal of Education, 38*(2). doi:10.15700/saje.v38n2a1465

Guri-Rosenblit, S. (2009). Distance education in the digital age: Common misconceptions and challenging tasks. *Journal of Distance Education, 23*, 105–122. http://www.ijede.ca/index.php/jde/index

Jung, I., & Latchem, C. (2012). *Quality assurance and accreditation in distance education and e-learning.* Routledge. https://doi.org/10.4324/9780203834497

Kaiser, G. (2006). Modelling and modelling competencies in school. In C. P. Haines, P. Galbraith, W. Blum, & S. Khan (Eds.), *Mathematical modelling (ICTMA 12): Education, engineering and economics* (pp. 110–119). Horwood Publishing.

Kilpatrick, J., Swafford, J., & Findell, B. (2001). *Adding it up: Helping children to learn mathematics.* National Academy Press.

King, B. (2012). Distance education and dual-mode universities: An Australian perspective. *Open Learning: The Journal of Open, Distance and e-Learning, 27*(1), 9–22. doi:10.1080/02680513.2012.640781

Koh, J. H. L. (2019). Articulating teachers' creation of Technological Pedagogical Mathematical Knowledge (TPMK) for supporting mathematical inquiry with authentic problems. *International Journal of Science and Mathematics Education, 17*, 1195–1212. https://doi.org/10.1007/s10763-018-9914-y

Makoe, M. (2018). Avoiding to fit a square peg into a round hole: A policy framework for operationalising open distance education in dual-mode universities. *Distance Education, 39*(2), 159–175. doi:10.1080/01587919.2018.1457945

Masenya, T. M., & Ngulube, P. (2019). Digital preservation practices in academic libraries in South Africa in the wake of the digital revolution. *The South African Journal of Information Management.* http://dx.doi.org/10.4102/sajim.v21i1.1011

Mendoza, D. J., & Mendoza, D. I. (2018). Information and communication technologies as a didactic tool for the construction of meaningful learning in the area of mathematics. *International Electronic Journal of Mathematics Education, 13*(3), 261–271. https://doi.org/10.12973/iejme/3907

Moore, M. G., & Kearsley, G. (2005). *Distance education: A systems view* (2nd ed.). Thomson Wadsworth.

Mullis, I. V. S., Martin, M. O., Foy, P., & Hooper, M. (2016). *TIMSS 2015 international results in mathematics.* Boston College. http://timss.bc.edu

Mullis, I. V. S., Martin, M. O., & Jones, L. (2014). Third International Mathematics and Science Study (TIMSS). In R. Gunstone (Ed.), *Encyclopedia of science education* (pp. 1075–1079). Springer.

Muyinda, P. B., Mayende, G., Maiga, G., & Oyo, B. (2019). Widely acclaimed but lowly utilized: Congruencing ODL utilization with its wide acclaim. *Universal Journal of Educational Research, 7*(2), 400–412.

Oladejo, M. A., Abiodun, M., & Gesinde, M. A. (2014). Trends and future directions in open and distance learning. *Journal of Education and Practice, 5*(18), 132–138.

Phoshoko, M. M. (2013). *Teacher's views on the use of contexts in transition to mathematics* (PhD thesis). University of South Africa.

Phoshoko, M. M. (2015). Experiences of role players in the implementation of mathematics teachers' continuous professional development in South Africa. *International Journal of Educational Sciences, 8*(1), 241–248. doi:10.1080/09751122.2015.11917610

Phoshoko, M. M. (2018). Teachers views on revisiting the operation of signed numbers using contexts: A case of three African teachers. Ubuntu. *Journal of Conflict Transformation, 7*(Special Issue), 63–85.

Sedega, B. S., Mishiwo, M., Awuitor, G. K., & Nyamadi, M. K. (2018). Pre-service teachers' perception of the use of Information Communication and Technology (ICT) in the teaching and learning of mathematics in three colleges of education in Ghana. *British Journal of Education, 16*(4), 109–119.

Shulman, L. S. (1986). Those who understand: Knowledge growth in teaching. *Educational Researcher, 15*(2), 4–14.

Simonson, M., Zvacek, S., & Smaldino, S. (2019). *Teaching and learning at a distance: Foundations of distance education* (7th ed.). Information Age Publishing.

CHAPTER 11

The Uses of Augmentative and Alternative Communication Technology in Empowering Learners Overcome Communication Barriers to Learning

Munyane Mophosho and Khetsiwe Masuku

Abstract

Learners with little or no functional speech (LNFS) often experience barriers with activity and participation in the classroom. Subsequently, they experience challenges accessing the curriculum. There is consequently a need to provide high level communication support for them to be able to participate fully. It has been established that commercially available information and communication technology (ICT), which includes augmentative and alternative communication (AAC), can be used as communication aids to mitigate the communication challenges that learners experience. Even though research has proven the benefits of ICT for learners with communication difficulties, the opportunities presented by ICT have often been underutilised. The underutilisation of these augmentative strategies is a result of policy, practice, educator skills, and knowledge barriers. The lack of awareness and training of educators and the inequalities that exists in education, health, and social development sectors further deprive students of their right to communication and education. In this chapter, we describe the different kinds of high and low AAC technology devices that can be made available to learners with LNFS. We also discuss the purpose of AAC for these learners, specifically their importance in addressing barriers to accessing the curriculum and participation. We furthermore discuss the challenges of implementing AAC in the South African context, while suggesting and recommending strategies that can be used to alleviate the barriers to learning using ICT.

Keywords

augmentative and alternative communication technology – learners with little or no functional speech – access to the curriculum – participation

© KONINKLIJKE BRILL NV, LEIDEN, 2021 | DOI: 10.1163/9789004447226_012

1 Introduction

The right to education for all learners is promised in both the Constitution of the Republic of South Africa and the South African Bill of Rights (Constitution of the Republic of South Africa, 1996). Access to education is also provided for in article 24 of the United Nations Convention on the Rights of Persons with Disabilities (CRPD) (United Nations, 2006) which South Africa ratified in 2008 (United Nations, 2016). South Africa acknowledges inclusive education as a fundamental right for all learners with disabilities (Department of Education, 2001). This is manifested in the implementation of the white paper 6, which has been dubbed the "post-Apartheid landmark policy which provides the vision and framework for transforming South Africa's divided and unequal education system into an inclusive one" (Barratt, 2016, p. 111).

Tomaševski, (2001) argues that the human right of inclusive education for learners with disabilities will be achieved when inclusive education is available (establishment of fully funded educational institutions for children with disabilities); accessible (educational facilities are within reach in terms of distance and finances); acceptable (the education offered is of the highest standard); and adaptable (meets the specific needs of each learner in the classroom). AAC therefore ensures that learners with LNFS can "access" an "acceptable" and "adaptable" curriculum.

The right for education for learners with disabilities is, however, far from being achieved in South Africa as learners with disabilities still encounter challenges related to all four of Tomaševski's (2001) pillars. Learners with disabilities struggle to access schooling, be it inclusive or in specialised education. Learning for learners with disabilities still occurs in separate environments, contributing to the further isolation of learners with disabilities. Mainstream education still occurs without adaptation and reasonable accommodation of the needs of learners with disabilities and education still comes at a hefty price for caregivers of learners with disabilities as a result of additional costs related to assistive devices and transportation costs.

The above-mentioned challenges are further compounded in learners with communication difficulties, including those with LNFS, because, regardless of the right to communication being provided for in the Constitution of the Republic of South Africa, for people with an acquired or congenital communication disability this right becomes elusive. LNFS experience more isolation due to their inability to communicate which leads to limited social participation, thus facilitating their exclusion and limiting functioning. Access to education is ultimately hampered as the LNFS will struggle to express and share their needs, wants, thoughts, and ideas. The educator may also struggle to understand the needs, preferences, and interactions of the learners.

The authors are of the opinion that "education should be for all learners and that no learner should be left behind". It is against the backdrop of these views that the authors therefore argue for AAC as a human rights tool that can ensure that LNFS are afforded the opportunity to access, be included in, and fully participate in the education curriculum that they would have otherwise not been able to access without reasonable accommodation. Musselwhite and St Louis (1988) put into perspective the role that AAC plays in facilitating access by saying "the aim of AAC is to enable learners with LNFS to attain their fullest potential through meeting their communication and learning needs with effective communication skills, facilitating inclusion in educational settings" (p. 213). In particular, AAC enhances communication by providing language for teaching and learning, enhancing language function goals such as requesting, enhancing educator goals, improving target vocabulary for specific activities or themes, and improving linguistic, operational, social, and strategic communicative competence (Light, 2003).

The challenges that surround the implementation of AAC in the South African context, such as budget allocations to provide and maintain assistive devices, the availability of AAC devices in multiple languages, lack of skills amongst educators to facilitate communication and curriculum support using AAC devices (McSheehan, Sonnenmeier, Jorgensen, & Turner, 2006), and safety of assistive devices when taken home by students, are acknowledged by the authors. These challenges can, however, be alleviated by providing intensive in-service educator training on AAC.

2   What Is Augmentative and Alternative Communication?

According to American Speech and Hearing Association (ASHA, 2017), Augmentative and Alternative communication (AAC) includes "all forms of communication (other than oral speech) that are used to express thoughts, needs, wants, and ideas. We all use AAC when we make facial expressions or gestures, use symbols or pictures, or write". AAC is supplementary communication or alternative, because it provides a medium that is not conventional (e.g. visual symbols in the case of communication books and speech generating devices) and that is different from what people typically use for face-to-face interaction.

AAC is a system of multiple components or modes for communication. It consists of symbols (objects, pictures, graphics, gesture, etc.); aids (electronic and non-electronic device); techniques (the way the message is transmitted); and strategies (most effective method of conveying a message) (Beukelman & Mirenda, 2013; Mophosho & Dada, 2015).

3 What Is the Aim of AAC and Who Can Benefit from It?

There is an increased need for AAC devices due to the increased number of children that need assistive devices in the classroom as well as in other communicative or social contexts (Sableski, 2000). AAC is aimed at addressing the communicative needs of an individual who presents with speech, language, and communication difficulties as a result of developmental or acquired disability, which limits their participation in an environment (Beukelman & Mirenda, 2013; Mophosho & Dada, 2015). For example, individuals with motor/ physical, cognitive, and sensory disabilities such as autism, Down syndrome, cerebral palsy (CP), motor neurone disease, deafblindness to name just a few may benefit from AAC (Beukelman & Mirenda, 2013). Learners with LNFS fall within these populations, therefore AAC can provide support for understanding this population as well as provide them an avenue for expression.

Not being able to communicate and be heard is not only severely isolating, but it is excluding, discriminating, and disempowering. It fundamentally limits participation across all spheres of an individual's life, including communication. AAC technology therefore, enables people with LNFS to access education and other social contexts and gives them the opportunity to be active members in a community.

3.1 AAC as a Tool to Facilitate Access to Education for Learners with LNFS

The United Nations (2016) submits that "the entire education system must be accessible, including buildings, information and communication, comprising ambient or frequency modulation assistive systems, curriculum, education materials, teaching methods, assessment and language and support services" (p. 8). AAC therefore guarantees that learners with LNFS can access the curriculum by affording them equal opportunities to access learning information and to also actively participate in the classroom context. That way this group of learners will have equal benefits and privileges that their peers without a disability enjoy.

The use of AAC can facilitate communication between teachers and children with special education needs and alleviate communication challenges which have been reported (Light & McNaughton, 2010). One of the core functions of AAC is to provide learners with the ability to develop ideas and communicate information (Banes & Coles, 1995). We communicate by using words, pictures, symbols, signs, and sounds. This is not related only to expression of ideas and creativity, but also the ability to comprehend all forms of communication. With AAC, learners can also be taught how to process and handle information. For instance, a case of a learner diagnosed with autism who presents with complex communication needs and relies on inappropriate methods of communication such as pulling their teacher or caregivers to the desired objects or being frustrated because they know an answer but have no means to express themselves. If given an AAC device such as a handheld VOCA like the big-MAC (pictured in Figure 11.1) with pre-recorded messages, he can become independent. AAC can be seen as a bridge to literacy development. Access to literacy also provides access to participation and independence.

3.2   *AAC as an Empowering Tool for Learners with LNFS*

AAC provides access to the power of communication technology and in so doing facilitates and provides opportunities for learners with LNFS to interact with other learners, their educators, families, and members of the society. In so doing they are able to make their voices heard, are involved in decision making, and thus have an influence on their environment, and to participate fully in society (Beukelman & Mirenda, 2013). AAC allows leaners with LNFS to access the education curriculum. The skills that are taught in schools give an opportunity for learners with LNFS to be independent and employable. One of the long-term goals for all learners, including those with LNFS, should be independence so that they can lead a dignified life.

3.3   *AAC as a Tool to Facilitate Inclusiveness and Equality*

Communication difficulties may lead to marginalisation and exclusion from social and educational opportunities. It infringes on the right to education for all, regardless of individual characteristics or difficulties (UNESCO, 2006, p. 13) and also on the right to communication (United Nations, 2006). Exclusion means being denied access due to disability. Exclusion from education may result in low literacy and low skills in adults with disabilities, thus continuing the vicious cycle of continuous exclusion from employment prospects leading to continuous poverty. The use of AAC is, therefore, crucial for the inclusion of learners with LNFS in both social and educational contexts. UNESCO (2006) proposes that in order for the goal of inclusive education to be achieved, learners with disabilities need to be provided with the necessary means to access and communicate information, these means might include ICT and AAC. Inclusion translates into increased participation. Technology provides the learner with LNFS an opportunity to interact with others in their environment. For example, digital technology has made life more accessible for people with disabilities in the following ways: apps can turn text to speech; software can be installed on mobile phones, tablets, iPads and iPods, allowing a person with LNFS to type and get an output of voice; and speech recognition software that allows a physically disabled individual, such as someone living with quadriplegia, to control their computer with a voice.

4 Types of AAC

According to Fosset and Mirenda (2007) there are two types of AAC devices: aided and unaided AAC systems. *Aided systems* are those which require external equipment such as objects, paragraphs, pictures, line drawings, and traditional orthography. Aided systems are further broken down into *low technology* and *high technology* devices.

Low tech options consist of systems and methods of communicating that are not battery powered and are usually cheaper to make. Common examples of low-tech systems include picture exchanging, printed word or alphabet boards, communication books, and sign language. Also, recorded speech devices (digital) can fall into this category if battery-powered with simple short messages.

FIGURE 11.1
BigMac

FIGURE 11.2
Eye-gaze alphabet board

High tech options include devices that are dedicated and non-dedicated to AAC, mainly technological devices such as the "Go talk" or iPad applications, and computerised speech generating devices (Beukelman & Mirenda, 2005).

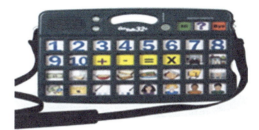

FIGURE 11.3   Go-Talk 4   FIGURE 11.4   Go-Talk 32

Unaided systems refers to the use of facial expressions, gestures, objects, pictures, symbols, sign language, written words and/or communication technology to augment speech, or to provide an alternative means of communication when speech is not possible or functional. Unaided techniques require the usage of the individual's body alone, such as body movements, manual signs, gestures, and facial expression (Fosset & Mirenda, 2007).

5   AAC and Natural Speech

AAC is not all or none, or a specific method of communication, it includes both verbal and non-verbal forms of communication. These multiple modes of communication can be used in combination to meet daily communication demands depending on circumstances. In addition, AAC can be used as supplementary or for repair if speech is not understood during communication. Research has proven that AAC use can promote an increase in speech with more successful communication opportunities (Light, 2019). Therefore, AAC is multimodal and multi-sensory in nature.

6   Determining Candidacy for AAC

Learners need to be assessed by a team comprising of caregivers, educators, speech language therapists, occupational therapists, and physiotherapists before they can be provided with support (DoE, 2014). According to SIAS policy, there needs to be screening, identification then assessment before support can be provided. Since most professionals who are able to screen and assess are based in the district, the process of finding support for a learner can be long and complex (Human Rights Watch, 2015).

6.1 Assessment Principles

Due to the complexity of communication disabilities, Beukelman and Mirenda (2013) suggest that a team approach is the best approach, with the individuals being assessed being accepted and given the role of "captain of the team". It is also important to understand that communication is multi-modal and multi-sensory communication. Children use their verbal skills to communicate part of their message and supplement for the portions of speech that are not sufficiently intelligible by using other modes of communication. Parents should be made aware that AAC augments speech rather than replaces the development of speech. This will allay their fears which are based on the myth that when a child uses AAC, that their child might stop communicating verbally.

6.2 Multi-Perspective Assessment Involves

A speech-language pathologist's role in AAC is to perform communication assessments and intervention on their own or as members of collaborative teams that may include the individual being assessed and the family or caregivers. It is of crucial importance that the team knows the child and understands their strengths and weaknesses (Handlemma & Harris, 2001). Assessment generally consists of:

- Initial interview: Inclusion of family members in the AAC process is pivotal. Bailey, Parette, Stoner, Angell, and Carroll, (2006) found that if family members are not included, this may lead to device abandonment. The interview should preferably be conducted in the family's first language. Otherwise, interpreters should be sourced.
- Needs assessment: Investigate if the need for the device is permanent or temporary. There is a need to determine if there are any comorbid disabilities such as autism (ASD), cerebral palsy, apraxia of speech, or intellectual disability. Identify and describe environmental or personal factors that serve as barriers or facilitators to participation and functioning (ASHA, 2016; WHO, 2014).
- Identification of individual strengths, participation and limitations in activity: The assessor should also note whether these are cognitive, language, sensory, physical/motor, or socio-emotional related. Formal or informal tests may be used by the multidisciplinary team. Furthermore, underlying strengths and limitations in speech production, verbal, and non-verbal communication should be idenfitied.

- Identify access methods: Make a determination of whether direct or indirect access methods are needed.
- Feature matching: Assess level of symbol representation. Determine appropriate AAC system features to recommend for the learner. Is it going to be objects/photos/pictures/words if literate? Aided or unaided modes of communication?
- Plan for follow-up (Beukelman & Mirenda, 2005, 2013).

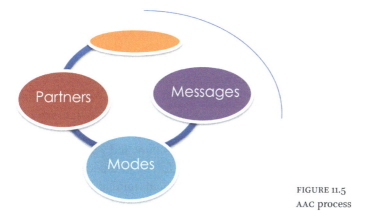

FIGURE 11.5
AAC process

Once the team has completed an assessment and screening of a learner with LNFS, the next step is to develop a plan for implementing communication intervention for the learner with LNFS to be able to communicate self-care needs; communicate emotional status; engage in social communicative interaction with familiar communication partners (friends and family); carry out communicative interactions in the school context and community; to enhance acquisition of language skills; acquire literacy skills; and have a good quality of life (Hamm & Mirenda, 2006).

7 Training for AAC System

School teams and DBST may recommend a variety of strategies such as Picture Exchange Communication (PECS), Prompt, TEACCH, and Makaton signs. In addition, low and high technology may be used in combination with unaided systems such as residual speech and manual signs or gestures. The major focus for education with learners with LNFS is to facilitate communication, learning, and participation (Handleman & Harris, 2001). After assessment and recommendations for an assistive communication device are made, then purchasing of the device and the training of the learner to become a competent communicator should start. Light (1989) states that communicative competence is "... the ability to communicate functionally in the natural environment and to adequately meet daily communication needs" (p. 143).

Light (2003) broadened the concept of communicative competence, and cautioned against just focusing only on operational, linguistic, social, and strategic competence aspects. Furthermore, it is of crucial importance to consider "... also a variety of psychosocial factors (e.g., motivation, attitude, confidence, resilience) as well as barriers and supports in the environment" (Light & McNaughton, 2014, p. 1). Some of these factors, barriers, and supports may include:

1. Operational competency: Direct instruction is required for a learner with a high- or low-tech device. Instruction should not only focus on developing good expressive skills but also on teaching the user how to operate and be able to navigate the device.
    –   On/off, charging, navigating, adding vocabulary, and volume.
2. Linguistic competency: A user has to be effective and participate using the symbols in class. Systematic instruction and training should include using language that is grade and age appropriate. The learner has to be able to use appropriate symbols on the device during interaction.
    –   Recognizing symbol sets, reading, manipulating linguistic codes, and being able to construct complex sentences. Learners should be supported during orientation and in learning how to use AAC to be able to convey messages in both verbal and written modalities.
3. Social competency: The learner should be taught when, how, and with whom to interact. Strategies such as modeling and using aided language input have been reported to be effective in teaching this skill (Senner & Baud, 2015).
    –   Pragmatics or what is often referred to as discourse skills such as initiation, turn taking during interactions should be part of training.
4. Strategic competency: The low- or high-tech user should be able to problem solve and learn how to use adaptive strategies to repair communication. This skill or competency is important for participation in curricular activities and conversations.
    –   Training should include how to use the most appropriate communication method and vocabulary for the situation.
    –   Developing compensatory strategies for effective communication within the AAC system, should be part of ongoing training.

8 Challenges of Implementing AAC

Even though the provision of AAC in South Africa is improving in special education (Tönsing & Dada, 2016), unfortunately not every learner with LNFS who requires an AAC device, especially a high-tech device, an access one (Dada, Horn, Samuels, & Schlosser, 2016; Van Niekerk & Tönsing, 2015). In fact, the World Health Organisation (2017) asserts that in developing countries such as South Africa, only between 5% and 10% of the people who require assistive devices have access to them. South Africa is unfortunately an unequal society, with 53.8% of the population reported to be living in poverty (Nicolson, 2015). The repercussions of this inequality are also visible in AAC intervention as affordability is still a factor in the issuing and maintenance of assistive devices in AAC practice (Dada, Murphy, & Tönsing, 2017; Van Niekerk & Tönsing, 2015; Van Niekerk, Dada, & Tönsing, 2019). The educational departments should therefore be consistent when factoring in the cost of issuing and maintenance of AAC systems, in accordance with their policies as stipulated in DoE (2007, 2010).

While the department of education has developed policy guidelines (DoE, 2007, 2010) aimed at guiding the national and provincial sourcing and managing of assistive devices in schools, it does not seem like these policies have been adequately implemented. This, coupled with the lack of consistency and set guidelines to follow during AAC assessment and intervention processes, hampers the successful implementation of AAC in educational contexts (Light & McNaugthon, 2015). In essence, the inconsistency of implementation of guiding policies on assistive devices, coupled with lack of funding earmarked for assistive devices and technology, suggests that although the South African government introduced major education reforms and adopted an inclusive education policy meant for learners with communication difficulties and other disabilities, access to quality learning remains at the margins of government transformation initiatives.

The assessment for the candidacy for assistive devices, even though conducted in a team, is usually facilitated by a speech language therapist (Thistle & Wilkinson, 2015). In the profession of speech language therapy, speech language therapists are over-represented in private practice and amongst those who do practice in public schools, only a minimum are proficient in the languages and cultures of the populations they serve (Kathard & Pillay, 2013). This implies cultural and linguistic barriers, which negatively affect the provision of AAC services (Dada, Kathard, Tönsing, & Harty, 2017), a practice which is contrary to the best practice in communication intervention proposed by Soto and Yu (2014).

There are currently 65 schools for learners with special educational needs across the 11 districts in the province. The majority of which do not go up until the 7th grade (46 out of the 64 schools, i.e. 72%) and very few that go up to the 10th grade (4 out of the 60 schools, i.e. 7%). Only 13 out of 64 schools reported having speech-language therapists, 10 out of 65 schools reported having audiologists, and 13 out 64 schools reported having a dual qualified SLTs and audiologists. The training of teachers to use an AAC device interactively needs to be prioritised as the shortage of SLTs and audiologists will not be resolved in the near future.

The attitudes of educators are key to the success or failure of the implementation of AAC technology for learners with LNFS. Bornman and Donahue (2015) lament that educators' attitudes towards the inclusion of learners with LNFS is often biased when compared to their attitudes towards learners with other disabilities such as Attention Deficit Hyperactivity Disorder (ADHD). Educators perceived learners with LNFS as burdensome (Bornman & Donahue, 2015). Factors contributing to these perceptions include: the evident gaps in the training of educators on specific disabilities (Manga & Masuku, 2020); the lack of skills necessary to facilitate AAC; and the fact that learners with LNFS may present with comorbid conditions such as intellectual disability, autism, language delay, global developmental delay, and behavioural difficulties (Marrus & Hall, 2017). Attitudes such as the one mentioned above infiltrate even to the level of families and communities (Van Niekerk et al., 2019). Such attitudes can only change when families and communities start recognizing that persons with disabilities, including learners with LNFS, have the potential to develop independence and be active members of the economy. This will be achieved when efficient and successful AAC strategies that ensure that these learners are included, accepted, and accommodated in an educational environment are fostered.

The successful implementation of AAC technology depends on the abilities and buy-in of the learner who uses the technology and their families (Van Niekerk, Dada, & Tönsing, 2019). For example, in some instances, it may be stressful for learners with LNFS to learn how to operate what may sometimes be sophisticated computer-based devices, especially if these devices have not been introduced into a family setting (Parette, Huer, & Brotherson, 2001). The lack of familiarity with an assistive device may pose a challenge to inclusion for these learners with LNFS in educational settings as learners may experience significant communication challenges with their peers and educators. Actually, Case, 2010) proposes that it is imperative that learners with LNFS "develop sophisticated literacy skills in order to maximize their participation with as wide a range of communication partners as possible" (p. 1).

Families may see the use of an AAC system as requiring additional caregiving responsibilities beyond daily routines, especially if families were not included as part of the team during the assessment for candidacy. The onus is therefore on SLTs to include families as part of their whole team. Expectations and the demands associated with the AAC system and the maintenance that comes with introducing an AAC device to a learner should be discussed with families as families should have the option to indicate choices and preferences (Van Niekerk et al., 2019).

The characteristics of the assistive devices themselves influence whether or not the device will be successfully used by the learner and their families. In particular, factors such as durability, portability, appearance, and comfort of the device are known to either be a barrier or facilitator to implementation of AAC devices (Van Niekerk et al., 2019). It is therefore imperative that these characteristics are factored into the discussion during the selection of devices as they have budget implications.

9   Solutions and Recommendations

It is incumbent upon the country to act on the CRPD as it is a universal, legally binding standard (United Nations, 2006). By ratifying the CRPD, the country has, in essence, committed to upholding its principles of ensuring that not only are the rights and dignity of persons with disabilities guaranteed, but also that persons with disabilities are respected, treated with dignity, have individual autonomy, are not discriminated against, are included, and are able to participate fully in a society that is accepting of them as equals (United Nations, 2006).

The Department of Basic Education needs to fully commit to operationalising Article 24 of the convention which guarantees that learners with disabilities can access education opportunities in an inclusive manner. They need to also implement Article 9 which mandates signatory states tensure that persons with disabilities are able to participate and live independently in their physical, transportation, and information and communication environments. It is acknowledged that South Africa has developed policies that have attempted to facilitate the inclusion of learners with disabilities, by mandating inclusive education and the provision of appropriate AAC devices to ensure that students with disabilities are able to fully participate equally in the curriculum (DoE, 2001, 2007, 2010); however, evidence suggests the implementation of these policies is questionable (Donohue & Bornman, 2014). As such, some learners who require AAC devices have them while some don't. There needs to be a realisation that for a learner with LNFS, an AAC device means access, participation, and independence (United Nations, 2006). Ultimately not having these devices means the lack of the above, implying exclusion.

AAC therefore lands itself as a human rights tool which ensures equality and justice for learners with LNFS (UNESCO, 2013; United Nations, 2006). It represents a human rights tool because it provides opportunities to access academic and social learning, employment, and participation for a group of people that would otherwise have been excluded from society. Ashington (2010) emphasises the need and value for state economies and societies in increasing the inclusion of persons with disabilities. In providing these technologies to learners in the South African context, Waddel (2008) and the United Nations (2006) propose three imperative considerations—availability, accessibility, and affordability—if AAC is to be made accessible to all learners who need it. This implies the need for a high level of commitment from the state to consistently fund the procurement, maintenance, and monitoring of AAC technologies for all learners who require them, so that no learner is left behind (DoE, 2015).

Over and above these considerations, it is important to consider the competence and confidence of educators in implementing and facilitating the use of AAC technologies with students in the classroom. Teachers play a pivotal role in supporting students using AAC systems in classrooms (Mukhopadhyay & Nwaogu, 2009). Therefore, teacher training is imperative to provide competence (Tonsing & Dada, 2016). In situ training coupled with modelling is proposed by De Bortoli et al. (2011) and Pasupathy and Bogschutz (2013) as the preferred and effective method of training. The classroom environment, in particular high student to teacher ratio, needs to be thought through, as it might negatively influence the successful implementation of AAC in classroom situations (Tönsing & Dada, 2016). Facilities must invest in the redesigning of classroom environments and caseloads to facilitate the implementation of AAC.

Ensuring a good fit between the abilities of the learner who needs an AAC device and the operational requirements of the AAC device allocated to them is important, even though this is not necessarily always the case (Naraian, 2010). This implies the need for thorough assessments to be conducted by trained professionals to ensure the allocation of appropriate AAC devices. A collaborative team approach including families, teachers, occupational therapists, and speech language therapists must be encouraged (De Bortoli, Arthur-Kelly, Foreman, Balandin, & Mathisen, 2011). Family-centered, collaborative intervention has been advocated as the foundation of successful AAC intervention (Alant, 2005; Calculator & Black, 2009). Learners with LNFS do not exist in a vacuum, they use their devices to engage with their peers, educators, families, and communities. Consequently, it is essential to provide communication training to educators, peers without disabilities, and families to enhance participation and interactions with a learner using AAC in both the schooling and home environment. Abramia and Mophosho (2021) suggest that there is a need for further training on AAC device use in the classroom involving all teachers, specialists, and parents who come in contact with the child, to improve facilitation initiatives.

Technology has become part of our lives in South Africa, thus AAC applications (apps) have become accessible. This phenomena has brought down costs and resulted in greater access to AAC. Learners with LNFS and their families do not have to wait for SLTs to prescribe high-cost AAC technologies; rather, they have the option to make their own decision and purchase the mobile or tablet applications (McNaughton & Light, 2013). These mobile devices (handheld devices) such as iPads and smartphones have become affordable for some families and are accessible to schools and communities.

10   Conclusion

Learners with LNFS have been previously excluded from accessing the curriculum and participating, due to their challenges with verbal speech, an infringement on their rights to access education and that of participation. ICT, in the form of AAC devices, is a solution to mitigating these barriers to learning while also providing an opportunity for these learners to function as members the society. AAC devices play an important role in the facilitation of expressive communication which, in turn, facilitates learning for individuals with LNFS. Although the value of AAC devices is emphasised, it is important to acknowledge that there exist barriers to implementing AAC and, as a result, as a country we have not yet done enough to ensure that all learners who require assistive devices can access them regardless of their socioeconomic status. It is also evident that for implementation to be successful there has to be coherence of multidisciplinary professions in order to provide an optimal impact on the learner. Educator attitudes and views are instrumental and can influence the facilitation of AAC technology. Education of all communication partners and educators on the implementation of AAC systems play a pivotal role in its successful adoption.

References

Abramia, A., & Mophosho, M. (2021). *Usage of augmentative and alternative communication devices in classrooms: Perspectives of facilitators in schools for students with special educational needs in Gauteng, South Africa.* Manuscript.

Alant, E. (2005). Support-based AAC intervention. In E. Alant & L. L. Lloyd (Eds.), *Augmentative and alternative communication and severe disabilities: Beyond poverty* (pp. 155–191). Whurr.

American Speech-Language-Hearing Association. (2016). *Scope of practice in speech-language pathology.* www.asha.org/policy/

Ashington, N. (2010). Accessible information and communication technologies benefits to business and society. *OneVoice for Accessible ICT.* http://www.onevoiceict.org/sites/default/files/Accessible%20ICT%20-%20 Benefits%20to%20Business% 20and%20Society.pdf

Banes, D., & Coles, C. (1995). *Information technology for all: Developing and information technology curriculum for pupils with severe or profound technology learning difficulties.* David Fulton Press.

Barratt, S. E. (2016). *Perspectives on the roles and responsibilities of an inclusive education outreach team in one rural education district of the Western Cape* (Unpublished master's thesis). Stellenbosch University.

Beukelman, D. R., & Mirenda, P. (2013). *Augmentative and alternative communication: Supporting children and adults with complex communication needs.* Brookes.

Bornman, J. (2016). AAC as a human rights vehicle: Implications for individuals with severe communication disabilities. *Augmentative and Alternative Communication, 32*(4), 235–238. doi:10.1080/07434618.2016.1252947

Bornman, J., Bryen, D. N., Moolman, E., & Morris, J. (2016). Use of consumer wireless devices by South Africans with severe communication disability. *African Journal of Disability, 5*(1), 202. https://doi.org/10.4102/ajod.v5i1.202

Calculator, S. N., & Black, T. (2009). Validation of an inventory of best practices in the provision of augmentative and alternative communication services to students with severe disabilities in general education classrooms. *American Journal of Speech-Language Pathology, 18*(4), 329–343.

Casey, M. (2010). *The bridge to literacy. A literacy approach for all students including those who use augmentative and alternative communication.* https://dl.acm.org/doi/pdf/10.5555/1926058.1926065?download

Dada, S., Horn, T., Samuels, A., & Schlosser, R. W. (2016). Children's attitudes toward interaction with an unfamiliar peer with complex communication needs: Comparing high and low-technology devices. *Augmentative and Alternative Communication, 32*(4), 305–311. doi:10.1080/07434618.2016.1216597

Dada, S., Kathard, H., Tönsing, K., & Harty, M. (2017). Severe communication disabilities in South Africa: Challenges and enablers. In S. Halder & L. C. Assaf (Eds.), *Inclusion, disability and culture: An ethnographic perspective traversing abilities and challenges* (pp. 169–193). Springer.

Dada, S., Murphy, Y., & Tönsing, K. (2017). Augmentative and alternative communication practices: A descriptive study of the perceptions of South African speech-language therapists. *Augmentative and Alternative Communication, 33*(4), 189–200. https://doi.org/10.1080/07434618.2017.1375979

De Bortoli, T., Arthur-Kelly, M., Foreman, P., Balandin, S., & Mathisen, B. (2011). Complex contextual influences on the communicative interactions of students with multiple and severe disabilities. *International Journal of Speech-Language Pathology, 13*(5), 422–435. doi:10.3109/17549507.2011.550691

Department of Basic Education. (2014). *Policy on screening, identification, assessment and support*. Department of Basic Education. https://wcedonline.westerncape.gov.za/Specialised-ed/documents/SIAS-2014.pdf

Department of Education. (1995). White paper on education and training in a democratic South Africa: First steps to developing a new system. *Government Gazette, 357*(16312). Government Printer.

Department of Education. (2001). *White paper 6: Special needs education – Building an inclusive education and training system*. Department of Education. http://www.education.gov.za/LinkClick.aspx?fileticket=gVFccZLi%2FtI%3D&tabid=1 91&mid=484

Department of Education. (2007). *Guidelines to ensure quality education and support in special schools and special school resource centres*. Department of Education.

Department of Education. (2010). *Guidelines for full-service/inclusive schools*. Department of Education.

Department of Education. (2015). *Report on the implementation of education White paper 6 on inclusive education*. Department of Education.

Department of Justice. (2006). *Constitution of the Republic of South Africa Bill*. Constitution Assembly.

Donohue, D., & Bornman, J. (2014). The challenges of realising inclusive education in South Africa. *South African Journal of Education, 34*(2), 1–14.

Hamm, B., & Mirenda, P. (2006). Post-school quality of life for individuals with developmental disabilities who use AAC. *Augmentative and Alternative Communication, 22*(2), 134–147. doi:10.1080/07434610500395493

Handleman, J., & Harris, S. (2001). *Preschool education programs for children with autism*. Pro-Ed Inc.

Human Rights Watch Report. (2015). *"Complicit in exclusion". South Africa's failure to guarantee an inclusive education for children with disabilities*. https://www.hrw.org/sites/default/files/report_pdf/southafrica0815_4up.pdf

Landbrook, M. W. (2009). *Challenges experienced by educators in the implementation of inclusive education in primary schools in South Africa* (Unpublished master's thesis). University of South Africa.

Light, L., & McNaughton, D. (2014). Communicative competence for individuals who require augmentative and alternative communication: A new definition for a new era of communication? *Augmentative and Alternative Communication, 30*(1), 1–18. doi:10.3109/07434618.2014.885080

Light, J., & McNaughton, D. (2015). Designing AAC research and intervention to improve outcomes for individuals with complex communication needs. *Augmentative and Alternative Communication, 31*(2), 85–96. doi:10.3109/07434618.2015.1036458

Light, J., McNaughton, D., Beukelman, D., Koch Fager, S., Fried-Oken, M., Jakobs, T., & Jakobs, E. (2019). Challenges and opportunities in augmentative and alternative communication: Research and technology development to enhance communication and participation for individuals with complex communication needs. *Augmentative and Alternative Communication, 35*(1), 1–12. doi:10.1080/07434618.2018.1556732

Manga, T., & Masuku, K. P. (2020). Challenges of teaching the Deaf-blind learner in an education setting in Johannesburg: Experiences of educators and educator assistants. *South African Journal of Communication Disorders, 67*(1), A649.

Marrus, N., & Hall, L. (2017). Intellectual disability and language disorder. *Child and Adolescent Psychiatric Clinics of North America, 26*(3), 539–554. https://doi.org/10.1016/j.chc.2017.03.001

McNaughton, D., & Light, J. (2013). The iPad and mobile technology revolution: Benefits and challenges for individuals who require augmentative and alternative communication. *Augmentative Alternative Communication, 29*(2), 107–116. doi:10.3109/07434618.2013.784930

McSheehan, M., Sonnenmeier, R., Jorgensen, C., & Turner, K. (2006). Beyond communication access: Promoting learning of the general education curriculum by students with significant disabilities. *Topics in Language Disorders, 26*(3), 266–290.

Mophosho, M., & Dada, S. (2015). The role of the speech-language therapist in the implementing of AAC in schools. In S. Moonsamy & H. Kathard (Eds.), *Speech-language therapy in a school context: Principles and practices* (pp. 197–214). Van Schaik Publishers.

Mukhopadhyay, S., & Nwaogu, P. (2009). Barriers to teaching non-speaking learners with intellectual disabilities and their impact on the provision of augmentative and alternative communication. *International Journal of Disability, Development and Education, 56*(4), 349–362. doi:10.1080/10349120903306590

Musselwhite, C. R., & St Louis, K. W. (1988). *Communication programming for persons with severe handicaps: Vocals and augmentative strategies.* Little Brown Company.

Naraian, S. (2010). Disentangling the social threads within a communicative environment: A cacophonous tale of Alternative and Augmentative Communication (AAC).

European Journal of Special Needs Education, 25(3), 253–267. doi:10.1080/08856257.2010.492936

Nicolson, G. (2015, February 2). South Africa: Where 12 million live in extreme poverty. *Daily Maverick*. https://www.dailymaverick.co.za/article/2015-02-03-southafrica-where-12-milli

Østvik, J., Balandin, S., & Ytterhusa, B. (2018). Interactional facilitators and barriers in social relationships between students who use AAC and fellow students. *Society, Health and Vulnerability, 9*(1), 1–14. https://doi.org/10.1080/20021518.2018.1438692

Parette, H. P., Huer, M. B., & Brotherson, M. J. (2001). Related service personnel perceptions of team AAC decision-making across cultures. *Education and Training in Mental Retardation and Developmental Disabilities, 36*(1), 69–82.

Statistics South Africa. (2014). *Stats SA profiles persons with disabilities.* https://www.statssa.gov.za/

Tomaševski, K. (2001). *Human rights obligations: Making education available, accessible, acceptable and adaptable* (Right to education primers No. 3). http://www.right-to-education.org/sites/right-to-education.org/files/resource-attachments/Tomasevski_Primer3.pdf

Senner, J. E., & Baud, M. R. (2015, October). *Chat with me: Pragmatic skill intervention in augmentative and alternative communication.* Paper presented at Closing the Gap.

Soto, G., & Yu, B. (2014). Considerations for the provision of services to bilingual children who use augmentative and alternative communication. *Augmentative and Alternative Communication, 30*(1), 83–92. doi:10.3109/07434618.2013.878751

Thistle, J. J., & Wilkinson, K. M. (2015). Building evidence-based practice in AAC display design for young children: Current practices and future directions. *Augmentative and Alternative Communication, 31*(2), 124–136. doi:10.3109/07434618.2015.1035798

Tönsing, K. M., & Dada, S. (2016). Teachers' perceptions of implementation of aided AAC to support expressive communication in South African special schools: A pilot investigation. *Augmentative and Alternative Communication* (Early online), *32*(4), 1–23. doi.org/10.1080/07434618.2016.1246609

United Nations. (2016). *Convention on the rights of persons with disabilities.* Committee on the Rights of Persons with Disabilities General Comment. https://www.refworld.org/pdfid/57c977e34.pdf

United Nations. (2006). *Convention on the rights of persons with disabilities.* https://www.un.org/development/desa/disabilities/convention-on-the-rights-of-persons-with-disabilities.html

United Nations Educational, Scientific and Cultural Organisation. (2013). *Opening new avenues for empowerment ICTs to access information and knowledge for persons with disabilities.* UNESCO Global Report. http://www.un.org/esa/socdev/enable/rights/convtexte.htmlUNESCO

Van Niekerk, K., Dada, S., & Tönsing, K. (2019). Influences on selection of assistive technology for young children in South Africa: Perspectives from rehabilitation professionals. *Disability Rehabilitation, 41*(8), 912-925. doi:10.1080/09638288.2017.1416500

Van Niekerk, K., & Tönsing, K. (2015). Eye gaze technology: A South African perspective. *Disability and Rehabilitation: Assistive Technology, 10*(4), 340–346. doi:10.3109/17483107.2014.974222

World Health Organization. (2014). *International classification of functioning, disability and health.* WHO. https://www.who.int/classifications/icf/en/

World Health Organization. (2017). *Assistive devices and technologies.* http://www.who.int/disabilities/technology/en/

Waddell, C. D. (2008, June). *Meeting information and communications technology access and service needs for persons with disabilities: Major issues for development and implementation of successful policies and strategies.* International Telecommunications Union. http://www.itu.int/ITU-D/study_groups/SGP_20062010/events/2007/Workshops/documents/18-waddell.pdf

Wilkinson, K., & Hennig, S. (2007). The state of research and practice in augmentative and alternative communication for children with developmental/intellectual disabilities. *Developmental Disabilities Research Review, 13*(1), 58–69. https://doi.org/10.1002/mrdd.20133

CHAPTER 12

Teleaudiology as Part of Efforts to Enhance Inclusivity and Equality through ICT in South African Schools: Some Considerations

Katijah Khoza-Shangase, Ben Sebothoma and Nomfundo Floweret Moroe

Abstract

Access to education has been a significant focus of the South African government, and online access has become urgent with the COVID-19 pandemic. Evidence of this is seen in initiatives such as the ECD programmes that the national government has adopted, as well as the recent migration to online and televised teaching and learning. Access, however, without similar emphasis on success is problematic and renders such access an unproductive and fruitless expenditure for all stakeholders involved, particularly for learners with barriers to learning. Efforts to facilitate success include access to therapeutic services that remediate barriers to learning, such as hearing impairment, language impairments, and auditory processing disorders that have an impact on learning. The use of teleaudiology is an important consideration for the South African schooling context. This chapter identifies audiology related barriers to teaching and learning and provides ways in which teleaudiology can be used in schools to facilitate empowerment, inclusivity, and equality, bearing in mind the goal of inclusive education within the South African context. What is covered has become even more relevant in the era of infectious conditions such as the novel coronavirus that calls for e-engagement and tele-interventions as a health and safety measure as well.

Keywords

equality – inclusivity – information and communication technologies – tele-audiology

1 Introduction

The DBE (2015) acknowledged challenges in the basic education sector that serve as barriers to the ability to provide quality education within the South African

© KONINKLIJKE BRILL NV, LEIDEN, 2021 | DOI: 10.1163/9789004447226_013

context. These barriers covered a range of challenges including inadequate quality, efficiency, and accountability nationally; lack of the use of existing interprovincial and inter-governmental structures to closely link policies, programmes and resources to affect quality improvement in the South African basic education system; insufficient curriculum coverage and delivery; poor retention; poor assessments; inadequate retrieval and usage of available learner and teacher support resources; over and above inadequate school infrastructure (DBE, 2015). Post-1994, the African National Congress led South African government spearheaded sweeping changes in government policies with the equitable and fair provision of services to all South Africans as a goal (South African History Online, n.d.).

This radical overhaul in policies included those in social development as well as educational service provision for learners with disabilities and/or special needs; with the development of an inclusive education system, consistent with the Constitution of the Republic of South Africa, Act No. 108 of 1996 (Republic of South Africa, 1996) being included (Dalton, Mckenzie, & Kahonde, 2012). Specifically, Section 29 (the Bill of Rights) states that everyone has the right to a basic education which the state, through reasonable measures, must make progressively available and accessible. This section also highlights that the state may not discriminate directly or indirectly against anyone on one or more grounds, including disability. A hearing impairment, leading to a communication disability, has a significant influence on both teaching and learning, hence the importance of ensuring that there are measures and strategies in place to manage such disabilities, helping eliminate discrimination. Forbidding discrimination on the basis of disability implies a call for embracing inclusive education, where the principle of inclusivity is a social model; as opposed to the special needs principle which is based on the medical model (Khoza-Shangase, 2021a). This model is not about learners with disabilities, but instead it is about the needs of all learners.

For the Department of Basic Education to abide by the Constitution of the Republic in as far as learners with special needs are concerned, access to therapeutic services for learners with disabilities need to form part of its Action Plans. This access is significantly challenged by South African contextual realities, including demand versus capacity challenges around healthcare professionals whose scope of practice is that of providing therapeutic interventions to children with disabilities; hence the importance of exploring alternative service provision models such as tele-health; specifically, teleaudiology for learners with hearing impairment. The current authors believe that adoption of such service provision models, that are information and communication technology (ICT) driven, would allow for learners with special needs to access intervention services wherever they are enrolled, thus facilitating inclusive education, which is the goal of the South African government.

2   Background

Numerous benefits exist to justify the investment and human value of inclusive education. Donohue and Bornman (2014) provide three key benefits, which the current authors also support as motivation enough for the use of ICT to facilitate and empower inclusivity and equality in schools. All relevant stakeholders—the learners, the teachers, and the parents—are comprehensively considered in these benefits: (1) for the learners: inclusive education nurtures a celebration of diversity amongst learners, where children gain a greater acceptance of themselves because of their exposure to peers from different backgrounds or those who are differently abled; (2) for the teachers: inclusive education inspires and demands continued professional development where the teachers acquire a larger, flexible, and varied skill-set of teaching methods that are able to cope with the diverse learning needs that the children present with; and (3) for the parents: inclusive education offers inspiration for their children with disabilities, where they see their children being provided with a chance to demonstrate their capabilities without being disadvantaged. Khoza-Shangase (2021a) offers a fourth benefit of inclusive education, that to the country as a whole. She argues that in line with the South African constitution "which does not tolerate diversity as a necessary evil; but affirms it as one of the primary treasures of our nation" (Judge Langa—Constitutional Court decision in MEC for Education: KwaZulu-Natal v Pillay), inclusive education ensures that diversity is seen as a contextual strength which provides South Africa with unique opportunities for development, innovation, and growth in all spheres of life (Khoza-Shangase & Mophosho, 2018).

Khoza-Shangase (2021a) makes mention of several policies, guidelines, and acts that guide inclusive education within the South African context, over and above the Constitution of the Republic of South-Africa No. 108 of 1996 (Bill of Rights, Chapter 2). Under policies, the Convention on the Rights of Persons with Disabilities (United Nations May 2008); the National Education Policy Act, 1996; the South African Schools Act, no. 84 of 1996; the White Paper 6: Special Education—Building an Inclusive Education and Training System, Department of Education (2001); and the Revised SIAS Policy (2014) are raised as important. Under guidelines, Guidelines for Inclusive Teaching and Learning (2010); Guidelines for responding to learner diversity in the classroom through curriculum and Assessment Policy statements (2012); Guidelines for

Full-Service/Inclusive Schools; Guidelines to ensure quality education and support in Special Schools and Special School Resource Centres; Integrated School Health Policy (ISHP); Care and Support for Teaching and Learning (CSTL) are highlighted as pertinent in inclusive education.

Lastly, under acts, the Children's Act No 38 of 2005, and Children's Amendment Act No. 41 of 2007 are included. As far as audiology and hearing impairment as a barrier to learning is concerned, Khoza-Shangase (2021a) highlights the 2018 Speech-Language and Hearing Professions Professional Board of the Health Professions' Council of South Africa's (HPCSA) Minimum Standards for the Hearing Screening in Schools Guidelines whose goal is to regulate hearing screening in schools to ensure that it occurs in a timely manner to detect, identify, and refer school age children for management of hearing impairment and ear pathology (HPCSA, 2018). All these documents have a goal of addressing the diverse needs of all learners who experience barriers to learning. The reader is encouraged to source these documents directly for further information.

According to the White Paper 6: Special Education—Building an Inclusive Education and Training System (2001), in order to make inclusive education a reality, a deliberate conceptual shift regarding the provision of support for learners who experience barriers to learning is required. In this context, barriers to learning are described as obstacles that inhibit access to learning and development. These difficulties can emanate from within the education system as a whole, and from the learning site and/or within the learner him/herself (Department of Basic Education, 2014). Barriers might, in one way or another, prevent the learner from giving a true account of his/her knowledge and skills when assessed and might require adaptive methods of assessment (Department of Education Republic of South Africa Directorate: Inclusive Education Curriculum, 2005; Assessment Guidelines for Inclusion, May 2002).

Such barriers can occur in isolation or in combination where they co-occur with each other and include, for example, internal learner barriers such as neurological, physiological, and genetic challenges; school barriers which are systemic challenges; and environmental barriers such as socio-economic difficulties. Specific to the internal learner barriers, neurological conditions such as ADHD, epilepsy, tics, Tourette's syndrome, autism, obsessive compulsive disorder, depression and anxiety disorders, and specific learning disorders have been documented as barriers to learning.

Deafness/hard of hearing, blindness/low vision, physical disability, multiple disability, and developmental delays have been listed as some of the physiological barriers to learning, with Down syndrome as a genetic barrier. Additionally, there are behavioural barriers to learning which include conduct disorders, anti-social behaviour, psychopathy, and emotional problems. Lastly, low cognition due to various causes including foetal alcohol syndrome and brain injuries also contribute towards barriers to learning in children.

To drive the implementation of inclusive education policies, the South African DBE (2008, 2011) adopted a strategy detailed in two sets of guidelines: The National Strategy on Screening, Identification, Assessment and Support (SIAS) (Department of Education, 2008) and the Guidelines for Responding to Learner Diversity in the Classroom through Curriculum and Assessment Policy Statements (Department of Education, 2011). While the SIAS guides inclusive education policy by defining the process of identification, assessment, and enrolment of learners in special schools, and curbs the unnecessary placement of learners in special schools, the Guidelines for Responding to Learner Diversity in the Classroom through Curriculum and Assessment Policy Statements provide practical guidance to school managers and teachers on planning and teaching to meet the needs of a diverse range of learners.

Furthermore, the SIAS provides guidelines on early identification and support, the determination of nature and level of support required by learners, as well as the identification of the best learning sites for support, while providing guidelines on the central role of parents and teachers in implementing the intervention strategy. Regardless of these policies and guidelines, the implementation of inclusive education in South Africa is slow and incomplete (Wildeman & Nomdo, 2007). The reasons for this slow and incomplete implementation of inclusive education within the South African context are numerous and relate to problems that affect the education system as a whole, the role of special schools, and other support structures and conditions of poverty, amongst others (Stofile & Green, 2006). Khoza-Shangase (2021a) also argues that failure to implement early identification and intervention of and for disabilities, such as hearing impairment through Universal New-born Hearing Screening, worsens the situation for the hearing-impaired learners.

Of the numerous challenges that have been reported in the basic education sector in South Africa, inadequacies in education of children with special needs are well documented. In their review of challenges of realizing inclusive education in South Africa, Donohue and Bornman (2014) argue that up to 70% of children of school-going age with disabilities in South Africa are not in school at any given point in time. This is in spite of the country's white paper that was designed to transform the South African educational system by building an integrated system for all learners utilizing a flexible and suitable curriculum that takes into consideration the diversity of the needs and abilities of learners; developing district-based support teams to provide systemic support for any and all teachers who need it; and strengthening the skills of teachers to cope with more diverse classes (Muthukrishna & Schoeman, 2000).

One of the key innovations involving ICT that could be of significant benefit in overcoming barriers to teaching and learning in an inclusive education context, is the use of telehealth for children requiring such services. With the recent novel COVID-19 (coronavirus) pandemic, where direct contact poses a health and safety risk for learners, especially those with disabilities, the use of telehealth alongside online learning and broadcast (TV and radio) support resources becomes unavoidable.

In low and middle-income countries such as South Africa, many people continue to experience barriers to health care services. While there are multiple factors contributing to these barriers (Khoza-Shangase & Mophosho, 2018), the establishment of teleaudiology was inspired by the extreme shortages of audiologists, speech-language pathologists, and ear, nose and throat specialists (Fagan & Jacobs, 2009; Mulwafu, Ensink, Kuper, & Fagan, 2017). The health professionals that are available in health centres are often located in big cities and private practices, where many people cannot access their services and the situation is even worse in the education sector where limited posts are available and are only in "special schools" such as Schools for the Deaf. Therefore, teleaudiology is becoming an alternative model of service delivery which intends to reach those that cannot travel long distances to these health centres; within the education sector, the current authors believe that teleaudiology can be explored as one of the strategies to improve access and success of children with hearing impairment within an inclusive education system through a hybrid model that engages the use of task-shifting where para-professionals are trained to perform some audiology tasks in the absence of the audiologist, though under the supervision of a qualified audiologist.

3   Teleaudiology Defined

Teleaudiology is a subset of telehealth. The current authors believe that the use of telehealth within the education system is congruent with the country's goals of embracing the 4th industrial revolution, as well as with the country's push towards e-learning which commenced in 2013 when the Deputy Minister of Basic Education, Enver Surty, officially launched an e-learning project at the Sunward Park High School in Boksburg. It became the first public school to transform learning into a fully digital platform, with the establishment of e-libraries to schools nationally as well as provision of connectivity in teacher resource centres through South Africa's Universal Service and Access Obligation (USAO) (South African Government News Agency, 2013).

In the 2019 State of the Nation Address, the President of the Republic (South African Government, 2019) pronounced that government will digitise the public education system over the next six years, where the department of basic education will provide pupils with digital textbooks and tablet devices. He stated that 90% of textbooks in high-enrolment subjects across all grades and all workbooks have already been digitised. "In line with our 'Framework for Skills for a Changing World', we are expanding the training of both educators and learners to respond to emerging technologies including the internet of things, robotics, and artificial intelligence" (South African Government, 2019). This is therefore an opportune time to explore the use of telehealth to assist in overcoming barriers to learning. In the context of this chapter, because the authors have a background in audiology, the main focus will be on tele-audiology.

Teleaudiology is a subset of telehealth that was established primarily to deliver audiological care in areas with limited access to health care due to a shortage of resources, such as remote rural areas. Krupinski (2015) described telehealth (i.e. teleaudiology) as the use of telecommunication technologies to reach out to patients, reduce barriers to optimal care in underserved areas, improve user satisfaction and accessibility to specialists, decrease professional isolation in rural areas, help medical practitioners expand their practice reach, and save patients from having to travel or be transported to receive high quality care. An obvious advantage of teleaudiology is that it may help overcome common barriers to getting hearing aids, such as cost and distance from service providers (Schweitzer, Mortz, & Vaughan, 1999).

4 Teleaudiology Possibilities

Swanepoel and colleagues (2010) provide a table (p. 199) that depicts the scope of application of possibilities for teleaudiology. This table delineates fields of application of telehealth in audiology, which include education and training, screening, diagnosis, and intervention. These authors then define the scope of telehealth applications and break these down under synchronous and asynchronous applications, with specific audiology functions and measures under each field of application. The current authors believe that information contained in this table can easily be adapted for telehealth in other disciplines as well within the Department of Basic Education, over and above just audiology. Each sector, for example, the education sector, would need to carefully select items in the table which are applicable to that sector as some items are applicable to teleaudiology within the healthcare sector only.

Teleaudiology within the education sector can use computer-based technology and internet connectivity to reach children with barriers to learning in various communities. This can be done in a variety of ways; which are described as either synchronous or asynchronous methods or a combination of both (hybrid method). Synchronous teleaudiology requires the service provider (audiologist) to be present, though in a different location to the learner, during the session e.g. video-conferencing, remote programming of hearing aids, etc. Hughes, Sevier, and Choi (2018) found that this method is useful for programming of hearing technologies such as cochlear implants. While synchronous teleaudiology has been found to be useful, it is anticipated that its implementation may not be feasible as yet within the South African context because of the limited number of audiologists for the population requiring audiological services.

Capacity versus demand issues, where lack of audiologists in comparison to the number of patients requiring audiology services, as well as challenges around network connectivity exist. In the first quarter of 2020, COVID-19 demands for online connectivity, where the population was under lockdown and all citizens needed to connect online for work or education, sharply revealed the connectivity challenges that South Africa faces. Steuerward, Windmill, Scott, Evans, and Kramer (2018) emphasise that synchronous telehealth technique requires the audiologist to be present during remote testing, and also requires computer network connectivity.

On the other hand, the asynchronous (save and forward) telehealth method can be used in the absence of the audiologist; where para-professionals, who form part of the task-shifting model of service delivery, can be trained to conduct certain audiological tests, save the results, and forward them to the audiologists at a later stage for analysis and management. This is one of the reasons why teleaudiology would be ideal for the South African basic education set-up where services of audiologists are not easily available. Studies have demonstrated the accuracy of asynchronous teleaudiology when compared to standard traditional face-to-face diagnosis made by qualified professionals (Biagio, Adeyemo, Hall, & Vinck, 2013; Biagio, Swanepoel, Laurent, & Lundberg, 2014).

Khoza-Shangase (2021a) recommends a combined use of synchronous and asynchronous teleaudiology (hybrid method) within the South African education sector. This is particularly important within this context when one considers the known challenges around network connectivity, particularly in rural and peri-urban areas, as well as the documented shortages of audiologists who may not be available for synchronous testing. Swanepoel et al. (2010) believe that asynchronous methods are more feasible for the South African context, especially in school settings. Furthermore, to use the combination of synchronous and asynchronous teleaudiology, there is a need to use para-professionals to mitigate against the notable shortage of audiologists in South Africa (Fagan & Jacobs, 2009).

Para-professionals can be used to increase access to quality hearing care. However, in order to achieve this, para-professionals need to be fully trained and empowered in order to effectively and ethically complete tele-audiological services. This training can form part of professional training programmes where a module on empowering students and ensuring inclusiveness and equality through ICT can be included. Biagio and colleagues (2013) trained para-professionals to conduct video otoscopy which can be analysed at a later stage. Findings of their study indicated that para-professionals can successfully capture acceptable video otoscopic images which could be analysed by the audiologist and/or ENT specialists to diagnose middle ear pathologies. Van Wyk, Mahomed-Asmail, and Swanepoel (2019) also trained 15 community care workers (CCW) to conduct hearing screening using the hearTestTM Smartphone application. Findings indicated that CCW can be trained to screen for hearing loss and reduce referral rates. In both studies, none of the para-professionals had any formal healthcare or other tertiary training. Given that South Africa has a high unemployment rate (Statistics South Africa, 2019), it is hopeful that individuals who are not currently employed may contribute to the provision of health care in the educational sector within a tele-health task-shifting model of service delivery for learners with barriers to learning.

Training for para-professionals is key in making sure that the use of teleaudiology succeeds within the educational setting. Therefore, careful planning of the program is crucial. A qualified audiologist must be responsible for planning and implementing this training program. Although the training can take place at the convenience of the para-professionals, the authors suggest that training environments must be conducive for learning. Based on research (Biagio et al., 2013; Van Wyk et al., 2019) training programmes for teleaudiology should include the following:
- Taking brief, but pertinent, ear and hearing related information (barrier to learning history).
- Positioning.
- How to administer and/or use equipment such as video otoscopy and screening equipment such as optoacoustic emissions.
- Communication skills.
- Record keeping.

At the moment, there are no guidelines on the training of para-professionals within the South African context, however, authors such as Mudzingwa (2015) and Lewin et al. (2010) have outlined basic training for community health care workers, who are described as para-professionals as they are defined as lay health workers who have received a limited amount of training on health care promotion and the provision of health care services to communities in which they reside (Lewin et al., 2010), while para-professionals are defined as trained volunteers to facilitate the telemedicine setup at the remote location. Therefore, in terms of qualifications, Lehmann and Sander (2001) and Glenton et al. (2013) report that para-professionals possess little or no secondary school education and do not have a tertiary education; however, they do undergo a much shorter duration and limited curriculum training relative to professionals.

In Africa, Lehmann (2004) states that para-professional training is generally provided by non-governmental organisations (NGOs) and the Department of Health. This training varies across programmes; for instance some para-professionals may receive training that is restricted to prevention and health care promotion roles. Others may receive training that prepares them to play a curative role. In most cases, the training for para-professionals is generally approved by the country's health department and the certification authority, but it is not considered to be a degreed tertiary certificate (Mudzingwa, 2015).

These para-professionals can therefore be valuable in the provision of services to learners with barriers to learning through the various teleaudiology methods described, with supervision by audiologists, not only from South Africa but also from the world, with adherence to the country's regulations aimed at protecting the public.

Despite the different methods of teleaudiology, the ICT innovation offers promise for early detection and identification of signs and symptoms of hearing impairments and ear pathology, auditory processing difficulties, as well as language impairments which might be barriers to learning for children; this promise extends to early and/or more regular interventions from professionals who are not stationed at schools. Swanepoel and Hall (2010) found that teleaudiology is used in a wide range of audiological assessments such as pure tone audiometry, otoacoustic emissions (OAE), and automated auditory brainstem response. These measures are used to assess hearing loss, outer hair cell function, and auditory nerve functioning respectively (Martin & Clarke, 2019). These are important measures in diagnosing hearing impairment in children; which, if missed, has serious consequences for the developing child, including learning.

5 Teleaudiology Relevance

The prevalence of disabling hearing loss is rising globally, with the authors believing this to be under estimated, particularly from the developing world context. In 2018, the World Health Organization (WHO) reported that there has been a 30% increase of disabling hearing loss between 2012 and 2018 (WHO, 2018). While disabling hearing loss in children is reported to be much lower than that in adults (World Health Organization, 2012), this number increases significantly when mild hearing loss and middle ear disorders, which may have the most significant impact on children's development, are included. South Africa reports a high prevalence of middle ear disorders in children (Biagio et al., 2014; Ramma & Sebothoma, 2016) and this highlights the importance of ensuring early identification and early intervention of these disorders in order to retard the progression to a more permanent and more severe hearing impairment. If middle ear disorders are not detected and treated early, they may cause hearing loss. As a result, there has been a concerted effort aimed at identifying early signs of hearing loss and middle ear pathologies in children in order to reduce or prevent their long term impacts. The National Institute on Deafness and Other Communication Disorders (2016) reported that 5 out of 6 children in the United States of America (USA) experience ear infections by the time they are 3 years. The current authors believe that strategies to prevent development of barriers to learning right from the ECD centres are crucial.

The impact of hearing loss has been documented to be far reaching. Studies have documented that children with hearing loss may have delayed speech and language development, delayed and/or impaired literacy development, psycho-emotional problems, cognitive developmental problems—all of which lead to vocational challenges later in life, thus impacting the quality of life of the affected family and individual. In the classroom, some studies have found that children with hearing loss easily become fatigued when compared to their hearing peers, and therefore are unable to concentrate in a classroom (Gustafston, Key, Horns, & Bess, 2018; Hornsby, Gustafson, Lancaster, Cho, & Camarata, 2017). Similarly, patterns of delayed development are also observed in children with recurrent and persistent middle ear disorders (Da Costa et al., 2018).

School-based hearing screening continues to be an important first step in identifying auditory pathologies in school aged children. The department of basic education and health in South Africa, through its integrated School Health Policy (ISHP), has recognised the need to implement screening programmes with the aim to identify potential barriers to learning (Integrated School Health Policy, 2012). School-based hearing screening forms an important part of this initiative and has been regulated by the HPCSA as well (HPCSA, 2018). However, school-based hearing screening programmes across the country have not been successful due to scarcity of resources and limited audiologists to conduct the screening (Fagan & Jacobs, 2009; Khoza-Shangase, 2021b); hence, the importance of exploring the use of teleaudiology in this context.

The potential applications and possible impact of teleaudiology within the South African education sector are significant. Khoza-Shangase (2021a) argues that the SA basic education sector may incorporate teleaudiology to increase access to services not only to South African audiologists, but also volunteer audiologists from across the world; thus, overcoming the capacity versus demand challenge existing within the South African context. Swanepoel et al. (2010) recommend exploring the use of the Teleaudiology Network,[1] a non-governmental/nonprofit organisation which developed this concept as a way to provide services to remote areas in developing countries where audiological services are unavailable.

6 Teleaudiology Challenges with Implementation and Solutions

Sufficient evidence exists that shows the various possibilities that telehealth has in enhancing patient care across many health care disciplines, including speech-pathology, audiology, medicine, physiotherapy, nursing, etc. (Swanepoel, Olusanya, & Mars, 2010; Dansky, Joseph, & Bowles, 2008; Jin, Ishikawa, Sengoku, & Ohyanagi, 2000; Tousignant, Moffet, Cabana, & Simard, 2011). The COVID-19 pandemic has further demonstrated the need and value of this approach to healthcare service delivery, with the HPCSA acknowledging and regulating its use. Despite this established clear value, telehealth presents with several challenges that need deliberating on and resolving.

In response to the coronavirus outbreak and its effects on closures of schools and universities, in 2020, UNESCO was quoted in the news as having highlighted a "startling digital divide" between the rich and the poor, with 43% of young people not having any access to internet. UNESCO further reports that these disparities are particularly acute in low income countries where 89% of learners do not have access to household computers and 82% lack internet access (fin24, 2020). Data specific to young people with disabilities who do not have access to both internet and household computers is not available; however, it can be assumed that their realities would be similar to or worse than the general household evidence. This has serious implications for all efforts around teleaudiology in schools if all stakeholders, including parents, are to be involved in intervention programmes as required.

As far as the use of health technology, as in the case of teleaudiology, is concerned, legal and policy landscape analysis evidence indicates that South Africa has no specific provision in the National Health Act on health technology assessment (HTA), with HTA being hardly and somewhat defined (South African Health Review HST, 2017). This is in the context of minimal telehealth capacity building that needs to be developed. Govender and Mars (2018) report on the paucity of published evidence on training and education of students in using and implementing telehealth services. If this gap exists at training level, implementation will experience significant challenges, hence the need for the South African government to utilise the opportunities provided by COVID-19 to ramp up all efforts to ensure curriculum enhancement on this aspect. Within the African context, where a significant need for telehealth has been demonstrated, evidence from a systematic review conducted by Edirippulige, Armfield, and Smith (2013) shows a lack of any record of education and training programmes on telehealth. This is despite the fact that telemedicine was recognised by the SA government in 1999, when the first phase of the SA National Telemedicine System was implemented (Mars, 2014), as important, although not successfully sustained.

South African healthcare acts, regulations, and policies are increasingly recognising the value of ICT in health, particularly in the context of 4th industrial revolution and COVID-19, and support the use of telehealth applications and technology within the healthcare service delivery model (Govender & Mars, 2018; HPCSA, 2020). This has led to the development of the National eHealth Strategy. In the South African National Department of Health's ten priorities (the 10-point plan) within the national service delivery agreement, ICT and sophisticated technology to advance patient care forms one of the priorities under health infrastructure improvement (Department of Health, 2012). All these efforts from the health ministry can be extended to the education sector so that there is overall benefit for inclusive education of learners diagnosed in the health sector when they join the education sector; thus, ensuring continuity of care which is currently significantly lacking.

Khoza-Shangase (2021a) states that the reality of limited educational opportunities in telehealth suggests that government must aim to promote capacity development in telehealth through education and research. Universities have been identified as key stakeholders to facilitate this capacity development process. Khoza-Shangase (2021a) argues for the introduction of telehealth into the education and training programmes of healthcare professionals, at both undergraduate and postgraduate levels, so that they are aware of, and can use, telehealth methods to provide healthcare to their patients. This will have direct benefits for the education sector as similar strategies can be applied there by professionals who are competently trained in the methodology (Rena, 2000; Rice, 2003) with sufficient research experience in the field (Edirippulige et al., 2013; Shulman, 1986). Related to this is the development of education and training courses that are well structured and prescribe minimum standards to provide the theoretical and practical competencies required for administering clinical and educational services via a telehealth model. This will ensure that where teleaudiology is implemented, it is done efficaciously and ethically, with a contextually relevant and contextually responsive evidence base. The current authors highlight this as a caution in the deliberations around implementing telehealth (audiology) in the basic education sector.

As part of preventive audiology, certain uses of teleaudiology have gained much needed momentum, these include identification of middle ear pathology and hearing loss as well as auditory processing problems through asynchronous teleaudiology (Olusanya, Okolo, & Adeosun, 2004; Swanepoel, Myburgh, Howe, Mahomed, & Eikelboom, 2014; Potgieter, Swanepoel, & Smits, 2018), with intervention through teleaudiology also showing increasing attention. In the South African context, recently, there has been a call to increase access to audiological services through hearing conservation programmes, an area that presents similar challenges to the education sector (Khoza-Shangase & Moroe, 2020). There has also been an increasing interest in the use of video otoscopy via asynchronous (save and forward) technique to assess and monitor middle ear disorders. Through this technique, para-professionals capture video clips or images of the external ear to the level of the tympanic membrane and send them to ear, nose, and throat specialists and/audiologists for further analysis. This technique has been shown to yield accurate diagnosis of outer and middle ear pathologies and facilitate early identification and intervention (Biagio et al., 2013; Sebothoma & Khoza-Shangase, 2018; Sebothoma, Khoza-Shangase, Mol, & Masege, 2021).

While identification of auditory pathologies such as hearing loss and middle ear disorders, and the implementation of appropriate management such as hearing aid fitting, forms an important part in the alleviation of barriers to success of learners, Khoza-Shangase (2021a) further argues that teleaudiology can also be used as a preventive and promotive tool, in line with re-engineered primary health care, to educate learners, teachers and parents/caregivers about ear and hearing care and about other barriers to learning such as auditory processing, language disorders, specific learning disorders, and so on. Noise induced hearing loss through exposure to hazardous noise levels of music, voice pathologies because of unhealthy vocal hygiene, as examples, are some of the self-induced and preventable health challenges that can benefit from such use of telehealth. As important as the preventive aspect of the audiologists and speech therapists is in their scope of practice, in the form of education and awareness, the demand versus capacity challenges of these professionals within the South African context prevents them from investing in anything other than secondary and tertiary level care. This is where telepractice, in conjunction with task-shifting, will bridge this gap in service delivery within the education sector.

As can be concluded from the review thus far, a number of challenges are anticipated in the implementation of teleaudiology within the South African education system. Over and above the key network connectivity issue and access to computers and ICT devices, challenges include computer competence and literacy of potential users (Carter, Horrigan, & Hudyma, 2010; Lamb & Shea, 2006; Picot, 2000), use of tele-practice within the prescribed ethical and legal prescripts (Grogan-Johnson, Meehan, McCormick, & Miller, 2015; Lamb & Shea, 2006; Picot, 2000), adherence to and understanding of the protocols and standards that guide good practice by the practitioners and para-practitioners (Grol & Grimshaw, 2003; HPCSA, 2020), adherence to the POPI Act around data management relating to online transmission, retrieval, and storage of data (Grogan-Johnson et al., 2015; POPI Act, 2013), as well as possible influences of linguistic and cultural diversity on its use (Khoza-Shangase & Mophosho, 2018; HPCSA, 2019).

Careful deliberations and planning around these challenges is key to successful implementation of telehealth to overcome barriers to education. Additionally, some concerns around the concept of teleaudiology include the ability of users to provide precise descriptions of issues they may have experienced in the "real world" such as overuse of care (e.g. unnecessary consultations), underuse of care (e.g. failure to referral for a necessary consultation), and poor technical or interpersonal performance (e.g. incorrect interpretation or inattention to hearing aid user concerns). However, data suggest that teleaudiology and conventional face-to-face audiology care around hearing aid services are comparable in terms of these concerns (Pross, Bourne, & Cheung, 2016).

7   Conclusion

Over 15 years following the unveiling of Education White Paper 6 (Department of Education, 2001), evidence suggests that most children with disabilities in South Africa remain excluded from receiving tuition in classrooms together with their typically developing peers. This lack of access, participation, and success within the basic education context in South Africa is regardless of inclusion of learners with disabilities into mainstream classrooms.

Evidence of barriers to achieving quality and inclusive education by learners with disabilities in South African schools exists. Such barriers include demand versus capacity challenges in the form of lack of resources, specifically rehabilitation professionals such as audiologists. This is illustrated by the significant mismatch between capacity and demand, especially within the basic education sector where not only audiologists' numbers are insufficient, but they do not match the demographic profile of the clients that they serve.

The current chapter deliberated on telehealth, in the form of teleaudiology and task-shifting, as one of the strategies to overcome access barriers in order to enhance success of inclusive education. It is believed that the use of telehealth will enhance educational outcomes leading to children with disabilities becoming productive and contributing members of society, showcasing their unique talents just like everyone else.

The impact of telehealth is increasingly evident in several areas of health care and its scope is continually broadening with advances in technology and internet connectivity and with the COVID-19 pandemic threatening to change human interactions; within South Africa, the already rolled out e-health through the recent HPCSA amended regulations around telehealth and e-education make this an opportune time to deliberate on inclusion of telehealth within South African schools. Teachers, therapists, audiologists, and parents need to find ways to plan and work collaboratively, for the greatest benefit to their learners; this includes embracing ICT in the form of telehealth as a way of bridging the existing gap.

Khoza-Shangase (2021a) argues that in the South African context, the application of teleaudiology within the South African education sector for learners with special needs is an exciting field with a broad scope of application possibilities including training/education, screening, diagnosis, and intervention. The fact that this service delivery model allows for services that are not bound by distance or location and can bridge the gap between patients isolated from the audiological services they require is a significant benefit. However, evidence proving contextual relevance and responsiveness of this service delivery model within the education sector, in conjunction with task-shifting, will need to be established. Such evidence gathering within the linguistically and culturally diverse South African context will ensure efficacy of the interventions provided. Furthermore, the Department of Basic Education's understanding and addressing of the diverse range of learning needs in South African classrooms needs sharper focus if positive learning and developmental outcomes are to be gained and exclusion of learners from the education system due to neglected learning barriers limited. This focus should include ensuring that ICT as a model of service delivery is included in professional training programmes to better prepare educators and all other relevant stakeholders in dealing with children with barriers to learning, thus empowering students and ensuring inclusiveness and equality in South African schools. The use of ICT innovations by the Department of Basic Education to increase access in order to facilitate success for learners with barriers to learning is a strategy worth exploring within the South African context.

Note

1 See www.teleaudiology.org

References

Biagio, L., Adeyemo, A., Hall, J. W., & Vinck, B. (2013). Asynchronous video-otoscopy with a telehealth facilitator. *Telemedicine and e-Health, 19*(4), 252–258.

Biagio, L., Swanepoel, D. W., Laurent, C., & Lundberg, T. (2014). Peadiatric otitis media at a primary healthcare clinic in South Africa. *South African Medical Journal, 104*(6), 431–435.

Carter, L., Horrigan, J., & Hudyma, S. (2010). Investigating the educational needs of nurses in telepractice: A descriptive exploratory study. *Canadian Journal of University Continuing Education, 36*(1), 1–20.

Da Costa, C., Eikelboom, R. H., Jacques, A., Swanepoel, D. W., Whitehouse, A. J. O., Jamieson, S. E., & Brennan-Jones, C. G. (2018). Does otitis media in early childhood affect later behavioural development? Results from the Western Australian Pregnancy Cohort (Raine) study. *Clinical Otolaryngology, 43*, 1036–1042. https://doi.org/10.1111/coa.13094

Dalton, E. M., Mckenzie, J. A., & Kahonde, C. (2012). The implementation of inclusive education in South Africa: Reflections arising from a workshop for teachers and therapists to introduce universal design for learning. *African Journal of Disability, 1*(1). http://dx.doi. org/10.4102/ajod.v1i1.13

Dansky, K. H., Joseph, V., & Bowles, K. (2008). Use of telehealth by older adults to manage heart failure. *Research in Gerontological Nursing, 1*(1), 25–32.

Department of Basic Education. (2014). *Screening, identification, assessment & support policy.* https://www.education.gov.za/Portals/0/Documents/Policies/SIAS%20Final%2019%20December%202014.pdf?ver=2015-02-24-131207-203

Department of Basic Education (DBE). (2015). *Action plan to 2019 towards the realisation of schooling 2030: Taking forward South Africa's national development plan 2030.* https://www.education.gov.za/Portals/0/Documents/Publications/Action%20Plan%202019.pdf

Department of Education. (2001). *Education White paper 6. Special needs education: Building an inclusive education and training system.* Government Printer.

Department of Education. (2008). *National strategy on screening, identification, assessment and support: School pack.* Government Printer.

Department of Education. (2011). *Guidelines for responding to learner diversity in the classroom through curriculum and assessment policy statements.* Government Printer.

Department of Health. (2012). *South Africa. eHealth strategy for SA (2012–2016).* Department of Health.

Donohue, D., & Bornman, J. (2014). The challenges of realising inclusive education in South Africa. *South African Journal of Education, 34*(2), 1–14.

Edirippulige, S., Armfield, N. R., & Smith, A. (2013). A qualitative study of the careers and professional practices of graduates from an e-health postgraduate programme. *Journal of Telemed and Telecare, 18*(8), 455–459.

Fagan, J. J., & Jacobs, M. (2009). Survey of ENT services in Africa: Need for a comprehensive intervention. *Global Health Action, 2*, 1–7.

Fin24. (2020). *Coronavirus | Half the world's locked-down pupils don't have a computer.* https://www.fin24.com/Economy/World/coronavirus-half-the-worlds-locked-down-pupils-dont-have-a-computer-20200421

Glenton, C., Colvin, C. J., Carlsen, B., Swartz, A., Lewin, S., & Noyes, J. (2013). Barriers and facilitators to the implementation of lay health worker programmes to improve access to maternal and child health: A qualitative evidence synthesis. *Cochrane Database of Systematic Reviews.* https://www.ncbi.nlm.nih.gov/pmc/articles/PMC6396344/pdf/CD010414.pdf

Govender, S. M., & Mars, M. (2018). The perspectives of South African academics within the disciplines of health sciences regarding telehealth and its potential inclusion in student training. *African Journal of Health Professions Education, 10*(1), 38–43.

Grogan-Johnson, S., Meehan, R., McCormick, K., & Miller, N. (2015). Results of a national survey of preservice telepractice training in graduate speech-language pathology and audiology programs. *Contemporary Issues in Communication Sciences and Disorders, 42*, 122–137.

Grol, R., & Grimshaw, J. (2003). From best evidence to best practice: Effective implementation of change in patient care. *Lancet, 362*(9391), 1225–1230.

Gustafston, S. M., Key, A. P., Horns, B. W. Y., & Bess, F. H. (2018). Fatigue related to speech processing in children with hearing loss: Behaviours, subjective, and electrophysiologyical measures. *Journal of Speech, Language, Hearing Research, 61*(4), 1000–1011.

HPCSA. (2018). *Minimum standards for the hearing screening in schools.* Health Professions Council of South Africa. https://www.hpcsa.co.za/uploads/editor/Userfiles/downloads/speech/guidelines/Minimum_Standards_for_the_Hearing_Screening_in_Schools.pdf

HPCSA. (2019). *Guidelines for practice in a culturally and linguistically diverse South Africa.* https://www.hpcsa.co.za/Uploads/SLH/Guidelines%20for%20practice%20in%20a%20culturally%20and%20linguistically%20divers---.pdf

HPCSA. (2020). *Guidance on the application of telemedicine guidelines during the Covid19 pandemic.* https://www.hpcsa.co.za/Uploads/Events/Announcements/APPLICATION_OF_TELEMEDICINE_GUIDELINES.pdf

Hornsby, B. W. Y., Gustafson, S. M., Lancaster, H., Cho, S. J., & Camarata, S., & Bess, F. H. (2017). Subjective fatigue in children with hearing loss assessed using self-and parent-proxy report. *American Journal of Audiology, 26*(35), 393–407.

HST. (2017). *South African health review 2017*. Health Systems Trust.

Hughes, M. L., Sevier, J. D., & Choi, S. (2018). Techniques for remotely programming children with cochlear implants using pediatric audiological methods via telepractice. *American Journal of Audiology, 27*(3S), 385–390.

Integrated School Health Policy. (2012). *Webpage*. https://www.health-e.org.za/wp-content/uploads/2013/10/Integrated_School_Health_Policy.pdf

Jin, C., Ishikawa, A., Sengoku, Y., & Ohyanagi, T. (2000). A telehealth project for supporting an isolated physiotherapist in a rural community of Hokkaido. *Journal of Telemedicine and Telecare, 6*(Supp 2), S35–37.

Khoza-Shangase, K. (2021a). Early intervention: Continuity of care for the hearing-impaired child that includes intervention at school. In K. Khoza-Shangase & A. Kanji (Eds.), *Early detection and intervention in audiology: An African perspective*. Wits University Press.

Khoza-Shangase, K. (2021b). Confronting realities to early hearing eetection in South Africa. In K. Khoza-Shangase & A. Kanji (Eds.), *Early detection and intervention in audiology: An African perspective*. Wits University Press.

Khoza-Shangase, K., & Mophosho, M. (2018). Language and culture in speech-language and hearing professions in South Africa: The dangers of a single story. *South African Journal of Communication Disorders, 65*(1), 594.

Khoza-Shangase, K., & Moroe, N. (2020). South African hearing conservation programmes in the context of tele-audiology: A scoping review [Special issue]: Occupational hearing loss in Africa: An interdisciplinary view of the current status]. *South African Journal of Communications Disorders, 67*(2). https://doi.org/10.4102/sajcd.v67i2.670

Krupinski, E. (2015). Innovations and possibilities in connected health. Journal of *American Academy of Audiology, 26*(9), 761–767.

Lamb, G. S., & Shea, K. (2006). Nursing education in telehealth. *Journal of Telemedicine and Telecare, 12*(2), 55–56.

Lehmann, U., Friedman, I., & Sanders, D. (2004). *Review of the utilisation and effectiveness of community-based health workers in South Africa. Joint learning initiative on human resources for health and development* (Working paper 4-1). http://hrh.uwc.ac.za/index.php?module=hrhlibrary&action=downloadfile&fileid=111930420852115

Lehmann, U., & Sanders, D. (2007). *Community health workers: What do we know about them? The state of the evidence on program activities, costs and impact on health outcomes of using community health workers*. University of the Western Cape.

Martin, F. N., & Clarke, J. G. (2019). *Introduction to audiology* (13th ed.). Pearson Education.

Mudzingwa, T. (2015). *Cost-effectiveness analysis of an HIV-adapted training and continuous quality improvement supervisory intervention for community caregivers* (Unpublished thesis). University of KwaZulu Natal.

Mulwafu, W., Ensink, R., Kuper, H., & Fagan, J. (2017). Survey of ENT services in sub-Saharan Africa: Little progress between 2009 and 2015. *Global Health Action, 10*. doi:10.1080/16549716.2017.1289736

Muthukrishna, N., & Schoeman, M. (2000). From 'special needs' to 'quality education for all': A participatory approach to policy development in South Africa. *International Journal of Inclusive Education, 4*(4), 315–335.

National Institute on Deafness and Other Communication Disorders. (2016). *Quick statistics about hearing.* https://www.nidcd.nih.gov/health/statistics/quick-statistics-hearing

Olusanya, B., Okolo, A., & Adeosun, A. (2004). Predictors of hearing loss in school entrants in a developing country. *Journal of Postgraduate Medicine, 50*(3), 173–179.

Picot, J. (2000). Meeting the need for educational standards in the practice of telemedicine and telehealth. *Journal of Telemedicine and Telecare, 6*(2), 59–62.

POPI Act. (2013). *Webpage.* Retrieved July 22, 2020, from https://www.justice.gov.za/inforeg/docs/InfoRegSA-POPIA-act2013-004.pdf

Potgieter, J., Swanepoel, D. W., & Smits, C. (2018). Evaluating a smartphone digits-in-noise test as part of the audiometric test battery. *South African Journal of Communication Disorders, 5*(1). doi:10.4102/sajcd.v65i1.574

Pross, S. E., Bourne, A. L., & Cheung, S. W. (2016). TeleAudiology in the Veterans Health Administration. *Otology & Neurotology, 37*(7), 847–850.

Ramma, L., & Sebothoma, B. (2016). The prevalence of hearing impairment within the Cape Town metropolitan area. *South African Journal of Communication Disorders, 6*(1). doi:10.4102/sajcd.v63i1.105

Rena, U. (2000). *Who will teach: A case study of teacher education reform.* Caddo Gap Press.

Republic of South Africa. (1996). *The constitution act No. 108 of 1996.* Government Printer.

Rice, J. K. (2003). *Teacher quality: Understanding the effectiveness of teacher attributes.* Economic Policy Institute.

Schweitzer, C., Mortz, M., & Vaughan, N. (1999). Perhaps not by prescription, but by perception. *High Performance Hearing Solutions, 3*, 58–62.

Sebothoma, B., & Khoza-Shangase, K. (2018). A comparison between video otoscopy and standard tympanometry findings in adults living with Human Immunodeficiency Virus (HIV). *South African Journal of Communication Disorders, 65*(1), doi:10.4102/sajcd.v65i1.591

Sebothoma, B., Khoza-Shangase, K., Mol, D., & Masege, S. D. (2021). The sensitivity and specificity of wideband absorbance in identifying pathologic middle ears in adults living with HIV. Manuscript in preparation.

Shulman, L. S. (1986). Those who understand: Knowledge growth in teaching. *Educational Researcher, 15*(2), 4–14.

South African Government. (2019). *President Cyril Ramaphosa: State of the nation address 2019*. https://www.gov.za/speeches/2SONA2019?gclid=CjwKCAjwr7X4BRA 4EiwAUXjbt-FiLEDoSuxrxjyuItH_KSJv3PA5ct8zXO1tmfPoBfXZAios5rnvhoCv9 UQAvD_BwE

South African Government News Agency. (2013). *Sunward Park high changes face of learning*. https://www.sanews.gov.za/south-africa/sunward-park-high-changes-face-learning

South African History Online. (n.d.). *South Africa's key economic policies changes (1994–2013)*. https://www.sahistory.org.za/article/south-africas-key-economic-policies-changes-1994-2013

Steuerward, W., Windmill, I., Scott, M., Evans, T., & Kramer, K. (2018). Stories from the webcams: Cincinnati children's hospital medical center audiology telehealth and pediatric auditory device services. *American Journal of Audiology, 27*(3S), 391–402.

Stofile, S., & Green, L. (2006). *Inclusive education in South Africa*. Van Schaik.

Swanepoel, D. W., Clark, J. L., Koekemoer, D., Hall, J. W., Krumm, M., & Ferrari, D. V. (2010). Telehealth in audiology: The need and potential to reach underserved communities. *International Journal of Audiology, 49*(3), 195–202.

Swanepoel, D. W., & Hall, J. W. (2010). A systematic review of telehealth applications in audiology. *Telemedicine and e-Health, 16*(2), 181–200.

Swanepoel, D. W., Myburgh, H. C., Howe, D. M., Mahomed, F., & Eikelboom, R. H. (2014). Smartphone hearing screening with integrated quality control and data management. *International Journal of Audiology, 53*(12), 841–849.

Swanepoel, D. W., Olusanya, B. O., & Mars, M. (2010). Hearing healthcare delivery in sub-Saharan Africa – A role for teleaudiology. *Journal of Telemedice and Telecare, 16*(10), 53–56.

Tousignant, M., Moffet, H., Cabana, F., & Simard, J. (2011). Patients' satisfaction of healthcare services and perception with in-home telerehabilitation and physiotherapists' satisfaction toward technology for post-knee arthroplasty: An embedded study in a randomized trial. *Telemed and EHealth, 17*(5), 376–382.

Wildeman, R. A., & Nomdo, C. (2007). *Implementation of inclusive education: How far are we?* (Occasional paper). IDASA.

World Health Organisation. (2012). *Global estimates on prevalence of hearing loss: Mortality and burden of disease and prevention of blindness and deafness*. https://www.who.int/pbd/deafness/WHO_GE_HL.pdf

CHAPTER 13

Educational Audiology within the Classroom: The Use and Importance of Information and Communication Technologies

Dhanashree Pillay and Ben Sebothoma

Abstract

Learners who are diagnosed with a hearing impairment face barriers when accessing auditory information within the classroom due to their atypical auditory system. The limited resources in low and middle-income countries, including South Africa, exacerbated by the large number of learners in classrooms with poor infrastructure which creates unfavorable classroom acoustics. Access to amplification devices such as hearing aids and cochlear implants is swayed towards the private healthcare sector, leaving the public healthcare sector with scarce resources. Learners who are diagnosed with a hearing loss are at a disadvantage when they are placed without support within a mainstream setting that is designed for a learner who is hearing. The inequality is exacerbated by a lack of educators who are equipped to meet the needs of learners who are diagnosed with a hearing impairment. The learner will soon become the educator and this chapter explores how learners can be empowered through ICTs that promote the inclusiveness of learners who are diagnosed with a hearing loss. This chapter also highlights the instrumental role that ICTs can play in educator preparedness when facilitating the learning process of learners who are diagnosed with a hearing impairment.

Keywords

audiology – deaf education – hearing impairment – information and communication technologies

1 Introduction

The World Health Organization (WHO) has estimated that there are approximately half a billion people globally with hearing loss, of which 34 million are children (WHO, 2018). Mulwafu, Kuper, and Ensink (2016) reported that hearing

© KONINKLIJKE BRILL NV, LEIDEN, 2021 | DOI: 10.1163/9789004447226_014

losses are most prevalent in low- and middle-income countries (LAMI), including sub-Saharan countries such as South Africa. Studies conducted in South Africa on the prevalence of hearing loss, including hearing loss in children, have indicated that hearing loss is high in many parts of the country (Louw, Swanepoel, Eikelboom, & Hugo, 2018; Ramma & Sebothoma, 2016). WHO (2018) estimates that the number of individuals diagnosed with a hearing loss will continue to increase and reach approximately one billion people worldwide. The prevalence of hearing loss within educational settings in the United States of America (USA) was 14.9% within the 6 to 19 years age group (Niskar, 1998). Mahomed-Asmail, Swanepoel, and Eikelboom (2016) reported that the prevalence of hearing loss was 2.2% in urban South African schools.

Given that LAMI countries such as South Africa are plagued with a myriad of risk factors that are only predominant in these regions, the continued increase of hearing loss is concerning. Olusanya, Akolo, and Adeosun (2004) found that the greatest predictors of hearing loss in children included foreign bodies in the ear canal, impacted cerumen, dull tympanic membrane, perforated tympanic membrane, and otitis media with effusion. These findings are supported by a study conducted in rural South Africa by Joubert and Botha (2019). The diagnosis of a hearing loss in LAMI countries is often diagnosed concurrently with the burden of other diseases such as human immunodeficiency virus (HIV) (Khoza-Shangase, 2017, 2010, 2020; Tshifularo, Govender, & Monama, 2013; Sebothoma & Khoza-Shangase, 2018). Learners who are diagnosed with a hearing loss and other comorbidities may experience additional barriers to learning. The cause of hearing impairments may differ but the impact of any hearing impairment is noticeable as a barrier in learning encounters. An unequal learning opportunity results from teaching environments that are ill equipped to provide support to the learner who is diagnosed with a hearing impairment. Learners can be diagnosed with a congenital or an acquired hearing impairment.

Maluleka, Khoza-Shangase, and Kanji (2019) conducted a study to describe the communication and school readiness abilities of learners who were diagnosed with hearing impairment. Findings of the study indicated that learners who had a delayed diagnosis exhibited some communication difficulties and they were not ready for school. Learners who end up in mainstream school systems regardless of their hearing loss may continue to experience auditory fatigue because of the need for extra concentration (Hornsby, Werfel, Camarata, & Bess, 2014). The impact of the inappropriate school placement of learners who are impacted by a hearing loss may affect the learners' ability to complete their studies (Pillay & Moonsamy, 2016), thus contributing to the high levels of unemployment in LAMI countries.

Noise induced hearing loss is one of the largest contributors to the diagnosis of an acquired hearing loss. Research indicates that university students increasingly expose themselves to high levels of noise through digital audio players such as MP3, iPods, and cellphones (McNeill, Keith, Feder, Konkle, & Michaud, 2010). Rawool and Colligon-Wayne (2008) found that college students tend to expose themselves to high levels of recreational noise, whether through headphones or during concerts. Approximately, 50% of college students who attend concerts choose not to wear hearing protective devices (HPDs) due to its negative impact on the quality of sound (Rawool & Colligon-Wayne, 2008). The continuous exposure to loud noise through digital devices may cause a hearing loss and contribute to a negative educational impact and quality of life.

Educational audiologists are required to assess and manage learners who are diagnosed with a hearing impairment in order to improve the chance for educational success in South Africa. Furthermore, educational audiologists are meant to provide educational support to educators to ensure that they are equipped with strategies to facilitate learning so that the learner who is diagnosed with a hearing impairment is not left behind. However, In LAMI countries there is a general shortage of audiologists and resources (Mulwafu, Ensink, Kuper, & Fagan, 2017). There are a significant percentage of audiologists in SA who work predominately in the private and tertiary hospital sectors, with a minimal number of audiologists within the needed public educational sectors. The general shortage of audiologists makes services inaccessible to learners in schools.

Although there is a call for universal audiology coverage, this may not be easily achieved in SA due to the challenges of demand versus capacity. While it is within the scope of practice for audiologists to work in schools, it can be argued that schools or educational settings are not yet the traditional spaces of practice for audiologists in SA. Given these challenges, the use of technology may be crucial in classrooms. Learners who are diagnosed with a hearing impairment face a visible gap between access to information and participation within educational settings. This gap can be eliminated with the use of ICTs within educational settings. The barrier of auditory deprivation within the classroom setting can be targeted through ICT to ensure that all learners are included. The needs of learners can be met on an individual basis to ensure equal access within learning environments. The learner who is diagnosed with a hearing impairment that is empowered through ICT may become the educator that is empowered. The transformation of teaching practices for learners who are diagnosed with a hearing impairment is overdue. Changes within educational environments must be reconstructed to afford equal access and participation to all learners. Through ICT, audiologists and educators can change the status quo of teaching methods in SA to ensure more inclusive and relevant teaching styles that overcome barriers to learning.

One such promising technology that can be harnessed to increase access, particularly in educational settings, is tele-audiology. Literature reports that teleaudiology is a method of delivering quality health to underserved areas through telecommunication technology (Swanepoel, 2015). Promising research conducted in the area of teleaudiology suggests that though analysis and diagnoses of auditory pathologies can be done by qualified ear and hearing professionals (Sebothoma & Khoza-Shangase, 2018), paraprofessionals can be trained to conduct tests, record results, and send them later for analysis (Biagio et al., 2013; O'Donovan, Verkerk, Winters, Chadha, & Bhutta, 2018). The promising prospects of teleaudiology have spurred the current authors to favour this method within an educational setting.

Learners who are diagnosed with a hearing impairment face barriers when accessing auditory information within the classroom in both mainstream classrooms and classrooms in special needs school settings. The limited resources in low- and middle-income countries including South Africa exacerbates the challenges experienced by learners who are diagnosed with disabilities including hearing impairments. The financial and economic inequalities in South Africa are clearly seen in the education sector as there is a lack of educators who are equipped to who meet the needs of learners, including those who are diagnosed with a disability. Resources are limited in the public education sector which creates a ripple effect on the burdened educator.

This chapter aims to provide a background to the current challenges experienced within the education sector, with specific attention to special needs education and hearing impairments. The chapter discusses the use of ICT as a tool to facilitate a transformation of the teaching and learning methods for learners who are diagnosed with a hearing impairment. The learner will soon become the educator and this chapter explores how learners can be empowered through ICTs that promote the inclusiveness of learners who are diagnosed with a hearing loss. Learners should be empowered to access ICT to create learning methods and environments that facilitate their active participation in classroom activities. This chapter provides recommendations on the instrumental role that ICTs can play in educator preparedness when facilitating the learning process of learners who are diagnosed with a hearing impairment. Student educators and student audiologists at higher education institutions may benefit from the recommendations for the use of ICTs within the teaching and learning environments.

2 Background

The facets that either shaped or were shaped by apartheid include religion, politics, liberation, economics and inequality through racial segregation and education (Bond, 2003; Maylam, 2017). The collapse of apartheid in the 1990's was a victory for the majority of the South African population; however, the consequences of apartheid rule were strikingly evident within the unequal education system. A significant disparity that exists within the South African education system is due to the legacy of a apartheid system that was governed by oppressive acts such as the Reservation of Separate Amenities Act, Bantu Education Act, Coloured Person's Education Act, Indian Education Act (Clark & Worger, 2016). The apartheid South African government did not foresee the abolition of apartheid; hence, the infrastructure capacity was proportionate to the white race only. Democracy highlights this point as there is a shortage of housing, education, jobs, and a struggling economic and health system, despite the freedom afforded to the SA population in 2020. The social, cultural, and educational impact of the apartheid regime is still being addressed in current times. The South African education system has however grown and developed over the past 20 years. Urban, peri-urban, and rural landscapes are clearly divided in terms of access to education and participation in educational environments in SA. The distinctive lack of equality is evident within the educational settings as the differences in infrastructure and support vary considerably between urban and rural locations. The lack of accessibility to information can be overcome with the use of ICT within learning environments. The landscape and location of educational settings may differ; however, the use of ICT can have a significant role in normalizing the access to information and encouraging the participation of all learners in the teaching space. Through ICT the historically created divides can be minimised, as ICT can play an instrumental role in overcoming barriers within educational and employment sectors.

In 2019 the South African education statistics reported 13,041,198 learners in ordinary schools, who were taught by 444,857 educators in 24,998 schools (SA Education Statistics EMIS, 2020). The South African Minister of Basic Education, AM Motshekga, described 27 goals of the Department of Basic Education (DBE) action plan during 2019, as the efforts made to improve the South African education system (Politics Web, 2019). Six thematic areas were discussed within the action plan (Politics Web, 2019):

- Improved quality teaching and learning through development, supply, and effective utilisation of educators;
- Improved quality teaching and learning, through provision of adequate, quality infrastructure, and Learning and Teaching Support Materials (LTSM);

EDUCATIONAL AUDIOLOGY WITHIN THE CLASSROOM

- Improving assessment for learning to ensure quality and efficiency in academic achievement;
- Expanded access to ECD and improvement of the quality of Grade R, with support for pre-Grade R provision;
- Strengthening accountability and improving management at school, community and district level; and
- Partnerships for educational reform and improved quality.

Minister Motshekga (Politics Web, 2019) highlights how the fourth industrial revolution impacts on teaching and learning, as learners must be prepared for the reality within the global sphere that is dominated by technological advancements. The goal of the DBE as stated by Minister Motshekga (Politics Web, 2019) is to:

> provide each learner and teacher with an ICT device with access to digitised LTSMs. The plan will be implemented in three phases commencing with Phase 1 that will target multi-grade, multiphase, farm and selected rural schools (2020–2021). The Second Phase will target quintile 1 to 3 schools (2022–2023), and Phase 3 will target quintile 4 and 5 schools (2024–2025). All special needs schools will be accommodated in all phases according to the type of disability. The aims and objectives of this intervention are entrenched in the e-education goals of White Paper 7, Action Plan to 2019: Towards the Realisation of Schooling in 2030, and the National Development Plan (NDP).

These aim to enhance the teaching and learning experiences of learners and teachers through ICT integration; ensure that learners have the ability to use digital technology and acquire 21st century skills; provide learners and teachers with digital content pre-loaded on appropriate ICT devices; promote the local industry in the economic growth by developing education specific devices; ensure that teachers have the relevant training to integrate ICT into teaching and learning; and support learning and teaching in special needs schools. A comprehensive ICT plan has been developed to provide a framework for an affordable and sustainable implementation of ICTs in education. The three-phased ICT school deployment model will ensure ICT compliance in all schools by 2025.

Learners in public schools are facing the barriers of large class sizes, a lack of books, school fees that are high, bad facilities, and a lack of educators (South African Market Insights, 2020). The use of ICT within the school setting can play a pivotal role in bridging the gap when there is a lack of educators as learners.

2.1 Special Needs Education in South Africa

The most recent statistics in South Africa reported that 119,403 learners were enrolled in special needs schools, where they are served by 10,059 educators, with the majority of special needs schools found in Gauteng (30.5%) followed by the Western Cape with 19.2% (SA Education Statistics, 2016). According to the SA Education Statistics report 2016, the total numbers of South African learners in 2016 who were categorised with an auditory impairment were:

- Deaf-Blindness: 23
- Deafness: 6215
- Hard of Hearing: 1202

In South Africa parents are faced with the high costs associated with purchasing hearing aids, special education, and medical services (Swanepoel, Störbeck, & Friedland, 2009). Strategies to combat hearing loss and the consequential cost in South Africa has included an increase in hearing screenings, efficient management of middle ear infections, and a state tender hearing aid price list which is more affordable to the individual who is not covered by the private medical aid system (Baltussen & Smith, 2012). Despite the efforts to fight against the effects of a hearing loss on the individual and the country's economy, it is evident that over two-thirds of individuals with a hearing loss reside in developing countries such as South Africa (Tucci, Merson, & Wilson, 2010). Developing countries have limited financial resources and strained healthcare and education systems that cannot cope with the increasing burden that is caused by illness, disease, and disabilities.

The burden of the increasing cost of assessment procedures to detect a hearing loss and the education and management costs of hearing aids is shadowed by the need for basics supplies of food and clean water (Kiyaga & Moores, 2003). The role of the audiologist is significant when assessing and managing an individual who is suspected of having a hearing loss. The need to holistically integrate aspects of financial burden into the service delivery is vital so that the individual with the hearing impairment obtains the best possible care.

Schooling and educational decisions form an essential aspect of parental responsibility (Kimmons, 2005). The educational decisions are based on access to schools in the area, cost of school fees, and future aspirations of the parents for the child based on the child's strengths and talents as well as a school that is equipped for the specificity of needs of the child (Pont, Goodman, & Steiger, 2001). Parents of a child with a hearing impairment are required to make an important decision about the method of communication for the child (Knoors & Marschark, 2015). The educational decisions made by parents of children who require amplification must be made in a supportive environment;

however, the already burdened audiologist within the healthcare sector may not have sufficient time to assist the parent. In South Africa there is an effective family support program called HI HOPES (Home Intervention—Hearing and Language Opportunities Parent Education Services). HI HOPES was established at the Centre of Deaf Studies at the University of the Witwatersrand in 2008, for families who receive the diagnosis of a hearing loss. The primary aim of the HI HOPES program is to inform and equip parents of infants with a hearing loss (Strobeck & Calvert-Evers, 2008). The program works to provide each family with a parent advisor who will assist with information in the following areas:

– Acceptance of the child's disability.
– Language assessment.
– Communication option: spoken language, signed language and SimmComm (signing and speaking).
– Hearing aids.
– Daily routines to maximise language acquisition.
– Cochlear implants.
– Play and concept development.
– Speech-language therapy.
– Literacy.

Parent advisors are matched to meet the needs of the family with special consideration of age, communication mode, religious views, and gender (Strobeck & Calvert-Evers, 2008). The consideration of biopsychosocial and spiritual aspects is evident in the pairing of families and parent advisors. Audiologists in South Africa are frequently from a different race or culture of the family, therefore the HI HOPES program assists in bridging the communication gap by matching the family with a parent advisor that can meet their communication and educational needs.

A rapport is established between the healthcare provider and the family so that there is a freedom to share experiences (Santhi, Aparna, Susan, & Winnie, 2013) and beliefs about the hearing loss. The initial lack of detection may have minimal consequences for a toddler; however, the consequences emerge as the child matures (Alpiner & McCarthy, 2000).

The cost and implications of cochlear implants is vast (Tucker, 1998) and very few candidates are implanted in the South African context. Swanepoel (2006) stated that cochlear implantation commenced in 1986 in South Africa with an increase in implantations annually. Cochlear implant candidates require a strong family system (Perez-Jorge, Rodriguez-Jimenez, Alegre de la Rosa, & Marrero-Morales, 2016) to support the process from fitting to mapping and aftercare of the implants. Cochlear implants can be highly successful; however, the lack of family support and educational support may lead to difficulties.

The financial implications for a South African learner with a cochlear implant relate to the follow-up programming and mapping of the cochlear implant, the transportation to the hospital, and accommodation costs if the family resides far away from the hospital (Moroe & Kathrada, 2016). There are only seven sites in South Africa that conduct a cochlear implant surgery (SACIG, 2017). Inclusive education is a topic of controversy as the resources and infrastructure required for the implementation thereof may not be available in the South African context. Mainstream schools that do not support the needs of learners who have hearing impairment will result in a higher number of learners who do not progress successfully (Griffin, 2013). The aims and objectives of inclusive education for individuals with a hearing impairment must be relevant and beneficial and should be supported. Hard of hearing/ Deaf learners need to be seen as individuals in their own right, without being compared to hearing learners (Young & Tattersall, 2007). The audiologist working within the education sector has additional factors to consider as opposed to those working within the healthcare sector.

Student audiologists and educators at higher education institutions are not empowered enough to offer services in the special schools, which results in unprepared audiologists and educators who are expected to provide services within the education sector. During the undergraduate training of student educators and audiologists, they should be taught to actively engage with transformation goals to challenge the barriers to learning so that inclusion and equality may then be afforded to all learners. However, the integration of ICT into the educational sector for learners who require amplification due to a hearing impairment is not an easy process.

2.2   The Hearing-Impaired Learner and ICT

South Africa has been changing rapidly post-apartheid; however, colonisation has resulted in inequality and unfair distribution of resources; the problems encountered are evident in the barriers experienced by learners even now in the 21st century. Change on the healthcare and education service provision is vital to facilitate a holistic and integrated paradigm for learners. The change in healthcare that is positive will require the definition of the concepts that are targeted.

The concept of integrated healthcare and education service delivery for the learner with a hearing impairment is dynamic.

The literature focuses on "integrated care" or "integrated health system"; however, the information is predominantly disease specific (Leatt, Pink, &

Guerriere, 2000). There is a dearth of literature pertaining to the performance of a well-run and functioning holistically integrated system that combines the healthcare and education of a hearing-impaired learner within the SA context. Integration within healthcare and education involves more than a healthcare provider who treats a person who has an illness. A multidisciplinary team approach is advisable as it will aid in the implementation of collective methods that support the use of ICTs. The players who are vital within a multidisciplinary team who work with a learner with a hearing impairment may include:

– The educator
– The educational audiologist
– The student educator
– The student audiologist
– The parent
– Fellow learners in the classroom
– Friends and peers

Learning and the sharing of knowledge within the classroom setting is a dynamic process. The access to information cannot be a privilege for some, whilst excluding those with a hearing impairment. Accessibility of information for the learner with a hearing loss must be a priority to reduce the digital divide by providing e-inclusion (Yeratziotis & Greunen, 2013). Student educators who are trained to employ ICTs within the teaching and learning environments will be prepared when they become the educators within mainstream and special needs schools.

The use and importance of ICT within an education setting has grown rapidly as computers and the internet are increasingly available (Strauss & Houw, 1991). Generation Z or iGen is the only generation that is born into the current internet era, with social media and internet access at their fingertips. They use technology as a vehicle to socialise and communicate on a daily basis. The use of ICT and technological platforms within the education sector is necessary to empower the current generation of learners who are accustomed to using technology for communication. The current learner will become a part of the workforce that uses ICT in every aspect of vocation as this is a developing trend within the workplace.

The use of ICT within the classroom will enable educators to use a communication method that is familiar to the learner, thus providing a transformed and relevant medium to education. Learners use technology and the internet to obtain information on a daily basis and it is vital to engage with such means within the classroom. There are challenges that exist globally with the risks associated with social media, the internet, and access to information, but the reality is that ICT is a growing sector and it should not be ignored in the South African context of education. The benefit of understanding and utilising ICT within the South African educational context includes the empowerment of the learner and the educator.

In South Africa, access to resources is limited; however, the lobbying for fair and equitable education platforms is highlighted by the higher education protests, governmental debates for inclusive education for all, and the increase in the building of schools. Despite the limited focus, there has been awareness of the need to develop ICT within programs for learners who are Deaf and HOH. Multimedia courses are being developed to teach sign language via e-learning with the use of a web-based interpreter that uses visual-gestured-spatial language (Jemni & Elghoul, 2008). Curriculum planning at higher education institutions should include courses on the use of ICT within the training programs to ensure that newly graduated educators are equipped and empowered with relevant and valuable knowledge to facilitate active learning via ICT methods when they enter the workplace.

The use of online courses will provide the learner with adequate time to go through a lesson and repeat areas that are difficult, a learner who cannot hear an educator within a mainstream setting may be able to connect to a direct sound source and hear the internet-based information in a solo manner. The SMILE: A Sign Language and Multimedia-based Interactive Language Course for the Deaf for the Training of European Written Language is one such project where language course applications are delivered online, which allows for easy and straightforward access to learning (Straetz et al., 2002). In South Africa there are few projects such as the SMILE to support the learner who is Deaf. The importance of such a project is evident as learners require support to ensure the completion of primary and secondary education, with no exception to the Deaf learner. A Polish project called Thetos5 effectively assists Deaf learners to translate written texts into animated sequences of Polish sign language using ICT (Straetz et al., 2002). The adaptation of the educational environment for a Deaf/HOH learner may create a user friendly and supportive environment that uses multimedia and technology to enhance learning. In South Africa, video conferencing is available via Skype, Zoom and Microsoft Teams; however, the transitions and access to such facilitates is a luxury within the higher education and corporate sector. The 4th industrial revolution highlights the need for the development of ICT within the basic education sector in South Africa. Deaf education requires a visual channel of input; therefore, ICT methods should be designed to attract and keep the learner's attention.

A study in Ghana by Dadzie-Bonney and Samuel K. Hayford (2017) revealed that 87.5% of the Deaf learners stated that their schools were well-equipped

EDUCATIONAL AUDIOLOGY WITHIN THE CLASSROOM

to use ICT. There were 77.5% of learners who needed the educator's guidance when using the computer to access information. A benefit to using ICT showed that 70.0% of the learners could save documents unto storage devices (Dadzie-Bonney & Hayford, 2017). There is a dearth of such studies in the SA context.

3 Recommendations and Conclusion

Despite the harsh realities of South African history that deprived many of basic education, there has been progress made in ensuring that the wrongs of the past are being made right. The Department of Basic Education has built more schools in previously disadvantaged areas to ensure that there is a growth in the number of children who obtain a basic education. However, the dearth of educators who are equipped and empowered to work in these schools creates a barrier within the education system. By exploring the use of ICT to educate learners, the gap can be minimised while more educators are sought and trained.

Deaf education has additional needs as there is growth in early identification and management programs for hearing loss in South Africa which positively impacts the child with a hearing loss as she/he is identified early. The shortage of special needs schools is evident in South Africa, however the child who was diagnosed early will still be a learner in need of an education in the country. While special needs schooling buildings are being constructed, it is recommended that educators and student educators be empowered to utilise the resources that are available. One important resource is the use of ICT to enhance the teaching environment within the current classrooms and buildings. Student educators can benefit from ICT during training with the use of simulated sessions of working within a special needs school. Training via ICT simulations will support the student educator by providing effective options to enhance teaching practices in a non-threatening environment.

The methods of teaching require scrutiny as the traditional verbal medium of instruction is not suitable for a Deaf/HOH learner. It is suggested that ICT can minimise the auditory barriers that exist for a Deaf/HOH learning. The use of ICT is vital in improving the learner's access to auditory information and assists in educator preparedness to facilitate the learning process of learners with hearing loss.

It is evident that integration within healthcare and education requires a multidisciplinary team approach. The use of ICTs by all players within the multidisciplinary team will aid in supporting and empowering Deaf/HOH learners and future educators.

The ICT growth globally and its use by the iGeneration mandates that there should be a growth of ICT usage to facilitate a better teaching and learning environment for the Deaf/HOH learner. There is a clear need to develop the current state of Deaf/HOH education in South Africa to allow the learner to achieve the best possible educational outcomes.

References

Alpiner, J. G., & McCarthy, P. A. (2000). *Rehabilitative audiology: Children and adults.* Lippincott Williams & Wilkins.

Baltussen, R., & Smith, A. (2012). Cost effectiveness of strategies to combat vision and hearing loss in sub-Saharan Africa and South East Asia: Mathematical modelling study. *British Medical Journal, 344,* e615. doi:10.1136/bmj.e615

Biagio, L., Swanepoel, D. W., Adeyemo, A., Hall, J. W., & Vinck, B. (2013). Asynchronous video-otoscopy with a telehealth facilitator. *Telemedicine and e-Health, 19*(4), 252–258.

Bond, P. (2003). *Against global apartheid: South Africa meets the World Bank, IMF and international finance.* Palgrave Macmillan.

Clark, N. L., & Worger, W. H. (2016). *South Africa: The rise and fall of apartheid* (3rd ed.). Routledge.

Dadzie-Bonney, P., & Hayford, S. K. (2017). Factors inhibiting students' ICT knowledge acquisition and utilization at Oguaa School for the Deaf in Ghana. *Rwandan Journal of Education, 4*(1), 34–46.

Du Pont, P. S., Goodman, J. C., & Steiger, F. S. (2001). *An education agenda.* National Center for Policy Analysis.

Griffin, C. (2013). Standing up for our children. Odyssey. *New Directions in Deaf Education, 14,* 26–28.

Hornsby, B. W. Y., Werfel, K., Camarata, S., & Bess, F. H. (2014). Subjective fatigue in children with hearing loss: Some preliminary findings. *American Journal of Audiology, 23*(1), 129–134. doi:10.1044/1059-0889(2013/13-0017)

Jemni, M., & Elghoul, O. (2008). *Using ICT to teach sign language.* Paper presented at Research Unit of Technologies of Information and Communication.

Joubert, K., & Botha, D. (2019). Contributing factors to high prevalence of hearing impairment in the Elias Motsoaledi Local Municipal area, South Africa: A rural perspective. *South African Journal of Communication Disorders, 66*(1), a611. https://doi.org/10.4102/sajcd.v66i1.611

Khoza-Shangase, K. (2010). Is there a need for ototoxicity monitoring in patients with HIV/AIDS? *African Journal of Pharmacy and Pharmacology, 4*(9), 574–579.

Khoza-Shangase, K. (2017). Risk vs benefit: Who assesses this in the management of patients on ototoxic drugs? *Journal of Pharmacy and BioAllied Sciences, 9*(3), 171–177.

Khoza-Shangase, K. (2020). Pharmaco-audiology vigilance in the treatment of patients with HIV/AIDS: Ototoxicity monitoring protocol recommendation. *Infectious Disorders – Drug Targets, 19*, 1–9. doi:10.2174/1871526518666181016102102

Kimmons, W. J. G. (2005). *A parenting guidebook: The roles of school, family, teachers, religion, community, local, state and federal government in assisting parents with rearing their children.* Author House.

Kiyaga, N. B., & Moores, D. F. (2003). Deafness in Sub-Saharan Africa. *American Annals of the Deaf, 148*(1), 18–24.

Knoors, H., & Marschark, M. (2015). *Educating deaf learners: Creating a global evidence base perspectives on deafness.* Oxford University Press.

Leatt, P., Pink, G. H., & Guerriere, M. (2000). Towards a Canadian model of integrated healthcare. *Healthcare Papers, 1*(2), 13–35. doi:10.12927/hcpap.17216

Louw, C., Swanepoel, D. C., Eikelboom, R. H., & Hugo, J. (2018). Prevalence of hearing loss at primary health care clinics in South Africa. *African Health Sciences, 18*(2), 313–320.

Maluleke, N. P., Khoza-Shangase, K., & Kanji, A. (2019). Communication and school readiness abilities of children with hearing impairment in South Africa: A retrospective review of early intervention preschool records. *South African Journal of Communication Disorders, 66*(1), 2–7. e1–e7. doi:10.4102/sajcd.v66i1.604

Maylam, P. (2017). *South Africa's racial past: The history and historiography of racism, segregation, and apartheid.* Routledge.

McNeill, K., Keith, S. E., Feder, K., Konkle, A. T. M., & Michaud, D. S. (2010). MP3 player listening habits of 17 to 23 year old university students. *The Journal of the Acoustical Society of America, 128*, 646. doi:10.1121/1.3458853

Moroe, N., & Kathrada, N. (2016). The long-term concerns post cochlear implantation as experienced by parents/caregivers of prelingually deaf children between the ages of 3 and 5 years in Gauteng Province, South Africa. *South African Journal of Child Health, 10*(2), 126–129.

Mulwafu, W., Ensink, R., Kuper, H., & Fagan, J. (2017). Survey of ENT services in sub-Saharan Africa: Little progress between 2009 and 2015. *Global Health Action, 10*(1). doi:10.1080/16549716.2017.1289736

Mulwafu, W., Kuper, H., & Ensink, R. J. H. (2016). Prevalence and causes of hearing impairment in Africa. *Tropical Medicine & International Health, 21*(2), 158–165.

O'Donovan, J., Verkerk, M., Winters, N., Chadha, S., & Bhutta, M. F. (2018). The role of community health workers in addressing the global burden of ear disease and hearing loss: A systematic scoping review of the literature. *British Medical Journal Global Health, 4*, e001141. doi:10.1136/bmjgh-2018-001141

Olusanya, B. O., Akolo, A. A., & Adeosun, A. A. (2004). Predictors of hearing loss in school entrants in a developing country. *Journal of Postgraduate Medicine, 50*(3), 173–179.

Pérez-Jorge, D., María, R.-J., Alegre de la Rosa Olga, M., & Marrero-Morales, M. S. (2016). Evaluation of the effectiveness of cochlear implant according to age of implantation. *Global Advanced Research Journal of Medicine and Medical Science, 5,* 237–242.

Pillay, D., & Moonsamy, S. (2016). Supernatural healing: Emotional reactions to healing loss in the South African context. In *Proceeding of the 2nd Biennial South African Conference on spirituality and healthcare* (pp. 207–226). Cambridge Scholars Publishing.

Politics Web. (2019). *Minister Angie Motshekga basic education: We are turning the tide.* Retrieved April, 2020, from https://www.politicsweb.co.za/politics/basic-education-we-are-turning-the-tide--motshekga

Ramma, L., & Sebothoma, B. (2016). The prevalence of hearing impairment within the Cape Town metropolitan area. *South African Journal of Communication Disorders, 63*(1), 1–10.

Rawool, V. W., & Colligon-Wayne, L. A. (2008). Auditory lifestyles and beliefs related to hearing loss among college students in the USA. *Noise & Health, 10*(38), 1–10.

SACIG. (2017). *South African cochlear implant group.* http://www.sacig.org.za/patients-corner/implant-programs/

Santhi, S. P., Aparna, S. G. R., Susan, K. Y., & Winnie, A. (2013). Measuring Prakash levels of stress and depression in mothers of children using hearing aids and cochlear implants: A comparative study. *International Journal of special Education, 28*(1), 37–44.

South African Education Statistics EMIS. (2020). *The 2019 school realities.* https://www.education.gov.za/Portals/0/Documents/Reports/School%20Realities%202019%20Final%20.pdf?ver=2020-02-07-101051-330

South African Market Insights. (2020). *South Africa's education statistics.* https://www.southafricanmi.com/education-statistics.html

Statistics in South Africa. (2016). *Department of Basic Education in 2018.* http://www.statssa.gov.za/?page_id=6283

Storbeck, C., & Calvert-Evers, J. (2008). Towards integrated practices in early detection of and intervention for Deaf and hard of hearing children. *American Annals of Deafness, 153*(3), 314–321.

Straetz, K., Kaibel, A., Raithel, V., Specht, M., Grote, K., & Kramer, F. (2002). *An e-learning environment for Deaf adults.* Institute for Language and Communication.

Strauss, W., & Howe, N. (1991). *Generations: The history of America's future, 1584 to 2069.* William Morrow & Co.

Swanepoel, D. W. (2006). Audiology in South Africa (Audiología en sudáfrica). *International Journal of Audiology, 45*(5), 262–266.

Swanepoel, D. W., Störbeck, C., & Friedland, P. (2009). Early hearing detection and intervention in South Africa. *International Journal of Pediatric Otorhinolaryngology, 73*(6), 783–786.

Tshifularo, M., Govender, L., & Monama, G. (2013). Otolaryngological, head and neck manifestations in HIV-infected patients seen at Steve Biko Academic Hospital in Pretoria, South Africa. *South African Medical Journal, 103,* 464–466.

Tucci, D. L., Merson, M. H., & Wilson, B. S. (2010). A summary of the literature on global hearing impairment: Current status and priorities for action. *Otology & Neurotology, 31*(1), 31–41.

Tucker, B. P. (1998). Deaf culture, cochlear implants, and elective disability. *Hastings Center Report, 28*(4), 6–14.

WHO. (2018). *Prevention of blindness and deafness.* https://www.who.int/pbd/publications/en/

Yeratziotis, G., & van Greunen, D. (2013). Making ICT accessible for the Deaf. In *IST-Africa 2013 conference proceedings.* International Information Management Corporation.

Young, A., & Tattersall, H. (2007). Universal newborn hearing screening and early identification of deafness: Parents' responses to knowing early and their expectations of child communication development. *Journal of Deaf Studies and Deaf Education, 12*(2), 209–220.

CHAPTER 14

Information and Communication Technologies to Facilitate Cognitive Skills Development of Learners Experiencing Barriers to and Learning

Nkhensani Susan Thuketana

Abstract

In contrast to their typically developing peers, learners experiencing barriers to learning have to contend, among other things, with physical, emotional, and psychological factors that inhibit their access to quality education. These factors not only hamper their access to the general curriculum in inclusive education contexts, but also perpetuate their exclusion and participation as equal members of society. They furthermore impede the acquisition of language and mathematics, which is essential for supporting learners' development and progress through school. The ability to learn, process, recall, and apply learned knowledge before deciding on a plan of action is key and encompassed in well-developed cognitive skills. When the ability to internalise and operationalise such skills is not inborn, they have to be taught. In the case of learners experiencing barriers to learning, the latter is the case. Inherent in the learners' disabilities are deficits that hamper executive functioning skills and their ability to learn. It is therefore crucial that 21st century teachers in inclusive classrooms be conscious of any impediments to child development and incorporate the use of information communication technology where necessary. They have to differentiate the curriculum to facilitate the development of cognitive skills and ensure the full participation of learners experiencing barriers to learning.

Keywords

cognitive skills – district-based support teams – executive functions – information communication technology – learner experiencing barriers to learning – perceptual skills – school-based support teams

© KONINKLIJKE BRILL NV, LEIDEN, 2021 | DOI: 10.1163/9789004447226_015

1 Introduction

Learners experiencing barriers to learning in South Africa, who have long been excluded from participating in mainstream education, are still suffering despite the inclusive education policy was ratified close to two decades ago. The policy adopted by the Department of Education in 2001 stems from the realisation that physical, environmental, social, and economic inequalities have contributed greatly to the struggle that atypically developing learners face in their academic journey. The policy specifically provides the framework to eliminate any intrinsic or extrinsic barriers that these learners may experience and that preclude their equal participation and access to quality education. Intrinsic barriers are innate in nature while extrinsic barriers are those in the environment that affect learners' participation, learning, and development (Gašpar, 2018).

A myriad of continuous needs assessment research conducted in the South African context constantly reveals issues that inhibit the inclusion of learner experiencing barriers to learning in full-service schools and repress the successful implementation of inclusive education. According to Chen, Anderson, and Watkins (2016), full-service schools are those whose ethos and principles strive towards creating conducive learning environments for all. They further suggest collaboration with families, communities, and interdisciplinary professionals to ensure holistic support for all learners to promote the successful implementation of inclusive education. This suggestion is in line with the whole-school evaluation (Booth et al., 2002) and systematic thinking (Tale & Room, 2017, p. 105).

Over the years, the literature has also identified issues pointing to teachers' negative attitudes (Naicker, 2018; Tanyi, 2016) towards the inclusion of learners experiencing barriers to learning in full-service schools. These negative attitudes were fuelled by teacher fatigue and adversely affected job fulfilment, and have resulted in teachers resigning from the profession (Robinson, Bridges, Rollins, & Schumacker, 2019). Additionally, Engelbrecht, Nel, Nel, and Tlale (2016), as well as Tanyi (2016), reported on negative attitudes among teachers, emanating from their use of training strategies that were incongruent with the pedagogic needs of learners in their classrooms. It has become evident that a paradigm shift away from investigating conventional issues towards providing solutions for the inherent challenges experienced by both teachers and learners experiencing barriers to learning is necessary.

In view of the above and in the context of the 21st century, this chapter advocates the beneficial effect of teachers using information communication technology (ICT) to facilitate cognitive skills development of learners experiencing barriers to learning in full-service schools. However, unless teachers understand child development and have the skills to use technology for the purpose, learners with disabilities will remain segregated. I will firstly discuss the background and theoretical stance within which my argument is grounded. Secondly, I will discuss the cognitive development (CD) concept as the foundation of language, literacy, and mathematical skills, and the developmental delays that learners experiencing barriers to learning present in a learning environment. The chapter will conclude with a discussion of ICT requirements/skills for teachers to improve the cognitive development of these learners, so as to enhance their equal participation, inclusion, and access to quality education.

2   Background of the Study

In these times of economic and social transformation, this chapter deems ICT as an essential resource to facilitate the cognitive skills development of learners experiencing barriers to learning. ICT is widely defined in the literature; however, this chapter aligns with the definition coined by Andrade and Doolin (2016) in their study on the use of technology with the purpose of socially including refugees to participate equally and learn the culture of their host country. The authors define technology as tools that by design are meant to facilitate development and equal participation for all. With the above background in mind, technology in this chapter is defined as any technological assistive device meant to close the participation gap that emanates from innate disabilities or from external causes experienced by learners experiencing barriers to learning. Assistive devices in the inclusive education context in particular are considered as all resources aimed at bridging the barriers to learning that exist between typically developing children and children with special needs. Thus, these devices facilitate curriculum access, participation, and social inclusion for the latter (Gašpar, 2018).

Education is a human rights issue that aims to promote the development and social participation of learners and adults, including those with special educational needs. Special educational needs in this chapter are conceptualised as the support requirements that atypically developing learners present within an inclusive education system. These requirements impede (among others) the progression of the learners through grades when compared to learners who experience little or no barriers to learning (Leppink, 2017).

South Africa is a signatory to the United Nations' Sustainable Development Goals (SDGs) that focus on eradicating poverty and providing quality education for all (Desa, 2016; Nilsson, Griggs, & Visbeck, 2016). Although different countries target different issues for intervention, SDGs provide the foundations from which the strategies can be theorised. To contribute to the realisation of these goals, White Paper 6 on Special Needs Education was developed in an attempt to build an inclusive South African school system and to eradicate inequalities and abolish the segregation of learners experiencing barriers to learning (Department of Education, 2001; McEwan, 2015). This resulted in teachers in South African schools being tasked with the responsibility to teach learners on a spectrum of educational needs. Inherent to teaching these learners is the obligation to be observant and responsive to their needs. However, teachers are often oblivious of special needs and the pedagogical knowledge required to support affected learners to develop to their maximum ability.

Teacher training and professional development in the context of inclusive education have been widely documented in both national and international literature (Chitiyo et al., 2019; Naicker & Stofile, 2018; Tanyi, 2016). Professional development is a constant process of becoming and linked to improvements and experiences congregated along the way. The aim is to reform teaching and learning so as to improve curriculum access for all learners, including those with special needs. Progress made internationally with the identification of pedagogic requirements for learners experiencing barriers to learning is notable in the literature. These requirements include curriculum differentiation and differentiated assessments (Department of Education, 2011, 2017); concessions to learners in need (Le Roux, 2016); the provision of interdisciplinary professional teams for support (Paget et al., 2016); and early identification of learning difficulties to facilitate the early development of learning skills (Barger, Rice, Simmons, & Wolf, 2018; Leppink, 2017).

In contrast, research conducted in South Africa has disregarded theoretical foundations such as the systemic requirements for the successful implementation of inclusive education. Contextual issues such as the socio-economic background of families, education level of the parents, and the belief systems of the communities within which learners grow up have been largely overlooked (Department of Education, 2001; Naicker & Stofile, 2018). Chitiyo et al. (2019), as well as Naicker and Stofile (2018), argue that most teachers in South Africa are not exposed to professional development opportunities to enhance their teaching skills. District-based Support Teams (DBSTs) are the assigned structures to support teachers and outsource professional support for learners experiencing barriers to learning; however, the organisational structures that should facilitate and support the improvement of teaching, learning, and assessment are often dysfunctional.

In addition to the factors mentioned above, the cognitive skills of most learners experiencing barriers to learning are underdeveloped (Kautz et al.,

2014). Cognitive skills are considered crucial in the learning process as they exert the brain to stimulate attention, memory, and the processing of information. There is a wealth of research reported in the literature aiming to understand the brain and its functioning, however, most investigations were conducted outside the context of child participation. Recently, with the development of scientific research, a paradigm shift to investigate brain functioning in the context of operation is recommended. Well-developed cognitive skills guide learning and ensure the accomplishment of set learning outcomes (Cirino et al., 2015; Goldstein, Naglieri, Princiotta, & Otero, 2014). Furthermore, cognitive skills nurture the acquisition of language and mathematics in learners and improve their retention of learned information in memory for future recall. Cognitive skills also support the working memory, which is the part of memory responsible for processing instantaneous information.

Although these abilities are intuitive, they have to be developed in learners who experience barriers to learning. Inherent in these learners are deficits that hamper their executive functioning skills and ability to learn. Learning difficulties emanate from various intrinsic and extrinsic factors, but watchful and receptive teachers who endeavour to create a conducive environment to learning are key to the identification of these difficulties. Despite the assumption that cognitive constructs are stable, Kautz et al. (2014) as well as Kirk, Gray, Riby, and Cornish (2015) argue that the training in these does not only benefit the targeted learners in full-service classes, but also equip all learners with the skills to transfer learned proficiencies to other contexts.

The current chapter is premised on Vygotsky's theory of cognitive development within the holistic inclusive education system and aims to highlight especially the importance of using ICT to facilitate teacher learner support in an inclusive education context. Teachers need to understand the skills required for learners to perform mental activities associated with learning, processing the learned information, and storing and recalling it when needed. Furthermore, teachers are expected to conceptualise what cognitive load is and how to use technology to bridge the gap between the actual load that the child can process and the content prescribed for their developmental grade. Cognitive load is defined as the amount of information that working memory can hold at one time. It is therefore key that teachers understand each learner's capability in order to pitch content to be taught and choose relevant technologies (Vygotsky, 1988). By design, learning is not linear but coiled and can benefit from a variety of processes, including peer and teacher support as advocated in Vygotsky's theory. With the above background in mind, this chapter aims to benefit student teachers aspiring to teach learners experiencing barriers to learning as well as in-service teachers in full-service schools' environments.

3   Vygotsky's Theory of Cognitive Development and Its Implications for Children with Special Needs

Vygotsky's theory of cognitive development is premised on the idea that a child learns when content is taught within the "zone of proximal development" or ZPD (Vygotsky, 1998). However, cognitive development and learning in instances where age is considered a criterion for admission, and where the curriculum is premised on the proposition of developmental age, results in serious disadvantages for children with special needs. The implication for children whose developmental and chronological ages are incongruent is that they have difficulty accessing the curriculum. When teachers are overwhelmed by the educational needs of these children and continue to employ homogeneous teaching strategies, the result is often to the detriment of the children with special needs in their class.

Vygotsky's theory, which argues that social interaction plays a fundamental role in the development of cognition, is characterised by different stages of cognitive development. Of interest is the assigned age for each of these stages. The stages have implications for how teachers need to differentiate the curriculum, teaching methodologies, and assessment strategies, so as to promote curriculum access for children with compromised cognitive skills development. There are discrepancies between the developmental and chronological ages for typically and atypically developing children. The development of the latter group is characterised by, among others, delays in respect of the perceptual and cognitive skills integral to their disabilities.

It is against the background articulated above that teachers in inclusive contexts need to be mindful of the cognitive requirements of all children in their classrooms. In so doing, teachers will be responsive to children's educational needs and employ the necessary technology to adapt the curriculum and improve its accessibility.

4   What Are Cognitive Skills?

Cognitive skills cannot be described in isolation from executive functions and perceptual skills, as they are intertwined (Danielsson, Henry, Ronnberg, & Nilsson, 2010; Kirk et al., 2015). Neuropsychology regards the brain and nervous system as influential for the development of cognition and behaviour. Danielsson et al. (2010) describe cognitive skills, among other things, as the individual's ability to demonstrate comprehension of learned and/or read text. The acquisition of cognitive skills is critical during the first years of life and essential for quality learning. It is important to note that cognitive skills are linked to the functioning of the brain. It is therefore crucial to identify the underdevelopment of cognitive skills already in the early stages when children develop word and concept formation, in order to remedy its manifestation. Ehrlich and Josselyn (2016) also postulate the elasticity of the brain and reiterate the need for early intervention.

Baddeley and Hitch (1994) and Goldstein et al. (2014) describe executive functions as "an umbrella term used for a diversity of hypothesized cognitive processes including planning, working memory, inhibition, self-monitoring, self-regulation and initiation carried out by prefrontal areas of the frontal lobe" (Goldstein et al., 2014, p. 3). Oppici, Panchuk, Serpiello, and Farrow (2019) describe perceptual skills as the ability of the brain to interpret and act on received stimuli, while Meltzer (2018) conceptualises executive functions as the mental process that are neurologically based to perform functions. What is common in the definitions above is that the brain is the core organ for regulating processes that constitute both learning and unacceptable behaviour.

It is therefore important to note that most disabilities are located in the atypical development of the central nervous system or the result of traumatic brain injury (TBI), both associated with brain functioning. From the multitude of challenges that may present in learning, cognitive skills must be considered alongside perceptual skills and executive functions. Cognitive functioning, learning, and decision making by children with special needs are affected because by atypical brain development. These children present with a spectrum of incapacities that include learning difficulties and unacceptable behaviour associated with neuro-disabilities. Paget et al. (2016, p. 225) define neuro-disability as an inclusive term that encompasses the investigated disabilities below and are mostly of a concomitant nature:

- Gross motor impairment; abnormal movements; speech, visual and hearing impairment following TBI or meningitis; multiple strokes; secondary hydrocephalus
- Diplegia and gross motor impairment due to TBI or meningitis
- Hemiplegia following TBI
- Gross motor impairment, generalised spasticity, incontinence, and speech impairment following TBI
- Hemiplegia, speech and visual impairment, and epilepsy following probable cerebral malaria
- Hemiplegia, speech impairment, cognitive impairment, swallowing difficulties following coma (underlying cause unspecified)
- Gross motor impairment, speech and swallowing difficulties following TBI, meningitis, or multiple strokes
- Global developmental delay post febrile illness in the neonatal period

Children with a conglomeration of the above disabilities present with different learning difficulties. This chapter will discuss three of these that manifest in a learning environment, namely dyslexia, dysgraphia, and dyscalculia. The discussion will integrate technology use so as to depict its importance and beneficial use by teachers who have to teach learners with developmental, perceptual functioning, and cognitive delays specifically.

4.1 Cognitive Delays in Inclusive Learning Environments

Children with special needs present a myriad of difficulties in the learning environment, and these often emanate from atypical cognitive development. The delays are more prevalent in full-service schools where teachers do not have the skills to identify early such difficulties and the associated ramifications. Whilst Goose and Van Reybroeck (2020) argue that there is no one-size-fits-all strategy to identify learning difficulties and provide therapy, teachers need to consider different variables to enhance the sustainability of the taught and learned skills.

The discussion below focuses on three of the learning difficulties that originate from cognitive development delays. The definitions of the concepts are discussed as a point of departure, after which the importance of providing ICT support for these children is deliberated, particularly in inclusive classroom settings.

Dyslexia is a language-based deficiency that manifests in spelling and reading comprehension challenges for children with special needs. Although D'Mello and Gabrieli (2018) and Kautz et al. (2014) regard heredity as one of the causal factors propagating dyslexia, they also mention cognitive and executive functioning skills as reasons for language acquisition difficulties. If brain functioning can be associated with cognitive and executive functioning, the causal effect of cognitive and executive functions on dyslexia can be assumed to be genuine.

Therefore, investigating the causal effects of dyslexia and the manifestation thereof is necessary for developing justifiable interventions. Furthermore, since teachers are at the centre of the teaching and learning process, their relevant expertise with regard to 21st century technology use is required (Andrade et al., 2016). Visual-motor integration, handwriting, and reading are intertwined in the exhibition of dysgraphia. Technology that promotes orthographic awareness and reading guides developed in collaboration with dedicated professionals are crucial to enhance reading and comprehension for learners experiencing barriers to learning.

Research has found that writing on paper uses the central and frontal brain regions and potentially more strongly link neuro-connections that facilitate cognitive development in children than typing information does. Feng,

Lindner, Ji, and Malatesha Joshi (2019) maintain that handwriting produces deeper learning and engages broader vocabulary use and emotional processing than when using a keyboard for writing. This has implications for children with dyslexia, dysgraphia, and other physical disabilities affecting their writing capability.

Lopez, Hemimou, and Vaivre-Douret (2017) state that although dysgraphia affects many children, it is under researched and little evidence is provided for a point of reference. Dysgraphia is on a spectrum that ranges from poor motor functioning and limited vocabulary to poor spatial organisation of letters in learners experiencing barriers to learning. Dohla, Wilmess and Heim (2018) agree and define dysgraphia as a "disorder associated with writing and spelling challenges" (p. 1). Whilst dysgraphia affects handwriting in children, it concomitantly includes difficulties with writing within spaces provided and the arrangement of words in text. These difficulties can be linked to the underdevelopment of fine motor skills as suggested by Paget et al. (2016). Dohla et al. (2018) furthermore associate dysgraphia with deficits of phonology, attention, vision, and hearing. Literature confirms the relationship between the aforementioned skills and neuro-disabilities, thus acknowledging their effect on learning.

Marshall et al. (2019) found great improvement in children with aphasia when word and voice prediction technology was used during writing activities. However, this did not mean that using such technology provided the same effect for all learners with disabilities. Ongoing research by teachers in full-service schools investigating a spectrum of learners experiencing barriers to learning is needed to recommend dedicated technology for specific disabilities.

Many scholars define dyscalculia as a difficulty understanding mathematical concepts and numbers. Moreau, Wilson, McKay, Nihill, and Waldie (2018) concur and state that 15% of the world's population struggle with this deficiency, which persists into adulthood when no intervention is pursued during early childhood learning. Interesting is that Moreau et al. (2018) also agree with D'Mello and Gabrieli (2018), Dohla et al. (2016) and Paget et al. (2016) in linking dyscalculia to neuro-functioning. These authors are also of the opinion that the deficiencies discussed in this section are interconnected: most children who struggle with dyscalculia are also dyslexic and present with dysgraphia.

The three learning difficulties discussed above are common in children with special needs. However, with appropriate assessments and the application of relevant intervention strategies such as the use of technological devices, these children may be able to access the prescribed curriculum and progress through school with other typically developing children.

Although technology use is discussed in this chapter as an intervention strategy to facilitate cognitive development and close the reading, writing and comprehension deficits in learners experiencing barriers to learning, it is not a panacea to solve these learning difficulties. Gaspar (2018) and Sande, Segers, and Verhoeven (2016) mention the use of dedicated hardware and software, cybernetic learning environments, and computer programs as some of the technological strategies and effective ways to reduce cognitive load and amplify quality learning for these learners. El Kah and Abdelhak (2018) as well as Sande et al. (2016) go further and argue that computer games are equally effective in developing executive functioning skills and inhibition and therefore for developing cognitive functioning in children. Inhibition is the ability of learners to be self-conscious and respond to stimuli in a responsible way. This can be assumed beneficial in most African contexts where technology and the infrastructural systems to support its functionality are underdeveloped. Games in these settings are an alternative for dedicated and high technology, which is defined as the most advanced type.

5 Information Communication Technology Skills Requirements for Teachers

ICT in the context of inclusive education can be used to scaffold learning, writing, reading, and the development of cognitive skills, depending on the child's educational needs. Teachers who use ICT also need to have the attributes to plan for content, knowledge, and the skills to enhance the holistic development of children in their classrooms. In their study, Dovis, Van der Oord, Wiers, and Prins (2015) report on the development of executive functioning (EF) skills by using computer games in children with EF deficits. It is against this background that this chapter argues that a wide spectrum of technological devices can be used to bridge the skills deficit in children and therefore proposes that teacher training be aligned to these requirements. On the other hand, since there are many technologies in the market, this chapter will not recommend any, but reiterate the following teacher guidelines as recommended by Adebisi, Liman, and Longpoe (2015, p. 18):

- Teachers should know that every child's assistive technology needs are distinctive. Children's needs should be matched with necessary technology rather than matching available tools to student needs.
- Teachers should teach needed technology skills before they are required. Thus, the children can then pay attention to regular classroom instruction rather than simultaneously learning the curriculum and the new assistive technology skills.

- It is very important that technology training for teachers make children better users of AT and maximises the impact of efforts and finances expended. Teachers should be up-to-date on AT skills acquisition. This training should include making teachers spend time researching and reading the recommended books and be current in the global use of assistive technologies.
- It is also important that teachers should have access to technical supports that might help in case of any system's crash or breakdown.
- The global trend now is collaboration and partnership among the multidisciplinary team that may include the assistive technology teacher, computer teacher, and computer maintenance professionals. This will help to ensure a functional/faultless assistive technology environment.

Furthermore, technology skills cannot be effective when taught in isolation. As early as 2009, Koehler and Mishra (2009) developed the Technological, Pedagogic and Content Knowledge (TPACK) framework to enhance teachers' capability to incorporate technology in the teaching and learning process. The novel contribution of the TPACK model is that it advocates that teacher training should encompass content, pedagogic, and technological knowledge in order to equip teachers with the skills to teach children with diverse educational needs. Furthermore, Koehler and Mishra (2009) suggest that it is the responsibility of higher education institutions to design teacher-training curricula to incorporate all of those. Furthermore, the authors suggest that the TPACK model holds promises for research to be conducted that will manage and mitigate challenges in education. The content, pedagogic, and technological knowledge skills are discussed below as intertwined and recommended beneficial for consideration in teacher training institutions.

Teachers in the foundation phase are expected to be content specialists, conversant with how theories, practices, ideas, and methodologies have contributed in the formulation of content to be taught (Koehler & Mishra, 2009). Chai, Koh, and Tsai (2010) agree with Gess-Newsome et al. (2019) and add that merging the training of the three knowledge systems for in-service teachers might enhance potential insights and point teacher training institutions towards emerging technologies.

However, research found that many teachers, particularly in South African inclusive settings, are trained only for teaching typically developing children (Engelbrecht et al., 2016; Naicker et al., 2018). These teachers possess the content knowledge for teaching specific grades but lack the skill to differentiate context and make it easily accessible to all learners in their classes.

As initially mentioned, pedagogic knowledge encompasses teachers' skill to differentiate between different types of teaching methodologies, styles, curricula, and assessments. Naicker and Stofile (2018) found inclusive pedagogic

INFORMATION AND COMMUNICATION TECHNOLOGIES 271

knowledge to be defunct and advocated that teacher-training institutions should develop training modules to counter the perceptions and attitudes perpetuated by in-service teachers in inclusive schools.

Although technology is not magic, it is an effective resource to provide learning support for children with underdeveloped cognitive skills. Alnahdi (2014) consider assistive technology essential to support the development of cognitive skills. Teachers should master not only the necessary content and pedagogic skills, but they should also be skilled to use technology to support those learners who have been identified as having learning difficulties to access the curriculum. However, the key requirement is the skill to not only use or provide technologies, but also to systematically outsource the interdisciplinary support required for children in need. Otherwise, the lack of collaboration may potentially create confusion among teachers and influence their attitude towards technology. The DBST is the structure responsible for coordinating services between schools, communities, and the Department of Education (Department of Education, 2005). Its role is to administer the screening, identification, assessment, and support of learners who experience barriers to learning, and as such, it is expected to assume these responsibilities. Unfortunately, the structure of DBSTs in many South African districts is found to be under-resourced.

To conclude, ICT offers a research platform to inform the modified TPACK model for contextual interventions and to provide teacher-training institutions with reference-based strategies to meet teacher training needs.

6   Recommendations

In the context of the need for the enhancement of inclusive education pedagogy skills, this chapter recommends that South Africa should adopt best practices from the international community. However, these strategies should be adapted to develop context-appropriate strategies for implementation in the wide range of diverse local school environments. The dearth in teachers' skill for inclusive education advancement and to support learners with delayed cognitive development succeed emanates from contrasting teacher training practices. Commitment towards learning based on the best scientific evidence from global experiences will assist in designing uniquely South African responses. Such a commitment will help to:

– inform teacher training content for student teachers in higher education institutions in order to produce teachers with the attributes for teaching in full-service schools (this will also inform modules for in-service and continuous professional development to upskill these teachers);

- encourage teacher reflection and cultivate professional skills in the use of technology to enhance the development of situational knowledge (in this case, context-relevant knowledge will be developed and curriculum access for all will be improved);
- inspire the sharing of best practices among teachers in the same vicinity, as well as promote their access to community-based resources to support learner experiencing barriers to learning;
- enhance the support needed for teachers and learners in availing resources, assistive devices, multidisciplinary teams and continuous professional development;
- power the DBSTs in pointing teachers to the relevant institutions for professional development (the facilitation of teacher development will thus bridge the pedagogic skills shortage in the South African school context in particular);
- enhance the collaboration between stakeholders in education, and thus facilitate the cultivation of community-based resolutions and delivery of sustainable development goals);
- strengthen teacher awareness to eliminate additional hindrances to the inclusion of children with special needs and develop the skill to use technology as an early intervention resource to stimulate cognitive development in all learners;
- create a blended learning approach that incorporates the training of members of the DBST in order to enhance the dual understanding of real challenges in full service schools.

7 Conclusion

Intrinsic and extrinsic barriers to learning are inherent and juxtaposed features of learners experiencing barriers to learning. This chapter illuminated the cognitive skills required for learning and the need for teachers to understand atypical development to improve curriculum access for learners experiencing barriers to learning in inclusive classrooms. The special educational needs of these learners are not confined only to physical, social, and emotional manifestations. The exosystem, including the cultural and belief systems in the communities from which learners hail, continuously presents situations from which context-relevant theories may be developed. Against the background discussed above, the collaboration of all stakeholders in education, including district-based support teams, teachers, parents, and communities, is paramount in achieving inclusive education benefits. In conclusion, appreciation

INFORMATION AND COMMUNICATION TECHNOLOGIES 273

of the value that ICT tools can contribute is strongly advocated, as the 21st century requires the application of innovative strategies for teachers in inclusive schools to eliminate barriers to learning for learner experiencing barriers to learning.

References

Adebisi, R. O., Liman, N. A., & Longpoe, P. K. (2015). Using assistive technology in teaching children with learning disabilities in the 21st century. *Journal of Education and Practice, 6*(24), 14–20.

Alnahdi, G. (2014). Assistive technology in special education and the universal design for learning. *Turkish Online Journal of Educational Technology-TOJET, 13*(2), 18–23.

Andrade, A. D., & Doolin, B. (2016). Information and communication technology and the social inclusion of refugees. *Mis Quarterly, 40*(2), 405–416.

Baddeley, A. D., & Hitch, G. J. (1994). Developments in the concept of working memory. *Neuropsychology, 8*(4), 485.

Barger, B., Rice, C., Simmons, C. A., & Wolf, R. (2018). A systematic review of Part C early identification studies. *Topics in Early Childhood Special Education, 38*(1), 4–16.

Booth, T., Ainscow, M., Black-Hawkins, K., Vaughan, M., & Shaw, L. (2002). Index for inclusion. In *Developing learning and participation in schools.* Centre for Studies on Inclusive Education.

Chai, C. S., Koh, J. H. L., & Tsai, C. C. (2010). Facilitating preservice teachers' development of Technological, Pedagogical, and Content Knowledge (TPACK). *Journal of Educational Technology & Society, 13*(4), 63–73.

Chen, M. E., Anderson, J. A., & Watkins, L. (2016). Parent perceptions of connectedness in a full-service community school project. *Journal of Child and Family Studies, 25*(7), 2268–2278.

Cirino, P. T., Fuchs, L. S., Elias, J. T., Powell, S. R., & Schumacher, R. F. (2015). Cognitive and mathematical profiles for different forms of learning difficulties. *Journal of Learning Disabilities, 48*(2), 156–175.

Chitiyo, M., Hughes, E. M., Chitiyo, G., Changara, D. M., Itimu-Phiri, A., Haihambo, C., Taukeni, S. G., & Dzenga, C. G. (2019). Exploring teachers' special and inclusive education professional development needs in Malawi, Namibia, and Zimbabwe. *International Journal of Whole Schooling, 15*(1), 28–49.

Danielsson, H., Henry, L., Rönnberg, J., & Nilsson, L. G. (2010). Executive functions in individuals with intellectual disability. *Research in Developmental Disabilities, 31*(6), 1299–1304.

Department of Education. (2001). *Education White paper 6: Special needs education: Building an inclusive education and training system.* Government Printers.

Department of Basic Education. (2011). *Curriculum and Assessment Policys Statement (CAPS): Foundation phase mathematics grade R-3*. Government Printers.

Department of Basic Education. (2017). *Responding to diversity in grades R to 9: Practical approaches to English & mathematics curriculum differentiation*. Government Printers.

Desa, U. N. (2016). *Transforming our world: The 2030 agenda for sustainable development*.

D'Mello, A. M., & Gabrieli, J. D. (2018). Cognitive neuroscience of dyslexia. *Language, Speech, and Hearing Services in Schools, 49*(4), 798–809.

Döhla, D., Willmes, K., & Heim, S. (2018). Cognitive profiles of developmental dysgraphia. *Frontiers in Psychology, 9*(1), 1–12. doi:10.3389/fpsyg.2018.02006

Dovis, S., Van der Oord, S., Wiers, R. W., & Prins, P. J. (2015). Improving executive functioning in children with ADHD: Training multiple executive functions within the context of a computer game. A randomized double-blind placebo controlled trial. *PloS One, 10*(4), e0121651.

Ehrlich, D. E., & Josselyn, S. A. (2016). Plasticity-related genes in brain development and amygdala-dependent learning. *Genes, Brain and Behavior, 15*(1), 125–143.

El Kah, A., & Abdelhak, L. (2018). Developing effective educative games for Arabic children primarily dyslexics. *Education and Information Technologies, 23*(6), 2911–30.

Engelbrecht, P., Nel, M., Nel, N. M., & Tlale, L. D. N. (2016). Teachers' perceptions of education support structures in the implementation of inclusive education in South Africa. *Koers, 81*(3), 1–14.

Feng, L., Lindner, A., Ji, X. R., & Malatesha Joshi, R. (2019). The roles of handwriting and keyboarding in writing: A meta-analytic review. *Reading and Writing: An Interdisciplinary Journal, 32*(1), 33–63.

Gašpar, D. (2018). ICT eases inclusion in education. In *Encyclopedia of information science and technology* (4th ed., pp. 2521–2531). IGI Global.

Gess-Newsome, J., Taylor, J. A., Carlson, J., Gardner, A. L., Wilson, C. D., & Stuhlsatz, M. A. (2019). Teacher pedagogical content knowledge, practice, and student achievement. *International Journal of Science Education, 41*(7), 944–963.

Goldstein, S., Naglieri, J. A., Princiotta, D., & Otero, T. M. (2014). Introduction: A history of executive functioning as a theoretical and clinical construct. In *Handbook of executive functioning* (pp. 3–12). Springer.

Gosse, C., & Van Reybroeck, M. (2020). Do children with dyslexia present a handwriting deficit? Impact of word orthographic and graphic complexity on handwriting and spelling performance. *Research in Developmental Disabilities, 97*, 103553.

Kautz, T., Heckman, J. J., Diris, R., Ter Weel, B., & Borghans, L. (2014). *Fostering and measuring skills: Improving cognitive and non-cognitive skills to promote lifetime success* (NBER working paper No. w20749). National Bureau of Economic Research.

Kirk, H. E., Gray, K., Riby, D. M., & Cornish, K. M. (2015). Cognitive training as a resolution for early executive function difficulties in learners with intellectual disabilities. *Research in Developmental Disabilities, 38*(1), 145–160.

Koehler, M., & Mishra, P. (2009). What is Technological Pedagogical Content Knowledge (TPACK)? *Contemporary Issues in Technology and Teacher Education, 9*(1), 60–70.

Leppink, J. (2017). Cognitive load theory: Practical implications and an important challenge. *Journal of Taibah University Medical Sciences, 12*(5), 385–391.

Le Roux, B. D. (2016). *Concessions and accommodations.* South African Teachers' Union.

Lopez, C., Hemimou, C., & Vaivre-Douret, L. (2017). Handwriting disorders in children with Developmental Coordination Disorder (DCD): Exploratory study. *European Psychiatry, 41*(1), S456.

Marshall, J., Caute, A., Chadd, K., Cruice, M., Monnelly, K., Wilson, S., & Woolf, C. (2019). Technology-enhanced writing therapy for people with aphasia: Results of a quasi-randomized waitlist-controlled study. *International Journal of Language & Communication Disorders, 54*(2), 203–220.

Meltzer, L. (Ed.). (2018). *Executive function in education: From theory to practice.* Guilford Publications.

McEwan, P. J. (2015). Improving learning in primary schools of developing countries: A meta-analysis of randomized experiments. *Review of Educational Research, 85*(3), 353–394.

Moreau, D., Wilson, A. J., McKay, N. S., Nihill, K., & Waldie, K. E. (2018). No evidence for systematic white matter correlates of dyslexia and dyscalculia. *Neuro Image: Clinical, 18*, 356–366.

Naicker, S. M. (2018). *Inclusive education in South Africa and the developing world: The search for an inclusive pedagogy.* Emerald Publishing.

Naicker, S. M., & Stofile, S. (2018). In search of an inclusive pedagogy in South Africa. In S. Pather & R. Slee (Eds.), *Challenging inclusive education policy and practice in Africa* (pp. 87–103). Brill Sense.

Nilsson, M., Griggs, D., & Visbeck, M. (2016). Policy: Map the interactions between sustainable development goals. *Nature, 534*(7607), 320–322.

Oppici, L., Panchuk, D., Serpiello, F. R., & Farrow, D. (2019). Response: Commentary: Long-term practice with domain-specific task constraints influences perceptual skills. *Frontiers in Psychology, 10*(85), 1–3.

Paget, A., Mallewa, M., Chinguo, D., Mahebere-Chirambo, C., & Gladstone, M. (2016). "It means you are grounded" – Caregivers' perspectives on the rehabilitation of learners with neuro disability in Malawi. *Disability and Rehabilitation, 38*(3), 223–234.

Robinson, O. P., Bridges, S. A., Rollins, L. H., & Schumacker, R. E. (2019). A study of the relation between special education burnout and job satisfaction. *Journal of Research in Special Educational Needs, 19*(4), 295–303.

Sande, E., Segers, E., & Verhoeven, L. (2016). Supporting executive functions during children's preliteracy learning with the computer. *Journal of Computer-Assisted Learning, 32*(5), 468–480.

Tanyi, M. E. (2016). Pedagogic barriers in Cameroon inclusive classrooms: The impact of curriculum, teachers' attitudes and classroom infrastructure. *Journal of Education and Practice, 7*(18), 1–12.

Vygotsky, L. (1998). *The collected works of L. Vygotsky. Child psychology* (Vol. 5). Plenum Press.

CHAPTER 15

Empowering Students Experiencing Barriers to Learning through ICT to Ensure Inclusiveness and Equality

Mbulaheni Maguvhe

Abstract

This chapter analyses literature on information communication technology (ICT), with a particular interest on its impact as an empowering tool which entrenches inclusiveness and equality in its quest to accommodate students experiencing barriers to learning. The aim is to highlight the impact and importance of ICT in the education of students experiencing barriers to learning in the inclusive education context. The analyses highlights that although ICTs are becoming the norm rather than the exception in many classrooms in the mainstream, a lot of students experiencing barriers to learning still feel they are deprived of general information communication technologies (ICTs) for reasonable accommodation to learning environments, and assistive devices which help in the facilitation of teaching and learning mediation. Reasonable accommodation is the provision of conditions and equipment as well as the environment that allows an individual with a barrier to perform his or her job effectively and efficiently. A worrying factor regarding this matter is that it is not only the paucity of the different technological resources that contribute to deficits in supply. More often than not, the attitudes of some people who should ensure and/or facilitate delivery of such technologies to students experiencing barriers to learning are also cited as possible hindrances, together with the self-denying attitudes of some of the possible recipients (students).

Keywords

assistive technology – barriers to learning – equality – inclusiveness – information and communication technologies

---

© KONINKLIJKE BRILL NV, LEIDEN, 2021 | DOI: 10.1163/9789004447226_016

1 Introduction

This chapter analyses and aims to show the impact of both assistive technology and information communication technology as empowering tools which entrench inclusiveness and equality in the quest to reasonably accommodate students experiencing barriers to learning in inclusive education settings. The target audience for this chapter includes, but is not limited to: teachers at inclusive schools, ECD and ABET practitioners, lecturers of TVET colleges and universities, parents of students experiencing barriers to learning, policy-makers, government officials, and researchers. Assistive technology and information communication technology are tools that can be used to eliminate or minimise barriers to learning (Department of Public Service and Administration, 2015).

Barriers to learning should be understood as anything that stands in the way of a student's ability to learn effectively. It is possible that a student may experience one or more barriers to learning throughout his or her education. Students experiencing barriers to learning will experience that barrier as an intrinsic barrier to learning and will require varying levels of support to accommodate their barrier in order to reach their full academic potential. Barriers to learning are not limited to intrinsic barriers. They can also be societal/environmental barriers. For example, extreme poverty, abuse, or neglect will all act as barriers to a student's learning. Barriers are by and large obstacles and impediments that prevent individuals from free movement, decision-making, association, and participation. Barriers may be environmental (physical) and could be created or perpetuated by attitudes and systems that limit functioning and create barrier's (Department of Public Service and Administration, 2015).

Students experiencing barriers to learning must be able to actively and competently participate in an increasingly digital world. According to Seale (2017) barriers broadly include physical, sensory, mobility, social, and cognitive impairments. However, it should be noted that a barrier does not define a single homogeneous group. Students experiencing barriers to learning and those living with disabilities show substantial variations regarding their experiences and attainment. Students experiencing barriers to learning are hindered from participating fully and effectively in society on an equal footing due to various attitudinal, communication, physical, and information barriers.

1.1 Assistive Technology and Information Communication Technology

An attempt to answer two key questions throughout this chapter will be made. First, how do assistive technologies and information communication technologies empower students in general and those experiencing barriers to learning in particular? Further, how do assistive technologies and information communication technologies ensure inclusiveness and equality? Dealing with equality and non-discrimination requires that institutions of learning take all appropriate measures to ensure that reasonable accommodations (fostered and enhanced through assistive technologies and information communication technologies) are provided in order to promote equality, inclusiveness, and empowerment by eliminating inaccessibility of information.

Focusing on education and learning requires of institutions of learning to ensure that accessible assistive technologies and information communication technologies are provided to students experiencing barriers to learning in the teaching and learning environment. The provision of accessible assistive technologies and information communication technologies seeks to address the issue of inclusion in different situations, including education. This inclusive, empowerment and equality measure, is an attempt to recognise the attendant need for reasonable accommodation which includes the provision of assistive devices to students experiencing barriers to learning in order to fully enhance their participation in the teaching and learning encounter (Department of Public Service and Administration, 2015).

Further, another central question in this chapter which needs an answer is: What is assistive technology and how does it differ from information communication technology? Simply put, assistive technology is an umbrella term which includes assistive, adaptive, and rehabilitative devices for people experiencing barriers or the elderly in their rehabilitation, daily lives, education, work, or leisure. On the other hand, information communication technology supports individuals experiencing barriers to enhance their social and economic integration in communities (European Platform for Rehabilitation, 2018–2022.) So, it is not possible when dealing with technology for individuals experiencing barriers to learning to put emphasis on either assistive technology or information communication technology. They complement and supplement each other in making the lives of these individuals easier and worth living. This is why these terms are used interchangeably in this chapter.

According to the Individuals with Disabilities Education Act Amendments (IDEA) of 2004, an assistive technology (AT) device refers to any item, piece of equipment, or product system, whether acquired commercially off-the-shelf, modified, or customised, that is used to increase, maintain, or improve the functional capabilities of a student experiencing barriers to learning. The term does not include a medical device that is surgically implanted or the replacement of such device (SEC 602[1]).

On the other hand, Department of Public Service and Administration (2015) suggests that assistive devices and technologies are any device designed, made, or adapted to help an individual execute a particular task. Products may be specifically manufactured or generally be made available for people experiencing barriers.

The federal definition is quite broad and encompasses devices that are electronic (e.g., computer, scanner, tape recorder) and non-electronic (e.g., pencil grip, large print books), so long as those devices are used to increase, maintain, or improve the functional capabilities of individuals experiencing barriers (Individuals with Disabilities Education Act Amendments (IDEA) of 2004; Department of Public service and Administration, 2015). Furthermore, the federal definition includes items such as computer-aided instructional software programs for reading or mathematics that can be used to remediate skill deficits.

Assistive technology includes electronic/computer technology that is used to compensate for specific learning barriers (e.g., speech synthesis for reading, voice recognition for writing). The technology may in some instances augment task performance in a given area of a barrier while in other instances it may be used to circumvent or by-pass specific deficits holistically. Assistive technology has the potential to maximise students' performance at an expected level based on general cognitive abilities (Raskind, 2013).

Assistive technology and information communication technology could be considered instrumental elements to normalise educational conditions and otherwise of students experiencing barriers to learning. Its empowering potential and entrenchment of inclusiveness and equality can be noticeable through its ability to give or guarantee equal access to the school curriculum. Technological advances in the recent past, have enhanced the integration and adaptation of people in general and students experiencing barriers to learning in particular in the field of employment (European Platform for Rehabilitation, 2018–2022).

Assistive technology and information communication technology in education play a pivotal role in giving access to and supporting high quality education for students experiencing barriers to learning. The advantages of assistive technology and information communication technology utilisation in the teaching and learning mediation process are a myriad as these offer alternative means of communication. Assistive technology and ICTs provide access to educational resources in a more convenient way and enhance teaching and learning.

Martinez (2011) posits that assistive technology/ICTs enable students experiencing barriers to learning to overcome obstacles of time and space. Assistive technology/ICTs supplement vital human functioning and support the development of important skills and contribute to the increased efficiency and effectiveness of educational processes by enabling students experiencing barriers to learning to fully and actively participate in teaching and learning mediation processes.

Of worth noting is that education is an essential sector for the prosperity of countries and societies worldwide. Telkom (2015) emphasises that education is one of the top priorities of governments. For education to be an effective tool for the future success of students, it must keep up with the latest developments in technology in general, and assistive technology/ICTs in particular.

This chapter is using the phrase/concept "students experiencing barriers to learning". One is aware that there are divergent opinions regarding the most appropriate use of the terminology. The justification to use the phrase/concept is that someone experiencing a barrier implies that the barrier is not necessarily a result of an impairment or condition, but can be caused society and its inability or reluctance to effectively cater to the needs of an individual. It is society that must effect change to remove that barrier. The focus of this chapter is on those students experiencing barriers to learning where assistive technologies and Information communication technologies are not integrated into the teaching and learning mediation, thereby impeding empowerment, inclusion, equality, equity, access to the curriculum, accommodation, and assessment.

This chapter focuses on the use of assistive technologies and information communication technologies in addressing barriers to learning. It attempts to highlight benefits and privileges that students experiencing barriers to learning can enjoy when using these technologies during teaching and learning mediation in various institutions of learning. It is therefore premised on the key concepts of a rights-based approach, foregrounding issues of social justice, equitable access, equal opportunities to benefits and services, and commitment to meeting the needs of the student fraternity. Since these concepts are prone to attracting divergent meanings, it is necessary to put them into context for this chapter. Walker (2003) notes that institutions of learning positively contribute to the shaping of shaping people's lives. He suggests that there are possibilities that these institutions of learning could produce "justice and injustice", "equity and inequality" if there is no adaptation or modification pertaining to programmes, environment, and practices. This is a wake-up call for communities to transform education systems to ensure respect for human rights and to guarantee the attainment of social justice (Mosia & Pasha, 2017).

Social justice, equity, and equality in this chapter are used in conjunction with Siemens' (2004) theory of connectivism. Social justice should be understood as justice applied to, for example, the distribution of wealth, opportunities, privileges, and resources within a society. Equity is the practice of striving to be fair and impartial. Equality refers to being equal particularly in status, rights, privileges, benefits, and opportunities. The theory of connectivism is a framework for understanding learning in a digital age. It puts emphasis on how internet technology such as web browsers, search engines, wikies, online discussion forums, and social networks contribute to new avenues of teaching and learning.

This theory sheds light on how technology has fundamentally altered the way knowledge has both been approached and acquired. According to Siemens (2004), this theory is contextualised in a digital era and characterised by the influence of technology in the field of education. Connectivism theory has shifted the focus of learning from the acquisition of knowledge by an individual and puts it squarely on the idea that knowledge is gleaned through sharing via networks. In other words, knowledge that has been stored in the internet can be accessed by anyone anywhere at any time as long one has the right gadget to access it.

1.2 *Global Perspective*

The number of students experiencing barriers to learning entering institutions of higher learning is on the rise. It is estimated that 8–10% of students in institutions of higher learning are registered with barriers in developed countries (Hardjikakou, 2007). Data from Higher Education Management Information System (HEMIS) in South Africa has shown a slow increase in enrolment (DHET, 2014; Siwela, 2017). Though the number of students experiencing barriers to learning in institutions of higher learning in South Africa is on the rise, they only constitute 1% of the student population. The United Nations has called for an increase in international promotion of inclusive and equitable quality education for all (UN, 2016). Therefore, widening participation in education is supported by among other things, legislative changes, inclusive education practices, the use of assistive technologies/information communication technologies, accessible facilities and programmes and, ultimately, an increasing belief among students experiencing barriers to learning that education maximises their opportunities for employment, independence, and enjoyment of productive and dignified lives (Hardjikakou, 2007; DHET, 2014; Siwela, 2017).

Transformation in South Africa has primarily focused on race and gender issues and disability has been overlooked despite the fact that South Africa is among other countries in the world to have ratified the Convention on the Rights of Persons with Disabilities (UNCRPD) in 2007 (Mutanga, 2007; DHET, 2014; Siwela, 2017). In addition, DHET (2014) and Siwela (2017) admit that access and inclusion of students experiencing barriers to learning receives very little attention or resources, leading to a small number of students experiencing barriers to learning accessing and graduating from South African institutions of higher learning. The disempowerment, exclusion from education, and unequal teaching and learning conditions mentioned above can be corrected through the proper utilisation of and access to information communication technologies and assistive technologies.

1.3 Emergence of Assistive and Information Communication Technologies

The boom of the information age has strengthened all continents', countries', and individuals' economic prosperity. Additionally, the transfer of information through emerging media upgrades has even revolutionised entertainment activities and created a whole lot of new ones. However, the dispersion that is prevalent in assistive technologies/information communication technologies is negatively influencing many aspects of global societies in education, training, employment, and many other spheres of life.

A number of scholars suggest that online communication is quite popular among young people (Price, Waterhouse, & Coopers, 2010; Eady & Lockery, 2013; Telkom, 2015). Internet and virtual environments are being integrated into young people's lives. Notwithstanding the fact that the utilisation of ICTs is a trend, Asuncion et al. (2009) and Fitchten et al. (2014) postulate that students experiencing barriers to learning may experience challenges and discrimination when institutions of learning expect them to utilise inaccessible information communication technologies as part of their teaching and learning mediation encounter.

Livingstone and Helpser (2007) and the European Platform for Rehabilitation (2018–2022) argue that the emergence of information communication technologies has rendered students experiencing barriers to learning vulnerable and marginalised. Concerted effort and unwavering support have been put into the maximisation of information communication technologies within institutions of learning in developed communities and it is rapidly spreading into developing communities. Some information communication technologies, such as Web 2.0 technologies and virtual learning environments (VLEs), are providing wider, anytime-anywhere access to formal learning to many students. That can be seen as a path towards empowerment, inclusion, and equality which is a quest to address barriers to learning.

This chapter thus examines the appropriateness and utilisation of assistive technologies/information communication technologies in institutions of learning, with a distinct aim towards the empowerment, inclusion, and equality benefits and privileges enjoyed or gained by students experiencing barriers to learning. The chapter takes full advantage of the ever rising voices of persons experiencing various forms of barriers in protest to marginalisation, ostracisation, and/or exclusion from access to information through the unavailability of assistive technologies or information communication technologies. Concern is also raised in association with matters in and around the level to which copyright and intellectual property rights must be entertained to prevent access to basic information which enables productive formal education, this can include accessible learning and teaching support materials. The Department of Public Service and Administration (2015) states that access is a means or way to locate, retrieve, understand, and appropriately use information. Therefore, an environment, service, or product (assistive technological and information and communication technologies) should allow access to as many people as possible, but in particular to people experiencing barriers (Department of Public Service and Administration, 2015).

1.4 Assistive Technologies/Information Communication Technologies and Inclusive Education

The demand in a large scale for inclusive education has increased and fostered major changes to both schooling and education. Students experiencing barriers to learning and special educational needs are now educated together with their peers within the local community. In many developed countries the number of students experiencing barriers to learning served in inclusive settings alongside students who do not experience barriers to learning is on the rise (Messiou, 2017; Lipsky & Gartner, 2006). Because of this, inclusive schools are required to adapt in order to accommodate diverse groups of students with a variety of needs (Messiou, 2017; O'Gorman, 2005).

It is important to point out that educational technology and ICTs when available and accessible play quite a significant role in creating and fostering a conducive learning environment for students experiencing barriers to learning. It is on this basis that the demand for assistive technologies is increasing tremendously because now more students experiencing barriers to learning are studying in mainstream educational settings (Connect a school, 2015; European Platform for Rehabilitation, 2018–2022). However, there is still a digital divide in many communities. This results from inadequate information communication technologies for addressing special educational needs and inclusive education classrooms.

Young people experiencing barriers in many communities often come from socially disadvantaged families and their educational attainment and life outcomes are most likely to be affected (Siwela, 2017; European Platform for Rehabilitation, 2018–2022; Lumadi & Maguvhe, 2013; Punie, 2008). From the technology point of view, this group is at increased risk of being part of a digital divide, i.e. having less or no personal access to the internet and not having

EMPOWERING STUDENTS EXPERIENCING BARRIERS

the skills required to maximise the use of online technologies for social, economic, and learning purposes.

A survey conducted in England found that many mainstream schools did not have access to technologies to support young people experiencing physical, sensory, or cognitive barriers (Becta, 2010; Lumadi & Maguvhe, 2013) WSIS (2010) has also reported that technologies are still not available to manage each barrier or for each person experiencing a barrier. Another study conducted by Hermans et al. (2008) revealed that integration of new technology into classes has been slow in progress while the dominant pattern in co-teaching has been that the special needs teacher takes subordinate role (Scruggs, Mastopieri, & Mcduffie, 2007; Lumadi & Maguvhe, 2013).

Most hardware and software are designed for the mainstream population. Technology designed for the mainstream population fail to take into account a wide range of capabilities people experiencing barriers have and, so, they are left out. Lumadi and Maguvhe (2013) caution that such technologies must be appropriate for the needs of students experiencing barriers to learning so that they can utilise them as well during the learning encounter.

1.5 Assistive Technology and ICTs as a Life-Long Empowerment, Inclusiveness, and Equality Requirement

Assistive technology and ICTs extend beyond the classroom, college, university, and other teaching and learning environments. For most people, this means the need for information to be provided in formats and mediums they can understand easily (e.g. in an easy read or symbol format) or an accessible website that can be read aloud using screen reading technology (Department of Public Service and Administration, 2015; Lumadi & Maguvhe, 2013). For others, this may be a device that talks and thus support communication, social interaction, or a device that translates sign language into text or provides automatic subtitles to video materials. In order for technology to support inclusion it must be available and accessible when it is needed and be fit for the purpose an individual needs it for (Maguvhe, 2014). One of the measures adopted globally to indicate the progress made in the use of technology for inclusion is the use of digital accessibility and assistive technologies.

2 Recommendations

This chapter has arrived at the following recommendations because education, training, and information are aspects of society. Assistive and information communication technologies should guarantee that those three important societal aspects are equally, easily, safely, and appropriately used or accessed by persons experiencing barriers. Further, those technologies foster inclusivity, empowerment, and equality (Department of Public Service and Administration, 2015). It is therefore recommended that students experiencing barriers to learning be equipped with life assistive technologies and information communication technologies to enhance their lives in different environments. In addition, it is further recommended that appropriate assistive technologies and information communication technologies that meet the unique needs of students experiencing barriers to learning be provided so that they can actively and fully participate in teaching and learning mediation encounters.

For coordinated use of information communication technologies and provision of assistive technologies it is recommended that a national policy be formulated by government or relevant departments including, but not limited to, the Department of Basic Education, Department of Science and Technology and others, to govern the accessibility of such technologies. Since government is the custodian of education, it must ensure that adequate assistive technology and information communication technology resources and equipment are provided to students experiencing barriers to learning at inclusive education schools. Therefore, it is incumbent upon government to provide equipment that is age appropriate, durable, and multi-purpose so that students do not have many gadgets to carry from one place to another.

It is also recommended to use educational technology and information communication technologies as long as they are available since they really make an impact in the creation of a productive teaching and learning environment. The use of assistive technology and ICTs by students experiencing print barriers is recommended since it compensates for the lack or loss of skills such as reading and writing. It is further recommended to use assistive technology and ICTs because of their power to transform education approaches (Lumadi & Maguvhe, 2013; Maguvhe, 2014). When education approaches are truly transformed, an inclusive learning environment becomes more conducive for all.

It is recommended that assistive technology and ICTs be used for communication purposes. Technological devices give a voice to the voiceless, such as students with limited or no speech. Students who receive assistive technologies and/or information communication technologies, should on a basic level know how to use, secure, and maintain them, and know where to get assistance when a problem occurs. The people who can give them support and assistance when problems with their assistive devices arise will be members of the school based support team at their respective schools. They will escalate the problem/s to the relevant authority should the need arise. They may also know places where they can send malfunctioning gadgets for repair or maintenance in their communities.

If funds allow, it is also recommended that posts for information technology specialists be created at the school level to give technical support and training on assistive technology and ICTs to students experiencing barriers to learning.

3 Conclusion

The literature review has revealed that the term assistive technology (AT) represents a very broad concept, and together with communication technologies such as ICTs encompass a broad spectrum of measures aimed at equipping individuals with means for life enhancement, be they persons experiencing barriers or not (European Platform for Rehabilitation, 2018–2022; Department of Public Service and Administration, 2015). While assistive technologies cover anything that could improve functional capabilities (Lumadi & Maguvhe, 2013; Maguvhe, 2014; Department of Public Service and Administration, 2015; European Platform for Rehabilitation, 2018–2022; Reed & Bowser, 2005; Bodine, 2003), information communication technologies are understood as technologies which aid education through improving ways of gathering information. Information communication technologies include computer software/programmes which enhance one's ability to interact with other people and to collect information and use it while assistive technologies include both low-tech and high-tech devices such as calipers and braces, to aid movement or other bodily function (WHO, 2009).

This chapter has also shown that for a coordinated use of information communication technologies and provision of assistive technologies there is need for a national policy governing the accessibility of such technologies (G3information communication technology, 2011). It has also emerged from this research that beyond the institutionalisation of relevant ICTs policies, there is need for positive attitudes towards the development of ICTs and AT use by both the teacher and the student (in education).

It has also been noted that it is quite feasible to use educational technology and information communication technologies as long as they are available since they really make an impact on the creation of a productive learning environment. It has also been noted through the search that the demand for information communication technologies is actually on the rise, confirming that prospective users find those materials worth investing in. The different information communication technologies are also useful for the education of younger students and students experiencing barriers to learning (Lumadi & Maguvhe, 2013; Maguvhe, 2014; Messiou, 2017; Starcic, 2010).

The literature search has revealed that the use of information communication technologies is beneficial to students with a wide range of needs, such as the need for assistance with cognitive processing, the need for critical thinking, or the need for team work. ICTs have also been observed to be helpful in promoting student-centred learning approaches (Department of Public Service and Administration, 2015; EC, 2008). It has also been shown that the learning speed of individuals has been seen to improve through the use of information communication technologies (European Platform for Rehabilitation, 2018–2022; Molnár et al., 2008).

A wide range of assistive devices is now available on the market for persons experiencing different types of barriers, such as the visually impaired, the Deaf and hard of hearing, the speech impaired, and the orthopedically impaired, and those with learning difficulties. However, some of the necessary assistive technologies and information communication technologies are still out or reach for many people.

References

Becta. (2010). *Harnessing technology survey 2010.* Coventry. http://dera.ioe.ac.uk/id/eprint/1544

Bodine, C. (2003). *Assistive technology: Access for all students.* Pearson.

Connect a School.org. (2015). *Connect a school connect a community toolkit module: Using information communication technologies to promote education and job training for persons with disabilities.* http://www.connectaschool.org/itu-module/15/331/en/persons/w/disabilities/connectivity/introduction/

Department of Higher Education and Training. (2014). *Department of Higher Education and Training plan 2014/15.* Republic of South Africa, Higher Education & Training.

Department of Public Service and Administration. (2015). *Policy on reasonable accommodation and assistive devices for employees with disabilities in the public service.* Braille Services of Blind South Africa.

Eady, M., & Lockyer, L. (2013). Tools for learning: Technology and teaching strategies. In P. Hudson (Ed.), *Learning to teach in the primary school.* Cambridge University Press.

EC. (2008). *The use of information communication technology to support innovation and lifelong learning for all – A report on progress.* EC.

European Blind Union. (2015). *Copyright and publication.* European Blind Union.

European Platform for Rehabilitation. (2018–2022). *Webpage.* www.epr.eu

Ferguson, D. L. (2008). International trends in inclusive education: The continuing challenge to teach each one and everyone. *European Journal of Special Needs Education, 23*(2), 109–120.

Fichten, C. S., Asuncion, J., & Scapin, R. (2014). Digital technology, learning and post-secondary students with disabilities: Where we have been and where we are going. *Journal of Post-secondary Education and Disability, 27*(4), 369–379.

G3information communication technology. (2010). *Convention on the rights of persons with disabilities 2010. Information communication technology accessibility progress report.* UN, Global Initiative for Inclusive Information and Communication Technologies.

Hadjikakou, K., & Nikolaraizi, M. (2007). The impact of personal educational experiences and communication practices on the construction of Deaf identity in Cyprus. *American Annals of the Deaf, 4*, 398–414.

Hermans, R., Tondeur, J., van Braak, J., & Valcke, M. (2008). The impact of primary school teachers' educational beliefs on the classroom use of computers. *Computers & Education, 51*, 1499–1509.

Individuals with Disabilities Education Act. (2004). *A comprehensive Guide to your rights and responsibilities under the Individuals with Disabilities Education Act (IDEA 2004): IDEA parent guide.* National Centre for Learning Disabilities.

Livingstone, S., & Helsper, E. (2007). Gradations in digital inclusion: Students, young people and the digital divide. *New Media & Society, 9*(4), 671–696.

Lumadi, M. W., & Maguvhe, M. O. (2013). Reimagining an augmentative communication: An inclusive curriculum angle. *International Journal of Educational Science, 5*(3), 245–254.

Maguvhe, M. O. (2014). Augmentative and alternative communication: Requirements for inclusive educational interventions. *International Journal of Educational Sciences, 7*(2), 253–260.

Martinez, R. S. (2011). Disability and the use of information communication technology in education: Do students with special needs recognize the support given by teachers when using technology. *Problems of Education in the 21st Century, 35*, 149–158.

Messiou, K. (2017). Research in the field of inclusive education: Time for a rethink? *International Journal of Inclusive Education, 21*(2), 146–159.

Molnár, I. T., Radványi, T., & Kovács, E. (2008). The usage of adapted information communication technology in the education of students with special educational need in different countries of Europe. *Annals Mathematicae et Informaticae, 35*, 189–204.

Mosia, P. A., & Phasha, N. (2017). Access to curriculum for students experiencing barriers to learning at higher education institutions: How does the National University of Lesotho fare? *African Journal of Disability, 6*, 1–13.

Mutanga, O. (2017). Students experiencing barriers to learning experience in South African higher education: A synthesis of literature. *South African Journal of Higher Education, 31*(1), 135–154.

O'Gorman, E. (2005, October 22–26). Setting standards for teacher education in special educational needs in Ireland. In *Proceedings 30th Annual Conference ATEE* (pp. 377–381).

Punie, Y. (Ed.). (2008). *The socio-economic impact of social computing. Proceedings of a validation and policy options workshop*. IPTS Exploratory Research on the Socio-economic Impact of Social Computing. Institute for Prospective Technological Studies (IPTS), JRC, European Commission.

Raskind, M. (2013). *Success attributes among individuals with disabilities*. Great Schools Inc. http://www.greatschools.net/LD/managing/success-attributes-among-individuals-with-learning-disabilities.gs?content=851&page=all

Reed, P., & Bowser, G. (2005). Assistive technologies and the IEP. In D. Edyburn, K. P. Higgins, & R. Boone (Eds.), *Handbook of special education technology research and practice*. Knowledge by Design Inc.

Scruggs, T. E., Mastropieri, M. A., & Mcduffie, K. A. (2007). Co-teaching in inclusive classrooms: A metasynthesis of quantitative research. *Council for Exceptional Students, 73*(4), 392–416.

Seale, J. K. (2017). From the voice of a 'Socratic Gadfly': A call for more academic activism in the researching of disability in postsecondary education. *European Journal of Special Needs Education, 32*(1), 153–169.

Siemens, G. (2005). *Connectivms: A learning theory for the digital age*. Elearnspace. http://www.elearnspace.org/articles/connectivism.htm

Siwela, S. (2017). *An exploratory case study of experiences of students with disabilities at a tvet college: Factors that facilitate or impede their access and success* (Unpublished thesis). School of Education, College of Humanities, University of Kwa-Zulu Natal.

Söderstöm, S. (2009). Offline social ties and online use of computers: A study of disabled youth and their use of information communication technology advances. *New Media & Society, 11*(5), 709–727.

Starcic, A. I. (2010). Education technology for the inclusive classroom. *The Turkish Online Journal of Educational Technology, 9*(3), 26–37.

Telkom. (2015). *Tomorrow starts today. Technology in education: Considerations and trends for the education sector*. tbsm@telkom.co.za www.telkom.co.za/bigbusiness

UN. (2016). *Inclusive education vital for all, including persons with disabilities – UN rights experts*. UN News. https://news.un.org/en/story/2016/09/537952-inclusive-education-vital-all-including-persons-disabilities-un-rights-experts

Walker, D. H. T. (2003). *Implications of human capital issues*. In D. H. T. Walker & K. D. Hampson (Eds.), *Procurement strategies: A relationship-based approach* (pp. 258–295). Blackwell Publishing.

World Health Organization, Regional Office for South-East Asia. (2009). *Self-care in the context of primary health care*. WHO Regional Office for South-East Asia. http://www.who.int/iris/handle/10665/206352

World Summit on the Information Society. (2010). *Outcomes document*. ITU.

CHAPTER 16

Summary

Mbulaheni Maguvhe and Ramashego Shila Mphahlele

1 Afterthought

With the estimated 50,000 pre-service teachers graduating from the ODeL institutions in South Africa, these students could be challenged to take co-responsibility for the teaching and learning process, and not merely be recipients of the teaching they are exposed to. This book hopes to create excitement for the implementation of ICT and ODeL. It can also minimise the "us and them" attitude and promote the notion that both students and lecturers are "lifelong learners" who are busy exploring and discovering the wonders of uncharted territory.

Although this book presented atypical South African case studies, e.g. UNISA and WITS, it is envisaged that other countries and institutions can learn from these case studies; however, not as the extreme example of excellence. The authors endeavoured to show how technological advances can play an instrumental role breaking down the barriers some students face to learning in all fields of education. Through this book the authors want to dispel the misconceptions and attitudes of many who believe that ICTs do not have a role to play in the lives of people who experience barriers. We hope this book will help people understand how ICTs can be used to promote the inclusion and equality of students who experience barriers to learning in an ODeL learning environment

2 Thesis of the Book

The chapters managed to address the misconceptions and attitudes of many who believe that ICTs do not have a role to play in the education of students and learners who experience barriers to teaching and learning. This book is premised on the view that ICT empowers students, fosters inclusiveness, and supports equality of people in general, but has particular strengths to offer those with disabilities. Reasonable accommodation in the form of ICT should always be linked to the inherent requirements of a particular learner and the specific tasks and specifications that the device has been procured to perform.

© KONINKLIJKE BRILL NV, LEIDEN, 2021 | DOI: 10.1163/9789004447226_017

ICT should add value to the performance and potential of learners with disabilities. Chapter contributors and editors strove to show that ICT have the ability to provide for the full and equal participation of learners with disabilities in school learning activities, with the intention of leveling the education playing field through equitable participation.

3 Summary of Chapters

This book consists of 15 chapters which have individually and collectively generated discourse on student empowerment to ensure inclusiveness through ICT. The chapters represent a number of larger topics that could be treated alone, but they were put together to follow a sequence and to complement each other by grouping them into two parts. The first part focuses on the identification of, and ways to address, barriers to learning in schools and ODeL. The common thread in all 15 chapters is student empowerment, which Pillay and Agherdien in Chapter 1 explicitly addressed with a conceptualisation of inclusivity, equality, and equity.

In Chapters 2 to 5, Mulovhedzi, Muzielwana, Mphahlele, Moonsamy, Mupawose and Adams articulated the barriers to teaching and learning as well as highlighted the underlying principles and definitions with an emphasis on the importance of exploring the possibilities which ODeL and ICT have for the teaching and learning process. The chapters emphasised the identification of learners who experience barriers to learning and the role of ICT in providing for their learning needs. Du Plessis, Mupawose, Moonsamy and Adams in the sixth and seventh chapters of Part 1 delineated the strategies for addressing barriers to teaching and learning using ICT. Hoosen and Crouch in closing the part, discussed a very important issue of critical pedagogies, bringing it into conversation with ideas about how ICTs, asking us to consider how they might shape the culture of an institution.

The second part of this book discussed the use of ICT to empower students in the specific areas of mathematics, speech language pathology, audiology and cognition. Ngoepe and Phoshoko presented the landscape regarding the use of ICT for mathematical participation and support. They both emphasised student empowerment where ICT should be seen as a discipline, not only as a tool to enhance the students' learning. Mophosho and Masuku focused on ACC, empowering students and learners at school level to overcome communication barriers. They outlined different kinds of AAC—low technology, high technology, no technology options. Khoza-Shangase, Moroe and Sebothoma put forward the teleaudiology implementation strategies as synchronous and

SUMMARY 293

asynchronous as well as how the combination of the two approaches is feasible in certain parts of South Africa. In the field of audiology, Pillay and Sebothoma described educational audiology within the classroom and how the use of ICT can empower students while also serving as a support tool to parents. Thuketana used Vygotsky's theory of cognitive development to describe the exclusion of learners experiencing barriers to learning. The last chapter by Mbulaheni Maguvhe wraps up this book by reinforcing student empowerment for those students experiencing barriers to learning. He problematised the limited or lack of AT and ICT integration and recommended inclusiveness and equality.

4 Call for Action

In this book academics discuss diverse topics related to ICTs, providing insight into best practices. They also give guidance to institutions of learning which offer distance education through the use of ICT, with an eye towards helping those who are concerned with the education of students who experience barriers to learning keep abreast of technological developments and events. Should educators and educational institutions truly want be a tool for empowerment, inclusion, and equity, all students (including those who experience barriers to learning) have to be exposed and enabled to ICTs which will help them fully participate in the digital world.

Index

#FeesMustFall 23

academic literacies 4, 73–84
access 1, 3, 7, 12–15, 20, 23, 24, 33, 42, 48, 49,
  58, 69, 70, 74, 75, 77, 79–84, 95, 98, 99,
  102, 103, 115–118, 123, 124, 128, 135, 137,
  139, 143, 153, 165, 174, 187, 204–207, 211
Africanisation 1, 89, 146
assessment 7, 21, 43, 58, 63, 70, 95, 100, 103,
  115, 116, 119, 120, 124–127, 129, 137, 178,
  206, 209–211, 213, 215, 225–227, 234,
  249–251, 261, 263, 265, 271, 281
assistive technology 7, 97, 101, 137, 269–271,
  278–281, 285–287, 224, 226, 228, 231,
  234, 255, 261–263, 265, 268, 280–285
asynchronous 13, 31, 77, 81, 115, 117, 119, 121,
  126, 129, 229, 230, 236, 293
audiology 5, 6, 101, 105, 223–226, 228–234,
  236–238, 244, 246, 247, 292, 293
auditory impairment 62, 250
augmentative and alternative
  communication 6, 204–217, 292

barriers to teaching and learning 1, 2, 4, 5,
  13, 27–29, 32–34, 57–70, 88, 89, 93–95,
  97, 162–165, 200, 228, 291, 292
blended learning 18, 20, 22, 23, 100, 197, 272

community of practice 6, 13, 23, 127, 184,
  189, 191–196, 198, 199
computer 6, 7, 19, 21, 23, 30, 31, 36, 37, 49, 66,
  68, 69, 84, 107, 118, 123, 137, 138, 163, 167,
  171, 198, 207, 214, 229, 230, 237, 255, 269,
  270, 280, 287
connectivity 6, 12, 31, 80, 83, 91, 119, 228–230,
  237, 238
constructivism 78, 92, 122, 125, 162, 166, 177
COVID-19 5, 12, 23, 79, 84, 98, 100, 119, 136,
  143, 228, 230, 234, 235, 238
critical realism 16–18, 24
culture 16, 18, 20, 22, 77, 83, 134, 135,
  140–142, 146, 150–154, 167, 170, 177,
  251, 262, 292

deafness 101, 102, 226, 233, 250
digital media 91

disabilities 5, 7, 28, 35–37, 43, 46–48, 60,
  61, 90, 97, 98, 100, 101, 106, 115–117, 119,
  124, 129, 162, 163, 165, 179, 204, 206, 207,
  210, 213, 214–217, 224–228, 234, 237,
  238, 247, 249–251, 262, 265, 266, 268,
  278–280, 282, 291, 292
diverse needs 29, 30, 145, 226

Early Childhood Education 168
early identification 3, 4, 6, 40, 42–53, 227,
  233, 236, 255, 263
Education White Paper 6, 43, 56, 70, 93, 237
e-learning 1–3, 20, 27–34, 37, 58, 98, 100, 103,
  107, 115, 116, 121, 139, 186, 196, 228, 254
epistemological access 74, 75, 79, 128
equality 1–4, 11–15, 18, 19, 22–24, 28, 41, 44,
  50, 52, 53, 59, 70, 123, 147, 163, 179, 200,
  207, 216, 223, 225, 231, 238, 248, 252,
  277–283, 285, 286, 291–293
equitable education 52, 116, 254
equity 3, 4, 11, 13, 15, 18, 19, 22–24, 90, 123, 135,
  147, 163, 281, 292, 293
evidence-based instruction 47
exclusivity 4, 90, 165

foundation phase 60, 270
Fourth Industrial Revolution 23, 74, 92, 115,
  118, 249
Full-Service Schools 70

genetic disorders 60, 61, 63

hearing impairment 117, 224, 226–228, 232,
  233, 245–247, 250, 252, 253, 266
Higher Education 2, 4, 5, 12, 13, 15, 16, 73–76,
  78–80, 82–84, 116, 118, 119, 134, 135, 141,
  144–146, 154, 164, 185, 186, 247, 252, 254,
  271, 282
Higher Education Institutions 12, 58, 75, 78,
  80, 185, 186, 247, 252, 254, 270, 271
human capital 93, 147
human right 90, 91, 139, 163, 204, 205, 216,
  262, 281

inclusion 1, 3, 12–15, 18, 20, 22, 24, 40, 42–44,
  46, 47, 49–53, 68, 70, 89, 90, 94–96, 98,

103, 107, 116, 162, 165, 177, 188, 196, 205, 207, 210, 214, 216, 237, 238, 252, 261, 262, 272, 279, 281–283, 285, 291, 293

inclusive classroom   48, 50, 93, 267, 272

inclusive education   4, 7, 47, 49, 51–53, 57, 58, 70, 90, 91, 93, 96, 97, 107, 204, 207, 213, 215, 224, 225–228, 235, 237, 238, 252, 254, 261–264, 269, 271, 272, 278, 282, 284, 286

inclusiveness   1, 2, 4, 28, 41, 44, 50, 53, 59, 70, 163, 179, 196, 207, 231, 238, 247, 277–280, 285, 291–293

inclusivity   3, 4, 11–15, 52, 93, 103, 223–225, 286, 292

inequality   1, 3, 5, 14, 19, 22, 23, 136, 145, 163, 165, 187, 213, 248, 252, 281

Information and Communication Technologies   1, 2, 4–7, 12, 13, 15, 16, 18, 19–24, 28, 33, 36, 37, 40, 44, 49, 50, 52, 53, 59, 64, 68, 69, 73–84, 89, 91, 92, 95, 98, 107, 115–128, 134–153, 203, 224, 238, 235, 237, 246–249, 252–256, 261, 269, 273, 278–288, 291–293

intervention   7, 15, 17, 24, 41, 43 44, 46–53, 65, 69, 70, 84, 95, 140, 150, 210, 211, 213, 214, 217, 224, 225, 227, 229, 232–234, 236, 238, 249, 251, 263, 266–268, 271, 272

language   5, 6, 42, 43, 61, 64–66, 74–80, 84, 101, 103, 118, 122, 123, 127, 205–214, 216, 226, 228, 232, 233, 236, 251, 254, 262, 264, 267, 285, 292

learning styles   7, 46, 75, 115, 120

lecturers   3, 82, 83, 161, 179, 278, 291

low- and middle-income countries   228, 245, 247

manifestations   62, 63, 69, 135, 266, 267, 272

marginalised students   116, 119, 138

mathematical proficiency   6, 185–188, 191–195, 199

Mathematics and Science teaching   161–163, 165, 179

online   14, 15, 18, 19, 28, 30, 31, 34, 79–83, 100, 105, 116, 117, 120, 128, 129, 136, 137, 139, 140, 143, 153, 164, 197, 199, 224, 228, 230, 237, 254, 282, 283, 286

online communication   197, 283

open and distance learning (ODL)   6, 184–187, 196

open, distance and e-learning (ODeL)   1–6, 27–37, 58, 59, 69, 70, 114–117, 119–122, 125, 126, 128, 129, 161, 178, 291, 292

paraprofessionals   228, 230–232, 236

parental involvement   50, 52

pedagogical content knowledge   92, 98, 99, 148, 149, 162, 175, 193, 195

pedagogy   5, 14, 74, 75, 77, 81, 82, 84, 115, 122, 135, 137, 138, 140, 143–145, 147–152, 170, 174, 175, 186, 193–196, 198, 271

policymakers   278

poverty   5, 11, 12, 20, 42, 95, 119, 136, 145, 146, 164, 207, 213, 227, 262, 278

practitioners   16, 41, 52, 63, 69, 164, 229, 237, 278

pre-service teachers   2, 4, 41, 59, 60, 69, 70, 171, 173–175, 177, 178, 291

prevention   232

procedural fluency   6, 188, 191, 192

scaffolding   13, 77, 128

School-Based Support Teams   44, 286

schools   2, 4, 6, 19, 29, 40–53, 58, 60, 64, 68–70, 75, 78, 80, 88–90, 92–95, 98, 104, 107, 124, 139, 164, 167–169, 173, 179, 176, 177, 179, 186, 204, 211, 213, 214, 217, 223, 225, 226–228, 230, 232, 234, 237, 245–255, 261–264, 267, 268, 271, 272, 278, 284, 286, 292

Screening Identification Assessment Support   43–45, 58, 70, 209, 225, 227, 271

sign language   118, 208, 209, 251, 254, 285

social justice   3, 12, 13, 15–18, 20, 24, 82, 90, 135, 281

social problems   64, 66

socioeconomic factors   18, 64, 74, 95

speech recognition software   106, 207

student empowerment   2, 134, 135, 139, 292, 293

student-centeredness   74, 143, 151

student-centred   2, 18, 20, 82, 84, 130, 135, 169, 177, 288

students   1–7, 11–23, 27–37, 40–44, 46, 47, 49–53, 59–63, 67, 69–71, 73–84, 89, 97–100, 103, 106, 114–130, 134–145, 147–153, 162–179, 184–189, 205, 215, 216, 231, 238, 253, 291–293, 277–289

support   1–3, 6, 7, 13, 15, 17–23, 33, 35–37, 41, 43, 44, 46, 48–50, 52, 53, 58, 67–70,

74–84, 91, 93, 95, 98, 102–105, 107,
115–117, 119, 120, 122–124, 128, 129, 137,
140, 152, 162, 163, 165, 166, 170, 171,
173–175, 179, 185, 194, 206, 209, 210–212,
224–228, 245, 246, 248, 249, 251–255,
261–264, 267, 269–272, 278–280, 284,
285–287, 291–293
synchronous   31, 77, 81, 103, 115, 117, 120, 127,
129, 229, 230, 292

teacher-centred   6, 82, 169
teacher training   52, 164, 173, 174, 176–179,
216, 263, 269–271
teaching and learning   2, 4, 5, 13, 27–29,
32–34, 57–70, 88, 89, 93–95, 97,
162–165, 200, 228, 291, 292
technological tools   34, 35, 171, 173
technology   1, 6, 12, 13, 23, 29, 30, 33–35,
49, 78, 80–82, 84, 88, 97–101,
104–106, 116, 122, 124, 135–139, 141,
144, 146, 149, 162–165, 167–176, 178,
179, 185, 187, 193–195, 197, 200, 203,

206–209, 211, 213, 214, 217, 229, 234, 235,
238, 246, 247, 249, 253, 254, 261, 262,
264, 265, 267–272, 278–288, 292
telecommunications   6, 30, 178, 229, 247
telehealth   7, 224, 228–231, 234–238
training modes   36
transformation   1, 76, 77, 89, 93, 116, 123, 130,
135, 138, 142, 144–146, 150, 213, 246, 247,
252, 262, 282

universal design   94, 97
universities   4, 5, 7, 13–16, 18–21, 23, 28, 29,
44, 52, 73, 75, 76, 79, 89, 101, 105, 117,
120, 127, 135–137, 140–144, 151–153, 161,
173, 178, 186, 187, 197, 234, 235, 246, 251,
278, 285

video conferencing   66, 230, 254
visual impairment   62, 99, 103–105, 266

Zone of Proximal Development (ZPD)   77,
265

Printed in the United States
by Baker & Taylor Publisher Services